The Eastern Mediterranean and the Making of Global Radicalism, 1860–1914

THE CALIFORNIA WORLD HISTORY LIBRARY

Edited by Edmund Burke III, Kenneth Pomeranz, and Patricia Seed

1. *The Unending Frontier: Environmental History of the Early Modern World,* by John F. Richards
2. *Maps of Time: An Introduction to Big History,* by David Christian
3. *The Graves of Tarim: Genealogy and Mobility across the Indian Ocean,* by Engseng Ho
4. *Imperial Connections: India in the Indian Ocean Arena, 1860—1920,* by Thomas R. Metcalf
5. *Many Middle Passages: Forced Migration and the Making of the Modern World,* edited by Emma Christopher, Cassandra Pybus, and Marcus Rediker
6. *Domesticating the World: African Consumerism and the Genealogies of Globalization,* by Jeremy Prestholdt
7. *Servants of the Dynasty: Palace Women in World History,* edited by Anne Walthall
8. *Island World: A History of Hawai'i and the United States,* by Gary Y. Okihiro
9. *The Environment and World History,* edited by Edmund Burke III and Kenneth Pomeranz
10. *Pineapple Culture: A History of the Tropical and Temperate Zones,* by Gary Y. Okihiro
11. *The Pilgrim Art: Culture of Porcelain in World History,* by Robert Finlay
12. *The Quest for the Lost Nation: Writing History in Germany and Japan in the American Century,* by Sebastian Conrad, translated by Alan Nothnagle
13. *The Eastern Mediterranean and the Making of Global Radicalism, 1860–1914,* by Ilham Khuri-Makdisi
14. *The Other West: Latin America from Invasion to Globalization,* by Marcello Carmagnani
15. *Mediterraneans: North Africa, Europe, and the Ottoman Empire in an Age of Migration,* c. 1800–1900, by Julia Clancy-Smith
16. *History and the Testimony of Language,* by Christopher Ehret
17. *From the Indian Ocean to the Mediterranean: Circulation and the Global Trade Networks from New Julfa, Isfahan, 1605–1747,* by Sebouh David Aslanian

The Eastern Mediterranean and the Making of Global Radicalism, 1860–1914

Ilham Khuri-Makdisi

UNIVERSITY OF CALIFORNIA PRESS
Berkeley Los Angeles London

University of California Press, one of the most distinguished university presses in the United States, enriches lives around the world by advancing scholarship in the humanities, social sciences, and natural sciences. Its activities are supported by the UC Press Foundation and by philanthropic contributions from individuals and institutions. For more information, visit www.ucpress.edu.

University of California Press
Berkeley and Los Angeles, California

University of California Press, Ltd.
London, England

First paperback printing 2013

Library of Congress Cataloging-in-Publication Data
Khuri-Makdisi, Ilham.
The Eastern Mediterranean and the making of global radicalism, 1860–1914 / Ilham Khuri-Makdisi.
p. cm.
Includes bibliographical references and index.
ISBN 978-0-520-28014-4 (pbk. : alk. paper)
1. Radicalism—Egypt—Cairo—History. 2. Radicalism—Egypt—Alexandria—History. 3. Radicalism—Lebanon—Beirut—History. 4. Cairo (Egypt)—History. 5. Alexandria (Egypt)—History. 6. Beirut (Lebanon)—History. I. Title.
HN786.C3K48 2010
303.48'4095609034—dc22 2009035397

Manufactured in the United States of America

19 18 17 16 15 14 13
10 9 8 7 6 5 4 3 2 1

To Nouhad and Kamal Makdisi

CONTENTS

ACKNOWLEDGMENTS

As the long odyssey of conceiving, researching, and completing this book is coming to an end, I would like to thank a number of individuals and institutions whose help and support have been crucial at various steps of this project. This book first began as a dissertation, and first thanks are due to my graduate advisor and members of my dissertation committee at Harvard University's Center for Middle Eastern Studies and the History Department: my mentor, Cemal Kafadar, for his inspiration, intellectual stimulus, encouragement to think outside the box, and unfailing faith in me; Roger Owen for sharing some of his immense knowledge of the field with me and asking eye-opening and crucial questions that forced me to think through my ideas with greater rigor; and Susan Miller for sharing her love of and expertise in urban history and providing me with unwavering support. I am also eternally grateful to the late Şinasi Tekin for patiently tutoring me in Ottoman Turkish, and to Bill Granara for his friendship and support over the years. Thanks are also due to Laura Saltz and the dissertation support group, and to Kathy Duffin at Harvard University's Writing Center. I would also like to thank the Center for Middle Eastern Studies for providing me with a dissertation research grant and summer writing grants and nominating me for a Foreign Language Area Studies grant my last year of writing the dissertation.

Research for this book was conducted in a number of much-loved cities and made possible thanks to the kindness and help of various people: in Beirut, the staff at the Greek Orthodox Archives and the Maronite Bishopric, the Lebanese National Archives in Hamra, the AUB Archives, the Beirut Port Archives, the Maqasid, and the Patriarchal School; in Cairo, the staff at Dar al-Kutub and Dar al-Wathaiq, the library at the Collège Sainte-Famille, and the staff at the CEDEJ and at the AUC

Special Collection Library; in Alexandria, the wonderfully friendly staff at the Alexandria Municipal Library, who provided me with an unforgettable work environment, and the archivists of the Syrian Orthodox Church, who kindly granted me access to their material. My thanks to the staff at the Başbakanlık archives in Istanbul and the Ministero degli Affari Esteri in Rome, and to the employees at the PRO in Kew. Finally, my deepest gratitude goes to the staff at Widener Library at Harvard, especially to those at the Philips Reading Room, which served as my home away from home for many years. I am also forever grateful for the heartwarming hospitality of Dana Sajdi, Shahab Ahmed, Malak Wahba, Hani Luqa, and Raja Adal in Cairo; the Yammine family in Alexandria; Zeynep Yürekli, Dilek hanım, Aslı Niyazioğlu, and Giancarlo Casale in Istanbul; and Andrea D'Avella and Maura Mezzetti in Rome. I thank them all for their friendship over the years.

My thanks also go to my department and colleagues at Northeastern University, especially to my chair, Laura Frader, as well as to my colleagues Kate Luongo and Denis Sullivan, whose encouragement and support have been vital over the years. I would like to thank the History Department's graduate students for their stimulating discussions over seminar tables and in my office of matters pertaining to Mediterranean historiography and global migration. I am grateful to the provost's office for granting me a Research and Scholarship Development Fund, which allowed for archival research in summer 2005. I was also extremely privileged to receive a Wissenschaftskolleg zu Berlin's AKME fellowship (2005–6), which provided me with the opportunity to work on my book. I wish to thank my colleagues at the ZMO in Berlin, particularly Ulrike Freitag for hosting me and Dyala Hamzah for very stimulating discussions, as well as for her friendship. The same applies to my friends and colleagues at Wiko: Hany Hanafy, Christine Hoffmann, Georges Khalil, and Dana Sajdi. Each one of them knows how indebted I am to them, and I thank them from the bottom of my heart for their intellectual complicity, academic help, friendship, and love.

I am deeply indebted to all the people who read parts or all of the manuscript at various stages of its existence and provided invaluable advice: Diana Abouali, Cemil Aydın, Nancy Baker, Sahar Bazzaz, Walid Bitar, Julia Clancy-Smith, Shirine Hamadeh, Dyala Hamzah, Zach Lockman, Kamal Makdisi, Dana Sajdi, Rhetta Wiley, and Sibel Zandi-Sayek. No words can adequately express what I owe intellectually to Edmund Burke III and Ussama Makdisi, both of whom read entire drafts more than once and made very substantial and helpful suggestions. I am also particularly grateful to Elizabeth Angell, who helped me considerably with chapter 1 and edited other parts of the final draft. I would also like to thank the two anonymous reviewers at the University of California Press for their comments, as well as Niels Hooper, Nick Arrivo, Cindy Fulton, and Judith Hoover for their splendid editorial work and seeing this book through to completion.

The comments and questions I received from graduate students and colleagues during presentations at SUNY-Binghamton and UC Santa Cruz were particularly incisive and stimulating, and I thank Donald Quataert and Terry Burke, respectively, for these two invitations.

I would also like to thank Diana Abouali, Sinan Antoon, Sahar Bazzaz, Suiling Cheah, Ayman Desouky, Leila Farsakh, Emine Fetvacı, Bill Granara, Shirine Hamadeh, Selim Kuru, Joe Logan, the "Olympians," Hashim Sarkis, Aaron Shakow, Mona Tayara, Ali Yaycioğlu, Sameh Wahba, and Sibel Zandi-Sayek for their invaluable friendship and support over the years. I am eternally grateful to my extended family in Beirut and elsewhere for always providing me with encouragement, warmth and generosity, good laughter, and fantastic food.

Finally, this book would never have seen the light of day without the full and unconditional love of my mother and brother, Nouhad and Kamal Makdisi, their unwavering faith, continuous support, unmatched intellectual stimulus, and tremendous humor. It is to them that I dedicate this work.

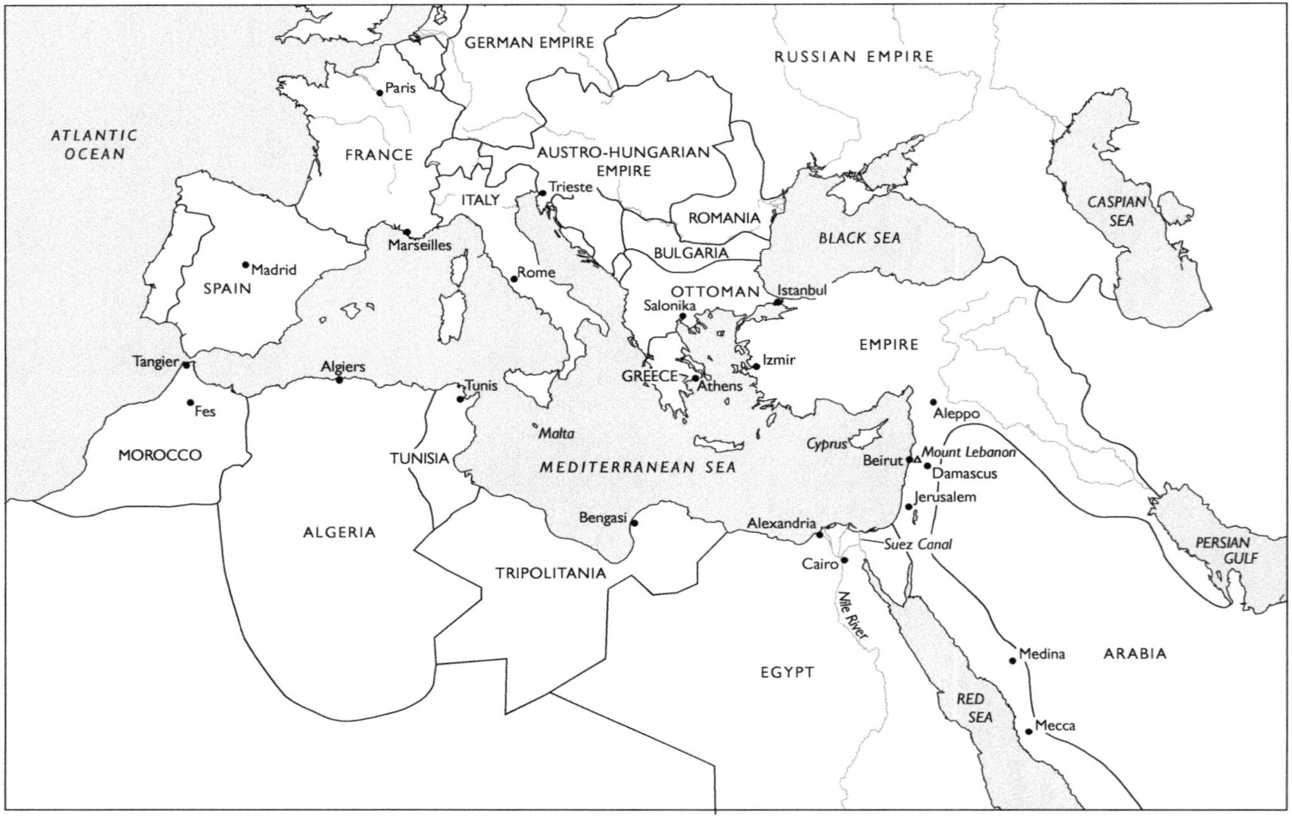

The Mediterranean world circa 1900.

Introduction

In the late nineteenth century and early twentieth a wide variety of radical leftist ideas began circulating among segments of the populations of Eastern Mediterranean cities, especially in Beirut, Cairo, and Alexandria, then among the most culturally and politically important cities of the Arab Ottoman world. These ideas, which are best described as selective adaptations of socialist and anarchist principles, included specific calls for social justice, workers' rights, mass secular education, and anticlericalism, and more broadly a general challenge to the existing social and political order at home and abroad. Those who embraced such ideas expressed them in articles, pamphlets, plays, and popular poetry (in Arabic, but also in Italian, Ottoman Turkish, and Greek), in literary salons and theaters, and during strikes and demonstrations, disseminating radical thought through educational, cultural, and popular institutions. They often combined radical goals with seemingly more moderate, liberal demands, such as the establishment of constitutional and representative government and freedom of speech, the curbing of religious and clerical authority, and resistance to European political and economic encroachments. The concepts of social justice that constituted central themes in leftist thought were rarely discussed in isolation from larger issues, but rather went hand in hand with a broader reformist agenda. Radicals in Beirut, Cairo, and Alexandria forged a culture of contestation in which they challenged existing and emerging class boundaries, redefined notions of foreignness and belonging, and promoted alternative visions of social and world order.

One of the most salient features of radical and leftist movements, as they were articulated in the late nineteenth century in the Eastern Mediterranean (and beyond), was their internationalism, spurred by a hyperawareness of and deep interest in world events. There certainly were many moments worthy of interest in the period under study: anarchist attacks in European capitals in the 1890s, the Russo-Japanese War of 1905, the arrest and subsequent execution of the radical icon Francisco Ferrer in Barcelona in 1909, the stellar rise of the German Social Democratic Party and its victory in 1912, and the 1909 attacks against British officials by Indian radicals, nationalists and others, to mention just a few. Each of these episodes represented a challenge to the status quo and to the existing world order; each was closely followed, commented on, and passionately debated (and in the case of the Ferrer affair performed) among radical intellectuals in Beirut, Cairo, and Alexandria. In other words, radicals and militants in these global, yet "(semi-)peripheral cities" were transmitting information about international issues, discussing them on the pages of periodicals, on stage, or in public gatherings, and hence appropriating them and *participating* in them. By doing so they were full participants in the making of a globalized world, albeit perhaps offering an alternative vision of this world or even challenging and subverting the version created and maintained by European imperialism. Radicals formed networks that were connected informationally, politically, and organizationally to international and internationalist movements and organizations that sought to promote leftist ideas and implement radical projects in various corners of the world. Beyond these formal and official connections, I argue, lay an entire worldview and way of being-in-the-world, a global radical moment that radical thinkers and activists in the Eastern Mediterranean partook in and helped shape.

Radicalism is a term I am ascribing retroactively to sets of ideas and practices that did not necessarily constitute an organized or official ideology in the period under study. It is a term that has historically been associated with a rather disparate set of ideas and movements, including English Chartists in the mid-nineteenth century, American populists around the turn of the twentieth century, and members of the Argentinian Unión Cívica Radical Party in the first half of the twentieth century.[1] Various political and social movements adopted the term, either by incorporating it into their movement's name or using it to describe the principles they stood for, and other movements and individuals were tagged with the label by their contemporaries or even retroactively. The term is used to refer to social movements, political parties (such as the French Radical Party during the Third Republic and the Argentinian Radical Party established in the 1890s), and more amorphous formations (as in "Radical Islamists"). What is almost always implicit in the notion of the radical is the existence of a mainstream and of a leap between this mainstream and radicalism, a gap that exists both in the vision of a better world and in the means used to turn this vision into a reality. As Anthony Giddens puts it, radicalism "meant not just bringing about change but controlling such change so as to drive history onwards."[2]

By adopting this term and applying it to the various ideas and networks discussed in this book, my aim is not to import terminology and apply it unquestioningly to a part of the world where, at the time, the term itself was not in regular use, but to connect what was happening in the Middle East and Eastern Mediterranean to contemporaneous global trends. I also seek to reclaim or appropriate terminology that has been associated strongly, if not exclusively, with leftist ideas and movements in the Western world, nationalist ones in the Third World, and politico-religious ones in the Islamic world, and hence question the separate taxonomies and forced boundaries used to classify ideas, practices, and social movements in different parts of the globe. Furthermore the vagueness of the term itself captures the lack of orthodoxy and rigid boundaries that was a key characteristic of the fin de siècle, whether intellectually, culturally, or socially. It suggests a Weltanschauung taking shape during a period of flux, in which different groups of actors in the non-Western world felt confident they could assemble their own visions of social and world order, borrowing, adapting, synthesizing, perhaps plundering ideas from "the West and the rest" and melding them with local practices and ideas to produce what might strike us today as a radical package marked by contradictions and limitations.

CONTEXTUALIZING RADICALISM IN THE EASTERN MEDITERRANEAN: GLOBALIZATION AND CHANGE, 1860–1914

What explains the emergence of this radical worldview in the Eastern Mediterranean? I have suggested that radicalism was connected to a period of flux. Between 1860 and 1914 cities of the Eastern Mediterranean and hinterlands, especially Beirut, Cairo, and Alexandria, underwent tremendous changes. Their populations swelled, their geographic areas doubled or trebled, and new neighborhoods emerged.[3] The cities were further incorporated into the world economy and became plugged into global information and communications networks, which allowed news from all over the world to reach them promptly, thanks to the telegraph, news agencies, a reliable postal system, and a plethora of periodicals. This incorporation into the world capitalist system was further intensified by the development of a transportation web with extensive railway expansion, the establishment of regular and frequent steamship lines, the construction of the Suez Canal in 1869 and accompanying large infrastructural projects such as port enlargements and construction, as well as the convergence of capital and the establishment of banks and international businesses. All of these changes meant that commodities, capital, and people flocked to these three cities with ease and regularity, linking them to the rest of the Mediterranean and the world. These changes, which are referred to collectively as the late nineteenth-century era of globalization (1870–1914 or 1920), occurred in tandem with local, internal reconfigurations triggered by both state and society. Concomitantly the specter of foreign interference and dominance, which peaked with the British Occupation of Egypt in 1882, magnified some of these processes and set off its own tremors. These overlapping and intertwined transformations unleashed profound convulsions in the cities and their hinterlands; at the same time they ushered in a moment pregnant with possibilities for the emergence of a new social order. Dramatic changes, simmering discontent, and great expectations triggered contestation as well as the "experimentation with new forms and ideologies of collective action," both rural and urban, which historians have identified as a "key feature" of the 1880–1925 period.[4]

Much of the contestation took place over land or was directly or indirectly linked to land issues. The land reforms introduced in Mehmet Ali's Egypt and by the Ottoman Tanzimat around the middle of the nineteenth century and the increased incorporation into the capitalist world system and subsequent domination of monocultures in much of the Eastern Mediterranean (cotton in Egypt, silk in Mount Lebanon, and tobacco in different parts of Syria) dramatically affected access to land. In Egypt the period between 1850 and 1880 "witnessed the removal of restrictions on private ownership of land; the right to sell and mortgage land; and authorization of foreigners to acquire land in Egypt."[5] By 1882 many Egyptian peasants, unable to pay the increasingly high land taxes, were losing their land, and would continue to do so over the decades. Simultaneously land was being consolidated in the hands of the very few: by 1913 "the large landowners represented only 0.8% of total proprietors, but held 44.2% of the land, whereas small landowners [who owned less than five feddans] increased in numbers (from 80.4 to 90.7% between 1897 and 1913)."[6] As one historian concludes, "This, alongside the abolition of slavery, laid the grounds for the emergence of a new class of wage-earner peasants."[7] It also led to large numbers of seasonal migrants, who commuted between their villages and Egypt's main cities.[8]

Although the story of peasants' access to land is neither a straightforward tale of dispossession (at least not in the case of Mount Lebanon) nor a tale of perpetual confrontation between new owners and old land users, one of its corollaries was rural migration. The figures for Mount Lebanon are astonishing: between 1890 and 1914 as much as a third of the population left for at least a period of a few years. Most headed to the Americas (particularly the United States and Brazil), leading to what must have been a serious shortage of peasant (and manufacturing) labor.[9] Emigration and return migration also led to remittances and to the establishment of entirely new villages made up of returnees or built thanks to their remittances, as well as new gender relations, new family patterns, and the transformation of some peasants into members of the middle classes.[10] Rural migration to the cities and emigration abroad seem to have eased some of the tensions and served as "a safety valve in the explosive countryside," as it did elsewhere.[11] At the same time, while many of these migrants took their grievances, their struggles, and their methods of contestation to new destinations, they also brought back with them new methods of collective action and new ways of challenging the status quo. It was not only peasants who were on the move, but also artisans, craftsmen, white-collar workers, and countless others, who converged on Beirut, Cairo, and Alexandria in search of employment. The development of the capitalist world economy, and the three cities' full incorporation in it, was inextricably linked to the establishment of a different and more expansive regional labor market than the one(s) that had previously existed in the Eastern Mediterranean. In the words of Reşat Kasaba, "The perennial nature of circulation of labor in the entire historical development of the capitalist world-economy makes it imperative that we explain this phenomenon as an integral part of that development rather than as an ex post factor of adjustment."[12]

The wave of migration included many people who eventually ventured farther than these three cities; many peasants who ultimately moved to South America most likely spent some time looking for employment in Beirut, for instance, before heading across the sea, and then across the ocean. Circulating labor also came from farther away: from various parts of the Mediterranean, such as southern Italy, Malta, and Greece, from the Ottoman and Austro-Habsburgian Balkans, and in a few cases even from distant parts of the British Empire, such as South Asia and South Africa.[13] The three Eastern Mediterranean cities were easily accessible to migrants, more so than many European and U.S. cities since the use of passports and nationality documents was still not standard. Even when such documents were officially required, the law was not systematically applied.[14] Significantly, though, this rather lackadaisical control at the entry ports and borders went hand in hand with stringent vagrancy laws, giving the state the power to arrest, forcibly relocate, or forcibly employ nonsettled ("sans domicile fixe") and unemployed people, practices in line with measures in Western Europe and elsewhere.[15] In the case of foreign subjects arrested as vagrants, the brunt of repatriation fell on consulates, maritime companies, or charitable immigrant societies.

At the same time this regional labor market was integrated into a larger, global market, as demonstrated by the migration flows of Italians, Greeks, and Syrians to North and South America. As with rural-to-urban migration, the great majority of people on the move were peasants turned urban workers, but their numbers also included artisans, entertainers (especially people in theater), and members of a new middle class. These latter categories of migrants often had cultural, if not necessarily economic capital, in part due to skills that were in demand in modern and expanding cities, including familiarity with foreign languages and modern (i.e., Western) training as journalists, doctors, lawyers, and administrators. The picture, then, is of a sudden shift and tremendous stretch (both geographically and quantitatively) in the regional labor market, which resulted in raised expectations for employment coupled with uncertainties about employment prospects and fixed employment and higher competition for jobs, all of which particularly affected the three cities in question and their hinterlands. Radicalism emerged within this ecology, a tremendously more competitive and volatile regional labor market, where movement seems to have been the norm rather than the exception.

THE MAKING OF THE POPULAR: NEW CLASSES, INSTITUTIONS, AND CATEGORIES

The late nineteenth century also saw the emergence and construction of new social configurations, categories, and classes. I suggest that radicalism should be seen partly through the lens of this development, namely, as the attempt of these new classes and groups to claim a greater role in the political, economic, and cultural life of their city and their state. One of these new configurations was the category of intellectuals, usually members of the middle class who had gained access to a specific kind of education deemed novel and modern, and who often were economically and politically frustrated as a result of being educated beyond their means. Unable to find the kind of employment worthy of their education, many, especially intellectuals formed in Beiruti institutions, chose to emigrate. Those who remained or returned expressed this frustration by taking over newly established urban institutions or protesting their lack of proper representation within the state. In the three cities under study radicalism was one possible repertoire (sometimes competing, overlapping, or intersecting with nationalism, in the case of Egypt) for middle-class intellectuals seeking to forge an alliance with the working classes through new conceptions of "the people" *(al-sha'b)*. Part of this alliance manifested itself in calls from members of the middle classes for mass primary and secondary education, as well as the promotion of self-help for workers and artisans through the establishment of mutual funds, artisanal and technical training courses, and a shared concern for the local economy. Among both middle classes and working classes in the cities under study, global and foreign capital and economic imperialism (whether or not directly accompanied by direct political imperialism) triggered a feeling that the economy was under siege and an awareness of fundamental asymmetries that were inherent in the international economic system. These fears were magnified by radicals' perception that their own state could not protect local interests and economies from this foreign penetration via international capital. Hence radicalism emerged within a matrix combining the desire to protect the local economy and local labor (and hence a necessary collaboration between intellectuals and workers); the rise of mass politics, or at least the possibility of mass politics, especially after the 1908 Young Turk Revolution in the Ottoman Empire; and the emergence of new classes whose place in society and in politics was not yet clearly defined.

At the same time as these emerging new classes sought to gain access to state and social power, they also secured or appropriated a number of the new key urban institutions (and spaces) that appeared in the second half of the nineteenth century. The synchronous development of these institutions magnified their individual impact; they included the (private) press, the theater, municipalities, new educational institutions, reading rooms, Masonic lodges, and scientific and literary clubs. Accompanying these institutions was the very rapid proliferation of cultural genres hailed as novel and transformative; the periodical, the play, and the novel would serve to disseminate new and radical ideas and articulate new notions of the public. Members of these new social classes moved among and shaped these urban institutions, these "new forms of sociable public [or semipublic] space," to borrow Chris Bayly's expression.[16] Masonic lodges in various parts of the Ottoman Empire, for instance, "were . . . places for the discussion and exchange of ideas about current themes: socialism, feminism, venereal diseases, progress of science, etc. Some mingled with politics, displaying a highly nationalistic discourse. . . . One of the[ir] goals . . . was to rid the Ottoman Empire of foreign penetration."[17]

This was certainly not the first time public spheres and public spaces had proliferated rapidly.[18] Nor was this an era of ruptures with the past; the transformations were just as often continuities and syntheses merging the new with the old. Older forms and spaces of sociability and cultural expression still occupied a central place in everyday life, especially for the overwhelming majority of common people—urban, illiterate or semiliterate artisans and skilled workers—as well as new middle classes. Such forms, including the local coffeehouse, the *hakawati* (one-person narrator) and the *karagöz* show (shadow theater), the bathhouse, public celebrations of religious festivities, encounters in the souks (the most frequented public place throughout the Eastern Mediterranean in the late nineteenth century), all provided space for discussion and interaction.[19] These traditional spaces and genres also merged with newer ones: newspapers were read out loud in coffeehouses and staged plays blended traditions and narratives from the modern theater with those of the *hakawati*.[20] What seems to have been different this time around was the emergence of a dominant and potent discourse on novelty, ushering in a new era in which different notions of the public were being explored and, in the process, in which notions of the popular and the local were used to fuse a newly constituted intellectual middle class with a bourgeoning modern working class. In other words, this was a time when new notions and concepts of the public were being formulated and visions of a new relationship between social classes defined, at least by intellectuals and public intellectuals, and especially by radicals.

THE *NAHḌA* REVISITED: A HISTORIOGRAPHICAL CHALLENGE

With this book I seek to contribute to the existing literature on the Left in present-day Lebanon and Egypt in the following ways. First, I aim to rehabilitate an understudied period, roughly 1870 to 1914, and give it its due importance in the history of the Left in the Middle East. Indeed although a number of studies have examined the emergence of the Left in both Egypt and the Levant, these have generally focused on the period after 1919–20 and the establishment of official leftist parties (socialist and communist), relegating the pre-1914 period to a mere backstage within the history of the Left. I suggest an alternative to this timeline and argue that the period 1870–1914 should be fully integrated into a narrative of the history of the Left, as it witnessed the initial articulation, dissemination, and implementation of many leftist ideas and projects, some of which would continue into the 1920s. Second, I emphasize the multiplicity of ideas, trends, and movements that made up the Left. The reader in search of a pure Left will be disappointed; in Egypt, the Levant, and throughout most parts of the world radicalism (and the Left) was more often than not a package of (sometimes inchoate) ideas and practices that were not codified, standardized, or homogenized, and in which cleavages between socialism, anarchism, social democracy, Fabianism, and other ideologies did not always or necessarily apply. Hence one of my larger aims is to prompt a rethinking of the meaning of the Left, too often associated with political parties and rigid official ideology and with notions of class consciousness and other traditional categories of the Marxist Left. Instead I seek to underline the multiplicity of Lefts that existed before World War I, before the Russian Revolution and the establishment of more orthodox, party-defined movements. Within these various Lefts, I argue, anarchism occupied an inspirational and tremendously important place. Third, I bring together various players and manifestations of the Left that are usually dealt with in different historiographical genres; this book is both an intellectual history of the Left(s) and a social history dealing with intellectuals, actors, workers, and political activists in Egypt and the Levant, both indigenous or foreign, exploring the connections among them all. Fourth, I place the history of the Egyptian and Levantine Left within regional and global frameworks rather than purely national ones.

By shedding light on this hitherto largely unknown radical history of the Arab Ottoman Eastern Mediterranean and emphasizing its connections and similarities with other parts of the world, the story told in this book challenges a deeply entrenched premise. That premise holds that the late nineteenth century and early twentieth constituted the antechamber of the rise of nationalism in the Arab world, and that all, or most, of the cultural and intellectual production of the period known as the *nahḍa* (or Arab renaissance) paved the way for a fully developed and inevitable nationalist denouement, with the collapse of the Ottoman Empire after World War I.[21] Leftist and generally radical ideas were not incompatible with emerging nationalist ideas at the time, whether in the Arab world or elsewhere. But the discussions about leftist concepts and the various radical experiments that took place during the period in Beirut, Cairo, and Alexandria have been either obliterated by a nationalist historiographical framework or forcibly incorporated into the nationalist narrative. I emphasize the contingency of the *nahḍa*'s nationalist turn and underline the variable currents of contestation, including calls for social reform, mass education, and a more just social and world order.

Through an exploration of radical ideas and practices, I seek to normalize the history of the Eastern Mediterranean and move away from exceptionalist narratives regarding the Arab world, the Ottoman world, and Islam. I also globalize this history, arguing that this was a world region deeply connected to other parts of the world through webs of people, information, capital, and commodities. I suggest that Mediterranean and Atlantic linkages—with other parts of the Ottoman Mediterranean but also with regions of Italy, for instance, and the United States and Brazil—must be systematically explored for a more complete picture of the Eastern Mediterranean in the late nineteenth century to emerge. Not only does this transnational, global lens allow us to fill in the blanks by disclosing hitherto unknown historical texture, but the adoption of this global lens allows (and predisposes) certain hidden histories to rise to the surface, histories that might not emerge with the exclusive application of narrower frames, be they national, imperial, or regional.

As I said earlier, the history of radicalism is an intensely local story; it is first and foremost about people interpreting and giving meaning to vocabularies, concepts, and practices that had recently emerged on the local scene. As such it is not a matter of importing but of adapting, and adaptations cannot take place outside of the local frameworks that give meaning to novel concepts, or local spaces and institutions such as the neighborhood coffeehouse, the theater, literary salons and clubs, periodical offices, and municipalities. Adaptations also obviously have to fit into existing and changing social relations, economic and political structures, and intellectual structures of meaning. In this book I examine how local inhabitants in the three cities under investigation discussed, reworked, and synthesized socialism and anarchism in ways that rendered these ideas meaningful to their local environment. By doing so I suggest an overall reconsideration of existing dichotomies pertaining to ideas and their proponents and suggest ways of moving beyond the binaries local/global and authentic/foreign.

NEXUS AND NETWORKS: AN APPROACH TO STUDYING THE RADICAL MOMENT

This book is "a tale of three cities."[22] I argue that, in order to understand the interest in and articulation and dissemination of radical ideas in the three cities under study it is necessary to use multiple lenses. The first consists of looking at the three cities together, as sites forming a nexus, a regional and connected space in which people and ideas moved. Here I have been in part inspired by contemporary writing on global cities, especially the work of Saskia Sassen and her school, who argue for the need to analyze multiple cities and their relationships to each other.[23] I underline the existence of a special relationship and a specific geography of contestation connecting Beirut, Cairo, and Alexandria, established by the movements of people (intellectuals, workers, and dramatists) between the three cities and providing channels for the circulation of radical ideas and practices between them. A second lens consists of analyzing this nexus in the context of its connections to other parts of the world, most notably to other shores of the Mediterranean as well as North and especially South America, and similarly following radical channels that spanned other geographies of contestation, such as those associated with Italian anarchism (which is explored in the second half of chapter 4) and Syrian diasporic periodicals (the subject of chapter 2 and part of chapter 4).

How can the channels be studied and mapped? I have already suggested that radicalism, in the Eastern Mediterranean and elsewhere, was a worldview and a set of ideas inextricably linked to movement and flows—of information, but also specifically of people. Migrant communities, Arab and non-Arab, played a crucial role in constructing and disseminating this radical worldview, and the resulting radical scene in the three cities in question emerged out of the interaction between locals and foreigners, among settled, immigrant, and migrant intellectuals, dramatists, and workers. Rather than focusing on individuals, I argue that radicalism in these three cities was shaped by the convergence of global and multiple radical networks and their intersection in these cities. By *network* I am referring to local and transnational institutions, organizations, and personal connections that established a system for the circulation of people, information, and ideas. Such a concept immediately conjures up intersections, overlaps, exchanges, and encounters. It incorporates the formal and the informal, the local and the international, and suggests a certain cohesiveness, albeit one that is not overly deterministic and allows for human agency. At the same time, using networks as a conceptual tool should not obliterate very real power dynamics and differentials of power; not all networks were the same, and not all people, materials, and ideas circulated freely or equally.

With this caveat in mind, thinking about networks has also allowed me to formulate an account of what was so particular about Beirut, Cairo, and Alexandria and the relationship between them. First, the three cities constituted poles of attraction to various global radical networks. Second, they provided conditions that allowed these networks to intersect. Third, these networks were able to reach out to at least parts of these cities' populations. Indeed although these networks allowed for the circulation of militant intellectuals, politicized workers, radical information in the form of periodicals, pamphlets, and theatrical performances, and so forth, their members did not operate in a vacuum. Instead they had deep connections to their own environment, allowing them to exchange ideas with more settled locals and engage in militant labor practices or establish radical institutions together. I examine the formation and intersection of social and intellectual networks in the following spheres of activity: the press, the theater, radical politics, labor migration, and social and labor unrest. Some of the networks I examine are those of Syrian intellectual reformers, Italian anarchists, Syrian and Egyptian dramatists, and trans-Mediterranean workers, all of whom converged on Beirut, Cairo, and Alexandria and circulated between them in the late nineteenth century and early twentieth. However, although I argue for the importance of a trajectory of contestation linking Beirut, Cairo, and Alexandria, I am not suggesting that such a trajectory was exclusive or isolated from other radical geographies. Although my focus in this book is the nexus formed by Beirut, Cairo, and Alexandria, and although this nexus was particularly important for the movement of ideas generally and radical ideas specifically, there certainly existed many different radical trajectories connecting these cities to other cities throughout the Ottoman Empire, the Mediterranean, and the world.

Chapter 1 sets the global stage for this book. Here I explore the emergence of what I have labeled a global radical moment and analyze the making of a global radical culture between 1870 and 1914. I identify global radicalism's key players around the world, noting the networks and institutions that helped them disseminate their ideas locally and globally, and the movement's main ideas and causes célèbres, its literary and political canons and reading lists. Specifically, I focus on the players, movements, and networks that had a direct impact on the story of radicalism in the three cities of the Eastern Mediterranean and emphasize the links between world regions that help explain the interconnectivity of these radicalisms and the making of a global radical moment.

In chapter 2 I argue that the press in general, and two periodicals in particular (*al-Muqtaṭaf* and *al-Hilāl*, both of which were founded by Syrians and were eventually based in Cairo), were central to the dissemination of radical leftist ideas throughout the reading populations of Beirut, Cairo, and Alexandria. These journals introduced their readership to socialism and anarchism by publishing articles on these subjects from the 1890s until 1914. I analyze the two periodicals' ability to bring socialism and anarchism to their readership by placing these two ideologies within a reformist framework that was becoming increasingly familiar and meaningful to their readers. Although I specifically examine the role of the press, both as an institution creating a network of intellectuals and as a medium for formulating and disseminating ideas, I also move beyond the press and position radicalism in relation to the *nahḍa.* I emphasize local agency in the appropriation of socialism and its adaptation into a larger social, cultural, and intellectual context. I also analyze the construction of a global Syrian diasporic press and its role in triggering local interest in radicalism.

In chapter 3 I argue that the theater was inextricably linked to the construction and dissemination of leftist ideas and that the stage reflected the progressive radicalization of a certain intellectual elite and allowed it to disseminate its ideas and gather support. At the same time the theater provided a unique forum for the consolidation of a coherent radical ideology. I underline the radical potential of the theater by examining vital social transformations that it developed and implied, such as the rights granted and appropriated by various segments of the population to perform, consume, and hence interpret topics that had hitherto been reserved for specific political and cultural elites, and the effects such phenomena had on the public sphere. After assessing this radical and subversive potential I analyze the actual politicization and radicalization of the theatrical repertoire itself and argue that the themes addressed by the theater were becoming progressively more radical. I place the emergence of radicalism in the context of mass politics, showing how the theater was not only the most effective tool for the education of the masses, but also provided the space for a rising radical bourgeoisie to construct a coherent ideology based on an alliance with the working classes.

In chapter 4 I analyze the construction of two radical leftist networks, one in Beirut and Mount Lebanon and the other in Alexandria. I focus on the ties between members of these networks, their building of a shared worldview, and the main radical ideas they put forth concerning workers, class conflict, mass education, workers' education, and related issues. I identify and explain the changes within these radical discourses and their connections to local as well as international issues. I assess these networks' ability to disseminate ideas in their own cities and in the other cities under study, through their own periodicals and by sponsoring highly visible and mediatized radical projects, including the establishment of free schools and universities to educate the working classes and the staging of plays promoting socialism and anarchism. I look closely at radical networks in Beirut and Alexandria and their relationship with more powerful reformist groups—in Beirut the mainstream *nahḍa* group, and in Alexandria a radical bourgeoisie with connections to the municipality and various other institutions. I discuss the success that radical ideas achieved in the two cities and the similarities between the structure of their radical networks.

In chapter 5 I analyze the role of workers in the radical movements of the three cities. I focus on strikes as one complex expression of radical ideas and argue that their emergence in the late nineteenth century and their popularity among workers in Beirut, Cairo, and Alexandria were linked to an interconnected set of social and economic factors, local and global, that caused labor categories in these cities to become fluid and unstable. This instability triggered discontent while simultaneously expanding communication channels between various labor categories, thus facilitating the circulation of radical ideas. I argue that the integration of certain cities and regions into the world economy created grievances among many members of the working classes in Egypt and Syria, and that strikes represented a new and effective way of expressing and addressing these grievances. I show that sites of globalization such as ports, railways, tramways, and tobacco factories were particularly prominent sites of labor contestation, and I link globalization and social and economic changes to workers' militancy and appetite for radical leftist ideas. I also focus on one central feature of globalization, international labor migration, and underline its radicalizing impact on local workers and on the three cities in question. I present Beirut, Cairo, and especially Alexandria as constituting sites of convergence and intersection for a multiplicity of labor traditions and workers' networks of contestation, both indigenous and foreign. I also analyze the relationship between class and ethnicity and argue that there existed various, if simultaneously limited spaces and opportunities for workers from different ethnicities, indigenous as well as immigrant and migrant, to interact with, exchange, and synthesize radical ideas and forms of militancy.

Given the multiplicity of media and institutions that figure in this book, it is only appropriate that I have used a wide array of sources in multiple languages. These sources can be grouped into five general categories: (1) periodicals, both well-known and relatively obscure, some of which have never previously been used as sources for historical research; (2) institutional archives, including Alexandria's municipality archives, the archives of educational institutions in Beirut, Cairo, and Alexandria, and the Beirut Port archives; (3) state and ministerial archives, including the Prime Ministry archives in Istanbul (the Başbakanlık Arşivi), the Dār al-Wathā'iq archives in Cairo, the archives of the Italian Ministry of Foreign Affairs, and published French consular reports on the province of Beirut; (4) literary and theatrical writings, many in the form of monologues; and (5) private correspondence and memoirs, some of which remains unpublished.

1

The Late Nineteenth-century World and the Emergence of a Global Radical Culture

In the last few decades of the nineteenth century, various groups of people throughout the world—workers, peasants, intellectuals, activists—began agitating for social justice, using similar and interrelated discourses and adopting similar terminologies and praxis and circulating their ideas through print, performance, and word of mouth.[1] Their activities fostered a plethora of ideas and practices pertaining to social justice, while simultaneously reflecting a convergence in the ways those ideas were articulated and implemented, and led to the establishment of an entangled worldwide web of radical networks. As a result, I would like to suggest, one can write about a global radical moment lasting roughly from the 1870s until the 1920s and about the making of a global radical culture during this period. In this chapter I examine the emergence of this global radical moment: its key players in the four corners of the world, the networks and institutions that helped them disseminate their ideas locally and globally, the movements' main ideas and causes célèbres, and their literary and political canons and reading lists. I focus on the players, movements, and networks that had a direct impact on the story of radicalism in Beirut, Cairo, and Alexandria and emphasize the links between world regions that help explain the interconnectivity of these radicalisms and the making of a global radical moment.

Most traditional histories of the Left have crafted their genealogies on the works of specific Franco-German (and occasionally British) thinkers. These genealogies start somewhere in the early nineteenth century, with ideas of the French Revolution overlapping with the effects of the Industrial Revolution and proletarianization. In this framework the seeds planted by Fourier, Saint-Simon, and Owen eventually climax with Marx's work and the establishment of the First International. After this peak the genealogies usually proceed by tracing the lines between the Second International, the establishment of socialist and social democratic parties, and the Russian Revolution and the dominance of communism and communist parties. My aim is different; it entails circumventing the whole project of genealogy and decentering it from northwestern Europe. Instead, starting with the 1870s and using a synchronic lens, I will try to conjure up a polyvalent, polyglot, and global leftist radical moment in which various, and very often unofficial, impure, and popular interpretations of the Left were gaining ground all over the world. This will in no way be a comprehensive study; rather, I select certain networks, schools of thought, and ideas as well as particular trends and developments affecting different world regions and intertwining their histories. I focus on those that had a direct manifestation in the Eastern Mediterranean, specifically in Beirut, Cairo, and Alexandria. These particular networks seem to have been both crucial and exemplary in spanning a global radical field and providing a radical matrix, or a radical package of ideas and practices. Hence rather than create a standard genealogy of the Left, I seek to show the matrix from which a global radical framework emerged. Some of the elements that shaped it were not always radical in nature but could nonetheless be vehicles for the articulation and dissemination of radical thought and praxis.

GLOBALIZATION, GLOBAL SHIFTS, AND GLOBAL LINKAGES: CAPITAL, LABOR, INFORMATION, IMPERIALISM, AND MIGRATION

The late nineteenth century ushered in developments that caused the world, or more accurately increasing numbers of regions, to become inextricably linked, responding to similar rhythms and flows *in sync.* The wave of globalization that began around the 1870s was associated with a deeper integration of regions that had been semiperipheral into the world capitalist system and the world economy, which made them more vulnerable to economic fluxes such as commodity production and price fluctuations, integrated their regional labor markets into a global market, and made them dependent on foreign investments and loans. Globalization meant faster and greater circulation of capital, commodities, and labor, as well as the building of necessary infrastructure: extensive railway networks, port expansions, the digging of the Suez Canal and the Panama Canal, the establishment of various steamship lines connecting the four continents, banks and money wiring services, and the like. The circulation of all these elements was not random or among equals; rather, capital, labor, goods, and to a lesser degree information usually followed paths suggested by, if not dictated by some form of political and economic imperialism. Between 1870 and 1914 this circulation also seems to have exacerbated inequalities between peoples, regions, and states, or what Chris Bayly terms the "differentials of power."[2] It also prompted a rethinking of both social order and world order. Globalization can thus be described as "a moment when crises in . . . global world orders produced an urgent attempt to rethink the very bases of politics, culture, and activism—on a local as well as a regional and global level."[3] Globalization was also connected to the growing and faster circulation of information and ideas through the increased flows of people, but also through new media: telegraphs, newspapers and periodicals, and postal services. As such it allowed for the emergence of specific and *global* forms of challenge and resistance to the status quo. It is within this framework that radicalism can be best understood, both as an indicator as well as a maker of globalization.

Let me offer three caveats. First, although I am generally arguing that radicalism, as it manifested itself in the late nineteenth century, was partly a global response to global changes, it is also important to understand it as more than a purely reactive movement and to characterize it (and the changes brought forth by globalization) as something other than a pure rupture. A second caveat concerns ideas and their material base. I am not suggesting an overly deterministic and materialist approach to the history of ideas, such as that the economic factors of globalization necessarily, or linearly, explain the various ideas (and therefore practices) that constitute radicalism. Rather, I argue that they certainly provided a framework for understanding why radicalism emerged as a worldview or mental structure. A third caveat is that by suggesting the existence of a global radical moment or culture, I am in no way pitting the global against the local nor suggesting a hierarchy of importance between the two in which the global would have the upper hand. Rather, I insist that the two are inextricably linked and so tangled in the period under study that they are necessarily complementary rather than opposite (albeit flawed) categories; as a result, they can be understood only in tandem.

THE WORLD WIDE WEB OF RADICALISM: THE LINKS THAT MADE THE MOMENT A GLOBAL ONE

In the late nineteenth century discussions and ideas pertaining to social inequality, wealth redistribution, the value of wage labor (versus capital), workers' rights, workers' housing, mutual aid associations, mass education, and generally the question of how to establish more just societies that would defuse the time bomb of class warfare became quasi-universal, transnational, and global. A multiplicity of communication channels circulated these discussions throughout various parts of the world. To explore some of the main communication channels, I suggest thinking of four interconnected units that played a central role in the articulation of radical leftist ideas and provided structures for their dissemination at a global level: international (and internationalist) organizations and associations, networks, nodal cities, and the printed word.

Any discussion on international organizations that articulated and disseminated radical ideas in the second half of the nineteenth century should include the International Socialist. Much has been written on the First International (1860–89) and the Second International (1889–1916), and my aim here is not to summarize the history of these organizations nor to add much to the body of writings on them. What I underline, in the case of the Second International, is the establishment of a structure that self-consciously and explicitly intended to spread socialism, help workers of the world unionize and gain rights, establish a global working-class consciousness, and, last but not least, foster the creation of socialist parties throughout the world. The extent to which the two Internationals were successful is debatable; certainly the International remained very much a European affair, with a handful of exceptions. What is undeniable, though, are the offices and services the Internationals provided, which were theoretically accessible to socialists all around the world: namely, political, financial, and infrastructural support to form workers' associations that would link to the International. Under "infrastructural support" came publications: pamphlets, booklets, and periodicals that would help spread socialism among the masses.[4] Furthermore the International Socialist Congresses, regularly held starting in the 1880s, and the establishment of International Trade Secretariats (many of which were based in Western Europe, especially in Germany), gave socialism visibility and respectability as increasing numbers of European socialist parties became successful national parties and played the parliamentary game, a point to which I will return.[5] However, if the International Socialist has figured prominently in the history of the Left, it has tended to overshadow another movement, whose principles and activities in fact gained much greater popularity outside of northwestern Europe. Indeed if there was one radical current which became global, or at least had a serious impact throughout the world in the late nineteenth century, it was anarchism.

Anarchism and Anarchosyndicalism

Around 1870 anarchism emerged as a major political ideology in Europe, most vibrantly in Italy and Spain.[6] Anarchism's main tenets were the elimination of private property and class differences and the economic and intellectual emancipation of workers. Visceral anticlericalism and the refusal to work within the system by playing the parliamentary card (in contrast to the policy followed by socialists in the 1890s) also occupied a central place. Following a "decade of regicide,"[7] political assassinations, and bomb attacks blamed, rightly or wrongly, on anarchists, after which many fled from repression during the concomitant rise in mass migrations, anarchism quickly gained ground throughout the world, from South America to East Asia. By the late nineteenth century anarchists and anarchist ideas were to be found, in different shades and degrees, in many parts of the world due to the strong connection between migration and anarchism. Indeed anarchism was *the* radical ideology that seemed to have had the greatest appeal for (or worked best for) workers on the move, as well as intellectuals in the diaspora.[8] Specifically, but not exclusively, it was associated with Spanish and especially Italian migrant and diasporic communities and networks, most strongly in South America but also in the United States, Europe (including France, Belgium, and England), and the Eastern Mediterranean.[9] Anarchists were particularly adept at establishing transnational networks of communications and exchange of information, propaganda, and militants. One of the most vivid manifestations of their success in this domain was the web of Italian anarchist periodicals circulating throughout various cities in Italy, as well as Alexandria, Cairo, Buenos Aires, Montevideo, Paris, and Paterson, New Jersey. This is not to say that anarchist ideas circulated exclusively within the confines of a diaspora, or exclusively along ethnic lines; there were certainly anarchist networks revolving around periodicals that were not exclusively connected to one specific diaspora but cut across ethnic and linguistic groups. Such was the case for Jean Grave's *Le Révolté* (which was initially founded by Kropotkin and subsequently was called *Les Temps Nouveaux*), one of the most famous and highly esteemed anarchist periodicals, issued in Paris after 1885, whose readership spanned continents and many ethnolinguistic groups, as attested by the subscribers' names, addresses, and letters to the editor.[10] *Le Révolté* seems to have been a central node for information and news connected to various anarchist networks.

Nonetheless, although such periodicals did exist and played an important role in the forging of connections between anarchists, many of the anarchist networks in the period under study were linked to a specific diaspora and to the activism of exiled militants. This was certainly not an exclusively European phenomenon. In the last decade of the nineteenth century and the first years of the twentieth Japanese anarchism (as well as socialism) was intrinsically linked to the presence and activism of Japanese militants in the United States, specifically in the San Francisco area, where "Japanese socialists and anarchists had found refuge from government repression in Japan, and were able to voice their dissent—in spite of the fact that their destinations were shaped by racial exclusion and discrimination. Also, the United States was where the labor movement in Japan 'had immediate roots.' "[11] Similarly the Chinese anarchist movement had strong connections to Paris as well as the United States and elsewhere.[12]

Anarchism's success as a global radical set of networks and a global radical movement can be attributed to the following features: the flexibility of its ideology; its work among and attraction to people from all classes, leading to its genuinely *popular* appeal; and its connection to migration and migrant labor, which represented a larger component of the global workforce than ever before, contributing to the geographic dissemination of anarchist ideas.[13] Indeed partly because of its fundamental aversion to centralized authority and because it was a movement that was often underground and whose members were constantly on the move, anarchism consisted of a rather flexible package of ideas. As a loose set of ideas it could offer something to everyone. Its malleability, perhaps even its emotionalism and its martyrs allowed people from diverse backgrounds to relate to it, as well as plunder from it whatever might suit their needs and prove resonant in their own local contexts. In some ways, then, it was a revolutionary movement (rather than an ideology per se) or a revolutionary mind-set, allowing for selective adaptations of bits and pieces from the long set of items on the anarchist wish list. Like the Spanish freethinker and educator Ferrer (an important character in this book), anarchism's supporters were often "plutôt qu'un révolutionnaire . . . un révolté."[14] Although certain anarchists and their followers were more intransigent regarding the purity of their doctrine, or the difference between it and socialism, the boundaries between these two ideologies were not always clearly demarcated before World War I. Partly because anarchism never quite became orthodox, the meaning of belonging to an anarchist organization was rarely formalized outside of Europe and South America. This meant that anarchists, even when they did have parties, were not as restrictive regarding membership.[15]

Instead anarchists had an equal opportunity approach when it came to doing propaganda work and spreading their message. In contrast to socialists, for instance, they did not favor urban skilled workers, but instead went to work in the city and in the countryside among skilled and unskilled workers, artisans, peasants; migrant, stable, and middle-class white-collar employees; artists and intellectuals. They tailored their multiple publications and messages according to their targeted audiences. Significantly, among audiences who were often illiterate their periodicals proved particularly successful thanks to their use of simple language and the fact that they "easily lent themselves to being read aloud."[16] Furthermore in the 1870s and 1890s anarchists in Spain and southern Italy were involved in massive rural uprisings, during which peasants occupied landholdings and destroyed land records and mobilized against the Church and its representatives, which sided with large real estate owners.[17] Later, in the first decade of the twentieth century, Spanish anarchists would often occupy and destroy Church property. This particular combination of anticlericalism and the struggle over land and property was to prove especially resonant in parts of the world experiencing similar battles, such as Mount Lebanon.

If the abolition of the state was one of anarchism's presumed main tenets, it was not necessarily the most evident goal to implement, and most anarchists focused their energies on spreading ideas about social justice, mutual aid, and general individual and social emancipation through propaganda work. Propaganda did not carry the pejorative connotations it has acquired today. It covered a full spectrum of activities, often, but not always, underground, ranging from casual conversations with workers to newspaper articles. It could also include acts of violence, especially political assassinations and various forms of terrorist attacks, which were categorized as "propaganda by the deed."[18] As Gramsci pointed out in the 1920s, no other previous or contemporary political movement had so emphasized the need to systematically spread its ideas among various sections of the population, especially among peasants and artisans, as did anarchism. Perhaps more than any other radical movement, anarchists were brilliant in their capacity to popularize their ideas and capitalized on increasingly popular media, institutions, and spaces: periodicals, reading rooms, theaters, and coffeehouse performances and discussions.[19] One of the strengths of anarchism was the great importance attached to popular performances and to "performing persecution," to borrow Elun Gabriel's felicitous expression.[20] Anarchists seem to have been particularly successful at using the stage to promote their ideas, canonize their martyrs, and set their narratives in plays and songs. The 1909 trial and execution of Francisco Ferrer was turned into a play in Beirut, in Paris, and most probably in many other cities.[21] Again, anarchists were certainly not the only radicals to employ such measures, but they ended up building an anarchist repertoire of themes and plays, many of which crisscrossed the world. Anarchists also managed to latch onto internationalist structures, whether or not they had been explicitly designed for anarchist use.[22]

Educating the Masses

The popularity of anarchism was also related to two specific concepts and sets of projects: mass education and mutual aid. Throughout the nineteenth century mass education was one of the main paths espoused and expounded by reformists and radicals in their mission to tackle the Social Question. The Social Question referred to the emergence of a class of paupers, the rise of unemployment, and the terrible working and living conditions of wage laborers, issues that, if unresolved, could destroy society. To appreciate the anarchists' contribution, both discursively and practically, to the topic of mass education, it is important to first underline the fact that belief in the primacy of education was not exclusive to them. The notion of educating the masses occupied a central place within a larger concept that was becoming popular globally: progress and civilization. Whether the masses were conceptualized as part of or constitutive of a class, a nation, a larger entity (such as empire or religion), or a society without necessarily belonging to a nation-state, educating them became the sine qua non of progress, evolution, and increased civilization.[23] Anarchists were particularly invested in mass education and were in fact pioneers in developing new visions pertaining to education, which they saw as the most important tool for building the kind of society they wished to establish. They envisioned mass education as the path to eliminating social inequalities, by offering an education and qualifications that would liberate workers economically as well as liberate and enlighten the masses intellectually and culturally and trigger an "intellectual rebellion" in society.[24]

Such a project was to take place in various spheres and in various forms, most obviously in schools: primary and secondary schools as well as night schools for adults and working children. Among the most successful educational projects of the early twentieth century were the modern school system established by the Spanish anarchist Francisco Ferrer and Leo Tolstoi's school. Both became models for schools established in New York, Cuba, and elsewhere.[25] Both educational projects were known and admired among radicals in the Eastern Mediterranean. Nonetheless, as I mentioned earlier, the unique power of anarchists lay in their appropriation of other institutions and other spaces for educational purposes: the stage, the press, public lectures, and popular universities. In an era characterized by an explosion of public and especially popular spaces and growing notions of publicity, anarchists used all kinds of old and new public spaces for didactic purposes. In Spain they established an informal education system using sites such as taverns, reading clubs, mutual aid societies, and especially radical newspapers such as *La Revista Blanca* (which was often read aloud), through which they made the education of the working class their priority.[26] In Cuba they used the theater, merging anarchist with gender issues, and targeted women.[27] Anarchists launched similar educational projects throughout the world. They believed in the need to first liberate the individual in order to liberate society.[28] Like many other radicals and reformists, anarchists viewed society as an organism whose health was contingent on the health of every unit within society; for them education was the quintessential way of improving individuals for the well-being of society.

Mutual Aid and Mutual Improvement Societies

Mutual aid was the second rubric that became strongly associated with anarchism in the late nineteenth century. The idea was to emphasize cooperation among workers, whether through labor cooperatives, unionization efforts, or mutual savings funds. Among other activities these funds would assist individual workers—artisans, factory workers, and others—in times of need, teach and hone skills, and establish agricultural cooperatives that gave out credit at very low interest rates. One of the key discussions for radicals and reformists in various parts of the world was how to guarantee the survival of employment sectors that were threatened with disappearance because of increased industrialization, mechanization, or competition from abroad, while striving to increase workers' productivity. Needless to say, such mutual improvement and mutual aid societies were not novel to the late nineteenth century, in Europe or in the Middle East. Furthermore mutual aid societies were not inherently radical, and certainly not necessarily anarchist. Nonetheless the anarchists were particularly successful at capitalizing on and radicalizing these institutions.[29] It is not a coincidence that the best known work on the topic was written by Piotr Kropotkin, one of the most important anarchists of the period; *Mutual Aid: A Factor in Evolution* was translated and read in various parts of the world, including Beirut, Cairo, and Alexandria.[30] By the second half of the nineteenth century these societies and the closely related mutual improvement societies were sprouting in various parts of the world, including Britain, Italy, the Eastern Mediterranean, Japan, and South

America.[31] Typically at the mutual improvement society meetings "one member would deliver a paper on any imaginable subjects—politics, literature, religion, ethics, 'useful knowledge'—and then the topic would be thrown open to general discussion. The aim was to develop the verbal and intellectual skills of people who had never been encouraged to speak or think."[32] Mutual aid and mutual improvement societies also established literary associations and amateur theatrical groups for the edification and entertainment of white-collar and blue-collar workers.[33]

Mutual aid was a particularly appealing institution because the concept fit into a larger, very influential worldview. In the late nineteenth century, as Darwinian ideas of natural selection, competition, and evolution became increasingly popular throughout the world, mutual aid emerged as a concept linking evolution, and hence progress and civilization, to cooperation rather than to competition. Such ideas were attractive in a world experiencing drastic changes, with massive economic restructuring and migration. Mutual aid seems to have become particularly appealing to workers who had just moved to the city and to immigrants in a new land. As José Moya points out, "Even if associations [such as mutual aid] existed in the place of origin, the 'mania' for them seems in most cases to have developed with migration."[34] In fact from the late nineteenth century until World War II, "in terms of wealth and number of members . . . they were the most widespread and important type of immigrants' associations. . . . Even in their modern form, they were already common in the Old World before the mass exodus began in the second third of the nineteenth century. . . . By the middle of the century, mutualism had become the dominant mode of organization in the European workers' movement." [35] Mutual aid also took a particular twist in the colonized world and in parts of the world where the state was deemed too weak to protect workers against foreign economic competition or penetration. In such cases, mutualism became associated with a form of economic localism: cooperation among local workers against unfair competition by stronger foreign parties.

Freemasonry

The emergence of new global radical networks and organizations, most prominently anarchist networks and the International Socialist, did not obviate older transnational or global networks that still played an important role in articulating radical thought or provided the necessary infrastructure to do so. Freemasonry deserves special mention, as it occupies an important place in the story of radicalism in the Eastern Mediterranean.

Needless to say, freemasonry (like mutual aid associations) was not necessarily inherently progressive or radical. According to one historian, in the late nineteenth century its ideology in fact shifted to become less radical, less interested in equality and fraternity and more supportive of British imperialism.[36] Other historians have countered that freemasonry was not an imperial ideology but "a decentralized system" that "facilitated intercultural connections throughout Asia and [the] Pacific and that these relationships would give rise to wholly unexpected consequences."[37] In places as far afield as Lagos, Calcutta, and Buenos Aires in the 1890s, freemasonry was seen as an institution inextricably linked to visions of social reform. It was often a bastion of subversive and anticlerical activity, whose members discussed socialism in lodges and were behind the staging of radical plays.[38]

ALTERNATIVE VISIONS OF THE WORLD ORDER COMING FROM THE SOUTH AND THE COLONIZED WORLD

Anarchist networks played a central role in articulating and globally disseminating radical leftist ideas in the late nineteenth century and early twentieth, but they were only one set of networks among others busily disseminating alternative visions of social and world orders and contributing to the making of a global radical moment. The period from the late 1880s until World War I was rich in anticolonial struggles and saw the establishment of networks challenging imperialism and engaging in what has been described as "universalist anti-colonialism."[39] Some of these anti-imperialist and anticolonial networks were nationalist; others were nonnationalist or included regionalist or pan-nationalist visions, such as pan-Asianism, pan-Africanism, and pan-Islamism.[40] These networks appeared both in the colonized homeland and in Asian and African diasporas. Among these networks contesting imperialism, part of the emerging global discourse was anti-Western critiques among Middle Eastern, Indian, Chinese, and Japanese intellectuals and the interaction between "various religious traditions and the experience of European colonialism . . . with peculiar Muslim or non-Muslim discontent with globalization, the international order, and modernization to produce shared anti-Western discourses in the twentieth century."[41]

Whether or not they were anti-Western, such movements could and often did intersect with radical leftist ideologies and networks, including anarchism. Many European and non-European anarchists joined or supported anti-imperialist struggles of various kinds, and some fought alongside nationalists and anti-imperialists in places as distant as Egypt, Greece, and the Philippines. Benedict Anderson has depicted the ties that existed among anarchists, anti-imperialists, and nationalists in and between the Philippines, Cuba, and various parts of Europe, rightly pointing out that "[anarchism] had no theoretical prejudices against 'small' and 'ahistorical' nationalisms, including those in the colonial world."[42] In Egypt a number of Italian anarchists, including Errico Malatesta, fought with the Egyptians and against the British in 1882.[43] Even when they did not directly take up arms against imperialism and colonial ideology, anarchists often stridently voiced opposition to them. One letter, sent from Algiers in 1907 to the anarchist periodical *Les Temps Nouveaux* in

Paris and signed "Un groupe de marins anarchistes," vividly described the beating and general abuse of Algerian boys, one of them a ship's boy *(mousse),* by French corporals. The letter concluded, "What must this poor lad think of French civilization and its superiority over Arab civilization?"[44] Another letter, sent from Tunis in 1908 and signed "Zuili," reported on a speech given by Andrea Costa, an Italian deputy, an ex-anarchist turned socialist, during his visit to Tunis. Costa's "chauvinist sentiments" *(esprit chauvin)* and exclusive focus on the condition of Sicilian immigrants in Tunis provoked the ire of Zuili, a local Italian anarchist, who "explained to him, through serious argumentation, that he was a phoney *[fumiste]* . . . to talk about patriotic feelings and deplore the conditions of Sicilians living in [Tunis], while that of the indigenous population that was spoliated since France's pacific penetration in Tunisia is much more pitiful [or miserable, *pitoyable*]."[45]

Hence in parts of the world under semi-imperial, imperial, and colonial rule, calls for a more just society based on greater equality between different classes very often merged with anti-imperial struggles. These various radical networks—anarchist, anticolonial, revolutionist—often intersected and were entangled, both in terms of people and ideas, though this would probably no longer be possible a few decades later, with the subsequent hardening of communism, nationalism, and other ideologies, which made these radical movements' eclectic bricolage impossible—or at least much more difficult.

One of the debates closely associated with anarchists in the late nineteenth century was about the use of revolutionary violence, specifically political assassination, which some anarchists viewed as "propaganda by the deed."[46] The wave of attacks on heads of state and prominent public figures was launched in 1878, peaked in the 1890s, and continued into the early twentieth century. By the 1890s political assassinations and bombings had become a fact of life throughout Europe, the Russian Empire, and to a lesser extent North and South America, Egypt, and the Ottoman Empire.[47] This put political assassination and the use of violence more generally on the table as an unavoidable subject of reflection. It was a hotly debated topic for anticolonial militants, many of whom engaged with anarchist writings on the subject and some of whom went to Europe explicitly to learn how to make bombs and other explosives.[48] In 1900, when Indian activists formed the Anushilan and Jugantar parties with the aim of liberating India from the British, their members, referred to by the British as "gentlemanly terrorists" because of their revolutionary and violent militant practices, displayed "an . . . enthusiasm for the writings of European revolutionaries, anarchists and nationalists (Mazzini, Garibaldi, Wolfe Tone and Marx)," which they combined with "indigenous forms of religious practice and physical training."[49] A few years later, in 1914, another Indian movement calling for a war of liberation against the British, the Ghadar movement, linked militant intellectuals in the Indian diaspora, in cities such as San Francisco, Hong Kong, Shanghai, Tokyo, Panama City, and Vancouver, with militant peasants and activists in the

Subcontinent. A "non-nationalist anti-colonial" movement and "a phenomenon of hybrid radicalism possible only in the context of diaspora," the Ghadar movement relied on "an eclectic—not to say opportunistic—array of strategic contacts" that allowed it to be inspired by Mazzini's Italian Risorgimento, while at the same time having "close ties of solidarity with Irish and Egyptian opponents of British colonialism, as well as with Pan-Asianist and, more problematically, with Pan-Islamist movements against Western imperialism." It was also "hooked into networks of anarchists and socialists in Europe, Japan, and North America, with a Bengali tradition of Kropotkinism as well as of guerrilla militancy."[50]

I am dwelling on Indian anticolonial networks and movements partly to give a sense of the bricolage involved in these radical movements and partly because such struggles, the ideas expressed by them, and the terminology of resistance and liberation they employed were in communication with and often shared by other anticolonial and anti-imperial movements. There was a particularly strong sense of solidarity and exchange of ideas and resistance tactics among regions subjected to the same imperial power, as Anderson has shown in the case of the Spanish Empire with Cuba and the Philippines and the revolutionary webs connecting them.[51] Of particular pertinence to radicalism in the Eastern Mediterranean is the fact that the period 1905–10 seems to have witnessed a convergence in strikes and anti-British mobilizations, especially between Egypt and Bengal, and a growing consciousness that all these liberation struggles were connected to one another.[52] Da'ud Muja'is, the main writer of *al-Ḥurriyya* and a member of a radical leftist network around Beirut, wrote in 1909 condoning the Indians' assassinations of British political figures, both on Indian and English soil: "The world is still in a continuous struggle *[jihād]* and upheaval that will only subside when all the people of the world will be liberated . . . and the barriers against this liberation, as high as they are . . . will eventually be destroyed."[53] For radical networks that had a presence in or an impact on societies subjected to direct foreign domination, it was the norm rather than the exception to meld anarchist ideas with anti-imperialist causes and to carefully analyze, pick and choose, and incorporate elements of the struggles, discourses, and methods put forth by many radical networks and movements: Italian anarchists, Russian revolutionaries fighting against the tsar's autocracy, and Indian, Egyptian, and Irish anti-imperialists.[54]

Nodal Cities

How and where did such entanglements and exchanges between radical networks actually take place? One such forum of exchange came via face-to-face encounters, many of which actually happened in what I call *nodal cities*. Such cities included imperial metropoles, particularly Paris and London. The role of imperial metropoles as centers for anti-imperial activism is well documented; the various anti-imperialist conferences held there, especially those organized by non-Europeans, nationalist, pan-nationalist, and otherwise, have all been extensively studied.[55] It was partly the confluence and intersection of various radical networks, some of them of political exiles in nodal cities, that globalized political and social struggles and created a common repertoire of concepts to frame them. Nonetheless such encounters transcended the focus of networks whose raison d'être was to fight imperialism. Iranian constitutionalists, Young Turks, exiled Russian nihilists, French and Italian anarchists, and many more met in world cities such as London and Paris, but also in neutral Geneva and in regional nodal cities such as Istanbul, Alexandria, and Tokyo.[56] Several such conferences and meetings took place between 1905 and 1911, labeled by Eric Hobsbawm "the little age of revolutions": the 1905 Russian Revolution, the 1906 Iranian Constitutional Revolution, the 1908 Young Turk Revolution, the 1911 Chinese Revolution. These cities harbored and brought together political exiles and militants from different parts of a region or an empire, guaranteed the circulation of printed material, and provided spaces for different radical networks to encounter one another and exchange ideas. These encounters in coffeehouses, clubs, study circles, and the like forged links and the establishment of lifelong connections between radicals from various continents.

It was often in such nodal cities that intellectuals and militants from the South became acquainted with or furthered their knowledge of radical movements and ideologies, partly through their interaction with European radical thinkers. For instance, it was in London that the Egyptian socialist Salama Musa became acquainted with Fabianism (a form of British socialism), and it was in Paris in the 1870s that Shibli Shumayyil, the first self-proclaimed Arab socialist, discovered Büchner's theories.[57] It was also in Paris that Li Shizeng, a Chinese anarchist, founded the World Society, which "would serve for decades as a conduit between European and Chinese anarchists[,] . . . would fashion the thinking over the years of most Chinese anarchists . . . [and] was to serve as a recruiting ground for [Chinese] anarchists."[58] The city was also the site of Li Shizeng's conversion to anarchism "as a consequence of his close relationship with the family of the famous French anarchist Elisée Reclus." This connection between Chinese anarchists and the Reclus family endured for years.[59] At the same time that many non-Western intellectuals became acquainted with or converted to radical ideas and ideologies in these (mostly European) world cities, their presence in these cities also contributed to the radicalization of the European intellectual circles they frequented. As Sara Blair has so aptly demonstrated, Bloomsbury became a literary and radical movement *because* of Bloomsbury the space, a liminal neighborhood in London that housed the Fabian Society and other radical and reformist societies and was home to University College, an institution attracting students from various parts of the empire, especially radical Indian students.[60]

These cities also hosted a number of study circles and international associations and conferences, which provided a forum for discussions on labor, workers' rights, capitalism, political economy, and related topics, often turning these into global discussions. Paris and London in particular were home to a growing community of social experts—sociologists, lawyers, economists, criminologists, and especially political economists—who convened study circles and founded periodicals that circulated beyond Europe, establishing links with intellectuals around the world who also belonged to or were interested in these new social disciplines. For a number of reasons, not least of which were imperial connections, North Africa and the Eastern Mediterranean were particularly plugged into such circles, especially the French circles. Such was the case, for example, for Charles Gide's *Revue d'économie politique,* founded in Paris in 1887.[61] Gide (1847–1932), a Christian socialist and a proponent of popular universities for free mass education and of agricultural and consumers' cooperatives (and hence mutual aid), was the author of a number of books on political economy (including *Principes d'économie politique*) that gained international fame. His works were translated into virtually every European language (including Polish, Russian, and Finnish), as well as into Ottoman, and articles summarizing his ideas appeared in Arabic periodicals. His books were available in French and English at the library of the Syrian Protestant College in Beirut, for instance.[62]

Whether or not some of the venues were explicitly designed as radical forums, they often ended up playing this role. For instance, the famous world exhibitions, a staple of the late nineteenth century, began to see booths for labor movements and radical groups as early as 1862. Of particular importance was the Exposition Universelle held in Paris in 1900, where the first International Congress on Mutual Cooperation took place; by then the concept of international solidarity and cooperation had become a major theme and a goal of labor movements in Europe.[63] The late nineteenth century was also the era of municipal socialism, whereby various radical projects were conceived and implemented by municipalities, the quintessential nineteenth-century urban institution. A movement that was particularly strong in Italy, where it was partly the product of a political alliance between the Italian Socialist Party and the radical middle class, municipal socialism led to the establishment of municipal councils that "concentrated their efforts on improving workers' living conditions and giving general support to the movement: a local finance policy based on fair taxation, assistance to democratic institutions, extension of free education and municipality services were the general characteristics of these administrations."[64] Municipal socialism seems to have quickly become popular elsewhere in the world, notably in Alexandria. By the late nineteenth century municipalities no longer operated solely within national boundaries; instead they became connected through international conferences and publications that sought to exchange (and compete over) strategies and policies regarding urban planning, low-income housing, health issues, poverty alleviation, and the expansion of urban public spaces. There was even a project (implemented in 1913) to establish a "municipal international," which, though Eurocentric, included municipalities from outside of Europe such as Alexandria and Buenos Aires.[65]

The late nineteenth-century French engineer Emile Cheysson described the "interpenetration of these reformist ideas and networks in the late 19th century as 'electric cables' connecting the industrial world in its entirety."[66] These connections spanned a much larger world than the industrial one, as intellectuals and professionals from the non-Western world visited these exhibitions, joined some of these networks, engaged with them and contributed to these discussions, or simply read about and were acquainted with ideas discussed in these forums. They wrote, translated, indigenized, and published articles on subjects such as mutual aid, labor unions, municipal socialism, and capitalism.

The Making of a Global Radical Culture

The late nineteenth century witnessed the efflorescence of a global popular radical culture and the establishment of a certain radical canon. The elements of this radical culture combined the historical with the fictional and cut across genres, regional cultures, and geographic boundaries. The most salient features were a historical narrative of radicalism that tied together key moments whose ideals, heroes, and martyrs would be celebrated across the world and a reading list of political thinkers, novelists, and playwrights whose works were translated into multiple languages. The historical narrative of radicalism connected various revolutions and rebellions, most of which were defeated by conservative forces, and led to the construction of a commemorative radical repertoire. There were regional differences in this canon, but this narrative was not exclusivist; radicals of different shades partook in the commemoration of these events. The unavoidable, perhaps most important event in this radical calendar was the French Revolution, whose ideologues Robespierre, Saint-Just, and Danton became the icons of many Arab, Ottoman, Indian, and South American radicals.[67] Also extremely significant were the revolutions of 1848 and the Paris Commune of 1871. In both cases, revolutionaries who had managed to flee repression sought refuge in South and Central America and throughout the Ottoman Empire, where they continued spreading the message of republicanism, equality, and socialism (in the case of the Commune) and collaborated with local radicals.[68] These two events generated not only a set of values, but also references, symbols, martyrs, and heroes for people who struggled for political and social emancipation.[69] The Commune in particular remained a key episode for radicals well after its day had passed. Indeed anarchists in Argentina, Egypt, and elsewhere distributed pamphlets commemorating the heroes of the Commune on its thirtieth anniversary.[70] Similarly the Dreyfus Affair and the Ferrer Affair also served to mobilize radicals. Finally, lest we forget, *the* international radical and leftist commemoration par excellence, May Day, "celebrates the memory of immigrant anarchists—not Marxists—executed in the U.S. in 1886."[71] It was thus the reaction to certain moments deemed pivotal and the construction of meaning and symbols commemorating these events in rallies, demonstrations, and theatrical performances that provided a common set of values and references to people who perceived themselves as radicals.

At the heart of this emerging global radical culture were two phenomena: translation and printing, of books but especially of periodicals. Translation, "a process which was central to globalization," was, as T. N. Harper succinctly put it, "rarely a search for pure meaning. It was an interactive process of borrowing. Translations of works . . . were unauthorized and not intended to be authoritative. Translators themselves became a vocal presence in the text; the aim was often 'translating the gist' and explicating the rest."[72] The inequality of exchange and of the power dynamics determining translations is evident and should be taken seriously, yet the degree of cross-fertilization and complexity that marked the use and development of these ideas is outstanding. Thus some of the main anarchist theoreticians, Bakunin, Kropotkin, Malatesta, Jean Grave, and Elisée Reclus (whose work as a geographer was also well-known), were translated (usually very selectively and loosely) into numerous languages.[73] Similarly Maxim Gorki, Leo Tolstoi, Eugène Sue, and Anatole France, among others, became bedside reading for radicals and aspiring radicals in the four corners of the world, a phenomenon that recalls Benedict Anderson's notion of the making of "transnational libraries."[74] The paths of translation were not necessarily linear and often involved multiple translations through various intermediary languages. Such is the case, for example, for some of the Arabic editions of Gorki's work, which were most likely translated from the Portuguese by a Syrian who had emigrated to Brazil, and which were published in 1906 in São Paulo.[75]

The radical credentials of Bakunin and Gorki are unquestioned, yet a hundred years ago a much wider array of authors were deemed to be radical or had their work interpreted through a radical lens. It might be somewhat baffling today to discover that Alexandre Dumas père's *Conte de Monte Cristo* was part of that radical reading list, but it was indeed; the story of false accusations, revenge, and ultimate justice was read out loud by cigar rollers in Cuba, devoured in its Modern Greek version in Istanbul in the 1840s, right after the French version had appeared, translated into Ottoman Turkish in 1871 to be serialized in the translator's satirical paper, *Diyojen,* and published in its Arabic translation in Cairo during the same year.[76] That novel as well as other writings by Dumas were also serially published by anarchist newspapers in Italian, French, and countless other languages. The works of Victorien Sardou and Eugène Sue have now sunk into oblivion, but in the first decade of the twentieth century their translation and adaptation to the stage triggered passions and thrust radicals into opposition against conservatives in many parts the world because people identified with their message of social justice and, in the case of Sue's *Juif errant,* the scathing attack on the Catholic Church and the Jesuits.[77] This need to reread authors who have been forcibly deradicalized but who were in fact read radically at a given historical moment also applies to Shakespeare, whose plays were translated into multiple languages and performed on various stages throughout the world in the late nineteenth century. In the context of England and, I would argue, elsewhere, Shakespeare should be "return[ed] . . . to centre-stage in working-class radicalism by considering his importance within popular politics and the role of the theatre in promoting radical reform, as a vehicle for radical ideas, or as a meeting place for reformers."[78] Other authors have in fact not only been deradicalized, but have been interpreted as promoters of free market and liberal economic thought. This has been the fate of Samuel Smiles, whose book *Self-Help* was a staple within the mutual improvement movement due to its emphasis on ways for individuals (especially workers) to pursue self-cultivation and liberation. *Self-Help,* which became a global best-seller in the late nineteenth century and early twentieth and was widely read and quoted in Japan, Egypt, and Britain, has been reclassified by Middle Eastern historians as a classical work of capitalist, liberal economics.[79]

I mentioned anarchists' belief in the need to first liberate the individual in order to liberate society and I underlined their focus on triggering an intellectual rebellion. Anarchists sought to bridge the gap between high and low culture through the theater and literature. Their faith in the implacable necessity of individual emancipation and growth as a sine qua non of social emancipation gave them faith in the "liberating powers of literature." In London's Jewish East End it was the anarchists who most effectively mobilized the "liberating power of literature" in Yiddish anarchist papers, where they published Yiddish translations of Molière, Herbert Spencer, Strindberg, Tolstoi, Ibsen, Chekhov, Gorki, Anatole France, and Kropotkin.[80] Similarly the periodicals of Alexandria's (Italian) anarchists invariably included translated passages of literary works by Tolstoi, Dumas, and Anatole France.[81] Through the establishment of free reading rooms, libraries, night schools, and plays, anarchists in London's East End, Alexandria, and elsewhere incorporated and popularized great masterpieces, teaching Shakespeare, Dante, and Tolstoi, and sometimes also lectured on Beethoven's Ninth Symphony.[82]

Yet this emerging radical global canon contained certain omissions that might seem odd today, with some authors conspicuously missing or underrepresented. Most striking, from our contemporary perspective, is the relative absence of Marx. Although the *Communist Manifesto* was translated into a number of languages (including Armenian), it is unclear how many people actually read it, or any of his other works, after Marx's death.[83] Only a few radicals and radical sympathizers active in the Eastern Mediterranean mentioned Marx or commented on his work; when some of them (such as Salama Musa and Farah Antun) did cite him, they did so quite briefly. In the case of Antun, the constant and consistent misspelling of

Marx's name (transliterated into Arabic as "Max") may suggest that Antun had only *heard* about Marx's theories before (or instead of) reading them.[84] The same was often true of radicals elsewhere. Upon his return from Europe to his native Philippines, the writer and revolutionary nationalist and anarchist sympathizer José Rizal brought with him his library, which consisted of the usual suspects: Dumas, Hugo, Sue, and Zola. But there is no mention of Marx.[85] This omission was certainly not confined to intellectuals or militants in the periphery, but seems to have been quite common among European radicals as well.[86] Marx's absence does not necessarily mean that radicals were not familiar with his ideas, but rather that other authors were more popular and considered more worthy of commenting on and summarizing for the people. Some of these writers had themselves integrated Marx's writings into their own, developing their own cannibalized version of his radical thought, or had written commentaries on Marx's writings, leading one historian of the European Left to conclude that "early socialist intellectuals [had] acquired garbled versions of Marx."[87]

PRINTING, PERIODICALS, AND THE MAKING OF GLOBAL IMAGINING COMMUNITIES

If books were important vehicles in the making of this global popular radical culture, it was periodicals that truly served as its cornerstone. In the late nineteenth century, probably starting around 1880, periodicals began appearing and multiplying exponentially around the world. The relationship between nationalism and print has been extensively explored, notably in Anderson's *Imagined Communities*, yet print, specifically periodicals, was often *the* main vehicle for all sorts of ideas. As such it was crucial to all forms of movements and ideologies in the late nineteenth century, allowing people to connect and create imagining communities and ties of solidarity across lands and seas. Such reading communities had existed for centuries before the advent of print through the circulation of manuscripts, and many of these reading and writing connections endured, occasionally forming a sphere parallel to that of print periodicals and occasionally merging or overlapping with them.[88] Nonetheless there was a quantitative as well as qualitative change in the kind of reading communities that emerged in the late nineteenth century. In newspapers and periodicals people all over the world read, and read *simultaneously*, stories on similar topics of concern and global events and reflected on the lessons they could draw from these events, hence simultaneously universalizing their own contexts and localizing the global. One of the main lessons radicals drew from world news was "how to 'do' revolution." Through newspapers Chinese nationalists "eagerly followed events in Cuba and the Philippines—as well as the Boer nationalist struggle against British imperialism, which Filipinos also studied—to learn how to 'do' revolution, anti-colonialism, and anti-imperialism."[89] Arab audiences read equally long descriptions of the Boer War, as well as briefer coverage of events in Cuba and the Philippines, and the Young Turks, while preparing for their 1908 revolution, closely followed news of the 1905 Russian Revolution and the 1906 Iranian Constitutional Revolution.[90]

Similarly noted with interest and covered by the press around the world were the spread of mass politics in Europe through the introduction of male universal suffrage and various important political victories by socialist parties in Europe in the 1890s.[91] The rather stellar rise of the German Social Democratic Party attracted a good deal of coverage in the Eastern Mediterranean press. The party reappeared on the political scene in 1890 after it had been banned for a few decades; it scored more and more votes until becoming Germany's strongest party in 1912. Newspapers and periodicals outside Europe not only reported on the socialists' successes; they also followed parliamentary debates and decisions, especially crucial changes in legislation and the implementation of important reforms. And it was not just the victories of socialist parties, but also a variety of militant social movements and radical activities that received coverage and were discussed in the pages of periodicals. Workers' strikes, trials of anarchists (such as that of Ravachol, the French anarchist and bomb thrower par excellence, tried and executed in 1892, and that of Ferrer in 1909), anticolonial struggles, ideas pertaining to mutual aid, social reform, wealth redistribution, and mass education—such topics received coverage (not necessarily positive coverage, of course) and comment in periodicals and newspapers almost everywhere, certainly in cities integrated into the world economy and connected to the rest of the world by telegraph.

Although visions of the world and interest in world news still followed specific geographies and favored certain regions over others—geographies, routes, and solidarities drawn by empires or diasporas—this still resulted in fairly extensive reporting about world affairs, especially for parts of the world, such as the Eastern Mediterranean, that were drawn into overlapping and competing empires, formal or otherwise. The region was subjected to imperialism or imperial interests by both the British and the French; was still part of another, different kind of empire, the Ottoman Empire; and hosted or refracted multiple diasporas, connecting them to many parts of the world and fostering interest and news exchange with these different corners of the globe.

What we see in this period, then, is the emergence of a global set of concerns and concepts, in which radicalism occupied a central place. Partly because they were global, partly as they became globalized, these concerns had enough flexibility to be useful and to be adopted in different localities. Hence the emergence of "a language of identification and common cause [that] serves to link social movements to each other. The metaphors and slogans work better if they are not too specific, so that the participants in each social situation can fill in their own details yet retain identification with those far away who must fill in quite different details. In 1789 'the rights of man' and 'abolition of feudal privilege' worked well; in 1989 'democracy' and 'multiparty elections' worked equally well."[92]

CONCLUSION

In this chapter I have sketched the contours of the complex and vibrant scene (or matrix) from which global radicalism emerged in the last quarter of the nineteenth century and manifested itself in a global radical culture. I emphasized the multiplicity of movements, institutions, and networks that articulated and implemented radical ideas and that had a global reach and could circulate ideas across lands and seas. This global radicalism went hand in hand with migration flows and allowed for local interpretations and accommodations of what radicalism meant. Radicalism was a package of ideas that worked at different registers: some of the discussions among radicals were highbrow and took place in learned circles and in cutting-edge and newly emerging disciplines (sociology, urban planning, political economy); others took place among peasants, artisans, and construction or industrial workers. Some radical ideas were published in elite periodicals for experts; others were distributed through pamphlets or periodicals accessible to the masses; still others were expressed on the stage, in coffeehouses, and in mutual aid societies and night schools. The rest of this book projects some of these radical beams back onto the Eastern Mediterranean; mutual aid societies, mass education, anarchism, freemasonry, anticlericalism, and anti-imperialism appear and reappear as discourses and presences in the three cities under study, perhaps in slightly different guises (or variations on the themes) and using a multiplicity of registers and languages. Chapter 2 picks up where this one stops: with the claim that the story of radicalism is inextricably connected to the story of periodicals and to the making of transnational and global communities of readers. My focus is on the coverage of the Left (and its radical attachments) by two influential, nonleftist Arabic periodicals (eventually) based in Cairo that played a central role in introducing reading audiences in Cairo, Alexandria, and Beirut to radical and leftist concepts.

2

The *Nahḍa*, the Press, and the Construction and Dissemination of a Radical Worldview

In the early 1890s Arabic reading audiences in Beirut, Cairo, and Alexandria began regularly (if not too frequently) encountering articles on socialism *(al-ishtirākiyya)* and anarchism *(fawḍawiyya)* in the pages of two formative and influential opinion-making periodicals: *al-Muqtaṭaf* (Beirut 1876–83; Cairo 1884–1952) and *al-Hilāl* (Cairo 1892–present).[1] Over the following twenty-five years, the two periodicals, both of which were by then based in Cairo and owned (and mostly written) by Syrians, published around fifty articles on socialism, anarchism, labor conflicts, workers' rights, and related matters. The series culminated in the last few months before the outbreak of the Great War with three long seminal articles on socialism, all unequivocally in support.[2] I begin this chapter by following the story of this coverage: how the Left was covered and interpreted by these two periodicals and what the meaning of such coverage was for reading communities in the three cities in question. I link this coverage of radical issues and the periodicals' desire to familiarize their readers with radical ideas (without necessarily endorsing them) to important developments pertaining to periodical (and intellectual) production: the formation of a class of Syrian intellectuals; the special relationship between Beirut, Cairo, and Alexandria and its pivotal role in the making of these intellectuals; and the globalization of this intellectual production through the establishment of a Syrian diasporic network of periodical writers and intellectuals. I revisit the *nahḍa* (usually translated as the Arab Renaissance, or Arab intellectual awakening), a period of intense intellectual production that has traditionally been interpreted as a precursor to liberal Arab nationalism, and suggest reading it instead as a global and increasingly radical phenomenon, which fits quite smoothly into the global radical moment discussed in the previous chapter. Contrary to a widely held belief, I argue that socialist and radical ideas were alive, often discussed and incorporated into the *nahḍa,* rather than being "inconsequential" topics confined to the work of a few lone intellectuals.[3]

POPULAR CULTURE AND WAYS OF READING

Before delving into an analysis of these periodicals' coverage of leftist and radical issues, a quick note on notions of literacy, readership, and accessibility is in order. Any discussion regarding the impact of any written material, published or otherwise, must take into account the low literacy rates of the period in Egypt and Syria. Although literacy rates in the Ottoman Empire were generally rather low, recent research has problematized both the notions of literacy and the various estimates of its prevalence.[4] Much more qualitative and quantitative research needs to be done on this subject, yet it seems that people who could read were not as few as previously estimated and that there was probably considerable variation in literacy within empires, regions, and even cities.[5] Some sources have suggested that during Sultan Abdülhamid's reign (1876–1909) the number of people in the Ottoman Empire who could read had tripled.[6] Reading rooms, that is, rooms containing books as well as periodicals and generally open for public use, were established by private and governmental initiative and were soon to be found all over Syria, from Beirut to remote villages in Mount Lebanon, as well as Egypt. At the same time, as I mentioned in this book's introduction, the proliferation of the printing press in the Eastern Mediterranean in the second half of the nineteenth century and the exponential increase in textual production, specifically in the form of periodicals, did not, or at least not immediately, supersede older ways of writing or reading. In the late nineteenth century periodicals in the Eastern Mediterranean were often read communally, as they were expensive and full literacy was confined to a select few.[7] This suggests that written (and published) material, especially periodicals, reached beyond the purely literate segments of society. Articles were read aloud and discussed in coffeehouses and probably in the workplace. François Georgeon captures this fluidity between the written and the oral, the literate, the partly literate, and the nonliterate, quite eloquently:

> The access to the written word is not exclusively reserved to those who know how to read and write. There exist, between the oral and written worlds, passages, mediations.... Very often reading is collective (in particular, the reading of a newspaper, which is done aloud by somebody who knows how to read (the imam, the school teacher, the officer, ...) in coffeehouses, and especially in these kiraathane, which literally mean "reading houses," which are half-way between European reading rooms and Eastern coffeehouses, and which began appearing in the 1860s. The end of the Empire thus corresponds to a period during which the fact of being alphabetized con-

> serves its prestige, but at the same time when the written word has lost its quasi-sacred character, and its inaccessibility to the masses.[8]

The implications of these blurred boundaries between written and oral, popular and intellectual are tremendous. In a chapter focusing on the intellectual, highbrow production of radical ideas—their introduction, popularization, and adaptation to reading communities in the three cities under study—this blurring of boundaries meant that, ultimately, information in periodicals was not confined to readers and intellectuals, but most likely spread to other segments of the population.

COVERING THE LEFT: *AL-MUQTAṬAF*'S AND *AL-HILĀL*'S ARTICLES ON SOCIALISM AND ANARCHISM

With this important caveat on the place of the written word in late Ottoman societies, we can now turn to analyzing the coverage of radical topics in *al-Muqtaṭaf* and *al-Hilāl*. *Al-Muqtaṭaf's* 1890 article on socialism, whose authors were most likely the periodical's owners, Sarruf and Nimr, was written in a polemical style and crowned with a combative title, "The Rottenness [or Corruptness] of the Doctrine of Socialists" ("Fasād madhhab al-ishtirākiyyīn").[9] An advocate of liberalism and free enterprise in the 1880s, the periodical generally promoted capitalism during that decade and exposed its readership to the basic premises of classical economic theory, although not necessarily adhering fully to liberal economic thought or unconditionally embracing capitalism, despite what a number of historians have argued.[10] At that time *al-Muqtaṭaf* forcefully argued that competition was natural, unavoidable, and necessary and that it lay at the heart of civilization, as did capitalism.[11] It was along these lines that the periodical attacked socialism in the 1890 article. Socialists, the article claimed, argued erroneously that "the current system increases the wealth of the wealthy and the poverty of the poor and . . . the wealth of the wealthy is taken from the poor," when in fact "the current system increases the wealth of the earth *[khayrāt al-arḍ]* and the wealth of both rich and poor together. . . . It does not concern one group *[farīq]* without the other. . . . The wealth of the rich is not taken from the poor, but from the wealth of the earth."[12] The article praised the individual whose thrift benefited all of society *(al-muqtaṣid)*, for he used his savings to build factories and bridges. It also pushed for "laws promoting individual freedom and rewarding the hardworking *[al-mujtahidīn]* so that they get out of the earth's wealth as much as they can."[13] Capitalism, it concluded, was a system geared at improving people's lives and decreasing the gap between rich and poor. By contrast, socialist principles were "damaging" *(muḍirra)* no matter how they were promoted.

Al-Hilāl was rather less polemical about socialism than *al-Muqtaṭaf*. However, it was quite evident where its sympathies lay during its initial years. Although the periodical often limited itself to objectively reporting events in Europe and to reproducing certain anarchist texts "borrowed" from European newspapers,[14] until the first decade of the twentieth century *al-Hilāl* had serious reservations about socialism and the Left generally.[15] For this journal, just as for *al-Muqtaṭaf,* socialism was unnatural and hence doomed to fail, an argument regularly repeated for years.[16] Socialism was unnatural because the equal distribution of wealth is unknown in the state of nature, which relies on competition; because it was unnatural, it was unjust: "Dividing the earth among people . . . will not last, because [this distribution is] contrary to general justice. Civilization occurs with . . . competition. . . . People are not equal, do not put equal effort into their work, and therefore it would not be fair that they all get equal share from the earth's produce."[17] Yet unlike *al-Muqtaṭaf, al-Hilāl* never depicted socialism as *morally* wrong, a judgment it occasionally made of anarchism, which it described in 1897 as a disease that needed to be eradicated and whose supporters were "evil" *(al-fawdawiyyūn al-ashrār).*[18] Rather, *al-Hilāl* presented the struggle for a more equal distribution of wealth as a lost battle or wasted energy.[19] Instead of obsessing over wealth redistribution, it argued (as did *al-Muqtaṭaf*) that socialists should focus their energies on promoting mass education, the genuine path toward reform and the betterment of society.[20]

Significant changes appeared in both *al-Muqtaṭaf* and *al-Hilāl* in the quarter of a century between the 1890s and the years before World War I. Both periodicals came to describe socialism in a decidedly more positive light, as it became increasingly equated with *reform* and ceased to revolve around the abhorred and feared call for wealth redistribution, an aspect of socialism that was shed in later articles.[21] The kind of reform socialism implied was familiar and desirable, sharing the same vision of society as the readership of *al-Muqtaṭaf* and *al-Hilāl.* Despite the occasional lapse into antipathy in *al-Muqtaṭaf*'s coverage of socialism and anarchism, various articles (even mere sentences and adjectives) suggest that as early as 1894 the periodical was becoming less Manichaean in its worldview. Indeed from 1894 onward *al-Muqtaṭaf* was suggesting that some aspects of socialism were actually positive. In a long article titled "Socialists and Anarchists" the author wrote "about the history of these two 'sects' *[ṭā'ifa],* their principles and the reasons behind their establishment, and assess[ed] . . . *the strengths and weaknesses of their principles, that which can be followed from their teachings, and what ought to be avoided.*"[22] The author concluded that, although socialists had "gone overboard in their demands . . . they helped in some ways, and were detrimental in others."[23] This was a marked departure from the periodical's position in 1890 that socialist principles were "damaging, in whatever way they were promoted."[24]

In fact as early as 1900 *al-Muqtaṭaf* was publishing articles by authors who were unabashedly sympathetic to socialism. In one such article that appeared in August of that year, the author, Khalil Thabit, engaged with socialist arguments and counterarguments, emphasizing that "moderate socialism has brought many positive things to the world."[25] Thabit, a graduate of the Syrian Protestant College (SPC) in Beirut (class of 1892) and a regular contributor to *al-Muqtaṭaf*, summarized an article that had appeared in *Contemporary Review* fifteen years earlier. He graphically described workers' exploitation in terms of sweat and blood and argued against a popular antisocialist argument that workers only had themselves to blame for their failure to achieve wealth. He concluded, "There are many among the rich who do no useful work, but . . . are fed by workers . . . with their labor and sweat. . . . Such people are more damaging to the social body *[al-hay'a al-ijtimā 'iyya]* than poor workers."[26] Significantly Thabit credited the "revolution of minds in Europe" *(thawrat al-khawāṭir fi Europa)* mostly to socialists; even if some of their demands were never to materialize, "[the socialists'] frankness and public declaration *[mujāhara]* of their opinions has . . . awakened the minds, and this . . . has led to workers' interests in their issues and has prompted governments to establish appropriate laws and associations in order to assist the needy among the workers."[27]

A similar reevaluation of socialism was taking place in the pages of *al-Hilāl*. By 1909 the periodical was overtly displaying its sympathies. In a five-page article on the Ferrer Affair, *al-Hilāl* portrayed socialism in a positive light and nonambivalently expressed its support for "moderate" socialism, which it equated with reformism.[28] It gave a synopsis of socialism in Spain, objectively summarized some of the ideology's main trends, and argued that socialism was crucial to the well-being of society because it served as a "warning to governments" to "protect the oppressed from the oppressor."[29] Opposing Francisco Ferrer's arrest in no uncertain terms, the article described the Spanish activist as a reformist, "a Spanish man who was nurtured on freedom and independence of mind,"[30] whose goals were praiseworthy. In particular the school system Ferrer established, which was geared toward mass education, was hailed by the periodical as "a modern school which spread the spirit of freedom and socialist principles."[31] Hence by 1909 *al-Hilāl* linked socialism, freedom, and independence of mind into one unified worldview.

This is not to suggest that the change in the periodicals' attitude toward socialism was linear and moving unhesitatingly toward an embrace of the subject. Generally, however, it seems that both periodicals began expressing more favorable opinions of socialism in the first few years of the twentieth century.[32] This shift culminated in the last few months before the eruption of World War I, when *al-Hilāl* published a long article explaining Marx's notions of surplus value and labor in a positive light and connecting them to social democracy, reform, and workers' rights and *al-Muqtaṭaf* published three articles unequivocally supportive of socialism.[33] Perhaps as significant, under the rubric of "questions and answers" in 1914 ("Bāb al-masā'il"), the periodical was not ambivalent about socialism's benefits and went so far as to assert that "socialism is the reaping *[istithmār]* of the earth's goods in a better way than that which is occurring today, and their distribution to people with more justice than now. . . . [It is] people's sharing of goods in equal measure."[34]

FROM REFORM TO SOCIALISM AND BACK: DOMESTICATING SOCIALISM, RADICALIZING THE *NAHḌA*

What explains this shift in *al-Hilāl*'s and *al-Muqtaṭaf*'s perceptions of socialism—or more precisely, their owners' willingness to publish articles by authors sympathetic to leftist ideas? And what does this shift to a progressive endorsement of leftist ideas indicate on a broader level? To tackle these questions, we first need to examine intellectual and periodical production in the late nineteenth century to see how the infrastructure and framework of intellectual production contributed to this shift, with repercussions far beyond the immediate readership of the two periodicals in question. The progressively (if cautiously) positive views of the Left displayed on the pages of these periodicals can best be understood if we read the *nahḍa* as a global intellectual production and grasp how ingeniously intellectuals of the period engaged with socialism and radical ideas, domesticated and hybridized them, and in the process created a local intellectual worldview and set of references that were simultaneously and self-consciously global.

The Nahḍa *and the Mantra of Reform*

If one were to attempt to define the *nahḍa* as it developed between the years 1860 and 1914 and was constructed in its three main centers, Beirut, Cairo, and Alexandria, reform would figure as its most dominant theme.[35] A conscious intellectual articulation of the need for reform and its manifestations by thinkers belonging to a variety of networks, groups, institutions, and intellectual traditions, the *nahḍa* was one geographic and linguistic module—a provincial, mostly Syro-Egyptian Arab manifestation—of a larger reformist project implemented by local rulers, administrators, and bureaucrats throughout the Ottoman Empire in the late nineteenth century. This larger Ottoman reformist movement, which was both local and imperial, aimed to modernize the state, institutions, and individuals in order to catch up with Europe and defend the empire against European hegemony.[36] The *nahḍa* was not interpreted monolithically and was not the monopoly of a single regional, religious, ethnic, or social category. The impetus for reform was shared by people forming a plethora of networks whose members intersected, collaborated, and shared various visions and implementations of reform. The pulse or vitality of the *nahḍa* was connected to specific cities—Beirut, Cairo, and Alexandria—that had privileged relationships with one another, allowing for the intersection and overlap of a number of reformist and radical networks. Although many aspects of reform were emphasized and interpreted differently by various reformist groups, there were significant common concerns and interests among *nahḍa* thinkers, which allowed for the formulation of a cohesive worldview. Central perhaps is the notion of reform as a total project and "l'horizon même de toute pensée hic et nunc."[37] This all-encompassing project aimed at modernizing religion. In the case of Islamic reform this meant looking for ways to purge Islam of elements deemed incompatible with the needs and reality of the present age. In the case of (predominantly but not exclusively Christian) secular reform in parts of Syria, it meant rethinking and curbing the authority of both local and foreign religious institutions over communal affairs; educational reform promoting secular and modern education, including female education; political reform underlining the need for constitutional and parliamentary politics; individual reform emphasizing the centrality of self-improvement and the use of logic and reason; and perhaps most important, social reform that would rid society of various internal and external "diseases" threatening its cohesion.[38] In place of an ailing society, reformists would build a strong social body *(al-hay'a al-ijtimā'iyya),* a healthy organism whose various divisions, including those generated by wealth disparity and sectarian tensions, would be eliminated or seriously eroded. It is partly within this framework of reform, with the idea of the healthy social body, that *nahḍa* reformists would progressively inscribe socialism, and in the process redefine the malleable project of the *nahḍa* itself.

Inscribing Socialism into the Nahḍa

Particularly striking in *al-Muqtaṭaf*'s and *al-Hilāl*'s coverage of socialism is the *manner* in which the periodicals broached the topic. Regardless of whether their articles were supportive or critical of socialism, they articulated the topic using literary devices, tropes, and epistemological and ethical categories that were familiar and appealing to their readers. One such tactic was to claim that both socialism and anarchism had existed in prior epochs and in different geographic or "civilizational" spaces; in other words, the periodicals searched for the roots of the two ideologies or comparable manifestations, especially in the Arabo-Islamic past.[39] Another tactic was to use a genre familiar to readers: biography.[40] Many of the articles on socialism and anarchism that appeared in *al-Muqtaṭaf* and *al-Hilāl* between 1880 and 1914 focused on the biographies of great socialist and anarchist thinkers, such as Saint-Simon, Owen, Reclus, and Proudhon. The articles typically gave a brief synopsis of the doctrines' most salient points, showed respect and admiration for these great figures, and steered clear of any deep ideological analysis.[41] On a few occasions both periodicals devoted entire issues to great European literary figures known for their radical positions, including Zola and Tolstoi.[42]

Socialism and, to a lesser extent, anarchism were brought home through formal as well as substantive devices. Although the coordinates of socialism and anarchism changed over time, *al-Muqtaṭaf* and *al-Hilāl* consistently framed them within interconnected discourses and tropes (signifiers) with which their readers were familiar or becoming familiarized and in which they were interested, even obsessed: civilization, natural science and natural law, progress, Darwinism, and modernity. The two periodicals, which proudly held on to their pretense of objectivity, thus demystified and reworked socialism and anarchism, making them fit comfortably in the larger Weltanschauung of the *nahḍa*, which they were busily creating as well as reflecting.

Significantly it was also within the framework spanned by the *nahḍa*'s favorite themes—the state of nature, the naturalness of competition and inequality, the social body's health, civilization and modernity—that *al-Muqtaṭaf* placed its (shifting) discourse on strikes in Egypt and the world, describing strikes as representing workers' unnatural and illegal quest for equality, inflicting damages or bringing benefits to society, and hampering or promoting civilization.[43] *Al-Hilāl* proceeded in a similar fashion. One article appearing in 1906 associated socialism with civilization by suggesting that the founding of a Japanese socialist newspaper was in and of itself a sign of civilizational progress.[44] Another article, which appeared in 1909, argued that worldwide socialist opposition to the Spanish government's treatment of Ferrer was civilized and symbolized the struggle against tyranny.[45] The article maintained that socialism was the consequence of progress and "enlightenment," since it "appeared as such when people got enlightened by knowledge and individual freedom spread in the age of reform, and the masses [the common people, *al-ʿāmma*] learned how to gather and how to ask."[46] The degree of civilization that allowed for socialism to emerge was linked to the masses' self-awareness, and was thus *modern* because it was connected to modern industrial inventions.[47]

Linked to the concept of civilization was the concept of the social body and its relationship to the individual. For the *nahḍa* civilization meant connecting individual interest to social interest; progress toward civilization was achieved when individuals had a strong and fruitful connection to the social body *(al-hay'a al-ijtimāʿiyya)*.[48] If individuals failed to secure this bond between their interests and that of the social body, if they broke away from it or exposed it to disease such as sectarianism,[49] society would become ill and civilization would be threatened. This discourse was an essential part of the *nahḍa* throughout the 1860s and 1870s, partly in the work of Butrus al-Bustani and Salim al-Naqqash, among others.[50] It was adapted to socialism as early as 1894 in an article explaining that "the aim, in socialism, is that the interest of each individual be linked to that of the community *[al-jamāʿa]*, as was the case in Greece and Rome."[51]

A Specific and Influential Example: Shibli Shumayyil's Writings on Socialism

Perhaps no article offers a better illustration of the way socialism was incorporated into the *nahḍa*'s web of natural science, civilization, Darwinism, and modernity than Shibli Shumayyil's long essay appearing in January 1913 in *al-Muqtaṭaf*.[52] Shumayyil (1850–1917) had been a regular contributor to *al-Muqtaṭaf* (and a number of other periodicals) from its time in Beirut. A doctor, polymath, and graduate of the Syrian Protestant College, he was also an unwavering and self-proclaimed supporter of socialism.[53] Written in a question-and-answer format, his essay summarized most of his ideas on socialism and sought to explain them in fairly simple terms, in line with *al-Muqtaṭaf*'s popularizing mission.[54] Socialism, he argued, was a way of preserving social harmony by ensuring that everybody got their rightful due from their labor: "Social organization should be such that all people will become useful workers, each benefiting according to their merit so that society would no longer have members doing nothing and others duped *[maghbūnūn]*, who will then be damaged and corrupted *[yushawwashūn wa yufsadūn]*."[55] Shumayyil argued that it was to the advantage of all parts of society (or this organism) to rid society of all that could lead to trouble and strife and thus endanger the social body's health. Exploitation posed one such threat; so did sectarianism. Significantly, in his advocacy for socialism and his efforts to convince his audience of socialism's merits, Shumayyil invoked not so much individual equality and other inalienable rights as the health of the social in general, which he knew to be a familiar trope and one of prime concern to his readers—and to himself.

As previously mentioned, the conception of society as an organism and the concern with its health were at the center of an Ottoman reformist discourse that was simultaneously formulated in Istanbul and influential among educated Ottoman subjects throughout the empire.[56] This organic articulation of society and the accompanying wish to remedy its ills had become a dominant theme throughout the world among socialists, social reformists, and anarchists. Shumayyil's organic conception of society, as expressed in his 1913 essay, bears a striking similarity to the influential French anarchist Elisée Reclus's comparison of the relationship between individual and society "to that of cell and body: each existing independently but completely dependent on the other."[57] Also, like the German scientist and philosopher Ludwig Büchner (1824–99), whose work he carefully read and translated, and in line with one of anarchism's main ideas, Shumayyil believed that cooperation rather than exploitation was the most advanced stage of evolution and should be society's highest aim, and that socialism was therefore the natural and rational application of evolution theory to human societies.[58] He emphasized the rational and scientific process by which this conclusion was reached and argued that it was proof of socialism's inherent modernity.[59] As a doctor and a scientist, he found attractive the idea that natural science offered a complete epistemology that could be applied to society. Natural science, he argued, provided "true knowledge *[al-'ilm al-ṣaḥīḥ]*" and "render[ed] rational judgment accurate *[yaj'al aḥkām al-qiyās al-'aqlī ṣaḥīḥa]*."[60] Hence the connection between natural science and socialism: society ought to be viewed as a comprehensive unit, as a body or an organism, and if any part of this body was dysfunctional or ailing it would ultimately affect the entire body and lead to its death.

DISCURSIVE AUTHORITY AND THE MAKING OF A NEW CLASS

To grasp the full magnitude and implications of these two periodicals' coverage of socialism, their progressive endorsement of it, and its inscription into the *nahḍa*, it is important to understand the weight these periodicals had and their place within a much larger matrix of intellectual production and opinion making. Various historians have surmised that, in absolute terms, these periodicals' distribution figures were not particularly remarkable.[61] However, though reliable distribution figures are notoriously difficult to determine, such statistics do not tell us much about *readership* nor, more broadly speaking, about *exposure* to the contents of these periodicals. Although their circulation figures were not extraordinarily high, their readership included many of the individuals and circles that both produced and consumed a large proportion of written goods in Beirut, Cairo, and Alexandria, both books and periodicals. From that perspective, what was printed on the pages of these two periodicals joined the reservoir of ideas that were consumed, recycled, reinterpreted, and generally engaged by a much wider audience than their own immediate readership.[62] Indeed, *al-Hilāl,* and even more so *al-Muqtaṭaf,* were not just any periodicals. They represented particularly powerful spheres that conferred legitimacy on ideas and discourses in the late nineteenth century and early twentieth in Beirut, Cairo, and Alexandria, but also beyond, including within the Syrian diaspora in the Americas. The two periodicals were at the center of what Bourdieu has labeled "le cercle enchanté de la légitimité." That is, the ideas expressed in their pages and the discourses constructed there were authoritative, for they were *recognized* as such and were expressed in a specific style that confirmed their authority.[63]

At the heart of *al-Muqtaṭaf*'s authoritative pronouncements and its claims to accessible, total, and universal knowledge lay the emergence of a new social class seeking to carve out its own discursive space and armed with the actual power to do so.[64] In the late nineteenth century in Syria a new class of intellectuals was emerging and constructing itself socially, economically, and culturally.[65] Though there were exceptions to the rule, members of this class tended to have the following characteristics. First, they had had access to a specific kind of education. They had attended, around the same time, the same handful of schools and colleges, most prominently the Syrian Protestant College and the Patriarchal School in Beirut, but also Butrus al-Bustani's al-Madrasa al-Wataniyya and al-Kulliya al-Wataniyya al-Islamiyya in Tripoli,[66] where they had acquired skills deemed novel and useful. With this education they constructed a rhetoric of difference and distinguished themselves from preexisting categories and institutions of learned men—at least rhetorically and when it suited their demands.

Second, partly through their educational experience they forged a shared worldview, or "collective consciousness,"[67] and in the process anointed themselves chief reformists. They established formal and informal associations such as the Syrian Scientific Society,[68] joined Freemason lodges, and continued the tradition of literary salons, all of which allowed them to discuss their ideas and build a shared worldview. For this class a necessary component of reform was engagement (and implicit or explicit comparison) with the militarily and politically dominant West, its ideas, institutions, and civilization. Engagement did not usually mean endorsement, but a close examination of how Western civilization worked. One task of this new class as chief reformists was to translate Western ideas for their audience in order to understand and become equal to the West. Another task was to assess the soundness of these Western ideas, to see whether they could be applied to reform Middle Eastern societies. From this perspective the investigation of socialism and anarchism, which were unavoidable political realities in late nineteenth-century Europe, was an inescapable task for any self-respecting *nahḍa* intellectual.

Third, it was mostly through their connection to and their capitalizing on another relatively new institution, the press, that these intellectuals managed to build and maintain this sense of distinction and worldview. Indeed the press was to serve as the perfect vehicle for their reformist project, as well as a tool for projecting their voice as one of authority. Keenly promoted as an educational tool and as the path, if not the index, to civilization, this relatively new medium constituted one field in which graduates of the aforementioned schools were present in a particularly high concentration.[69]

These journalists could thus disseminate their worldview and recruit new members. Through its access to its own legitimizing institutions, most prominently the press, and its reliance on a professional and personal network (the two of which were in fact inseparable), this new intellectual class was equipped with its own symbolic and cultural capital as well as a relatively autonomous means of achieving authority and legitimacy—at least one autonomous from traditional institutions, such as state and religious institutions.[70] It was thus capable of and willing to challenge the authority of traditional bodies, namely, state and religious institutions, as well as established elites, and it often did so through the promotion, or at the very least investigation, of radical ideas and practices. Socialism was one of them.

Historians of intellectuals in France and the United States have connected the formation of intellectuals as a class with radicalism. Christopher Lasch, writing in the 1960s, and Christophe Charle, writing in the 1990s, have both done so, the latter linking the emergence of intellectuals as a class to the cause célèbre of the Affaire Dreyfus, a landmark in radical politics, and casting the use of the public petition, as with Zola's "J'accuse," as a central moment in the formation of intellectuals—who are, in Charle's definition, necessarily public.[71] Something rather similar was happening with the emergence of intellectuals in the Arab world. The defense and open discussion of radical ideas using a specific language (created in the moment) as well as the *publicity* of this process allowed them to constitute themselves as a class. However, this is only part of the story; in the case of these *nahḍa* intellectuals, what contributed to their formation, and also amplified their interest in and sometimes endorsement of radical ideas, was migration.

Migration and Intellectual Production

The late nineteenth century marked the beginning of Syrian emigration and migration, especially to Egypt and North and South America, a phenomenon that affected large segments of the population.[72] Peasants were by far the most affected numerically and otherwise, but lists of graduates from a few Beiruti schools in the 1870s and after, most prominently graduates from the Patriarchal School and SPC, reveal the existence of two major trends: the employment of large numbers of these graduates in the field of journalism in Syria and throughout the world, but most strongly in Egypt, and the particularly high rates of emigration among the pool of graduates.[73] Indeed an astonishingly high number of graduates from these schools left Syria, either immediately after graduation or shortly afterward, and a large percentage among them headed to Egypt, where they worked mostly as doctors, businessmen, and journalists. According to the SPC's annual reports, by 1904 almost half of the school's graduates were residing in Egypt, in contrast to a third who remained in Syria. The remaining number had immigrated to the Americas, especially to the United States.[74]

These Syrian intellectuals retained their special link to the press in their countries of immigration. Soon after settling in their adoptive country they founded newspapers and journals in Arabic. The total figure for Syrian periodicals founded between 1880 and 1908 reached nearly 300, of which 129 were in Egypt, 29 in North America, 34 in South America, and 37 elsewhere.[75] Only 68 of these periodicals (23 percent) were based in Syria itself, a figure that represented fewer than half the number of Syrian periodicals in Egypt.[76] Almost as soon as they were established in Beirut, the two institutions most central to the emergence of an intellectual network, self-proclaimed modern educational institutions and the press, were geared toward serving the local and the global simultaneously. It is remarkable that so many, if not all the institutions that made the *nahḍa*—the press, educational institutions, and freemasonry and other organizations (and, as we shall see in the next chapter, the theater)—had the potential from the beginning to be international and global and were thus promptly adapted to a highly mobile group of people.

A Special Relationship: Syria and Egypt and Exile Politics

Among the reasons for these graduates' departure for Egypt was the fact that their newly acquired modern skills were very much in demand in a province of the Ottoman Empire that had become increasingly autonomous under Mehmet Ali and his successors (especially Isma'il). Egypt's rulers sought to establish a modern state and actively recruited educated Syrians to fill positions in various ministries and as modern doctors, journalists, interpreters, and translators. With the British Occupation of Egypt in 1882, educated, often multilingual Syrians were in even greater demand.[77] The strong presence of Syrian intellectuals and periodical owners in the *mahjar* (lands of immigration), especially Egypt, was in part connected to political repression and stifling censorship in their place of origin.[78] Abdülhamid abolished the Ottoman Constitution in 1878, and many newspapers were shut down, banned, or severely constrained by the censor (the much dreaded *mektupci*). Even when publishers left for Egypt or the Americas, the periodicals they produced abroad were often banned from entering the empire. (Initially there was hope that the 1908 Young Turk Revolution would reverse these policies of censorship, but in the long run little seemed to change.)[79] As a result many intellectuals and publishers opted to emigrate and continue promoting their reformist agenda in exile. There was thus an important and conscious political decision behind many Syrian intellectuals' choice to emigrate, a decision to continue reforming Syrian politics and society from abroad. The Syrian press outside Syria would often overcompensate and use the freedom of expression it enjoyed to the extreme by discussing subversive topics and promoting radical ideas that would not have made it past the censor in Syria.[80] The claims made by many Syrian intellectuals regarding the stifling censorship to which they were subjected in Syria, and their need to escape political repression and muzzling, should not be taken at face value. This (often retroactive) narrative of fleeing repression and censorship is part of the collective *imaginaire* of *nahḍa* intellectuals; as such it is constitutive of a shared group identity.

Regardless of whether or not they were interested in promoting subversive ideas regarding political and social authority while still in Syria, many of these intellectuals could not help but be shaped by the cities that hosted them. Both Cairo and Alexandria were vibrant political and cultural centers for local reformist and radical networks revising social relations, seeking to modernize religion and revamp religious institutions, to rethink politics, and often eventually to challenge the British Occupation. Among all of these reformist networks and movements, Salafi Islamic reformers certainly deserve special mention.[81] Cairo and Alexandria were also magnets for groups and networks of migrant and immigrant activists, especially political exiles (a condition that was often self-imposed) from all over the Mediterranean and beyond. The two main Egyptian cities harbored networks of exiled revolutionaries and political theorists who plotted coups and revolutions, articulated reform programs, formulated new ideologies of contestation, and published pamphlets and periodicals, many of them multilingual. Between 1880 and 1914 Egyptian cities became important bases for exiled Muslim radicals such as Jamal al-Din al-Afghani and his followers, as well as Young Ottoman and Young Turk reformists, Armenian socialists and nationalists, Russian leftists who had fled their country after the 1905 revolution, Italian anarchists, and probably countless other groups. Syrian intellectuals and periodical writers in Egypt were thus part of a much larger matrix of political activists in Cairo and Alexandria. Moreover with respect to the production and circulation of periodicals and the formulation of reformist and radical agendas, the two Egyptian cities were organically connected to the Syrian public sphere, especially in Beirut and Mount Lebanon.[82]

Al-Muqtaṭaf *and* al-Hilāl *and the Geography of Contestation*

Among the intellectuals who fled to Egypt supposedly in search of freedom of expression were Ya'qub Sarruf and Faris Nimr, the founders of *al-Muqtaṭaf*, and Jirji Zaidan, the subsequent founder of *al-Hilāl.* The three of them traced their decision to move to Egypt to the notorious Lewis Affair, which erupted at Beirut's Syrian Protestant College in 1882.[83] In July of that year, during a graduation speech titled "Knowledge, Science and Wisdom," Edwin Lewis, professor of chemistry and geology at SPC, mentioned the positive scientific contribution of Darwin's work, thus igniting the fury of SPC's old guard American missionaries, who forced him to resign. Lewis's resignation was followed by a five-day student and faculty strike in solidarity with the professor.[84] In addition to the strike, forty students left the college as a consequence of the affair, although many of them ultimately returned to the college. Among those who left SPC and Beirut altogether was Zaidan, who had been a student at the time, as well as the science instructors Nimr and Sarruf, who relocated *al-Muqtaṭaf* to Cairo after publishing it in Beirut for seven years (1876–83)—but not before printing Lewis's speech in its entirety in August 1882.[85]

The Lewis Affair was a complex episode whose significance and repercussions were not limited to the debate over Darwinism and natural selection. An in-depth analysis of the event itself is beyond the scope of this book; what is important for our purposes is the strong ideological and personal connections that existed between *al-Muqtaṭaf* and *al-Hilāl* and Darwin's theories, which in the 1880s and until 1914 constituted a main tenet of radical thought in Beirut, Cairo, and Alexandria.[86] Indeed *al-Muqtaṭaf* was central in disseminating evolutionary theory throughout the Arab world, first through objective reports, and then through the passionate and partisan writings of Shibli Shumayyil.[87] The periodical's coverage of Darwin's theories was so extensive that Salama Musa wrote in his memoirs that Sarruf was "obsessed with evolution theory, [and] there were articles about it in every issue."[88] From that perspective, it is no surprise that the discussions of socialism and anarchism in *al-Muqtaṭaf* (and to a lesser extent *al-Hilāl*) were couched in terms of natural law, evolutionary theory, and natural selection theory.[89] Moreover in the eyes of *nahḍa* intellectuals the battle over Darwinism as manifested through the Lewis Affair epitomized many crucial struggles: for freedom of speech, for the curbing of clerical and missionary authority in the realm of knowledge, for equal treatment of native instructors employed by an American missionary institution, and for the supremacy of science. Reform and contestation thus developed in a complex matrix that combined many causes, a matrix into which socialism could be fit.

The Lewis Affair, the move from Beirut to Cairo of the three publishers, and the establishment of these two periodicals on Egyptian grounds paved the way for the establishment of a geography of contestation linking the three cities. On the one hand, these events gave progressive, if not radical credentials to *al-Muqtaṭaf* (and later *al-Hilāl*) as periodicals willing to challenge authority, at least in their pages, by carrying the banner of freedom of expression. On the other hand, they confirmed the image of Egypt as a country that allowed for such (conditional) freedom of expression, despite, or even perhaps because of the British Occupation. The subversive freedom offered by Egypt was not lost on the American missionaries at SPC; as one of them dryly wrote on the occasion of Sarruf's departure from the college, " 'Going down to Egypt' has never proved wholesome."[90] From that point on both *al-Muqtaṭaf* and *al-Hilāl* would accumulate a subversive, yet simultaneously deeply authoritative cultural capital that placed them at the center of an extensive matrix of intellectual production spanning multiple continents.

PERIODICALS AS COMMUNAL AND GLOBAL PRODUCTIONS

While *al-Muqtaṭaf*'s and *al-Hilāl*'s intellectual credentials, pedigrees of contestation, and willingness to publish provocative and subversive articles (alongside very unthreatening pieces, one should hasten to add) were becoming firmly established in the 1890s, the two periodicals also began to respond to and reflect important changes in periodical production and circulation. These included the expansiveness of Syrian migration to North and South America, Egypt, and beyond (including Haiti and the Philippines); the truly remarkable efflorescence of Arabic periodicals in the diaspora; the overlap of professional and personal connections in this group of people who had been educated together in Beirut and its surroundings; and the establishment of a mechanism for the communal production and circulation of periodicals and articles (both opinion pieces and translations of articles that had appeared in Arabic and non-Arabic periodicals). All these features led to an extremely tight-knit, extensive, and far-reaching web of intellectual production and a global forum of readership. This global web meant greater and wider circulation of topics, articles, and discussions that appeared in important Syrian periodicals, of which *al-Muqtaṭaf* and *al-Hilāl* were founding members. It also would have an impact on the topics deemed of interest and their coverage.

Even before the migration of large numbers of Syrian intellectuals, periodical production had more often than not been the fruit of communal efforts. The owner and editor of a periodical would mobilize his relatives and friends to help him write, edit, and translate articles. As a consequence it was often unclear who the actual author of an article was. This was partly in line with past writing practices and the endurance of different notions of authorship that saw literary production as a communal rather than a necessarily individual effort. More important, the constant threat of censorship in Ottoman Syria during the Hamidian era privileged communal (and often anonymous) production and contributed to the spirit of adventure, camaraderie, and collaboration. Such communal production meant that certain topics transcended a single author and essentially were written by an anonymous mass that the periodical personified. Perhaps this also granted such periodicals greater power than individual authors had, anointing them with an authorial authority that could not be easily crushed.[91]

Migration made the production of periodicals even more of a communal enterprise, but this time on a global level. This development can be gauged from the articles published in the periodicals themselves in Egypt, Syria, and North and South America, but also from the correspondence of periodical editors, owners, contributors, and readers. There was a whole common reservoir of news and articles that were made available to Syrian publishers throughout the world, and the publishers themselves would send their own articles or copies of their periodicals to one another. It is striking how self-referential these authors and the work they produced and circulated were. In fact the articles, subjects, texts, and authors read and discussed among this intellectual class, Egyptian and Syrian, were surprisingly few and were highly intertextual; the same article, or responses to and variations on it, appeared in various periodicals, and authors did not limit their contributions to one periodical. Periodicals took articles from one another, cut and pasted, translated and plagiarized, with little care for the (Western and expanding) notion of copyright or intellectual property, ultimately creating a common public repertoire of news and articles. Examples abound of articles published and republished on different continents, including opinion and reportage. One example is an article on siriculture and silk worms that appeared in a Syrian periodical in São Paulo after it was published in a periodical in New York, following its publication in the original periodical, whose title and place of publication remain unknown.[92]

This public repertoire was created not only by writers, but also by readers around the world, usually immigrant acquaintances who would read news items and articles they deemed interesting in Syrian, but also Brazilian, American, and Egyptian periodicals, then translate these articles or send them on in their language of publication.[93] The readers also played a central role in shaping the content of periodicals through the questions they sent in.[94] Looking at the "Question and Answer" sections of *al-Muqtaṭaf*, *al-Hilāl*, or some of the numerous other Syrian periodicals, such as Farah Antun's *al-Jāmiʿa*, one is struck by the scope of questions concerning recent scientific discoveries, trivia about specific world regions, articles on various political systems and archaeological discoveries, and the geographic span of the readership: readers from Buenos Aires, Winnipeg, and villages in Mount Lebanon and Upper Egypt would send in questions to the periodicals' owners.[95] *Al-Hilāl*'s Brazilian readership was substantial enough for the periodical to give detailed instructions regarding subscription payments, and this was the case for many other periodicals as well, which had agents (usually friends and relatives) throughout the Americas as well as in Syria and Egypt.[96] Of interest is the fact that many of *al-Hilāl*'s and *al-Muqtaṭaf*'s articles on socialism and anarchism were written *in response* to readers' questions: "What are the socialist and nihilist associations which are constantly mentioned in newspapers, and what are their origin?" asked two readers in 1897.[97] Several readers specifically asked for *al-Hilāl*'s *opinion* on various radical ideologies, indicating just how authoritative the periodical had become a mere couple of years after it had been founded: "Do you consider the demands of socialists just, and is socialism beneficial to civilization? What is your opinion on this matter?"[98] Another reader asked, "What is your opinion about the future of anarchists? Will states continue to let them be or annihilate them?"[99] The two periodicals obliged with articles (or short answers) responding to the readers' queries. Similarly an article on Tolstoi was inspired by a group of readers keen to know *al-Hilāl*'s opinion of the Russian philosopher.[100]

THE DIASPORA PRESS IN BRAZIL

Significantly, many, if not most of the questions addressed to *al-Hilāl* and *al-Muqtaṭaf* concerning socialism and anarchism came from Syrian readers in the Americas, especially Brazil.[101] Brazil had become a popular destination for Syrians from the 1890s onward, with around 100,000 Syrians immigrating there between 1891 and 1916.[102] It was also *the* non-Arab country (or realm) with the highest number of Arabic periodicals; if Tarrazi is to be trusted, this figure totaled ninety-five publications by 1922.[103] From 1900 on Syrians in Brazil, specifically in São Paulo, would on many occasions demonstrate their exposure to, interest in, and endorsement of radical and socialist ideas. They also penned and published what were probably the earliest translations of Tolstoi's and Gorki's works into Arabic.[104] Syrians in Brazil also occasionally wrote articles on radical topics for *al-Muqtaṭaf* and *al-Hilāl*.[105] Brazil had a very active and visible anarchosyndicalist movement in the late nineteenth century and early twentieth, and its cities, even more so than Cairo and Alexandria, figured prominently on the map of world (and specifically Italian) anarchism.[106] Accompanying and fanning this interest was the Syrian (Arabic) press in São Paulo, whose owners were constantly in touch with other Syrian intellectuals throughout Syria, Egypt, and North and South America. The Arabic press of São Paulo, which counted three bi- or triweekly periodicals in 1904 and was continuously expanding in the first decade of the twentieth century, constituted the third largest (really ex eco, in second place) immigrant or foreign language press in the city, after the Italian and equal to the German press. In 1904 its total distribution figure was 23,000 copies per month.[107]

One of these periodicals, *al-Munāẓir*, was founded by Naʿum Labaki, known for his strident anticlericalism and his criticism of privilege conferred by wealth.[108] Another periodical, *al-Afkār,* was founded in 1902 (and may have lasted until 1943) by Sa'id Abu Jamra, who contributed at least one article on anarchism to *al-Hilāl.* A graduate of the Syrian Protestant College, where he studied medicine, Abu Jamra settled in São Paulo, where he was the first Arab doctor.[109] The periodical, whose subtitle was *Scientific, Literary, Health-related and Informational (Majalla 'ilmiyya wa adabiyya wa ṣiḥḥiyya wa ikhbāriyya),* saw its mission as the publication of articles "for the purpose of benefiting working men and women" *(li ifādat al-'āmilīn wa'l-' āmilāt),* although it is not clear whether Abu Jamra explicitly meant blue-collar workers.[110] A third periodical, *al-Farā'id,* subtitled *Scientific, Literary, Social, and Novelistic (Majalla 'ilmiyya adabiyya ijtimā'iyya riwā'iyya),* was founded in 1910 by Ibrahim Shehadi Farah, who had translated and published one of Gorki's short stories. A look at the issues that came out in 1911 confirms its owner's radical sympathies. The opening article of that year was a biographical piece on Tolstoi (who had passed away a few months earlier), which was soon followed by a translation of "the best article written on Tolstoi" by a certain Vance Thompson, a translation of one of Tolstoi's essays, and a eulogy of the Russian philosopher by the Egyptian poet Hafiz Ibrahim.[111] The periodical also serialized Gorki's short story "The Bakers" and reproduced a long speech by Enrico Ferri, a well-known Italian social scientist and criminologist who was a member of the Italian Socialist Party and the editor of its organ, *Avanti.* That year Ferri visited São Paulo and presented his work, which was profoundly shaped by his socialist convictions.[112] Farah most likely later published and distributed Ferri's speech on its own, since he mentions that the periodical made 500 British pounds from it.[113] There was clearly interest in Ferri's ideas among Arabic readers in Brazil and beyond. Hence the South American connection seems to have played a key role in triggering the interest of Arabic readers in socialism and anarchism in Beirut, Cairo, and Alexandria, as well as in the Americas.

The radical activities of the Syrian Brazilian press and readership were not limited to translating radical writings into Arabic, but seem to have also included backing and promoting two main Syrian radical authors whose writings became somewhat canonical among Arabic readers sympathetic to the Left. They were Farah Antun and Amin al-Rihani, both of whom were originally from Syria (specifically present-day North Lebanon and Mount Lebanon). Antun had moved to Alexandria, where he founded and edited *al-Jāmi'a* from 1899 until 1906, before relocating to New York, his base until 1909. He continued to issue *al-Jāmi'a* there, with the help of his sister Rosa and her husband, Niqula Haddad, a self-proclaimed socialist and the author of articles and later books on socialism. A year after his return to Cairo in 1909 Antun terminated *al-Jāmi'a* and began writing for Egyptian nationalist periodicals.[114] As for Rihani (whose father had sent him, along with his uncle, to the United States in 1888), he spent the years 1905–11 based in Mount Lebanon but moving between his village of Frayke, New York, and Egypt.

Both authors occasionally contributed articles to *al-Muqtaṭaf* and *al-Hilāl,* writing on subjects such as the French Revolution and reform. The two periodicals would occasionally mention and review their works, including articles and books sympathetic to socialism. The writings of these two authors became a central part of the repertoire of articles circulating among Syrian periodicals, partly thanks to their tireless efforts to send copies to fellow intellectuals and publicists in the diaspora.[115]

Antun and Rihani began endorsing socialism as early as 1900.[116] Antun did so using various genres (from political articles to novels), most of which appeared in installments in *al-Jāmiʿa,* where he also popularized and explained Marx's theories.[117] But if Antun was sympathetic to socialism, he had absolutely nothing positive to say about anarchism (at least not in 1900), which he seems to have associated almost exclusively with political assassination—unlike, for instance, Shumayyil, who engaged with anarchist ideas and seriously explored (and almost justified, at least certainly understood) the reasons behind anarchists' use of violence.[118] Rihani's endorsement of socialism was also evident early on and was manifested in a lecture he gave in New York in 1900, in which he described the nineteenth century as " the century of civilization *[tamaddun],* light, democratic and *socialist* principles, and Christian mercy."[119] Like Antun and Shumayyil, among others, Rihani saw socialism as a marker of civilization and considered socialist parties to be guarantors of peace.[120] Like them, he also contributed articles to *al-Muqtaṭaf* and *al-Hilāl,* as well as to a plethora of other periodicals, some fairly small enterprises.[121] He also wrote books and articles in English and contributed articles to periodicals and newspapers such as the *Atlantic Monthly, Forum,* and Michael Monahan's progressive *Papyrus,* as well as to the French daily newspaper *Le Temps* (the ancestor of *Le Monde*).[122]

The Brazilian connection played an important role in shaping and encouraging the radicalism of both Antun and Rihani. Antun's knowledge of Tolstoi was partly mediated through the Brazilian *al-Munāẓir,* in whose pages he read "captivating excerpts from [Tolstoi's] philosophy, one of them entitled 'The Only [True] Christian.' "[123] It also was most likely none other than Labaki, the owner of *al-Munāẓir,* who introduced Antun's work to the Syrians in Brazil.[124] A few years later Antun claimed that part of the reason he relocated from Alexandria to New York was to get closer to his readership in North and South America. He noted *al-Jāmiʿa*'s three hundred subscribers in Brazil alone and his thousands of readers there. His popularity was so great among Syrians in Brazil, he claimed, that "[his] emigrant brothers in Brazil . . . suggested offering *al-Jāmiʿa* a printing press."[125]

Rihani engaged in a lifelong correspondence with Labaki beginning in 1901. Labaki, who had harshly criticized the Maronite clergy, had been vilified by the Church and its supporters in São Paulo. He and Rihani shared a deep hatred of *taʿaṣṣub* (sectarianism, or religious fanaticism), as well as a strong anticlericalism.[126] For Rihani, hope for reforming the Syrians, both in Syria and in the diaspora, came mostly from people like Labaki in Brazil. In one of his (extremely long) letters to

Labaki, after lamenting the power of the clerical camp among certain journalists in New York, Rihani wrote, "I had thought that the sun of freedom would shine on our beloved homeland from Egypt or Paris or Geneva, but it seems I was mistaken. For two years, I have been in seventh heaven of hope from what I have seen from the Syrian community here [in New York], as one stance for the defense of its trampled rights, and I had told myself that it is in the Syrians of New York that there is the seed of the future nation, but my hope has now vanished. . . . These seeds are in the South of the New World. *The light that we need will shine on our miserable nation from the firmament of Brazil.* . . . You *[al-Munāẓir]* are fighting our battle; how can we simply look on from the margins?"[127]

The Brazilian connection through the Syrian diaspora points to one of many routes of radical ideas that contributed to forging a global radical moment. An analysis of the web of Syrian periodicals sheds light on the emergence of a global public forum in which readers had access to information from multiple continents and could engage with and debate, in the global (and virtual) public space provided by periodicals, interests triggered by contact with their host societies, as well as by their preoccupation with reforming the homeland socially and politically. Not surprisingly, radical ideas—including the two most powerful radical ideologies of the fin de siècle, socialism and anarchism—figured in this global and international public forum. The interconnectivity of themes, discussions, and articles in this context and the formation of a global web of intellectual production contributed to the increased coverage and endorsement of socialism and other radical themes in periodicals such as *al-Muqtaṭaf* and *al-Hilāl* by linking them to readers and writers in the diaspora, in societies where such ideas were widely discussed and had many adherents. *Al-Muqtaṭaf* and *al-Hilāl* occupied a privileged position within this strikingly small and extremely extensive global intellectual infrastructure. A very large proportion of the articles produced by Syrian diasporic periodicals passed through these two periodicals, which mentioned, referred to, summarized, or commented on them. The metaphor of a web is useful here, although it was a web with certain key nodes that served as convergence and distribution hubs for articles, authors, and authority—a role that these two periodicals played.

RECENTERING EGYPT: THE IMPORTANCE OF PLACE IN THE ARTICULATION AND DISSEMINATION OF RADICAL IDEAS

Although Brazil and North America occupied an important place in the forging of this radical corpus of concepts, articles, and authors, both the process and the end result were intrinsically linked to Cairo and Alexandria. The *nahḍa* might have been a global production, but the local never ceased to matter. It was precisely *because al-Muqtaṭaf* and *al-Hilāl* were located in Egypt that the editors of these two periodicals and many of their core contributors took radical ideas seriously, even if they did not always endorse them. It was in Egyptian cities that the main intellectual heavyweights of this global web, and of other intellectual networks as well, were based or converged. At a very basic level it was first and foremost the amenities and infrastructure that Egypt provided—steamships, a reliable postal system (or rather many different postal systems), and a relatively free press—that allowed for the circulation of questions, articles, periodicals, books, and people, coming from many continents. This was also the locus of an older and still vibrant infrastructure of intellectual production and dissemination, the enduring legacy of Cairo's unique historical place at the center of intellectual production for centuries and with which newer Egyptian institutions producing knowledge intersected and overlapped. None of these flows and syntheses, none of this free public discussion would have been possible without Egyptian cities, especially if we recall that Syrian periodicals in Syria were rather heavily censored (at least until 1908) and that many of the periodicals issued in the diaspora were barred from Syria.

This core group of intellectuals based in Egypt took socialism and radicalism seriously partly because many of the people around them were either doing so or were seriously contesting the existing social order. In discussing the coverage of radical ideas in Beirut, Cairo, and Alexandria, I have singled out *al-Muqtaṭaf* and *al-Hilāl* for a number of reasons, mostly because of their influence and the fact that they were both leaders within as well as symptomatic of an entire production network. Cairo, Alexandria, and Beirut were cities progressively incorporated into the world economy and into an expanding capitalist system. Starting in the 1890s and picking up momentum a decade later, the cities were the sites of strikes and other forms of workers' militancy, as well as the establishment of anarchist cells and even a popular university featuring courses and lectures on Proudhon and Bakunin. Furthermore Cairo and especially Alexandria served as nodal cities, attracting various radical networks and allowing them to intersect and exchange ideas through a multiplicity of communication channels. Although I have analyzed the role of Arabic periodicals, especially through the formation of a global Syrian network of intellectuals and periodical owners, in covering, articulating, and disseminating leftist ideas, periodicals are only part of a much larger story of networks, institutions, and individuals converging in the three cities in question.

Perhaps most important, it was because of the organic connection the intellectuals associated with *al-Muqtaṭaf* and *al-Hilāl* had with Egyptian intellectuals, and more generally with the reading populations in Cairo, Alexandria, and Beirut, that this global intellectual web, and specifically its coverage of the Left, mattered. Indeed this Syrian diasporic public forum was not closed. Many contributors to these periodicals, especially to the Egyptian *al-Muqtaṭaf* and *al-Hilāl*, were indigenous Egyptians. In fact one of the most vocal socialists among the contributors to the two periodicals was an Egyptian (Copt), Salama Musa. In his memoirs Musa described his finding old issues of *al-Muqtaṭaf* (and *al-Jāmi'a*) as one of the most formative moments of his life. His articles and occasionally lively discussions about socialism in the two periodicals (including his heated exchange on the topic with Sarruf and Nimr in 1910)[128] eventually turned into the first published book on the subject in Arabic (it came out in 1913), which was more than a series of compiled essays. In addition to including writings by non-Syrian writers, this global Arabic public sphere reached deep into Middle Eastern literate societies, especially in Egypt. By one count, roughly one-fifth of all periodicals published in Egypt before World War I belonged to Syrians (who represented a very small percentage of the total Egyptian population).[129] The most widely read and influential periodicals—*al-Muqtaṭaf, al-Hilāl, al-Manār,* and, among the dailies, *al-Ahrām*—had all been founded by Syrians, and in 1914 they were still owned (and mostly written) by Syrians.

The thinkers who were decisive in covering the Left and constructing a positive image of it were an organic part of Egyptian intellectual society. *Al-Muqtaṭaf* and *al-Hilāl* were read by indigenous Egyptian intellectuals, many of whom were influential; that is, their opinions were respected and their voices heard either because they occupied positions of power or because they had access to educational institutions, publishing houses, periodicals, or salons. The authors who contributed sympathetic articles on socialism and the Left were themselves connected to larger segments of Egyptian society, and many were individuals with tremendous intellectual authority within Egyptian society. Shibli Shumayyil discussed his ideas with Rashid Rida, the prominent Syrian Muslim reformist and owner of *al-Manār,* and high-ranking Egyptian officials such as Prince Muhammad Ali Halim and Ahmad Zaki Pasha.[130] He also published articles on socialism (and related matters) in a number of different periodicals, casting his net relatively widely.[131] Similarly Amin al-Rihani would regularly send his articles to Egyptian friends, including the poet Hafiz Ibrahim and the mufti Muhammad Abduh, when he did not read them out loud in front of them in Cairo.[132] Farah Antun was also connected to a larger intellectual circle in Egypt, including the nationalists, through his work at *al-Liwā'* upon his return to Cairo in 1909. Clearly the supporters of radical and socialist ideas whose articles appeared in *al-Muqtaṭaf* and *al-Hilāl* (some of whom, like Shumayyil and Musa, explicitly saw themselves as socialists) formed a *permeable* group that had a certain intellectual weight.

They shared contacts and interactions with individuals who belonged primarily to other reformist networks but were ultimately part of the same web of intellectual production. Hence the discussions on socialism and support for socialism in these periodicals were not the product of lone voices with no impact on their local societies or intellectual communities, but instead were the work of individuals, networks, and institutions embedded in an intricate and extensive web of thinkers and their public that transcended geographic, communal, and religious boundaries. By the beginning of World War I the Arabic reading publics of Beirut, Cairo, and

Alexandria had become familiar with socialist and radical ideas and viewed them as an integral part of this reformist worldview that the *nahḍa* had come to represent.

ORDERING KNOWLEDGE: AN ALTERNATIVE EMPIRE OF INFORMATION

The radicalism of this international Syrian press was in fact much more far-ranging than its mere coverage, and even endorsement, of radical ideas and activism. For one thing, it connected Egypt and Syria with news from all over the world. The reading public in Beirut, Cairo, and Alexandria were exposed not only to great world events, but also to a variety of topics deemed important by readers and writers living on different continents. The distant became as much a part of everyday life as the local, and the information deemed worth knowing was far vaster than that provided by a national press. A quick browse through the issues of the first five years of *al-Hilāl* (1892–97) shows, on the same pages, announcements regarding the activities of benevolent societies in Cairo, Damascus, and Beirut, articles on mental illness, general knowledge about Brazil, and comments on scientific discoveries. It was the juxtaposition and the constant oscillation between the local and the international, between the provincial and the truly worldly, the general and the specific, the lay and the professional that made *al-Hilāl* and other periodicals subversive, for they violated all sorts of boundaries. The information and ultimately knowledge that they made accessible to the reading population was gathered not through the mechanisms or the logic of states and empires, but through alternative channels. This information was not organized according to an official (if implicit) hierarchy of importance by which knowledge was ranked. If such an importance was acknowledged by writers and readers of periodicals, it was precisely in the violation of the limits set by the Ottoman state or local institutions such as the Maronite clergy regarding permissible topics of discussion. But even more dangerous, perhaps, was the way this global press functioned as an alternative node of knowledge. This fluid, transnational authority, whose readers asked for its opinion on various matters (recall the questions addressed to *al-Hilāl* and *al-Muqtaṭaf* about socialism and nihilism), was beyond the regulation and the control of any state or institution. It began to displace formal institutions in creating a canon of knowledge, so much so that old issues of periodicals were used in Syrian and Egyptian schools as science textbooks.[133]

The vitality of this translocal, transregional, global intellectual network and its importance for the Syrian diaspora as well as Egyptian and Syrian societies suggest that we need to reinterpret this entire period from a different perspective than that which has dominated Middle Eastern historiography to date. Namely, rather than reading the *nahḍa*, this period of great intellectual and cultural effervescence in the

Arab world, as a chapter within the larger text of Arab or Syrian nationalism, we should instead consider it within a global perspective and view the Syrian diaspora's role not as the making of national culture but as an effort engaging mostly in the production of global radical culture. This is not to suggest that the emergence of nationalism, specifically Syrian nationalism, was not in and of itself a global radical production; in many ways it was precisely that.[134] However, nationalism can be seen as one possible historical interpretation, turn, or outcome of such a diasporic and subversive culture, and one that ought to be contextualized within a larger picture of contention shaped by local as well as global movements.[135]

CONCLUSION

The mainstream press, particularly the influential periodicals *al-Muqtaṭaf* and *al-Hilāl,* played a large role in introducing socialism and anarchism in a form and language understood by the literate public in Beirut, Cairo, and Alexandria. Because of their special place within the *nahḍa,* these periodicals wove socialism into the reformist framework of contention that was in the process of being constructed. *Al-Muqtaṭaf* and *al-Hilāl* were fundamental to the making of a trajectory and a geography of contestation that linked Beirut, Cairo, and Alexandria, making these cities central nodes in the propagation of radical ideas, such as Darwinism and socialism. Furthermore Egypt served as a crucial extension of the Syrian public sphere, allowing for the free expression of radical ideas whose expression was prohibited in Beirut.

An international network of Syrian intellectuals and the circulation of periodicals created an international public forum and a "diasporic public sphere."[136] These cities not only existed in a special relationship to one another, but also occupied a central position on the map of this Syrian diasporic world, and hence had privileged access to the knowledge and information contained within this diasporic network. This access had a radicalizing effect on the development of these cities' local public spheres, as this network appropriated and subverted domination tools, that is, tools used by empires and states to order and circulate knowledge, thus defining for themselves a space for communication and discussion beyond the reach of state or empire.

Before 1914 the emerging global and radical public sphere developed through the press bridged the distance between local and international and contributed to making Beirut, Cairo, and Alexandria global cities, whose populations (or segments thereof) learned fairly rapidly what was happening in the rest of the world, felt connected to that world, and considered themselves entitled to interpret and hence participate in events taking place on the global scale, such as the Russo-Japanese War and the execution of Ferrer in Barcelona. The theater emerged around the same time as the press and also contributed to the making of an internationalist and radical public sphere in Beirut, Cairo, and Alexandria. Plays and monologues were written and performed about Japan's victory over Russia in 1905–6 and about the life and trial of Ferrer in 1909. The potential subversiveness of the theater and its role in the construction of radicalism in and between the three cities through the use of the stage as "the press for the people" is another means by which their populations participated in contemporary international events.

3

Theater and Radical Politics in Beirut, Cairo, and Alexandria 1860–1914

A CURIOUS AFFAIR: THE FERRER PLAY OF 1909

In the last days of October 1909 a play celebrating the life and work of Francisco Ferrer was performed in Beirut.[1] Ferrer, a Spanish social and political activist, a freethinker whose ideas combined elements of anarchism and socialism, had been executed a few days before. A pedagogue, he had created a modern curriculum and established modern schools in Barcelona based on the principle of "class harmony," a project very similar to the ideas behind the Université Populaire that appeared in France at the same time.[2] Ferrer's pedagogy and ideology enjoyed tremendous popularity throughout the world; they combined freemasonry, freethinking, a strong class consciousness, anarchism, and anticlericalism.[3] He became an icon of the world's leftist movements in 1909, when he was falsely accused by the Spanish Church and condemned to death for his alleged involvement in an anarchist terrorist attack. His trial and condemnation triggered demonstrations and protests throughout the world, from Italy to Mexico.[4]

In Beirut the play about Ferrer was improvised on the spot. The script was written in four hours by Daud Muja'is and Emile Khuri and was promptly memorized by the actors. Remarkably the cast consisted of sixty people, most of whom must have been nonprofessional actors recruited locally. 'Aziz 'Eid, a well-known Syrian actor based in Egypt who had a predilection for controversial plays, played the leading role.[5] The cast also included Petro Pauli, a member of the Beiruti intelligentsia and an amateur actor who, a few weeks earlier, had appeared with 'Eid in another political performance.[6] The play, which Muja'is proudly branded the first of its kind in the world, was presented by Jam'iyyat Iḥyā' al-Tamthīl al-'Arabi on the stage of the New Theater; "it was greatly appreciated by the people who filled its seats. . . .

The history of the last Spanish Revolution was acted and that of the martyr Ferrer, his imprisonment and condemnation, with an explanation of his principles and those of true socialism. . . . The play was written by two local authors so that it serve as a school for the people *[al-sha'b]* who still ignore everything about the principle of general freedom *[ḥurriyya 'umūmiyya]*, and of general brotherhood."[7]

In the first act Ferrer appeared on stage draped in a banner covered with slogans: "Liberty, Fraternity, Equality," "No poor ever hungered without a rich man profiting from it," and "Long live the free popular schools."[8] Ferrer gave a ten-page speech on socialism *(khuṭba ishtirākiyya)*, while "the people" on stage "kept interrupting him with screams of excitement . . . asking for freedom and justice, and protesting against the Marrakech campaign."[9] At one point the battle between the soldiers and the people became so heated that some actors were slightly injured.

Intellectuals gave speeches during the intermission and after the play.[10] The poet Shibli Mallat, owner of the newspaper *al-Waṭan*, recited a poem titled "The Eternity of Ferrer" ("Khulud Freira"); Felix Faris, owner of *Lisān al-ittiḥād* and a well-known member of the local branch of the Committee of Union and Progress, explained what socialism is. There were other speakers as well. The audience was delighted; "the play had won a place in their emotions and thoughts which no other play before had ever achieved."[11] The troupe was asked to perform it again on November 21, at the request of a large number of literati.[12] It is unclear whether this second performance ever took place. What is clear, though, is that members of the clergy (most likely the Maronite clergy and the Jesuits) were extremely upset by the performance's strong attack on the Spanish clergy for its persecution of Ferrer.[13] "There were many protests; actors and authors were brought to court, but were eventually acquitted. The matter had a ripple effect *[L'affaire eut du retentissement]*."[14]

The Organizers of the Ferrer Play and the Emergence of a Radical Network

The performance of the Ferrer play in Beirut was not an isolated expression of support for leftist ideals. There existed an entire network of radical leftist intellectuals in Syria active in Beirut and Mount Lebanon in the first years of the twentieth century. By the time of the Ferrer play in 1909, members of this network actively sought to eliminate poverty, promoted social justice, denounced the exploitation of workers on moral and economic grounds, were fiercely anticlerical, identified with international leftist icons, or at least European ones, and referred to themselves and were referred to as radicals or socialists. Members of this network were involved with the periodicals *al-Nūr* (Alexandria 1904–8) and *al-Ḥurriyya* (Beirut 1909–10?). They promoted and diffused radical ideas through newspapers, as well as through a wider social network that connected them to the *nahḍa* core. This network was equipped with the means to formulate ideas and the actual power to disseminate and apply them via the establishment of free reading rooms, schools for workers, and industrial and agricultural exhibitions. More important, members of this network were profoundly convinced of the primacy of the theater in promoting social justice by denouncing exploitation and educating their audiences about socialism.

The emergence of this specific leftist network and its role in the formulation and dissemination of leftist ideas is the subject of the following chapter; in this chapter I seek to explain the emergence of the *theater* as a central organ in the formulation and dissemination of radical leftist ideas. I analyze the nature of the relationship between social and political contestation and the theater and the evolution of that relationship between 1860 and 1914 in Beirut, Cairo, and Alexandria. The Ferrer play, in its subject matter as well as in its practice, was in many ways the *culmination* or epitome of various theatrical trends. The references to revolutions, the French Revolution in particular; the appropriation of contemporary events for the stage; the anti-imperialist stance; the virulent anticlericalism; the blurring of the line between audience and actors, amateurs and professionals; the participation of large numbers of average people in the role of the Crowd on stage, battling against figures of authority; the use of the theater for political speeches and rallies; the theater as a press for the masses—all these elements present in the Ferrer play of 1909 were the result of historical developments that occurred both within the framework of the theater and within society during the period under study. The theater was inextricably linked to the construction, formulation, and diffusion of leftist ideas; that is, not only did the stage *reflect* the progressive radicalization of a certain intellectual elite and allow it to diffuse its ideas and gather support, it also provided a unique means of expression and a forum for the *formulation* of a coherent radical ideology, hence playing an essential role in allowing the construction of a leftist radical discourse.

But before examining the specific relationship between the stage and radical politics, let us begin by assessing the place of the theater in the social, political, and cultural life of Beirut, Cairo, and Alexandria.

THEATER FEVER

Around the turn of the century Beirut, Cairo, and Alexandria were seized by a theatrical frenzy. A plethora of performances were regularly mounted, and people scrambled to squeeze into theaters or simply to congregate in front of a makeshift stage that often consisted simply of wooden planks.[15] Amateur troupes proliferated in schools, literary societies, and among friends,[16] their performances indulgently attended by dignitaries and average subjects alike. The number of plays written or translated by intellectuals and regular bourgeois, the quest by average citizens for rehearsal space, the sheer volume of pages devoted to discussing theatrical matters in the press or in municipal reports give a sense of the theater's importance and ubiquity in the lives of elites and nonelites alike at the beginning of the twentieth century in these three cities. What were the reasons behind such a theater craze?

The Nahḍa *and the Theater: The Construction of a Discourse*

When, in the first half of the nineteenth century, readers in the Arab world uncovered Europe through the eyes of prominent literati (al-Jabarti, al-Tahtawi, al-Shidyaq), they were subjected to lengthy descriptions of an artistic genre about which they knew close to nothing. For these literati and many others after them, the discovery of the theater in London and Paris (*tiyatro, marzaḥ, marsaḥ,* or *masraḥ* in Arabic) caused tremendous excitement and unleashed many thoughts.[17] Wishing to explain this new genre to his fellow Egyptians, al-Tahtawi described plays as "an imitation of what has occurred."[18] He then elaborated: whereas the plays he saw were often entertaining and humorous, they in fact dealt with serious matters: "In truth, these plays [*al'āb,* literally games] are serious issues in the manner of comedy *[hazl]*. . . . In them, a human being sees good deeds and bad deeds, the praising of the first and the condemnation of the second, so much so that the French say that it [the theater] inculcates morality *[tu'addib akhlāq al-insān wa tuhadhdhibuha]*."[19]

The moral dimension of the theater to which Tahtawi alluded in the 1830s, and therefore its inherent seriousness, would remain a dominant discourse throughout the late nineteenth century and early twentieth. But what exactly did morality mean, and what did it imply? What other traits were attributed to the theater? It seems fitting to begin searching for an answer to these questions by turning to the pioneer of Arab theater and examining his thoughts on the matter. In February 1848 Marun al-Naqqash (1817–55) gave an opening speech in Beirut to the first ever performance of a play in Arabic: *Al-Bakhīl,* an adaptation of Molière's *L'Avare.*[20] Praising the progress made by the inhabitants of "our realm" *(ahāli bilādina),* Naqqash pointed out that the inhabitants of the West *(ahāli al-bilād al-ifranjiyya)* were still ahead in terms of "science, art, order and civilization."[21] This discovery paradoxically gave Naqqash hope: "Through reading and hard work, perhaps we will understand the source of their greatness . . . and lift the veil off our continuous poverty."[22] The East's backwardness, he suggested, lay in the following causes. First, the inhabitants of these lands had shed their love for their country and displayed a visible lack of concern for *public interest ('adam al-tafshiya 'ala al-naf' al-'āmm)*;[23] they were purely self-interested and paid no attention to the needs of their fellow countrymen *(abnā' jinsihi[m])*. Naqqash contrasted this selfishness with the Europeans' love for their country, which they strove to improve through their actions, notably by spending money and subsidizing worthwhile projects that benefited the country as a whole. Second, Naqqash blamed his fellow countrymen's laziness for the country's backwardness. This laziness was inexcusable, he argued, for the following reason: "There is in this realm a very high number of noble students . . . eager and articulate . . . but they are content with their success, and rely on their friends [for any initiative]."[24] Third, he maintained that progress required patience, whereas in Syria, "everybody is too impatient to plant the seeds today in order to have trees tomorrow."[25]

Naqqash thus equated progress with transcending private interests for the common cause of public interest. What better way to promote and enhance public interest than through the theater? Like Tahtawi, he had discovered during his travels in Europe that the theater was more than entertainment. If plays were, "on the surface, [about] entertainment and humor," in reality they were "[about] truth and reform *[min ẓahiriha majāz wa mazḥ wa bātiniha ḥaqīqa wa iṣlāḥ]*."[26] Even the rulers were attracted to the theater, and they gained political wisdom through it. Implicitly, then, Naqqash was arguing that the theater, by triggering soul-searching among individual spectators, would ultimately benefit society as a whole, because a truly moral person tamed his selfish nature and did not push for his personal interests at the expense of society's.

Thirty-odd years after Marun al-Naqqash's opening speech, as the theater began to gain ground among wider intellectual circles and notables, his nephew Salim elaborated on the connection between the theater and public interest in a seminal essay on "the benefits [or merits] of plays or theaters," which appeared in *al-Jinān* in 1875.[27] He repeated the argument put forth by Marun, that the reason for and the manifestation of Europe's primacy in the realm of civilization was its early promotion of theater. He also elaborated on his uncle's concept of public interest *(al-naf' al-'āmm)* by introducing the concept of a social body *(al-hay'a al-ijtimā'iyya)*, which would be the catalyst for progress. The theater would be a vital maker of this social body. Salim Naqqash began his long essay by linking the rise of civilization with the concept of collaboration, of man's need to work with other men in order to satisfy his basic needs of safety and food. This collaboration led to the creation of a social body *(hay'a ijtimā'iyya)*.

> And when the number of human beings increased, so did their needs, and the importance of *hay'at al-ijtimā'* increased as a consequence . . . and he who knows about the condition of man in ancient times and his condition now, is bewildered by the progress made by humanity. . . . The cause of civilization is the wellness of *hay'at al-ijtimā'*, without which man would have stayed in his savage condition *[al-hamajiyya]*. The Europeans knew this before us, and they devised ways to improve it [the social body]. Among these ways [were] theaters. For the theater is the mirror that shows man a representation [or imitation, *timthāl*] of himself, so he sees his vices *['uyūb]* and shortcomings and avoids them. . . . People gathered there, and their meetings were devoid of divisiveness and fanaticism *[ta'aṣṣub]*. They made the theater a means to unite, pushing away that which divided them. And this sometimes brought innumerable benefits, and other times, great damage. This has to do with the difference of principles *[mabādi']* it displays.[28]

Salim Naqqash thus associated the theater with progress and civilization. Progress would be achieved both individually and socially: individually, through the spectator's heightened moral consciousness, and socially, through the *gathering* of individuals in front of a stage and their *common* shared experience of the performance. This interaction between individuals who shared space and spectacle was itself a form of collaboration that made the individual transcend the self, "push away that which divided" him from this fellow spectators, and form a social body. Salim had thus gone a step beyond his uncle's conception of the theater and public interest by identifying a necessary organ in the making of public interest, the social body, and explaining how the theater played a key role in its making. Without a social body, Naqqash argued, there could be no civilization. Civilization *(al-tamaddun)*, which was at the heart of his concerns,

> means a language that instills in man the morality of urban dwellers *[akhlāq ahl al-mudun]*, and transports him from a state of roughness [or lack of refinement, *khushūna*] and ignorance to a state of sociability [or pleasantness, *ans*] and knowledge, but this definition does not encompass all that which we mean when we use the term *tamaddun*. I say that its more accurate meaning is that of life improvement, and the formation of the *hay'at al-ijtimā'*.[29]

Civilization was thus not merely about social and individual progress, but about life improvement, a philosophical project that was more than the sum of its social and moral parts. Naqqash elaborated on ways the social body could guarantee life improvement:

> We want to specify it *[tamaddun]* even more, by saying that it is a call for the tying of people to works, as well as the reason of their strength and the way to improve their condition. *It is also a way to divide their wealth among them with justice [qust wa 'adl]*. . . . Suffice it to say that civilization is the connection of private interest to public interest *[al-tamaddun huwa irtibāt al-maṣlaḥa al-khuṣūṣiyya fi'l-maṣlaḥa al-'umūmiyya]*; that is, man, in his activities, should attend to the interest *[maṣlaḥa]* of all the people of his kind *[abnā' jinsihi]*; where such ties and assistance exist, there will we find civilization, and where we see man tending only to his own interests . . . there will there be roughness [or barbarity, *khushūna*] and weakness resulting from the love of the self.[30]

Naqqash thus connected private and public interests and spelled out the need for individuals to tend to the interest and well-being of "people of their kind" if they wanted to achieve civilization. But what exactly did he mean by "people of their kind"? He suggested the "love of the homeland" as a way to tie public and private interests; he remarked that the Europeans had understood the effect the theater had on strengthening such a feeling:

> The love of the homeland *[al-waṭan]* is among the best ways to tie private interests to public ones. . . . This is what people understand by *tamaddun*, which Europeans spread through acting rooms. [These rooms, i.e., the theater] are the means to spread principles that are the basis of the country's progress and its means of civilization. They

> have achieved great art with their plays *[tafannanū kathīran]*, and their rulers have helped them do so.[31]

Salim Naqqash's homeland was not "the nation," but a land that welcomed foreigners and integrated them into this homeland.[32] The love for one's homeland implied recognizing what was good for it, including welcoming and supporting those whose work contributed to the creation of a social body, especially through the theater. Thus in a well-thought-out argument Naqqash moved from the notions of social body and civilization to the love of the homeland. He argued that he, a Syrian, would contribute through the theater to leading Egypt on the path of civilization by increasing Egyptians' love for their country and the creation of a social body. For that purpose, he insisted, the theater's benefits to Egyptian society would materialize only if the performances were in Arabic.[33]

Salim Naqqash's seminal essay was one of the earliest elaborations of the idea that the theater constituted a vital tool for progress, civilization, and the making of a social body. It is not difficult to grasp how reformist his conception of the theater was: the theater was essential in shaping a social body, without which civilization could not be attained; it bridged individual and social reform, allowed people (as individuals and as groups) in the audience to unite, transcend their divisions, and join forces for the sake of public interest. All these elements were promises of a new society, one that broke loose from an earlier society that, in Naqqash's view, was ridden with self-interest and social divisions. In that respect his vision was perfectly compatible with the general ethos of *nahḍa* reformists and supporters—politicians, intellectuals, and notables—who embraced the theater wholeheartedly, just as they embraced the press, as a vehicle for the dissemination of reformist ideas that would lead to the formation of a social body and would thus benefit society.

The discourse linking the theater to progress, social reform, and civilization became a dominant feature of the *nahḍa* throughout the period under study. Even thirty years after Salim Naqqash's essay was published the theater was still being hailed as the central institution for the advancement of civilization.[34] One reason his views on the theater were so influential was that he himself was not merely a man of the theater, but a true intellectual and a prolific author whose writings were taken seriously and were widely read. And not only was he a central figure in the world of the theater, but he also founded newspapers, was a member of and in close contact with various intellectual networks, and could disseminate his ideas through institutions as well as by informal, noninstitutional means.

Although Salim Naqqash's views on the theater and on society were compatible with the principles of the *nahḍa*, he pushed a more radical envelope. First and foremost, he tied the development of civilization—to which the theater was essential—to wealth distribution, arguing, "Civilization . . . is also a way to divide their [the people forming a social body] wealth among themselves with justice."[35] This was most likely one of the earliest assertions of a direct association between wealth distribution and civilization in the period under study; the fact that it was made in a discourse on the theater is highly illustrative of the intrinsic connection between the theater and radical thought. Second, Naqqash's efforts to link radical thought with the development of the stage were magnified through his long-lasting association with Jamal al-Din al-Afghani, one of the most radical intellectuals of the 1870s and 1880s. Indeed the Muslim radical also viewed the establishment of an Egyptian theater as the most effective way of promoting radical ideas and raising the political consciousness of the populace.[36] He advised a number of thinkers, including Ya'qub Sannu'a, whose name is inextricably linked to the Egyptian theater, to found a popular Egyptian theater for this purpose.[37]

In summary, the discourse linking the theater to social responsibility, reform, and civilization was constructed and diffused among *nahḍa* reformists. Many aspects of this discourse contained seeds of radicalism, and in the 1870s and 1880s a strong association emerged between the stage and the radical core composed by al-Afghani's disciples. But the idea of the theater as a maker of civilization and hence a vital organ for the formulation and diffusion of ideas was not confined to a handful of intellectuals. Rather, it was an idea held in common by members of various social classes and institutions who hastened to engage in theatrical patronage, production, and consumption. Across social categories and classes, the theater was universally accepted, in theory and in practice, as a most effective vehicle for the dissemination of ideas promoting social responsibility and reform. However, this omnipresence of theatrical activities could also be potentially subversive and radical.

INSTITUTIONS AND THE PROMOTION OF THEATRICAL PRODUCTION AND CONSUMPTION

Two institutions, the press and the municipality, helped disseminate the idea that the theater was associated with progress and civilization. Like the theater itself, both were *new* institutions that emerged around the same period, and their impact on society was shaped and magnified by their overlap. The press adopted and spread the discourse formulated by *nahḍa* intellectuals that linked the theater to social change and promoted the use of the theater as a yardstick for cultural progress: "It is known that plays *[al-riwāyāt al-tashkhīṣiyya]*, called theatricals *[al-tiyatrāt]*, are amongst the most important indications of progress and one of the most important reasons for the reform of customs and the implantation of historical wisdom in the minds of the people," wrote *al-Jinān*.[38] A year later *al-Ahrām* continued on the same subject, emphasizing the role of the theater as a consolidating element of society and expressing its satisfaction with Arabs who acknowledged the theater's importance, studied it, and by doing so contributed to "civilizing" their own culture.[39]

The press's support for the theater was not merely discursive and theoretical; it was manifested in a practical manner by actively rallying the population behind the theater. In the 1870s, when the Arab theater was still a novelty in Egypt, newspapers such as *al-Ahrām* published articles explaining the meaning of comedy in the hope of convincing readers to attend performances given by Arab troupes.[40] Later they published scripts, synopses, and reviews of plays performed, so as to whet readers' appetite for the actual performance; some periodical offices even sold tickets for theatrical performances.[41] Periodicals actively sought to promote certain troupes that they deemed talented, especially if they were on the verge of bankruptcy.[42] The press's great concern throughout the period under study was to convince people of means to lend the theater moral and financial support, a campaign perhaps most tirelessly led in the late nineteenth century by *al-Ahrām*, whose owners, the Taqlas, were themselves particularly interested in the theater.[43]

The municipality also offered strong support and patronage to the theater and helped promote it discursively as well as practically. The municipality represented a liminal space between the state and civil society in which civic ideas could be discussed in a forum that was somewhat different from yet related to the state. Unlike other completely civil institutions such as the private press, the municipality was actually endowed with the legal power to implement policies, and its discussions on the theater were often translated into tangible policies that had a significant impact on the practice of the theater and contributed to bringing it to the masses—or at least a sizable part of the urban population. The discussions and decisions pertaining to the theater during meetings of Alexandria's municipal council shed light on the vital role of the municipality in promoting the theater for the masses.[44] One should obviously keep in mind, however, that although Alexandria's case suggests the kind of debates on the theater that must have taken place in other cities, such as Cairo and Beirut, the theater in Alexandria occupied a particularly privileged position in the life of both the municipality and the city. The uniqueness of the Alexandrian theater was related to a number of factors that were specific to that city: the presence of a significant nonindigenous population (roughly a quarter of the city's population in 1900) and its overrepresentation on the city's municipal board, the existence of a group of bourgeois radicals who occupied positions of power in the municipality and the city, and the presence of a sizable Italian community.

The Italian community of Alexandria had historical links to the theater as actors, authors, builders, sponsors, and spectators.[45] The first troupes to tour Egypt in the early nineteenth century were Italian. Throughout the nineteenth century and early twentieth Italian troupes were a continuous fixture in Egypt and major port cities of the Ottoman Empire. Their repertoire included not only highbrow classical plays, nor even plays destined for upper-class audiences, but also a lively tradition of Commedia dell' Arte, a combination of humor and social criticism. It seems that members of the Italian community in Alexandria were avid theatergoers, and this epithet was certainly not reserved for people of means.[46] Another element that helps explain why Alexandria was a hotbed for theater is the fact that many members on the board of the municipality were progressive notables who, among other things, had been instrumental in establishing a unique project in the Ottoman Empire and the Eastern Mediterranean: the Free Popular University, the Université Populaire Libre d'Alexandrie, a unique venture that sought to educate workers and whose statement of purpose and curriculum emphasized the didactic role of the theater. Partly because of these factors, many elements that were propitious to the theater in general, and to a social theater or a theater *for the masses* in particular, converged in Alexandria. This convergence was to have serious and radical repercussions on the stage.

The scope of Alexandria's theatrical craze emerges in the pages of the city's municipality reports, which reveal heated and frequent discussions indicating just how seriously the theater was taken and confirming how widespread the discourse linking theater and reform had become among Alexandria's multiethnic bourgeoisie. Beginning in the municipality's formation in 1892, council members, both indigenous and foreign-born, engaged in lengthy and often passionate discussions on theatrical subvention: Which troupes and theaters should the municipality subsidize? Did the municipality need to fund both European and Arab theaters?[47] How could the city justify spending money on plays when there were more pressing issues to deal with: entire neighborhoods to revamp, sewer systems to expand, and hospitals to build? A number of municipal members pushed for municipal subsidies for Arab as well as European troupes from 1894 onward. When an Egyptian member of the municipality expressed his desire to have part of the theatrical subsidies channeled to an Arab theater, his opinion was seconded by a European, although the latter suggested that an "indigenous troupe" be granted one-fifth of the sum allocated to its European counterpart.[48] Although the municipality systematically privileged European over local troupes, the imbalance of subsidies decreased over the years as more subsidies were granted to Arab troupes.[49]

Over time the reports show a heightened sensitivity to issues of class. Various municipality members initially opposed the subventions, protesting that the theater would benefit only a fringe of the population, culturally as well as economically.[50] They argued that the money should be put toward popular entertainment, such as street fests.[51] Ultimately, however, their reservations were put aside; by the beginning of the twentieth century the theater had won the support of all municipal members. A number of them tirelessly insisted on promoting theatrical activities that would benefit both rich and poor, Europeans and Egyptians. In 1906 the debate about the construction of a new municipal theater and the choice of the site led various members to display overt working-class sympathies, and the municipality pledged to subsidize the price of seats so that "the theater would be affordable to all."[52] This pledge was formalized in the proposal of 1909: the new municipal theater "would be placed at the service *[mis à la disposition]* of the indigenous population as well as Europeans of all nationalities, while remaining within the reach of all wallets."[53] During this debate some members of the municipality even tried to turn the theater into an institution serving first and foremost members of the working class: "M. Stross a très bien exposé le but d'un théâtre qui est un établissement pour l'éducation et le délassement du peuple, où les classes moins aisées en plus grand nombre que la classe riche, viennent s'instruire et se récréer après le labeur de la journée."[54]

It is striking how central a topic of discussion the theater was during Alexandria's municipal meetings. Certainly no other cultural institution was as carefully examined or triggered as intense a debate as the theater. In the eyes of the municipality the theater was a city maker, just as for intellectuals of the *nahḍa* the theater was a social body maker. It brought different people together: rich and poor, Egyptians and Europeans, Christians, Muslims, and Jews. It allowed the inhabitants of the city to feel that they were one audience, forming one public that not only attended spectacles but was itself a spectacle. This diverse public eager to absorb culture was to be the living proof of Alexandria's modern (and European) aspirations.

There was yet another aspect behind the city-making quality of the theater. The theater generated capital that would be channeled to various echelons of society and would therefore benefit the entire economy of the city, bringing in tourism and luring investments.[55] The municipality's view of the theater was thus twofold. First, it sincerely believed in the social values of the theater and saw the theater as a maker of society, an educator of the masses, and a generator of public life. It linked progress and civilization to the development of the theater and imputed Europe's superiority to its promotion of that institution, exactly as Arab intellectuals of the *nahḍa* had done. Second, the municipality held the theater to be the symbol of and the tool for a certain kind of city; in some ways it viewed the theater as the cultural equivalent of the stock market, since both confidently asserted the city's adherence to a certain set of modernist and European values.

In an epoch obsessed with the gaze of Europe, Alexandria, like so many other cities of the Ottoman Empire (and of the Habsburg and Russian empires), displayed its modernity with a certain urgency. It had to be able to compete with or at least be on par with European cities.[56] But there was more to this story. Alexandria's municipality was also clearly attuned to the endorsement of socialism by various European municipalities and the emergence of municipal socialism. In 2000 its library still held a very significant number of publications from the late nineteenth century on municipal policies: booklets, reports, periodicals issued in French, Italian, and other European cities, and books examining the intersection between urbanism and social welfare. Alexandria's municipality associated two central features with European and modern cities: public consumption of culture and public concern for the working class—or, more accurately, a public display of interest in its fate. In European cities this second feature had been translated into projects such as building low-income houses and popular education. Alexandria's municipality discussed the possibility of building low-income houses, but the project failed to materialize.[57] For Alexandria's municipality, the theater served as the perfect display for public consumption of culture, as well as an eloquent reminder of the municipality's campaign to educate the working classes. Its other project was sponsoring the Free Popular University.

From Discourse to Practice: The Popularity of Theatrical Activities

The efforts of the press and later of the municipality helped to ensure that the discourse that made the theater one of the major paths (if not *the* path) to progress was internalized by large segments of the populations of Beirut, Cairo, and Alexandria, and theory was soon put into practice. The result was that the sponsorship, production, and consumption of theater truly permeated all levels of public life. Professional troupes proliferated at a bewildering speed,[58] and so did amateur performances. Virtually every school in Syria and Egypt, local and foreign, Christian, Muslim, and Jewish, was busy putting on performances and inviting parents as well as governors and other dignitaries to attend them.[59] Their repertoire ranged from the sacred to the profane, and sometimes these two categories overlapped. Charitable institutions also staged theatrical performances, asking troupes to perform for free for fundraising.[60] This seems to have been common practice from the theater's early years; the sum raised by Marun al-Naqqash after his first performance in Beirut of *Al-Ḥasūd al-Ṣalīṭ* (between 1850 and 1854) went to help the poor.[61] Similarly the Jewish Cairene Charitable Society (al-Jamʿiyya al-Khayriyya al-Isrāʾiliyya) put on a performance at the opera in April 1881 to raise money for the poor of its community.[62]

Patronage was not confined to institutions. Often notables invited actors to give private performances at their houses, sometimes to celebrate a birth or a marriage.[63] Some financed the translation, writing, and printing of plays, sometimes by their own printing press, and then distributed these plays for free.[64] Or they would secure a much needed venue for theatrical activities; most theaters in Alexandria, and probably also in Beirut and Cairo, were commissioned privately rather than being state-sponsored.

Although there is ample documentation regarding theatrical patronage, sources that could shed light on audiences are sorely missing. Who actually made up the audience at most of the performances? Who made up the general public? The masses? It seems that theatrical performances were generally extremely well attended, and some theaters in Egypt could and often did hold as many as two thousand spectators.[65] Indeed *al-Ahrām* reported that people scrambled to get tickets for the performance of *Al-Ḥasūd al-Ṣalīṭ* by Salim al-Naqqash's troupe in 1876 in Cairo; every seat was sold.[66] Theaters in Syria also held huge numbers of spectators. When the Ottoman state lifted a temporary ban on the theater in Syria in 1906,

Egyptian troupes flocked back to Damascus. Sa'id al-Qasimi and Khalil 'Azm described the inhabitants of Damascus going en masse to attend these performances.[67] When *Ḥādithat jarīḥ Bayrūt* was performed in Damascus in 1911, the size of the audience far surpassed the theater's seating capacity. According to a contemporary witness, "The room which could fit 800 people contained those 800, with another 300 people standing."[68] An important feature of all these performances is that they brought together people from various ethnic, religious, and class backgrounds. In the case of the play sponsored by the Jewish Cairene Charitable Society, the actors were Jewish, the audience included Muslim high dignitaries, and the training for the actors, who were all amateurs, was provided by the Christian Yusuf al-Khayyat.[69] Audiences during many performances commissioned by charitable institutions included members of the underprivileged classes.

A Potentially Subversive Institution

As I mentioned, the theater had radical and subversive elements. From its introduction into the Ottoman Arab provinces around the middle of the nineteenth century, it had been viewed as a sign and a catalyst of progress and reform, and such an association had become internalized by large segments of the cities' populations. The theater also created a public that was likely more mixed religiously, ethnically, and socioeconomically than that of many other artistic or cultural gatherings; at least it had a strong potential for bringing together individuals, groups, and classes that mingled less with one another in other settings. This new public could engage in defining itself and making its own public sphere; through the theater its members could also (at least in theory) communicate across class and ethnic divisions in a space that was not defined by state or religious institutions. There were other potentially subversive aspects to theatrical production and consumption as it developed in the Ottoman Arab provinces between 1860 and 1914: the fact that the theater in the period under study did not become the exclusive fiefdom of professionals; the making of a transnational network of dramatists, continuously on the move and specifically between Egypt and Syria; related to the previous point, the special role played by Syrians in the world of the theater and in the formulation of radical, leftist thought in Egypt; and the theater's contribution to the public sphere, particularly through the proliferation of private theaters that could potentially be used for extratheatrical activities.

How did all these features contribute to the theater's potential subversiveness and radicalization? The appropriation of the stage by a general, nonprofessional population, as illustrated by the efforts to found a theater in a village at the outskirts of Beirut and the establishment of an amateur theatrical association by employees of the Egyptian post in Alexandria,[70] meant many things: the access of the masses to a modern, reformist institution, their acquisition of a theatrical repertoire that was very often radical in and of itself, and, most subversively, the legitimacy to interpret and adapt a script and the right to improvise scenarios. A Western genre whose production was initially reserved for an educated elite, the theater had let loose a middle-class and intellectual culture onto a population that was subjected to this culture's hegemony at the same time that it was actually empowered to dissect, analyze, represent, and subvert it. As such, the theater was not only the vehicle for a dominant elite to disseminate its ideology, but also the means by which commoners appropriated elite culture. It also provided contesting and marginalized groups, especially disgruntled workers, a space for gathering and holding political meetings.

Another potentially radical feature of the theater in the late nineteenth century and early twentieth was the perpetual movement of actors between Syria and Egypt and the formation of training and recruiting networks.[71] Given that Arabic performances had begun earlier in Syria (in the 1850s) than in Egypt (in the 1870s), Syria was a natural recruitment pool for actors. In fact until 1914 Syrians more or less dominated Egyptian theater as both actors and directors. They trained newcomers and formed an entire generation of actors; they also managed, owned, and built theaters, sometimes grand ones such as the Zizinia and the Teatro Rossini in Alexandria, as well as less prestigious but very popular theaters such as Qordahi's and Iskandar Farah's in Alexandria and Cairo, respectively.[72] The presence of Syrians was fundamental in articulating the need for an Egyptian as well as an Arab theater, and they did so first through the Beiruti *al-Jinān* in the early 1870s and then through Syro-Egyptian papers. Their support for the theater can also be seen in the number of translations, adaptations, and publications of European plays, as well as in the speeches given by intellectuals and professionals praising theatrical performances.

Many troupes based in Egypt, such as Qabbani's, recruited actors and stage designers while on tour in Syria and brought them back to Egypt.[73] This was particularly true for actresses; it is said that Qordahi, returning in 1894 to Alexandria from a tour in Syria, brought back with him eleven actresses.[74] A great number of actors and actresses recruited or trained in Syria opted to move to Egypt. By the turn of the century there was a plethora of Syrian troupes in Egypt; some lasted only two or three years, but others achieved great fame and formed schools of acting.[75] Professional actors, Syrians and non-Syrians alike, maintained a strong connection with Syria, went on tours there, and even spent entire summers in Beirut and pleasantly cool Mount Lebanon, fleeing from the Egyptian heat.[76] The troupes moved constantly between the two provinces, creating a repertoire, a language, and a network of people, all of which continuously circulated.[77] The memoirs of two famous actors, Badi'a Masabni and Najib al-Rihani, vividly depict the fluidity of the theatrical world, the constant branching out of actors to form their own troupes, the head-hunting and snatching of various stars from one troupe by another, the incredible amount of plagiarism that took place between troupes in Syria, Egypt, and even Brazil, and the constant examination of each other's work and acquisition of various techniques from one another.[78]

The movement of people, the establishment of an actors' network, and the making of a transnational repertoire and a transnational *popular* culture that went beyond merely local issues, all seem to have encouraged the theater to deal with radical themes. Perhaps this was partly due to the special relationship that developed between certain stars and members of a radical middle class in Beirut, Cairo, and Alexandria. Many famous actors, such as 'Aziz 'Eid and Salama Hijazi, were recognized by their contemporaries as *nahḍa* intellectuals; they frequented learned circles and were close to the major intellectuals and reformists of their period. 'Eid in particular seems to have had strong ties with Beiruti radicals; in the span of a few weeks he held the leading role in two political plays performed in that city in 1909.[79] Given that 'Eid and his troupe performed a play titled *The Masons* in Cairo (one of the performances took place in Hijazi's theater) and given his involvement in the Ferrer play a couple of years after that, it is also highly likely that 'Eid was a Freemason and had close contact with Freemason circles in Beirut, Cairo, and Alexandria.[80] Iskandar Farah also seems to have had serious radical connections; more than once he put his theater at the disposal of striking workers and their middle-class representatives and spokesmen. Furthermore his plays, which were clearly politically sensitive, were often forbidden or interrupted in midperformance by policemen, especially around 1909–10.[81] It is worth noting that Salama Hijazi, Iskandar Farah, and 'Aziz 'Eid worked together at various points in their careers.[82]

The emergence of the theater also provided an additional public space that was to significantly strengthen and expand the public sphere and hence bring forth potentially subversive and radical changes. The production and consumption of plays and the new kind of crowd that the theater created implied that the public was discussing and interpreting topics hitherto restricted to certain religious and political elites. Moreover the creation of a new physical space contributed to the expansion of the public sphere. Activities within theaters and on stage were by no means confined to theatrical performances, and theatrical locales often served as a stage for political speeches, rallies, and gatherings. This was certainly not unique to Egypt and Syria in the late nineteenth century and early twentieth. Throughout the world strikers and anarchists held meetings in theaters and in ballrooms.[83] In Egypt and Syria some of the political speeches in theaters were impromptu; after one politically charged play on Cretan independence, one spectator was "moved by the spirit" and broke into a political *khuṭba*, "giving an impassioned speech in which he mentioned freedom and demanded it. . . . The excitement increased among the spectators. . . . The chief of police stopped the speaker from finishing his speech . . . then he took [him] along."[84] Other speeches might have been more rehearsed, such as al-Afghani's famous speech in Alexandria's Zizinia Theater in May 1879, in which he is said to have advocated the separation of political and religious authority in Islam.[85] The Egyptian nationalist leader Muhammad Farid recalled making his first major speech at Salama Hijazi's theater on Junaynat al-Bahri Street in April 1908.[86]

Like older spaces, such as coffeehouses, the theater was vital to the construction of a working class because it provided the necessary space for the development of a "working-class public sphere."[87] Theaters provided a locale for workers, strikers, and labor union organizers, all of whom seem to have made a habit of meeting there. In March 1902 the Cigarette Workers' Association, composed of both local and foreign members, met in Alexandria's Tiyatro 'Adnan, and in 1908 its Cairene branch opted for Iskandar Farah's theater on 'Abdulaziz Street; the spokesman on behalf of the striking workers in 1901 was himself the artistic director of many troupes, as well as a translator and writer of various plays, who would go on to found his own troupe a couple of years later.[88] Similarly in 1911 striking tobacco workers negotiated the terms of a settlement with their employers in Cairo's Harmonia theater.[89]

The Need to Regulate and Control Theatrical Space

Given the potentially subversive role that the theater could and did indeed play, it is not surprising that the state sought to control it, regulate access to it, and monitor its repertoire. In fact both the Egyptian and Ottoman states tried initially to rid themselves of the subversive potential of the theater by banning it altogether. When the ban was lifted the authorities attempted to regulate it. In Egypt the Ministry of Education issued a decree in February 1888 forbidding students from participating in theatrical activities. The reason it gave for its crackdown on the theater was the desire to preserve social order.[90] The Ministry claimed that the students' excessive attraction to the stage was affecting their academic performance, leaving the state with no option but to forbid students from participating in the "unseemly profession" and threatening them with expulsion from school.[91]

The argument that the theater posed a serious threat to the existing social order was not confined to the state. According to the authors of *Qāmūs al-ṣināʿāt al-shāmiyya* (The Dictionary of Damascene Crafts [or Professions]), actors and theater directors in Syria were paying so much attention to their profession that social chaos was imminent: performance places became overly crowded—hence turning into both health and security hazards—and moral havoc ensued, as "many corruptions *[mafāsid]* resulted from it: the craftsman who worked all day would spend a day's salary on the theater, leaving his family to starve."[92] These arguments were very similar to those put forward during the seventeenth century against coffeehouses, then new and popular spaces in the Ottoman Empire.[93] Indeed both spaces were attacked by their opponents for serving the opium of the masses; coffee, tobacco, and plays were all avidly consumed, dispossessed the poor of their money, and made the masses lazy and unproductive. The social chaos triggered by the theater, claimed the authors, justified government intervention and the subsequent banning of plays. For reasons that remain unclear, however, the ban was short-lived, and the state decided instead to try to control the theater by regulating the space within it and prohibiting the performance of selected plays.

In Egypt the first article of *Niẓām al-masraḥ* (Theatrical Regulations, or Regulations Concerning the Theater, 1874, covering regulations, laws, and amendments on proper and legal behavior in theaters) strictly ordered that "the theater be placed under the supervision of the local authorities, regardless of [its] owner."[94] There followed a series of articles spelling out the proper conduct for both actors and spectators. Actors had to show respect for the public in their gestures as well as their dialogue; whoever broke this rule would "be tried and put in jail immediately after the end of the play."[95] Spectators had to reciprocate by remaining silent: Article 2 stipulated, "Whoever makes any noise . . . for [any] reason . . . will be immediately kicked out."[96] This would serve as a first warning; if the culprit repeated this breach of etiquette, "he [would] be [permanently] forbidden entry to the theater."[97] Article 4 elaborated on the concept of noise control; it specified that it was absolutely forbidden to "whistle, or produce noise by banging with a stick or with feet, or *tashwīsh* [interference, mostly whispering loudly]." Another article categorically forbade smoking in the theater. The state, being prescient enough to realize that it lacked the imagination to think of all the ways order could be threatened in a theater, wisely added another clause: "In cases not mentioned and not legislated, the necessary procedures will be taken, depending on the kind of violation."[98] Finally, for added protection, just in case all these articles did not dissuade potential troublemakers from misbehaving, the state ordered that "eight soldiers *[shāwūsh]* [be] posted inside the theater, to implement orders given by the chief of police."[99]

A couple of decades later, when municipalities were put in charge of regulating all spaces within a city, another set of laws completed the control over the theater. In Alexandria as in other cities in Egypt and the Ottoman Empire, the Règlement sur les théâtres of 1904 repeated the same restrictions regarding noise control; even more categorically it insisted on the moral content of plays performed, stating, "All shows and all representations of an immoral nature will be formally forbidden. The police have a right to suspend representations or shows of this kind."[100] The new Règlement also stipulated that "no theater could be erected without the municipality's previously written authorization."[101]

Banning and censorship were other tools with which the state exercised its control over the theater. The Egyptian Règlement sur les théâtres ordered that "prior to the performance, every theater manager should submit the repertoire of shows and representations . . . to the city's governor, and get his approval."[102] Similar measures were adopted in the Ottoman Empire generally and in Syria specifically; *al-Ahrām* reported that a letter was dispatched from Istanbul to the vilayet of Beirut, ordering that "political newspapers . . . be monitored [or censored, *turāqab*] by the Ministry of Information . . . and theatrical plays . . . be sent to the Asitane [Istanbul] to be monitored *[turāqab]* there before they are performed."[103] These measures, however, did not mean that the dichotomy between approved good, moral plays and rejected bad, subversive, immoral plays was clear-cut; in fact the history of censorship and banning is much more complex than that. Many plays written between the 1880s and 1914 probably never saw the light of day; they were either not published or not performed. And certainly quite a few plays were performed only once before the government decided that they were dangerous and therefore ought to be banned. But there was no merciless logic or master plan deciding the fate of plays. Many a play that *ought* to have been banned in Egypt—because it truly contained subversive material of a nationalist, pro-constitutional, or leftist nature—was not, whereas some seemingly innocuous plays were.

The state thus legally and theoretically seized control of the new space generated by the theater as well as the theatrical repertoire; however, whether it chose to apply the law systematically and whether it *could* always do so is a different matter. Regardless of whether the Egyptian and Ottoman states succeeded in controlling theatrical space and repertoire, the elaborate infrastructure of control is significant in and of itself. Thus the government's decision to ban certain plays, interrupt others in midperformance, or simply close down a theater may be viewed as an indication of the theater's real or perceived subversiveness and radicalism. Furthermore, as previously suggested, the theater's impact on the public sphere was magnified by the rise of other, new civil institutions, particularly the press.

Like the theater, the press had appropriated the right to present, discuss, and interpret local and global themes and events that had hitherto been reserved to limited spaces of discussion determined and monitored by the state. The press often leaped to the theater's defense if it felt that the state was threatening this new public domain by intervening in theatrical affairs. For instance, many newspapers vehemently disapproved of censorship and of police interventions during theatrical performances, warning both the state and the population that such measures were the first steps toward absolute tyranny.[104] Reporting on the state's decision to ban a play or intervene during theatrical performances rendered such a decision *public* and made the state accountable to the public, or at least the reading public, for its decision. The audience informed and concerned by such decisions became much larger than the limited number of individuals directly affected by the banning. The publicity of the state's decisions allowed the theater to gather support from the population, as illustrated in the case of the play *Dinshaway*, which revolved around the shooting of Egyptian peasants by British soldiers. When the play was suddenly banned by the state in 1908, after it had been performed for months, its author addressed a letter to *al-Ahrām*, reporting to the editorial staff that the Ministry of the Interior had issued a decree prohibiting the play's performance.[105] *Al-Ahrām* published the letter and openly expressed its solidarity with the author, at the same time rallying support from its readership; it would later play a similar role in rallying the population's support for strikers by publishing their petitions.

The alliance between the press and the theater must have been partly strengthened by the fact that these two spheres were run by the same individuals. As discussed earlier in this chapter, a great number of journalists were also involved in the theatrical world (Naqqash, Ishaq, and Sannuʿa, to name just a few). The concomitant emergence of the world of the press and that of the theater and the municipality, and the overlap between them, magnified the tremendous social impact of these institutions.

From Social Theater to Radical Theater: The Politicization and Radicalization of the Theatrical Repertoire

By the early twentieth century a potentially radical discourse linking the theater to profound reform had become widespread and internalized in Beirut, Cairo, and Alexandria. This discourse was accompanied by new and potentially subversive practices among actors and spectators. Did this radicalization manifest itself through changes in the theatrical repertoire in Egypt and Syria? How can we quantify it? Did certain themes emerge at one point and become predominant? Were there differences in the content of plays performed in Syria and in Egypt? What about the audiences' responses to theatrical performances? What light do they shed on the radicalization of the theatrical repertoire and that of society generally? How can we measure an audience's radicalism? Unfortunately, because we lack sufficient information concerning the performances of these plays, the majority of these fundamental questions cannot be satisfactorily answered. Most scripts of the period are no longer available, and many plays were performed without a script; we therefore have no way of analyzing their content. Despite all these difficulties, and on the basis of the limited number of available texts from the period, information concerning their banning, and titles suggesting the themes of the plays, it seems that between 1860 and 1914 the subjects addressed in theatrical performances became increasingly political and radical. Moreover the audience's reaction to theatrical performances appears to have followed a similar pattern.

The first plays performed in Arabic in the mid-nineteenth century were translations of European plays adapted to a local setting; that is, names of characters were Arabicized, local references introduced, and songs added.[106] These adaptations were usually based on works by three seventeenth-century playwrights—Molière, Corneille, and Racine—who form the basis of the French theatrical canon. Later adaptations around the turn of the century included translations of Shakespeare. The fact that the first performance of a play in Arabic was an adaptation of Molière's *L'Avare* reflects a trait that characterized the Arab theater in its first decades. Most plays, both translated and freshly composed, were morality plays revolving around a character's negative trait that was exposed and condemned, such as avarice, greed, or dishonesty. Such plays were often set in the classical Islamic era, drawing their inspiration from or literally adapting for the stage a story from *A Thousand and*

One Nights.[107] Their format was often akin to operettas, in the sense that the historical context was hastily painted and the focus was on the characters rather than the historical setting, even when the play claimed to be historical.[108]

By the 1890s plays adapted as well as freshly written had become more decidedly social, critical, and political.[109] Eighteenth-century French Enlightenment works were translated and adapted to the stage or served as inspiration to plays set in a local context but dealing with the same topics. Voltaire's works and adaptations of Rousseau's novels into plays were extremely popular.[110] European (mostly French) contemporary or near contemporary novels were also widely translated and adapted to the stage, including the work of Victorien Sardou.[111] Significantly, among the most popular plays performed in the three cities of focus in the early twentieth century were stage adaptations of Alexandre Dumas's works, many of which were social critiques calling for class equality. Among Dumas's most popular adaptations was *Ibn al-sha'b,* also known as *Nubūgh wa ikhtilāl, aw riwāyat fannān* (*Kean, ou Désordre et génie,* 1836), which was performed from 1905 to 1907 in Egypt and Syria.[112] This play, alongside many of Dumas's work, was translated by Farah Antun (1874–1922), the founder of *al-Jāmi'a,* a radical and a socialist thinker. As I suggested in chapter 1, the growing numbers of translations and adaptations of Shakespeare also attest to increased radicalization, since Shakespeare became part of a radical canon in the late nineteenth century as he became associated with reformist and radical causes. This was certainly the case in late Victorian England, but it most likely was not confined to England. During this period Shakespeare's work was perceived as being full of "narratives that spoke strongly to contemporary radical concerns. Radicals were particularly inspired by the tension between town and countryside present in his plays, his celebration of national traditions, his tense relationship with Christianity, and the concern for the landscape and the national past manifested in all his writings. . . . Above all, Shakespeare's plays were seen as expressive of a pre-modern natural order and a balance within society that was violated by land monopolists, enclosers, and 'regaling tax-eaters.' "[113]

Such a radical twist was apparent not only in translated plays. Plays freshly written also pointed to a shift in the theater's perceived mission, as the main theme moved from individual redemption to social reform. More accurately the link between individual and social reform had been made explicit, and the theater sought to bridge the private and the public and to make the private part of the public domain. Under the guise of rehashing the same old popular stories, the stage was actually presenting didactic plays that bluntly exposed the problems riddling Egyptian and Syrian societies: class rigidity, patriarchy, and the need for women's education.[114] One monologue, *Fatāt al-'aṣr* (The Contemporary Girl), called for female education while criticizing bourgeois values: "By education I do not mean embroidery, piano or drawing; leave such things to the people of Paris. My desire is that the girl be . . . able to read and know many things in writing and cooking." It wisely concluded, "Education is better than guineas, it never abandons those who have it."[115] Other plays, such as Isma'il 'Asim's *Ṣudq al-ikhā'* (The Honesty of Brotherhood), were more overtly political in nature, criticizing Egyptian society's blind imitation of the West, condemning Western education, calling for the establishment of Egyptian girls' schools rather than Western schools, and promoting the teaching of science in Arabic rather than Western languages.[116] Perhaps the apogee of social theater was reached by Farah Antun, whose work promoted a combination of anti-imperialist, Arab proto-nationalist, and socialist values, and advocated social and moral reforms through the depiction of vice, especially the seduction of young women, gambling, and drinking.[117] Many plays promoted a strongly anti-capitalist message, in which Big Business in the form of the stock market, banks, and real estate speculation usurped the right of the middle and working classes to access their country's wealth.

Significantly, topics of social justice, such as the call for wealth redistribution and criticism of rigid class structures, were almost never tackled independently or in isolation from larger issues. Rather, they went hand in hand with a larger reformist agenda that included criticism of the East's facile imitation of the West, the call for curbing the power of local and foreign churches (or even a frank attack on them), the promotion of female education, and the demand for an Ottoman constitution. Reform was therefore a package in which class issues were but one item. Social radicalism, as it emerged in these cities but also in many other parts of the world at that time, maintained this multiplicity of issues. These causes were all interconnected in the minds of their promoters and accepted as such by the wider public. There were many implications for this plethora of causes presented and defended together. First, this packaging helps explain the broad support for radical ideas among a certain reformist but not necessarily radical public; indeed if social justice was one cause among many—and very often not the most prominent one—it became more diluted and hence more palatable for the general bourgeois public. Second, because class issues were almost never extracted from a larger reformist agenda and singled out, there did not develop a discourse focusing exclusively on class at the expense of any other category (ethnic, national, clerical or anticlerical, and so on). Hence causes such as the Ferrer Affair could trigger tremendous passion in Beirut in 1909 because they combined a critique of existing social hierarchies with a vociferous anticlericalism and an attack on European colonial expansion.

Staging the Revolution

Several themes were addressed by the theater as it became progressively more politicized and radicalized in the first years of the twentieth century. One theme was revolution, especially the French Revolution.[118] In the last decades of the nineteenth century "The Marseillaise," probably the strongest signifier of the French Revolution, had been appropriated and adapted to the local stage (at least its tune was).[119]

By the early twentieth century a number of plays adapted from French authors emerged on the market and became clear favorites in Beirut, Cairo, and Alexandria.[120] Among the figures who contributed most to bringing home the French Revolution was Amin al-Rihani, whose study came out in 1901 and was widely circulated and discussed.[121] Perhaps the most important advertiser of the Revolution was Farah Antun, who in *al-Jāmiʿa* (1897–1906), the periodical he founded in Alexandria, helped his readers discover "a new world . . . the world of European literature which we did not know before. . . . Arabic literature was that of authority and tradition and customs whereas . . . *European literature, especially French literature, was that of the revolution* . . . the literature of the mind that feels and of the heart that thinks, the literature of Voltaire and Rousseau and Diderot."[122] Most notably Antun's translation and adaptation of *Ange Pitou,* one of Dumas's novels on the French Revolution, was to leave a lasting impression on all those who read it. Salama Musa wrote, "[I did not] know of a single conscious person who did not read this story and who was not transformed by it and by the rest of Antun's work."[123]

More than merely reflecting the growing concern and interest in the French Revolution among intellectuals, the stage was actually *fundamental* in allowing for and even pushing for the radicalization of a certain group of intellectuals. This radicalization came precisely through an internalization of the French Revolution and the intellectuals' participation in the Revolution as spectators and *actors.* Thanks to the theater, radicals and aspiring revolutionaries throughout the Ottoman Empire began to engage in role-playing on stage, assigning to themselves the roles of Saint-Just, Danton, and Robespierre. This internalization of and apprenticeship in revolution, first conducted through the performance and firsthand experience of the French Revolution, gave the Saint-Justs and Robespierres of Beirut, Cairo, and Alexandria a preview of mass leadership. Not only did the stage serve to disseminate these ideas to a larger audience, but it also allowed the masses to learn their part in the revolution and rehearse their role as the revolutionary Crowd. By being on stage or in the audience witnessing a revolution, revolutionary leaders as well as the masses learned their roles and internalized the revolution's inevitability in human progress. The theater was thus pivotal in allowing radical actors, thinkers, and playwrights as well as the masses to imagine, rehearse, live, and glorify the revolution.

Partly as a result of the theater, some time around the turn of the century the French Revolution stopped being a thing of the past. Whereas a previous generation of Ottoman Turkish and Arab reformers had referred to the principles of the French Revolution (or more accurately, to the values of the Enlightenment), called for their application in the empire through the restoration of the constitution,[124] and conceived of the French Revolution as *the* pivotal moment in history and its point of reference, a new generation was emerging that not only engaged with the principles of the Revolution, but actually *lived and internalized* 1789 by identifying individually and associating others with the heroes (or even the villains) of the French Revolution. One letter written by Shibl Damos to Amin al-Rihani in 1901 captured precisely this state of mind, as the author expressed his wish that he might live to see his own (Ottoman or Syrian) revolution: "Will we be able to live to see this great sight, will I survive to see you its Danton, and I its Robespierre, but differently from what Danton and Robespierre were for the French Revolution. I am dying for something similar to happen, but . . . I fear that [we will have to wait a long time for the revolution]."[125] Perhaps even more telling is that when the Unionist coup was proclaimed in July 1908, many people broke into "The Marseillaise,"[126] or that Jirji Zaidan devoted most of *al-Hilāl*'s April and May 1908 issues to the French Revolution.

The internalization and staging of the French Revolution was in fact a dress rehearsal for the imminent and much awaited Ottoman Revolution.[127] Şükrü Hanioğlu has written of the Young Turks' "preparation for a revolution," and indeed around 1900 and throughout the empire a radical fringe among reformists, including the circle around Rihani, began seriously investigating the concept of revolution in order to set the stage for the forthcoming revolution, Ottoman or otherwise. George Hubayqa, a friend of Rihani based in Cairo, informed him in a letter that he had been "studying the subject of revolutions; how they are brewed *[tutbakh]* and who makes them," and was trying to get information on the following questions: "How is it possible for an *umma* [nation] to revolt *[tathīr]*; what does it need in terms of money and knowledge and experts? . . . How is it possible to establish a new government?"[128] Having identified these topics as being "among the most important topics which reformists should know about before they start shouting . . . for revolutions and encourage people to bear arms," he asked Rihani to send him a reading list and some books.[129]

If these thinkers could only fantasize about their own revolution in the first few years of the twentieth century, by 1908 the fantasy had become reality. The Young Turk Revolution brought with it a constitution, general euphoria, and a series of plays celebrating it to the Egyptian and Syrian markets. Many of these plays were the work of well-known Syrian intellectuals in Egypt; they were performed both in Syria and Egypt and enjoyed great popularity. Antun Gemayyil's *Abtāl al-Ḥurriyya* and Najib Kan'an's *Fatāt al-Dustūr* were among the most popular of that genre; it is said the latter's depiction of Midhat Pasha provoked great enthusiasm from the public.[130] Regular people were recruited for the revolutionary crowds or the People's Army in these plays, just as they had been recruited for the performances of the French Revolution and other plays.[131] One of Rihani's correspondents assured him that if he wished to have *Abdulḥamīd fī Atīna*, his play on the 1908 Unionist coup, performed in Zahle, a town in present-day Lebanon, "all of Zahle's inhabitants [would play the] soldiers."[132] The battle on stage between the soldiers and the people, the great majority of whom were amateur actors recruited from among the population, became so passionate during the Ferrer play that some of the actors were slightly injured. The line between audience and cast would become even more blurred when the audience, forgetting itself, would suddenly erupt onto the stage and join the revolutionary crowd there.

The masses' participation in the staged revolution might have been one of the reasons for the Young Turks' opposition to the performance of plays celebrating the 1908 Revolution and Abdülhamid's dethroning. The play *Al-Dustūr al-'uthmāni,* which denounced Abdülhamid's spying network and celebrated the Constitution and the Unionist coup, was suddenly banned in October 1909, after many performances and having enjoyed great popularity. Even more striking, when in 1908 Amin al-Rihani decided to stage *Al-Sujanā' aw Abdulḥamīd fī Atīna,* his play celebrating the end of Hamidian rule, he encountered great opposition from Unionists in Beirut. Pleading with the president of the Beirut Commercial Court for assistance, Rihani argued, "Abdülhamid is today like any other prisoner. Why can't we perform his role on stage, so that people in the future will know about his bad deeds?"[133] Part of the answer perhaps pertained to the Unionists' deep suspicion of the masses, crowds, and revolutions.[134] For them the staging of the constitutional revolution presented a terrible danger; not only did it grant the masses a role as the people, but it also made them participate in the performance—and hence discussion and analysis—of contemporary events.

Theater's Appropriation of the Contemporary: The Stage as a Press for the Masses

Besides performing the revolution, a new trend had appeared on stage starting around 1907–8: the performance of contemporary events, both local and international.[135] The theater abandoned seventeenth-century France and Abbasid Baghdad and turned to the present. Plays were set in twentieth-century Alexandria, Beirut, Istanbul, or Barcelona, commenting as much on large-scale international events, such as Beirut's bombardment by the Italian fleet in 1911, as on the daily practices of Alexandria's rich and famous. One monologue, *Al-Bank al-Zirā'i* (The Agricultural Bank), bluntly named and denounced the Alexandrian bank's owners, the Soussa brothers, as "silk-clothed pashas" who "have taken your money and ours" and "steal the money of the poor and drink people's blood with their meat."[136] Significantly it might have been the same Soussa brothers, the owners of a small cigarette factory, who stood out in their refusal to join a syndicate and improve the working conditions of their employees.[137] Thus the stage served as the press of the masses, offering access to information on local and global political developments, for instance on employers' fairness or lack thereof, as well as carrying a political message for the workers. At the same time it granted nonelites and aspiring elites the right to participate in the making of their own history as equal players, observers, and public commentators. It also served as a court of the people; the arm of justice might not be long enough to reach bankers stealing the money of the poor, but the public naming of these "silk-clothed pashas" was a kind of trial, providing some form of punishment of the culprits and hence justice for the oppressed.

The staging of nonlocal contemporary events must have triggered the audience's deep empathy with the suffering of world populations and masses. By reporting on strikes and the living and working conditions of the proletariat in various countries around the globe, the press must have contributed to the creation of a sense of solidarity among workers in different realms; stage performances of contemporary scenes of oppression and suffering must have had a similar effect. In fact Egyptian and Damascene audiences responded very strongly to plays such as *Ḥādithat jarīḥ Bayrūt* (The Incident of the Wounded of Beirut), about Italy's invasion of Libya and the subsequent bombardment of Beirut in 1911.[138] One contemporary witness described going to a performance of that play in Damascus in 1911 as "the first terrifying political incident" of his life: "The [theater] room which could fit 800 people, contained those 800, with another 300 people standing. . . . The play was supposed to come after the performance of another play. There were some delays after the entr'acte. . . . After some time, the director appeared with the chief of police and announced that the performance of the play had been forbidden. . . . The public was furious, and speeches were given . . . in which it was suggested that the play be performed by force. . . . Then the police intervened, and the troupe spent the night in prison."[139] Similarly, Beiruti audiences empathized greatly with Ferrer's plight and his persecution by the state and the Church. The radicalizing effects and implications of transposing contemporary (and international) events onto the stage were not lost on the state. Indeed many of the plays treating contemporary events—those celebrating the Young Turks' Revolution and Abdülhamid's exile, the Ferrer play, and *Ḥādithat jarīḥ Bayrūt*—were censored, banned, or interrupted in midperformance by the police. In some cases troupe members risked serving time in prison.[140]

THEATER AND ANTICLERICALISM IN SYRIA

The Ferrer play of 1909 was subversive and radical because it represented the culmination of various radical trends within the theater: the organizers behind the play staged the revolution, prompted the participation of the people in it, appropriated contemporary events, and reserved the right of the people to interpret them unofficially. To top it all, they also offered a biting criticism of the Church, which led to clashes between actors and the clergy. In fact the frequent opposition to theatrical performances by various clergy was one salient feature of the theater in Syria, as compared to the relative quiet of its Egyptian counterpart.[141] Although some form of challenge to the Church's authority was to be found among all denominations,[142] it was mostly the Maronite Church and Catholic missions, especially the Jesuits, that were most severely targeted. The antagonism between Church and stage simultaneously contributed to and reflected the growing wave of anticlericalism that swept over Beirut and Mount Lebanon. Already a relatively widespread phenomenon in the first years of the twentieth century in Beirut and Mount Lebanon and among the Syrian diasporas in North and South America,[143] anticlericalism was on the rise among commoners and intelligentsia alike until 1914 and constituted a serious force for the Church to reckon with. The battle between individuals for and against the clergy took place in periodicals and books as well as on stage, but the theater was perhaps the main vehicle for the expression of anticlerical ideas.[144] This feature significantly affected the theater's radicalization; indeed anticlericalism went hand in hand with the promotion of radical policies and ideas, such as land and wealth distribution, a challenge to existing social structures, and an anticapitalist discourse calling for the East's protection from Western economic, religious, cultural, and political encroachments.

Antagonism had not always characterized the relationship between Church and stage. In fact when the theater first appeared in Syria in the 1850s, the Church quickly understood its mobilizing and proselytizing potential. It did not hesitate to appropriate the stage for the setting of morality plays and the propagation of Christian, and specifically Catholic, dogma, and the relationship between Church and stage was synergistic between 1860 and 1880. But starting in the 1880s the Church regularly voiced its disapprobation of certain performances. In August 1888 the play *Al-Sirr al-khafiy,* performed by the Jewish School of Beirut and written by its principal Salim Kuhin, was severely criticized for its immoral content by *al-Bashīr,* a leading newspaper and the organ of the Jesuit college.[145] A few years later, around the turn of the century, major clashes erupted between Church and stage, and tensions remained high until 1914.[146] During these years and especially after 1908 the relationship between Church and stage in Beirut and Mount Lebanon became openly antagonistic.

What were the roots and manifestations of anticlericalism in Syria? Put succinctly, the late nineteenth century was a trying period for the Church, in particular the Maronite Church and Catholic missions. The authority of the Maronite Church had already been severely eroded by the peasant revolts in Mount Lebanon in 1858–60,[147] and the sectarian violence of 1860 in Mount Lebanon triggered an unshakable belief, especially among the educated elites, that the Church's authority had to be limited and confined to certain domains. In the following decades the power of the Church was further eroded by the establishment of various community councils *(majālis al-milla),* secular bodies of notables who challenged the exclusive authority of the clergy over communal affairs. In various instances communities—often poor, rural communities in Mount Lebanon—complained that the Church sided with the rich and that its clergy were uneducated and did not tend to the needs of the population. Within the clergy itself a strong populist movement emerged, accusing the higher ranks in the Church of distancing themselves from the people and being lured by worldly riches. There were repeated calls to seize Church property as the expansion of agriculture and a general economic crisis meant that employment opportunities had reached their limits.[148] The foundations of the Maronite Church were further shaken by the wide appeal of freemasonry and the challenge posed by Protestant missionaries, which gave dissatisfied populations the powerful bargaining card of conversion.

In this context the theater seems to have become one of the preferred vehicles of the anticlerical camp to promote its ideas, and the stage became a major battlefield. As the anticlerical movement increased in popularity the Maronite Church's rather desperate attempts to crush it became increasingly ineffective. The performance in Beirut of the play *Le Juif errant* in 1911, one of the high points of anticlericalism, vividly illustrated the tension between the clerical and anticlerical camps. It also shed light on the Church's feeling of being under siege and, given the degree of its overreaction, its ultimate weakness. The play, performed by a French visiting troupe organized by the head of the Beiruti Masonic lodge, Jirji Dimitris Sursock (who corresponded with Rihani), was based on a tremendously popular mid-nineteenth-century novel by the French author Eugène Sue.[149] It combined calls for social justice with a biting criticism of the Jesuits and their accumulation of wealth. Its performance in Beirut was guaranteed to cause a commotion, and commotion indeed best describes the events that preceded, accompanied, and followed its staging. Periodicals close to clerical circles (especially to the Maronite Church and the Jesuits) mounted a campaign to prevent the performance and urged the Ottoman authorities to ban it. The wali of Beirut refused to do so, referring to the new Constitution, which guaranteed freedom of speech. This was not enough to deter the clerical camp, and the play itself was interrupted in midperformance by pro-Jesuit medical students at the French Jesuit college Saint Joseph, who unleashed "small glass tubes with terrible and poisonous smell" into the theater.[150] Following the performance the clerical camp organized a widespread petition-signing campaign, protesting against the play and at the Ottoman state's decision to allow it to be performed.[151] The protest campaign was so effective that it gathered nearly four thousand signatures from Beirut and Mount Lebanon, reaching the most remote villages, the great majority of whose residents would never see the play.[152]

Thus far my focus has been the subversive potential of the theater as a genre and as a space. Plays became more radicalized and certain major radical themes emerged in the repertoire that also arose within a larger context of political and social transformations, which the theater reflected as well as triggered. The relationship between the theater and radical politics was strongly connected to the rise of mass politics and the emergence of a new class. Indeed the theater played a vital role in the making of a new, radical bourgeois class and allowed this class to conceptualize, formulate, and diffuse a coherent discourse, and in particular to construct an alliance with the working class.

THE RISE OF MASS POLITICS AND MASS EDUCATION

In the early years of the twentieth century a conceptual shift occurred as social, intellectual, and political elites throughout the Ottoman Empire began positing new social and political categories. Rather than speaking exclusively on behalf of their religious community (millet), class, or neighborhood, social elites and aspiring elites systematically began to include peasants and urban working classes into their political discourse. They sought to establish contacts with previously marginalized groups and to mobilize them by diffusing their political messages among them. However, elites and aspiring elites first had to reform, discipline, and educate members of these groups in order to lay the groundwork for the successful diffusion of their ideas.

Many historians have framed this educational impetus as mostly (or solely) manifesting itself among nationalists, especially Egyptian nationalists.[153] In fact this didactic impetus was not confined to one ideological movement: members of all groups with a political project put forth a discourse of social reform, a vision of a mass movement (be it *al-umma, al-hay'a al-ijtimāʿiyya,* or another formulation of the social body), and emphasized the need to begin reforming the masses through education. In the early twentieth century these groups included Syrian and Egyptian secular intellectuals seeking to reform their societies broadly or with a leftist radical bent, Muslim reformists, Italian anarchists and anarchist sympathizers among Alexandria's bourgeoisie, and nationalists.

In some ways *all* these movements—which, at least until 1914, did not form fixed or mutually exclusive categories—were radical; all of them sought to incorporate the masses into their political projects and their visions of a different society; all of them had a rhetoric of wealth distribution, whether the undeserved wealth of the indigenous or of the nonindigenous elites (foreign companies, Levantine and European capitalists, and so on); and all of them asked for a change in the relationship between state and society. Furthermore all of them were seen by the state, as well as other institutions, as posing a threat to their authority and potentially disturbing the status quo.

For these new movements the theater was an essential, if not the main tool for reforming, disciplining, and educating the masses. In particular the education of the working class, as a distinct category, was becoming the focus of various mass movements. A dominant historiographic trend pertaining to workers' education in the Ottoman Empire, specifically Egypt, has overemphasized the role of nationalist parties in establishing night schools for workers and has placed nationalists at the vanguard of such projects. Such an analysis is in fact inaccurate. In Egypt as well as Syria projects to educate the working classes had materialized earlier and involved the extensive use of the theater. In the Middle East perhaps the first such project and the first clear use of the theater in educating the working classes came with the establishment of Alexandria's Université Populaire Libre in 1901, which offered a great number of classes and lectures on the theater, including a history of the theater (in French and Italian).[154] The fruit of a local initiative, the UPL's views on the theater were in line with the philosophy of the Parisian headquarters of that same institution, which thoroughly embraced the idea of social liberation through art and believed that the theater was the most effective tool for that purpose.[155] In Syria the revolutionary potential of the theater for mass education, especially political education, was formulated quite distinctly as early as 1904 by members of the *al-Nūr* circle, who five years later would put on the Ferrer play.[156] Between 1904 and 1909 this group certainly saw in the theater one of the most important forms of social art. Its members were constantly involved in theatrical activities; they regularly published theatrical reviews, gave public lectures on the merits of the theater, wrote scripts, adapted novels into plays, produced plays, and acted in them.[157] In fact by the time of the Ferrer play, this group had arguably come to conceive of the theater as *the* most effective vehicle for the masses' political and social education.[158]

The idea of the theater as a school for the masses was not novel, but it had undergone serious changes from its earlier formulation. As previously discussed, the discourse of the theater as a school for individual morality as well as social consciousness was present since the theater first made its appearance in Syria and later in Egypt.[159] The theater was also to contribute to individual progress by sharpening the mental tools of the audience; it was "a sort of school, in which are gathered humor, witticisms, distinction and knowledge."[160] However, this sort of school differed considerably from that which proponents of mass ideologies pushed for. In the 1860s and 1870s Salim al-Naqqash and others had focused more on bringing together individuals from various religious backgrounds at a time when the main concern in the eyes of reformists was sectarian division rather than class tensions. It is only at the beginning of the twentieth century that the concept of the masses was first formulated, let alone that of the working classes. In other words, the rise of mass politics propelled the theater to the front of mass education, and specifically working-class education. By 1910 the theater had become so inextricably associated with workers' education that *al-Hilāl* could, in all seriousness, make the analogy between the formation of Arab troupes and the establishment of free schools specifically targeting workers, arguing, "This [the formation of Iskandar Farah's Arab troupe] is a venture whose educational fruits will not be less valuable *[la taqill fi thamarātiha al-adabiyya]* than the establishment of a big school that educates youth for free."[161]

In the context of mass politics one group in particular was to benefit from what the theater had to offer. Consisting of radical and intellectual middle-class individuals, this group used the stage for two purposes: the construction and formulation of a coherent radical ideology—a task central to the group's existence as such and one that might have remained unaccomplished were it not for the stage—and the dissemination of this ideology to larger audiences. It was precisely because this group combined radicalism with bourgeois values that its impact was strongly felt. Various components of the ideology that it promoted on stage appeared in Sulayman Hasan al-Qabbani's compilation of popular monologues performed in Alexandria in the first decade of the twentieth century.[162] Published around 1914 by this Alexandrian actor, the booklet *Bughiyat al-mumaththilīn* included a number of popular monologues and lyrics, a brief introduction on the art of the theater and its emergence in various parts of the world, and a series of essays on appropriate behavior in the theater. The striking aspect of these monologues is their authorship: out of twelve monologues whose authors were named, at least seven were the work of Syrians from Egypt,[163] including Dr. Ibrahim Shududi (the author of three monologues) and Tanios 'Abduh. Both Shududi and 'Abduh seem to have had a serious radical connection; if the periodical *al-Iqdām* is to be believed, Shududi was a member of the Socialist Party, supposedly founded in Cairo by Shibli Shumayyil in 1907.[164] A dentist in Tanta, he was famous for his *zajals* and was asked to write plays for the rising star Najib al-Rihani some time around 1914.[165] The three monologues dealt quite radically with a number of social issues. Tanios 'Abduh, the owner of the Alexandrian periodical *al-Sharq*, seems also to have been a member of Shumayyil's entourage.[166]

Among the most striking aspects of the monologues is the articulation of a discourse seeking to construct an alliance between the middle and working classes and linking individual morality to the economic well-being of society. The monologues depict indigenous and nonindigenous upper classes as hopelessly debauched. In one long monologue privileged heirs *(al-wārithīn)* are accused of squandering their fortunes in coffeehouses on hashish, drinking, and women.[167] These effeminate, obscene dandies, who wear pink and swing their hips and whose trousers hug their thighs so tightly they can barely move,[168] are not merely squandering their inheritance on roulette and female dancers. They are in effect dispossessing Egyptian society of a capital that is rightly its own, since they spend their money on non-Egyptians who send it to their homeland rather than reinvest it in the Egyptian economy: "Look at Mr. Christo [the owner of the coffeehouse], sitting like a sultan on his bank, constantly cashing money. His work gets better everyday. He is protected from the law by the consulates, and is getting fatter collecting our money, which he sends to Greece."[169] In fact there is nothing Egyptian about these Egyptian upper classes; not only do their financial excesses not benefit the Egyptian economy, but they themselves have become indistinguishable from the nonindigenous upper classes, speaking a language punctuated by French and Italian and leading equally debauched and dissolute lives.[170] Their spouses even read Zola's *Nana*, surely a marker of their immorality![171] Not only do loose morals lead to individual perdition but, more gravely, they guarantee the economic ruin of society. Members of the middle class are warned of the consequences of such behavior in case they are tempted to taste the forbidden fruits: "If he is an industrialist, he becomes . . . dishonest, cheating in his profession . . . and if he is a doctor, he fries [kills] his patients."[172]

Dismissing the upper classes as hopelessly debauched—with the only glimmer of hope provided by women, thanks to female education[173]—this group regarded the middle and working classes as providing the only remaining hope for society. For these classes to blossom and save their society from collapse, however, they needed to be mobilized for work; hence the monologues' praises and incantations about the virtues of work: "Have you not seen beehives, how everybody works in there, no distraction and no boredom. Egypt is a hive, a fertile ground *[al-mar'a al-khaṣib]*, and you are the bees"; and "Let us roll up our sleeves, produce and revive industry, and bring back a lost greatness."[174] It is not enough to rely on the Constitution *(dustūr)*, the writers warned; although political freedom is necessary, it needs to be accompanied by hard work in order for Egypt to be truly civilized:

> Ye Egyptians! Enough excitement *[ghurūr]* and screams *[fugūr]*; you are in the era of civilization
> roll up your sleeves and say long live the *dustūr;* may it become freedom
> freedom does not mean getting distracted *[tawashshash]* and drunk, this isn't freedom
> . . . freedom means knowing one's duty.
> roll up your sleeves *[shammir]*.[175]

To regain past grandeur and pride and become civilized, Egyptians had two options. The first was to follow the Japanese model: "Show the West that we, like the Japanese, refuse to [suffer] insult and contempt."[176] The other option was to literally *become* the West. As the wounded in *Jarīh Bayrūt* proclaimed, "I wish I did not hasten to die before my due time, [but lived to] see the East rise, despite the attacks of time, and recover its majesty . . . [until] the characteristics of civilization *[ṭabāi' al-'umrān]* take hold of them [the people of the East], and *the East becomes West.*"[177]

Thus rather than be a space for leisure, the theater was to tirelessly educate the masses about the merits of work. Theatrical activity itself epitomized this work ethic because the establishment of amateur troupes sought "to prevent the wasting of free time in places of entertainment."[178] The middle-class radicals who appropriated the stage promoted it as the antithesis of the coffeehouse; whereas both public and private morality were lost in the coffeehouse, they were gained in the theater, and whereas Egyptian capital and potential labor were wasted in the former, they were being channeled toward the well-being of Egyptian society in the latter. The theater was not depriving people of entertainment; it was simply offering a different type of entertainment. Unlike coffeehouses, which catered exclusively to debauched men, theaters focused on providing family entertainment, and theatrical performances were often open exclusively to family members.[179]

Many monologues had an undeniably anticapitalist tone; banks in particular were blamed for impoverishing not only the average person but the entire city.[180] These banks refused to lend honorable people (who were owed money that they were unable to recover) the necessary sum to avoid bankruptcy. In one play a character says, "The banks of this realm have connived . . . to cut my source of gain and add to my misery."[181] Banks were not alone in dispossessing the local population of its capital; every other tool of capitalism was part of a system that would ultimately lead to the destruction of Egyptian society. And all these tools—stock market, land value, salaries—were interconnected. In the words of one character, "I have gained what you have wished upon me, poverty has bitten me; you have . . . lowered my value. . . . I have lost my fortune. . . . Am I to blame if I complain about my hardships? I have one thousand proofs and reasons: the loss of money in stocks and stock market and that of valuable credit; the collapse in the value of land and the rise in rent and the cost of living; the banks' stubbornness and the rise in interest; the halt in payments and the end of security."[182] The only way out of the system's built-in injustice was the establishment of a new basis for society, one that required an alliance between the middle and working classes on the grounds that these two classes constituted the workforce. The task of reviving the nation's economy thus became incumbent upon them. This was the alliance a radical middle class sought to forge on and off the stage.

The theater had thus become one of the main sites for the formulation and dissemination of radical and middle-class, bourgeois ideals—radical because the plays challenged the legitimacy of the ruling classes by showing them to be irredeemably debauched and effeminate, jeopardizing the economic well-being of Egyptian society. The ruling upper classes deserved neither their wealth nor the right to power. The underlying message was that all upper classes, local as well as foreign, harmed the local economy and hence deprived the middle and working classes of what was legitimately theirs—the local upper classes by squandering local fortunes and filling the pockets of individuals who would remove this money from the Egyptian market, and the foreign upper classes, especially bank owners, by bluntly exploiting the natives.[183]

These features, though radical, were at the same time quintessentially bourgeois. The new system would maintain class distinctions even more strictly than those upheld by the previous social system, in which rich and poor were at least equal in the eyes of vice. Indeed one of the reasons for criticizing coffeehouses and places of perdition was that they were sites in which rich and poor intermingled and were even turned into equals: "You see the effendi sitting with an ass, and the bey sitting with a porter *[shayyāl]*"; "The youth drowns in Azbakiyya, the heir as well as the servant *[mustakhdim]*."[184] Rather than eliminate social codes and class distinctions, middle-class radicals sought to impose a new set of codes by which everybody could abide. Ultimately members from various classes could, if they behaved accordingly, become bourgeois, for being bourgeois meant having a work ethic and conducting oneself in a specific way publicly and privately. The theater was the site of apprenticeship of some of the bourgeoisie's most valuable gestures; there individual behavior was tamed into bourgeois social behavior. Hence the selection of press articles at the end of the *Bughiyat* inculcating good bourgeois behavior in the theater and covering topics such as the merits of speaking softly, refraining from aiming one's binoculars at women in the audience, and getting to the theater on time.[185] The manners to be displayed at the theater were *Western* bourgeois manners; indeed a few articles on good manners were originally written in a European language.[186] If *al-Hilāl* is to be believed, these lessons in bourgeois conduct were relatively successful; whereas during earlier performances actors had to contend with an unrefined public that laughed during tragic moments, fell asleep during serious dialogues, and chatted throughout the performance, later performances hosted a more refined public, and this in turn positively affected the quality of the acting.[187]

CONCLUSION

A privileged relationship existed between radicalism and the stage in Beirut, Cairo, and Alexandria around the turn of the century. Not only did the theater serve as a tool to express radical ideas and disseminate them to society, particularly to the masses and working classes; it also provided a necessary forum for the conceptualization, articulation, and internalization of such ideas and hence played a vital role in the making of a radical middle class. From its introduction in the Arab provinces of the Ottoman Empire in the mid-nineteenth century, the theater was conceived of as an important organ for social reform. By the late nineteenth century the discourse associating the theater with progress and civilization had become widespread not only among intellectuals, but also among the general populations of Beirut, Cairo, and Alexandria. This fact, as well as the ensuing omnipresence of theatrical activities, contributed to making the theater a potentially subversive genre.

As it developed in the three cities in the late nineteenth century, the theater implied and triggered deep social transformations. Among these were the population's appropriation of the theater and the de facto right of nonelites and aspiring elites to perform, consume, and thus interpret topics that had hitherto been reserved for specific political and cultural elites. As a consequence the public sphere expanded and was strengthened. Such a transformation was subversive and radical in and of itself, a fact that is confirmed by the elaborate mechanism of control and regulation of theatrical space and repertoire, devised by both Egyptian and Ottoman states. Additionally the making of a transnational network of actors who were constantly on the move and were often in close contact with radical leftist circles in Beirut, Cairo, and Alexandria must have privileged the incorporation and integration of radical global and internationalist elements into the theater's repertoire.

Around the turn of the century plays became more politicized and radical than earlier ones had been; they challenged existing class structures, promoted social justice, and called for the end of tyranny and imperialism. Certain themes became especially popular: the French Revolution and revolutions in general, local and global contemporary events, and in Syria anticlericalism. The theater allowed radicals and the masses to imagine, rehearse, live, and glorify revolution, and the staging of revolutions assigned to both intellectuals and the masses their roles as leaders and revolutionary Crowd. With the adaptation of contemporary events the stage became the press of the masses, offering access to information on local and global political developments. It granted nonelites and aspiring elites the right to participate in the making of their own history as equal players, observers, and public commentators. The emergence of mass politics and the rise of a new class comprising middle-class radicals sealed the symbiosis between stage and radicalism and provided the middle class the necessary space for the construction and dissemination of a coherent ideology that relied greatly on the promotion of an alliance between the middle and working classes.

My focus in this chapter and the preceding one was the role of two new and popular institutions, the press and the theater, in the construction and dissemination of radical culture in and between Beirut, Cairo, and Alexandria. By radical culture, I have mostly referred to the making of a radical mental universe of contestation, which predisposed certain groups within these cities to act as well as think in a subversive and radical manner and produced a radical canon. This canon circulated through periodicals and plays and contributed to the creation of a geography of contestation connecting the three cities. The press and the theater were also closely associated with the emergence of a new class of radical middle-class intellectuals. They allowed members of this group to construct themselves through the articulation of an ideology of reform and challenge the status quo and the existing sources of authority (particularly state and religious institutions). The two institutions also allowed this emerging group to disseminate its radical ideology, as well as imagine, construct, and appeal to a larger audience, namely, the masses.

4

The Construction of Two Radical Networks in Beirut and Alexandria

In the previous two chapters I analyzed the role played by two relatively novel institutions in the articulation and dissemination of radical ideas: the web of periodicals centered around *al-Muqtaṭaf* and *al-Hilāl* and the theater. In this chapter I focus on two self-proclaimed radical networks, one predominantly based in Beirut and Mount Lebanon and an Italian anarchist network in Alexandria. I analyze the establishment and maintenance of these networks and their ideas concerning workers, class conflict, mass education, and other related topics. Specifically I tackle the following questions: How were these radical networks constructed? What made the ideas they promoted radical, and how did they change over time? To what extent were these networks successful in disseminating their ideas in their ambient urban environment, but also beyond? What was it about Beirut and Alexandria that allowed for the construction of such networks, and what local and international factors explain the resonance of such ideas in the two cities? I analyze the deep similarities between both networks in terms of structure, ideas, and activities and suggest explanations for their analogous developments and the implications of their presence, activities, and similarities on radicalism in the Eastern Mediterranean.

We have already encountered members of the first of these networks: they were the ones behind the Ferrer performance discussed in chapter 3. The Ferrer Affair was not an isolated incident; rather, it was the work of a network of radical intellectuals in Syria, which emerged in Beirut and Mount Lebanon in the first years of the twentieth century, was active there until 1912, and had connections to Egypt (and beyond). By the time of the Ferrer play in 1909, members of this network were actively promoting ideas of social justice, had developed a discourse that viewed workers, if not as a class per se at least as a prominent category or subcategory deserving special attention, identified with leftist European icons, and viewed themselves and were viewed as radicals and socialists. This network had the ability to disseminate its views locally and globally through periodicals it issued between 1904 and 1910, as well as through various projects it sponsored, such as theatrical performances. There might have been other networks involved in disseminating radical ideas in the Beirut–Mount Lebanon area, but this network had the power to move from theory to practice; it established free reading rooms, founded schools for workers, and mounted performances and exhibitions. Before analyzing the ideas put forth by this network, let me begin by introducing its members and exploring their worldview through their main organs for articulating and circulating their ideas: *al-Nūr,* a periodical published in Alexandria (1904–8), which was followed by *al-Ḥurriyya* (1909–10), published in Beirut.[1]

AN INTRODUCTION TO THE MEMBERS OF THIS NETWORK

The main protagonists of this network revolved around Daud Muja'is and the two periodicals he founded and directed, *al-Nūr* and *al-Ḥurriyya.* Little is known about Muja'is himself, and barring a few exceptions, almost all the direct information on him and on this leftist network emanates from his publications, or from people affiliated with it.[2] Another important figure in this network was *Al-Nūr*'s owner, Faris Mushriq. A friend of Amin al-Rihani, Mushriq had returned from the United States to Mount Lebanon in the first years of the twentieth century and established its first Masonic lodge in 1904, the same year *al-Nūr* began appearing.[3] Other members of the network included some well-known figures, such as Jirji Niqula Baz, a doctor, a graduate from SPC, and a regular contributor to various periodicals, his own *al-Ḥasnā* as well as *al-Muqtaṭaf* and *al-Hilāl;* and Iskandar 'Azar, an intellectual who was part of the older generation of reformists and who had been close to the Ottoman statesman and reformist Midhat Pasha and to Salim Naqqash and Adib Ishaq.[4] Other rising stars were Khairallah Khairallah; the poet Shibli Mallat; Sayyid Husayn Wasfi Rida, *al- Ḥurriyya*'s correspondent in Cairo and the Islamic reformist Rashid Rida's brother; as well as Labiba Hashim, Felix Faris, Shibl Damos, Jirji 'Atiyyah, and Emile Khuri, who had coauthored the Ferrer play.[5] All these figures and others contributed articles to the two periodicals. Amin al-Rihani was also part of this network; he was in touch with most of its members, corresponded with them, and shared and inspired many of their ideas.[6] The figures covered by *al-Nūr* and *al-Ḥurriyya* were fairly standard radical authors: Amin al-Rihani and Farah Antun were the two local figures,[7] and Leo Tolstoi was the network's favorite international intellectual. The network seems to have also been connected to Na'um Labaki, the owner of the Brazilian *al-Munāẓir* (which I discussed in chapter 2), who moved back to Mount Lebanon in 1909.[8]

This group was more than the sum of its parts: its power and identity did not emerge solely from the individual weight of its members, but also from the group as a unit. Indeed its members seem to have functioned as a group socially, intellectually, and politically.[9] It is also almost certain that each of these figures was affiliated with a Masonic lodge; they also were affiliated with the Shams al-Birr society, a progressive Protestant Sunday school not devoid of Freemason connections.[10] Most of these individuals belonged to the same social class: an educated elite, but a class educated beyond its financial means, since its members were not independently well-off and seemed to lack the opportunity to become so, and sometimes even to find regular employment. Like many *nahḍa* figures, most members of this network did not belong to the merchant class, although they often found patrons to subsidize their literary and political endeavors. They occasionally taught at one of Beirut's numerous schools or were bank or company clerks; their chances of landing a job that would allow them to use their skills beyond clerical or journalistic paths seem to have been very limited, given that in order to make ends meet they offered their writing, editing, and translation services.[11] At some point virtually every member of this network issued his (or her) own periodical.

One important characteristic of this group is that its members had the power to disseminate their ideas. As individuals, they were very well connected to a broader reformist network in Beirut and Mount Lebanon; Jirji Baz and Iskandar ʿAzar in particular were constant presences on the Beiruti literary, social, and cultural scene, giving numerous talks during school plays and inaugural speeches for charitable institutions and ceremonies honoring various literati. They moved as comfortably among social and intellectual elites as among more common mortals and in that sense were public intellectuals of a middle caliber who were equally visible in low-profile social gatherings and on the grander, highbrow *nahḍa* literary scene. Their activities in benevolent societies seem to have brought them into contact with members of the working classes, and they were often able to disseminate their ideas to them through speeches and lectures. The picture that emerges, therefore, is certainly not that of a marginal or marginalized group, but rather of a close-knit group with ties to a much larger network with established intellectual and social legitimacy, whose own members were very visible on the social activist scene of Beirut and Mount Lebanon, constantly moved between these two social and geographical spheres, and founded and sat on committees for various educational, moral, and medical benevolent institutions. Many of their projects were noticed (and sometimes criticized) by periodicals in Beirut, Alexandria, and Cairo. The Beiruti *Lisān al-ḥāl* chastised members of this group for "taking Ferrer's side without knowing anything about his life except that he is a symbol of anarchists," and strongly insinuated that the network's political sympathies were well-known. The publishers of and contributors to *al-Muqtaṭaf* and *al-Hilāl* reported on the network's activities.[12]

Members of this group were thus intellectually and socially close to more mainstream *nahḍa* figures and shared many features with them. They contributed to periodicals and also founded their own. They strongly believed in the theater as one of the highest forms of social art, wrote plays, and often acted in amateur performances.[13] They participated in transcommunal projects.[14] And they adhered to the credo of *nahḍa* reformists, urging a general reform that focused, first and foremost, on the need for an Ottoman constitution as well as educational, social, and religious reforms. Hence the basic premises of this group were deeply familiar to the more mainstream *nahḍa* reformists, which must have ensured a certain receptivity of their reform package among larger *nahḍa* audiences, even as the network became more radicalized. This was a network whose members considered themselves Ottoman patriots and whose mission was to serve both the Ottoman Empire and Mount Lebanon specifically.[15] The fact that it benefited from the support and patronage of the mutasarrif of Mount Lebanon Muzaffer Pasha (1902–7) probably allowed this network to implement some of its projects quite effectively, as well as offered it protection against the many enemies it made on the way.[16]

REGIONAL AND GLOBAL CONNECTIONS

Like many Syrian periodicals appearing in the late nineteenth century and early twentieth, *al-Nūr* and *al-Ḥurriyya* (and, by extension, the network around them) had strong ties to the outside world: with Egypt and with the larger world of the Syrian diaspora in the Americas. To begin with, *al-Nūr* was published in Alexandria, and its director and owner were based in Mount Lebanon, where it maintained an office.[17] There are many possible explanations for this. First, by issuing their periodical in Egypt, Syrian radicals would be free to publish whatever they wished rather than abide by the mutasarrif's orders, deal with state censorship, or face the wrath of the Maronite clergy and the Jesuits.[18] Second, *al-Nūr* (and later *al-Ḥurriyya*) wanted to be a periodical for Syrians throughout the world. It seems to have succeeded, judging by its subscribers' countries of residency (Brazil, Haiti, Mount Lebanon, even South Africa).[19] It therefore needed to ensure regular delivery of its issues throughout the world and to be able to receive Syrian periodicals and letters from the *mahjar* (countries of immigration). The various postal services in Alexandria were more capable of offering such a guarantee than their Beiruti counterparts, since they were not under the severe scrutiny of the *maktubji* (the Ottoman censor). Thus Egypt was to *al-Nūr* what it was for a great many Syrian periodicals: it served as a crucial extension of Beirut's and Mount Lebanon's public spheres and was an unmatched center for intellectual production as well as an informational hub that shaped the intellectual life of Beirut and its vicinity. Many members of the network had spent time in Egypt as residents or visitors; others maintained an ongoing conversation with a number of seminal radical thinkers in Egypt, such as Shibli Shumayyil.[20]

THE EMERGENCE AND DEVELOPMENT OF A DISCOURSE ON WORKERS

Workers were a major theme addressed by members of this network. Workers initially appeared in the periodicals as subtexts to three main rubrics that remained central topics of discussion until 1910: the establishment of secular and free educational institutions, the need to remedy a local economy in crisis, and the desire to curb European political, economic, and religious encroachment into Syria.[21] Already in 1904 *al-Nūr* began supporting the establishment of night schools for the education of "youth whose work does not allow them to study during daytime."[22] Night schools had been introduced by the Ottoman state at least as early as 1892 throughout the empire and specifically in the province of Beirut.[23] Although *al-Nūr* did not yet name workers (or conceive of them) as constituting a distinct class or even category, this was an early articulation of a discourse that, if it did not exactly single them out, at least carved a discursive space in which to place workers and workers' education. Significantly *al-Nūr*'s views on mass education differed somewhat from the standard *nahḍa* views on the matter. Unlike other *nahḍa* reformists who, in the first few years of the twentieth century, generally called for the education of society, an amorphous and unspecified general audience, *al-Nūr*'s network made it clear that, by establishing night schools, it specifically targeted the education of workers and their children. However, workers were placed in a category dependent on two other categories in need of education: the poor and the middle classes. Indeed workers were to be educated primarily for two reasons: because they were poor and the poor needed to be educated, and because workers were part of an unnamed and vague entity whose other half was the middle class. The fate of the working class was hence connected to that of the middle class, and educating one necessarily entailed educating the other.

From the beginning *al-Nūr* displayed a certain social awareness that, though not class-based per se, was to a certain extent quite progressive and critical of social inequalities. The call for educating both the urban and rural poor, and specifically the working poor, was made on the pages of *al-Nūr* in 1904 and remained a constant topic throughout the period under study. Almost every issue carried an article arguing for the need to reform education, establish free and civil schools to educate the poor, and found associations to help the needy. One article published in 1905 reminded *al-Nūr*'s readers of society's real prerogatives: "We are in need of real schools that teach us our needs and how to respond to them; we are in need of shelters *[malāji']* and hospitals, and most pressingly for industrial and agricultural associations to decrease the number of poor."[24] In fact by 1907 *al-Nūr* was even suggesting a taxation plan and a new budget that would allow for the establishment of schools specifically for needy students.[25] This discourse was partly motivated by the perceived economic recession and unemployment. We know from a number of contemporary sources that businesses in Beirut and Mount Lebanon had gone bankrupt and that the number of poor was visibly on the rise. As a port city Beirut seemed to attract migrant, destitute workers from the rest of Syria, as well as the Eastern Mediterranean. One contemporary observer commented, "Il y a ici une pauvreté indescriptible. Beyrouth devient tous les jours davantage le rendez-vous de toutes les misères que les petites villes de Syrie chassent. On vient ici dans l'espoir trop souvent déçu de trouver un gagne-pain plus facile dans un port de mer de plus de 100,000 âmes. . . . J'ai vécu treize ans en Palestine où la pauvreté de nos coreligionnaires est si grande, jamais je n'y ai vu une pareille misère, un tel dénument."[26]

Al-Nūr itself devoted many articles to bankruptcy and unemployment, graphically describing the miserable lives of the unemployed and the destitute.[27] However, the picture of economic recession so vividly painted by the periodical might have been somewhat inflated, given that poverty and bankruptcy were not exactly new in the early 1900s. In fact *al-Nūr* might have "rediscovered poverty," just as poverty had been rediscovered in late Victorian England by Charles Booth and a number of social reformists.[28] Furthermore the reality of this recession is itself questionable; it seems that various parts of Syria, especially Beirut and Mount Lebanon, both of which had been integrated into the world economy, were in fact generally experiencing a boom between the mid-1890s and 1907, but that this boom was benefiting a select few, and wealth disparities were on the rise. Of particular significance, though, is this perception of a recession, and the very real and strong sense of economic unease and insecurity. It is in this context of malaise that *al-Nūr*'s conception of a local economy began taking shape.[29] Accompanying it was a discourse emphasizing the need to remedy the malaise, and salvaging the local economy hence became *al-Nūr*'s priority. Although this implied that improving the fate of the working classes was subservient to more pressing needs, it also guaranteed the working classes some attention since they clearly had a role to play in boosting local production.

If *al-Nūr*'s mission of salvaging the Syrian economy was to be successful, the working classes had to be prepared, for they held a central role in the rescue mission. Not only did the network around *al-Nūr* construct a discourse on the need to educate workers; it actually pioneered many didactic projects that specifically targeted workers via the establishment of night schools and reading rooms and the promotion and organization of industrial and agricultural exhibitions. Although the details are unclear, the periodical likely had a hand in founding a night school in Shuwayr, an important village in Mount Lebanon, in 1904.[30] The purpose of this establishment was to attract "all students regardless of their religious denomination" and "spread sound manners and knowledge *[al-tahdhīb wa'l-'ulūm]* among the youth whose work does not allow them to study during daytime."[31] Arabic, mathematics, geography, and music courses were offered, as well as basic French and English. All these disciplines were taught for free, and needy students were given the necessary school supplies. In its first year the Shuwayr night school had twenty-five students age fifteen and older.[32] Other night schools were expected to follow the example set in Shuwayr, including one in Muḥaydtha, a village in Mount Lebanon.[33]

Another project devised to educate the working classes (as well as the middle classes) was the establishment of free reading rooms.[34] Reading rooms were more or less public libraries, some of which were established by the Ottoman state, while others were the fruit of local initiative, individual or institutional. Often affiliated with an educational institution, they put books as well as local and international periodicals at their readers' disposal. The campaign for establishing reading rooms was launched by *al-Nūr* in its first year of publication. In virtually every issue from then onward, the periodical would extol the social benefits and civilizing effect of libraries generally.[35] When a committee was established in 1904 for the foundation and eventual management of reading rooms, it was headed by none other than Faris Mushriq, the publisher of *al-Nūr*, and included Jirji Baz.[36] The committee's efforts were to bear fruit, for the first reading room was inaugurated in Shuwayr in September of that year. The example was followed in Beirut and even in remote villages of Mount Lebanon. The reading room founded by *al-Nūr*'s group held

> over five hundred volumes, among the best literature, history and religion books, most of them in Arabic. There is also a set of maps . . . and a big one of Syria and Lebanon. Five Egyptian newspapers are offered, and three magazines, nine newspapers from the *mahjar* [countries of immigration], fifteen local newspapers, and *The Times* and *Le Matin*. . . . It also receives telegraphs daily; has the portraits of all of the mutasarrifs of Lebanon, as well as that of the great sultan, and a history tree with the most important historical figures *[sic]*, from Adam to Jesus . . . and another *silsila* [genealogical tree, or lineage] of all the Ottoman sultans. [It is estimated that] over 1,800 people read there.[37]

Most significant, *al-Nūr* saw in the reading rooms a space and a tool that would benefit society generally, as well as workers specifically, since it would "inculcate good manners in the men of the future, and [would] *expand the skills [or knowledge] of today's workers [madārik al-ʿummāl]*."[38]

Workers' education was becoming even more imperative as their status was changing within *al-Nūr*'s discourse. Not only were workers to save the local economy through their labor, but, starting around 1906, they were seen as constituting one of the most potent bargaining powers for the local economy in the face of increased European encroachment. While the exploitation of local workers by foreign companies had been criticized in 1904, it was not really at the center of *al-Nūr*'s concerns. The network's writings on workers' exploitation had then served as mere illustrations of a larger phenomenon of European political, religious, and economic domination.[39] But a marked change of tone began to appear in *al-Nūr* around 1906. Rather than merely deploring the injustice of unequal salaries for local and foreign workers, *al-Nūr* began arguing that the dependency that existed between foreign companies and local workers was in fact reciprocal. This argument served two purposes: it reminded foreign companies of their reliance on local workers, and it informed local workers of their intrinsic power vis-à-vis foreign companies:

> We need them [foreign companies] and they need us [but] we do not realize it; among these, the railway company . . . employs [indigenous labor] for its most important tasks, most difficult positions and hardest jobs. Despite all that, it prefers the foreign coal burner or the doorman to them; and if there are foreigners and locals to be found in the same post, the foreigner's wages are higher and so is his rank. . . . *Our intention is not to . . . trigger a rebellion [fitna] or a strike [iʿtiṣāb] between the company and its workers . . .* but we ask the company's board of administration to assist these poor people *[masākīn]*, look at them with a just eye, give them what they deserve, and make their rights equivalent to their obligations. We are not demanding that it return the blood of those it exhausts in its service, and are not pressuring it to consider national blood equivalent to foreign blood. . . . We are asking for justice for those who stay up all night and work all day and . . . whose lives are constantly threatened by machines.[40]

Labor had thus become an intrinsic part of the local economy, but this time, in an economy under siege from foreign capital, it could serve as a bargaining chip—in fact, perhaps as the most potent bargaining chip for the local economy's defense. Workers had gained significance within that discourse, and their labor had acquired value not only in and of itself, but as capital to be used against European penetration. This conceptualization of workers as having bargaining power was the result of two trends: on one hand, it was a realization of very *locally* rooted facts, the specific economic situation of Syria and the realities of Western penetration; on the other, it marked the transcending of this very local reality (or the universalization of the local) since it was tied to the articulation of a *more abstract conception of labor,* which indicated a more sophisticated grasp of economic principles. Both these discursive developments would push the conceptualization of workers in a more radical direction.

Starting in 1906 *al-Nūr*'s writings on the exploitation of local workers began to shift from a purely moral to an increasingly and self-consciously economic perspective, while simultaneously depicting exploitation in much more graphic and violent terms.[41] Labor emerged as a significant force to be reckoned with, not only socially but also economically, as an integral part of capital. Exploitation was thus broached as a problem of economic inefficiency rather than sheer immorality, to be contrasted with the path to economic optimization, which lay in "the balance between the power that workers spend [on their work] and the power they get out of their work. . . . If these two forces are in equilibrium, then work becomes long-lasting and profitable."[42] The development of a more theoretical and abstract conception of workers and labor was accompanied by the formulation and adoption of a new language concerning labor: terms such as *al-yadd al-ʿāmila* (labor, literally *main d'oeuvre*) and *ra's māl* (capital) began appearing on the pages of *al-Nūr* and *al-Ḥurriyya*. These terms and others were duly explained week after week, and in January 1910 *al-Ḥurriyya* began publishing a series of articles by Khairallah Khairallah and introducing its readership to basic economic notions ranging from capital and profit distribution among owners and workers to balance of trade.[43] Khairallah would begin each article by objectively explaining various economic concepts and policies, clearly the result of his readings on political economy, most likely Charles Gide's work, given the occasional French term inserted in the text and the general content of the articles. He would then argue for one economic policy over the other. Among the policies Khairallah favored was profit distribution among workers, factory owners, and intermediaries.[44]

Khairallah's articles illustrated this network's radical turnaround concerning workers. To begin with, the network developed an abstract language with which to describe labor and was promoting it in its periodical. It moved away from viewing workers and labor relations primarily from the perspective of a simple dichotomy between local and foreign. Indeed, rather than depicting the condition of labor as the result of European oppression, *al-Ḥurriyya* presented it as the outcome of *class* dynamics and negotiations between workforce and capital. Furthermore by 1910 the network sought to teach workers ways of improving their work conditions, rather than showing them how to work. Articles covered the benefits of establishing emergency funds *(ṣundūq iḥtiyāṭī li waqt al-ḥāja)* and mutual funds and the advantages of actively fighting for the codification of labor laws.[45] Perhaps more important, the group wished to inculcate in workers the value of their labor in negotiations with their employers.

The vision promoted by Khairallah was that of a class-blind legal system that would eventually lead to a classless society. It was with this goal in mind that he wrote his articles: "It is time that there be justice [and a legal system based on] . . . true justice, and not justice built on selfishness . . . but one built on fraternity . . . with which we will create a fraternity in rights, *no poor and no rich, no worker and no capitalist [mutamawwil]*."[46] A fairer treatment of workers by employers, which included dividing the profits between them, was one step toward this utopian society. At the same time as he seemed to be addressing workers and giving them instructions for improving their working conditions, Khairallah wished to convince the middle classes—his main readers, after all—of the merits of this classless, or at least more just society. He repeated time and again that fair labor conditions and profit distribution would lead to a more efficient economic system, and hence was to the employer's benefit.[47] This form of socialism, which in fact was quite close to the ideas pertaining to mutual aid that anarchists and socialists were promoting in various parts of the world, was not only more efficient for the middle classes; it also pointed to a higher degree of *civilization* than one based on injustice and exploitation. As befitting intellectuals obsessed with reform and ultimately civilization, Khairallah's articles appeared under the heading "Letter on the Origin of Civilization."[48] While the road to civilization had taken various paths, Khairallah followed a number of eminent reformists who argued that social justice and wealth distribution were indexes of civilization, and his intellectual lineage included illustrious thinkers such as Salim al-Naqqash and Shibli Shumayyil.

If Khairallah did not explicitly spell out part of the rationale behind the new equal and efficient society he promoted in this series of articles, others did. Around the same time, Muja'is and Mushriq began publishing articles in *al-Ḥurriyya* and elsewhere describing and denouncing world economic inequality and uneven trade agreements between nations. The solution was simple: to consume locally produced goods.[49] Hence not only were mutualism and cooperation the path to a classless, more just society based on brotherhood, but they also were to provide a response against unfair competition. Powerful foreign countries, companies, and a world order that favored them had triggered local workers' exploitation and gross underpayment, privileging foreign workers and forcing out local businesses. The end result was unfair trade, in which Syria was exporting people, capital, and skills abroad (into countries of immigration) and receiving Western knickknacks in return.[50]

THE RADICALIZATION OF CONNECTED DISCOURSES

Between 1904 and 1910 the radicalization of the network's discourse on workers was accompanied by a more radical coverage of a number of issues. This radicalization affected all the interconnected themes dear to Muja'is and his network. On a local level it manifested itself in a shift from secularism to blatant anticlericalism, as well as a strong attack against the Unionists and the mutasarrifiyya regime in Mount Lebanon in the years following the constitutional revolution of 1908.[51] On a global level it was accompanied by an increased interest in and explicit identification with international leftist movements such as socialism and anarchism, as well as more forceful attacks against imperialism and colonialism and a growing sense of the global dimension of anti-imperialist struggles. These themes were interconnected and linked to concepts of social justice that were in the process of being reformulated by this network.

The network's radicalization was perhaps most vividly expressed in its changing views on the local Church. Whereas *al-Nūr* had always advocated secularism, the content and tone of its advocacy was becoming increasingly vociferous in the first decade of the twentieth century. By 1907 *al-Nūr* had ceased being merely critical of the clergy and had become frankly anticlerical. The periodical had always been wary of certain aspects of organized religion; from 1904 on it had constantly warned against religious intolerance *(al-ta'aṣṣub al-dīni),* that "divisive disease that has generally attacked the hearts of Lebanese."[52] However, until roughly 1907 the main focus of its attacks was Western clergy and missionaries, which it accused of spreading the seeds of sectarian division and seeking to impose a monolithic and foreign interpretation of Christianity on the local population.[53] Behind the schools foreign missionaries were establishing, *al-Nūr* argued, lay imperial conquest: "'Those who come holding the Holy Bible in their right hands come bearing the cannon in their left one,' as Yuhanna the emperor of Ethiopia told American and English missionaries in his country."[54] The local clergy—Greek Orthodox and especially Maronite—were initially criticized primarily for their impotence in protecting the local population and truly meeting its needs.

Progressively, however, *al-Nūr* moved from criticizing the local Church's impotence to actively suggesting ways of reforming it, before frankly attacking it, accusing it of maintaining the population in a state of ignorance, abusing its authority and increasingly violating people's rights, and stealing and mismanaging a fortune that was not rightfully its own to begin with.[55] By the time the Ferrer play was performed in 1909, members of this network were bluntly attacking both local and foreign Churches. The local Church was attacked because it had forgotten its original duties and needed to be reminded "that the money of the people is for the people, for its education in order to eliminate poverty, and for the education of orphans; it is not for the building of palaces and the purchase of silk and crosses inlaid with diamonds."[56] Foreign Jesuits and Protestant missionaries were attacked because "foreign priests are teaching us a lesson that kills our patriotism *[waṭaniyya]* in order to replace it by a foreign *waṭaniyya*. . . . There might have been an excuse for this before the Constitution, [but this is no longer the case]."[57] This degree of anticlericalism was not confined to the network around *al-Nūr* and *al-Ḥurriyya:* the network connected anticlericalism with social justice, and the fierce attack on the Church's wealth was cited as proof of financial mismanagement. Such attacks became even more pressing after 1907, as the expansion in agriculture and a general economic recession meant that employment opportunities had reached their limit. Members of *al-Nūr's* network made repeated calls to seize Church property, especially land.[58] In the face of such challenges the Maronite Church in particular seemed increasingly unable to preserve its authority. As early as 1905 an edict by the Maronite patriarch, Monsignor Hoyek, condemning freemasonry and threatening to excommunicate "all the members of this society, its supporters, and those who did not report the names of their leaders," was met with "mocking public demonstrations of liberal groups in the streets of the villages and towns of Kisrawan, testifying to a significant loss of deference toward the Church and the person of the Patriarch in this traditional Maronite fiefdom."[59]

To appreciate the intensity of the struggle between the Church and radicals in the first decade of the twentieth century, we need to keep in mind that the rural areas in the Ottoman Empire were still feeling the effects of the Ottoman Land Code of 1858. Although the situation varied from place to place, the Land Code triggered a panoply of issues: the dispossession of smallholders in certain cases, the raised expectations of peasants, and general uncertainty and contestation about the exact interpretation and implementation of the Code, especially as it pertained to access to land and to its surplus.[60] In Mount Lebanon and in many parts of what are today Lebanon and Syria, the effects of a new land system, coupled with the full integration into the world economy, triggered serious unrest.[61] As Khater describes it, "An accumulation of population pressure and a crisis, due to competition, in the silk manufacturing . . . led to a crisis of land. As young peasant families inherited smaller and smaller plots of land, they also had to contend with decreasing prices of silk."[62] In many parts of Mount Lebanon peasants made numerous and vocal claims regarding land, arguing specifically for their right to access to collective grazing land *(mushāʿa),* which they linked to the notion of a common good.[63] In Mount Lebanon the Kisrawan peasant uprising of 1858–61 threatened to reverse the entire social order in the area.[64] This was not the end of convulsions and contestations; in the 1890s, as many documents eloquently testify, the battle for control over land was still raging in different parts of the mountain (Kura, Batrun, and Kisrawan) between traditional village elites and the Church, on one hand, and commoners and newcomers, on the other.[65] One notable feature was the request by peasants and small landholders to have access to land hitherto belonging to the Church. That anticlericalism constituted such a central element of radicalism was not specific to Mount Lebanon, of course; land seizure constituted a crucial battle for radicals in different parts of the Mediterranean, such as in Sicily and Calabria, where anarchists participated in peasant rebellions and land occupation in the 1870s and again in the 1890s. The group around *al-Nūr* clearly supported (and was probably directly involved in) land claims against the Church and feudal lords, and they harshly criticized the Unionist government after the Revolution of 1908 for not settling these claims. The issues were brought together and attacked in an article by Husayn Rida, who exclaimed, "Who then can blame us for raising our voices with those shouting, those seeking to uproot the oppressive forces of aristocracy and theocracy in Lebanon, while we see the [awful] consequences of deceitfulness, coercion, and inaction?"[66] Paraphrasing the "philosopher of poets," the great medieval poet Abu'l 'Ala' al-Maʿarri, Rida then warned, "We have gotten restless . . . with this negligent government and with this silent people."[67] The periodical strongly backed a local leader, Jirji Zuwayn, who openly confronted the Maronite Church, and whose supporters occupied the monastery of Mar Ruhana in Kisrawan in a battle over the control of *awqāf* (charitable and religious endowments).[68] Incidentally, Zuwayn's attack on the Church was accompanied in 1910 by a vociferous denunciation of the mutasarrif's corruption and Zuwayn's subsequent arrest. It is no coincidence that *al-Ḥurriyya*'s last (extant) issue came shortly after the periodical had unequivocally supported Zuwayn in his anticorruption and anticlerical campaigns. The mutasarrif sued Mujaʿis (or perhaps *al-Ḥurriyya*?) for insulting him and, tellingly, for "inciting the people to revolt *[taḥrīḍ al-shaʿb wa daʿwatuhu ila'l-thawra]*." It is not clear what the outcome of the suit was.[69]

Thus by 1907 both local and foreign Churches were under fire from *al-Nūr*'s network. In this new discourse divisions between local and foreign had become secondary, just as the local-foreign dichotomy in the discourse on workers had made way for a more theoretical understanding of labor. More accurately, a different conception of the local was being articulated, one that made the local synonymous with serving local interests. Just as the Syrian local upper classes had been dispossessed of their locality for failing to invest in projects beneficial to the Syrian economy, and the local Egyptian upper classes had suffered a similar fate, as expressed in a number of contemporary popular songs and monologues, so the local Church, by going against the interests of a population whom it maintained in a state of ignorance and dispossessed of its wealth, had turned into an Other.

The othering of the local Church was further intensified by the perceived cooperation between the Maronite Church and the Committee of Union of Progress after 1909, an accusation regularly mounted in the pages of *al-Ḥurriyya.*[70] Such sentiments were not exclusive to this specific network. The Unionist revolution of 1908 accentuated anticlericalism overall and pushed various groups that had been vaguely sympathetic to leftist ideas further left. In Mount Lebanon and Beirut the initial euphoria triggered by the proclamation of the Ottoman Constitution was followed by disappointment, then disillusionment. By 1909 the gap between expectations and reality had begun to show: censorship was back, strikes had been banned, misery was still rampant. What then had changed, asked the contributors to *al-Ḥurriyya:* "What is the meaning of the constitution, if the peasant ignores it; what is the meaning of freedom, if the harvester in the field cannot enjoy it? . . . This [begging] boy walks in Ittiḥād Square in front of the garden of Freedom, as if nothing has changed. . . . The rebellious heads *[ru'ūs mutamarrida]* are still rebellious, and Abdülhamid has become one thousand Abdülhamids."[71] Equally if not more worrisome were certain measures taken in 1909 and 1910 by the local Ottoman authorities threatening the autonomous status of Mount Lebanon, especially the mutasarrif's decision to enforce a new law passed by the Ottoman Parliament that would subject the press in Mount Lebanon to increased censorship.[72] All these issues—anticlericalism, mass education, workers' rights vis-à-vis foreign companies, and resistance to European cultural, political, and economic encroachment—were part of a general package of contestations and grievances that converged and overlapped after 1905 and were given an even stronger boost after the disappointments of the Unionist revolution.

THE INTERNATIONAL BENT

Another radical development was the network's growing familiarity and identification with international leftist worldviews and ideas. Between 1905 and 1909 part of this radicalization was linked to and reflected in the network's awareness of the rest of the world, specifically its increased familiarity with international leftist movements. *Al-Nūr* had paid very little attention to world affairs in the first few years of its life, and its articles dealt almost exclusively with local matters pertaining to Mount Lebanon and, to a lesser degree, Beirut. This was somewhat paradoxical given that the periodical purported to be self-consciously international and targeted a readership of Syrian emigrants spread all over the world. Yet until the end of the century's first decade it remained very much a provincial periodical. In fact one of the very few exceptions to this lack of interest in world events was its coverage of the Russo-Japanese War of 1905, which was passionately and even obsessively covered by *al-Nūr,* just as it had been by every other periodical in the Ottoman Arab provinces. From 1904 until roughly 1907 the network's radicalism was thus very local; it did not align itself with international leftist movements and did not even refer to them. This provincialism is perhaps best illustrated by *al-Nūr*'s complete silence on the failed Russian revolution of October 1905. Indeed for a radical periodical that passionately called for the need to eradicate poverty, educate workers and the needy, limit European capitalist penetration, and curb the power of the clergy, this silence is indicative of *al-Nūr*'s initial provincialism and of a worldview based on purely local references. The lack of interest in world affairs was particularly striking given how tumultuous and revolutionary the period 1905–8 had been in the East, from the failed Russian revolution of 1905 to the Iranian Constitutional Revolution of 1906 and the introduction of constitutions and the challenges to state authority throughout the region. All these radical changes were felt very strongly by Ottoman reformists, who hoped their state would be next.[73]

Around 1907 the Syrian radical network began venturing beyond local matters and working to tune its ideology to that of international leftist movements. That year its members organized a May 1 celebration, the first of its kind in Syria and, with the possible exception of Alexandria and Istanbul, one of the earliest throughout the Ottoman Empire.[74] The "fête socialiste," as its chronicler Khairallah described it, was organized by none other than Daud Muja'is and two other people whose identity remains a mystery.[75] It brought together "une trentaine de jeunes gens d'élite, marquants pour leur instruction et leur position sociale" who, armed with a gigantic red banner, paraded and gave speeches on the shores of Dbayeh, a coastal village adjacent to Beirut.[76] Besides the May 1 celebration there were other signs of identification and engagement with international leftist figures and ideologies. The intense coverage devoted by *al-Ḥurriyya* to the Ferrer Affair and the performance of the play itself, the socialist speeches accompanying it, and the Jean Jaurès quotes published by the periodical all attest to the degree to which the network had come to identify and engage with the international Left.[77] Another indication of this network's international bent was the adoption of a certain leftist economic jargon by *al-Ḥurriyya* and the periodical's abstract conceptualization of labor.

Furthermore around 1909 the Syrian radical network began to express interest in, sympathy for, and identification with specific anarchist ideas and modes of action. The Ferrer Affair was one such display, preceded by *al-Ḥurriyya*'s publication of a series of articles authored by a certain Stavinsky Polikivitch and titled "The Philosophy of Bombs."[78] As discussed in chapter 1, although the use of political violence, in particular the planting of bombs, was certainly not confined to anarchism, the two were not exactly disconnected.[79] Polikivitch's articles were clearly on revolutionary anarchist and nihilist practices. Although information about this mysterious character and his relationship to *al-Ḥurriyya*'s network is lacking, it is clear that the periodical's editors had consulted Polikivitch on the topic and asked him to express his opinion on the "famous 'Aley bomb," in which the target of the bomb, the mutasarrif of Mount Lebanon, emerged unharmed.[80] Polikivitch seems to have been a seasoned revolutionary activist; he had, by his own admission, spent ten years in prison (it is not clear where) for engaging in such actions.

What is significant about Polikivitch's article is that it was one of the first fairly sophisticated reflections on revolutionary praxis to appear in *al-Ḥurriyya.* His main investigation concerned the use of violence for revolutionary purposes and the distinction between "revolution" and "chaos."[81] Although his main argument was not terribly original—he argued that violence (or more specifically "terror") was legitimate, but only as a last resort—its elaboration was quite systematic. Examining the degree of oppression that justified the use of violence in Russia and Spain, he then coldly assessed the pros and cons of various instruments of violence: the revolver, the dagger, and the bomb.

> [The bomb is] not the weapon which a sanguinary killer uses; rather, it is synonymous with the terrorizing [terrible] expression through which a pressured force releases itself from oppression. And the expression *[ta'bīr]* is often just; it is the spirit of the present age, as long as it does not abandon the realm of rights or harm the interests of others. The French revolution has announced these rights for the first time, and has done so with the blood of its king . . . and the Ottoman revolution has sanctified it *[qaddasatha]* by crushing the throne of its oppressor.[82]

The international brand of leftist thought that anarchism represented had a specific resonance, given local realities. Members of the radical network and anarchists worldwide shared a common enemy, the Church, which many European anarchists had identified as a prime target. The Spanish brand of anarchism that received attention in *al-Ḥurriyya* during the Ferrer Affair had successfully called for the destruction of a significant amount of Church property.[83] It is clear in *al-Ḥurriyya* that members of the network were fascinated by this use of violence against the Spanish Church and approved of it, describing it as retaliation against a particularly ruthless institution that had tortured and oppressed the Spanish poor for centuries.[84] Besides fitting well into the growing anticlerical movement in Beirut and Mount Lebanon, anarchism had yet another local appeal: it was viscerally feared and hated by the Unionists. As previously mentioned, there had been increasing opposition in Mount Lebanon to the government of the Young Turks and to their policies, as early as 1909. As Hamit Bozarslan points out, although many Young Turks were initially attracted to anarchist ideas—mostly through their adulation of the French Revolution, their desire to dethrone and even assassinate Abdülhamid, and their embrace of biological materialism—they soon developed a deep fear of anarchism and what it meant: empowering the masses, eliminating political parties, and destroying the state. As Abdullah Cevdet made clear:

> Anarchists are a party whose objective is to uproot all sorts of government from earth. They await the weakening of their government so as to be able to topple it with greater ease. As for us, toiling so that our Ottoman government regain its power and find, once more, its place and grandeur, we act in a manner diametrically opposed to the anarchists' ideas. To destroy the state, us? [On the contrary], we want to reinforce it.[85]

The Young Turks' need to distinguish their ideology from anarchism went as far as determining the kind of weapons they used. They favored the revolver, "lourd de toute une symbolique révolutionnaire, . . . à la bombe. Il constitue la ligne de démarcation entre les Jeunes Turcs et les courants anarchistes. Il assure une mort propre et individuelle."[86] From that perspective Polikivitch's words and value judgment on the difference between dagger, revolver, and bomb, and *al-Ḥurriyya*'s publication of it, are particularly revealing: "The dagger and the revolver on one hand, and the bomb: the first two are individual weapons, the second is a mass weapon *[silāḥ jamāʿāt]*. . . . It is the weapon of the oppressed masses in countries of increased oppression, such as Spain . . . and Russia."[87] It is understandable that radicals opposed to or disappointed by the Young Turks and their policies in Mount Lebanon and Beirut were attracted to anarchism. Although anticlericalism and opposition to the Young Turks did not fully explain the resonance of anarchist ideas among the Syrian radical network, they certainly contributed to anarchism's growing appeal.

ANTI-IMPERIALISM AND THE USE OF VIOLENCE

Around the same time, the network's radical and international bent also manifested itself in the adoption of a vociferous anti-imperialist discourse. Beginning with *al-Ḥurriyya*'s first issue (July 11, 1909), a series of articles examined imperialism and compared the British imperial project in India and Egypt. One article bluntly stated that "the aim of imperialists/colonialists *[mustaʿmirīn]* is well known: they consider the colony a milking cow *[baqara ḥalūb]* to be milked for as long as possible," and pointed out that Indians were "working towards national liberation more actively than . . . our brothers . . . the Egyptians, and establishing schools funded by wealthy Indians," which were unmatchable steps when it came to the liberation of peoples and individuals.[88] In their struggle for national liberation the Indians did not content themselves with establishing schools, the article continued, but founded India House, an organization that advocated political assassination as a necessary means for liberation. Political assassination, in that case, was morally and legally sound and good *[ḥalāl]*, and those who engaged in it "followed the paths of saints *[fi sulk al-qiddīsīn wa'l-awliyā']*."[89] *Al-Ḥurriyya*'s coverage of Indian resistance movements and assassination attempts continued throughout 1909; in each article the author (most likely Muja'is) approved in no uncertain terms the use of violence for national liberation. Hailing as a hero Madan Lal Dhingra, the student who killed Sir Curzon Wylie in London and was subsequently hanged, the author asserted that Lal Dhingra's single action was greater than if "a million Indians bore arms to liberate India."[90]

Accompanying its scathing attack on imperialism and its support of violence in liberation struggles was *al-Ḥurriyya*'s equally strong denunciation of incompetent, corrupt leadership that weakened countries and hence paved the way to their subjugation by a Western power. Such was the case of the Moroccan ruler Abd al-Hafiz, who had merely "inherited power" and whom *al-Ḥurriyya* scathingly attacked for his weakness, tyranny, torture of his opponents, and violation of Moroccan notables' rights and traditions, all of which, the periodical argued, had facilitated the task of French and Spanish occupation. Unlike an unnamed Istanbul newspaper that had condemned foreign intervention in Morocco but simultaneously cautioned against criticizing Abd al-Hafiz, arguing that this would be akin to backstabbing him, *al-Ḥurriyya* did not mince words: it was too late to offer rulers counsel and reform advice, it roundly argued. It had become necessary to spell out the truth, and unlike the Istanbul paper it could not fathom how "a Muslim journalist . . . could seek to please these tyrannical rulers and kings with words. Is he not acquainted with the saying of Ibn al-'Abbas to the caliph: 'I spent the night looking for a word by which to please my Sultan but not anger my Lord, but I could not find one?' "[91] For Muja'is (whose family belonged to the Orthodox Christian community), all these liberation struggles were linked: "The world is still in a continuous struggle *[jihād]* and upheaval that will only subside when all the people of the world will be liberated . . . and the barriers against this liberation, as high as they are[,] . . . will eventually be destroyed."[92]

A related topic *al-Ḥurriyya* covered while engaging with the theory and practice of political violence was the Wardani case.[93] In February 1910 an Egyptian nationalist, Ibrahim Nasif al-Wardani, assassinated the (Coptic) Egyptian prime minister, Butrus Ghali, on grounds that he was collaborating with the British Occupation. From *al-Ḥurriyya*'s perspective the assassination was not an act of religious extremism or fanaticism *(ta'aṣṣub)*, as many were claiming. It was simply not possible, the article argued, for "a person who studies at the university level and reads natural sciences and Darwin and Spencer's philosophies . . . [to] be a religious fanatic." The only remaining interpretation was that "the man is a political assassin, or an 'anarchist' *[fawḍawi]*, and this is what he confessed to, and what the investigation has yielded." If this is the case, then "Wardani is justified in doing what he did, because anarchists in every part of the world believe that present laws are inappropriate for human society, and consider that they do not have to abide by them. However, such a principle . . . cannot become the norm unless everybody or at least the majority of people become anarchists, and this is not presently the case." According to Muja'is, Wardani represented the will of hundreds of thousands of Egyptians who considered Egyptian independence a right. Where he differed (and erred) was in his increasing inability to realize that "independence was a process for which the nation has to be prepared through education, among other means. While in London, Russian nihilists and Italian and Egyptian anarchists taught him lessons. . . . He returned to Egypt with a flame in his heart, not realizing that the Egyptian nation is not one that revolts asking for its rights." Wardani's error was to believe that he alone, through his solitary act, could "lift [or awaken] the people"; this was sheer "madness . . . to see virtue in one's opinion, and want to lead a nation to [independence] by leash [or by force, *bi zimām*]; to ignore the period of nurturing [raising] the nation *[ḥaḍana]*, [which is necessary] for its awakening *[nahḍa]*." As a consequence of his act, Wardani "deserves to die, but he does not deserve to be calumniated; his action . . . is very likely to trigger tremendous reform *[iṣlāḥ]* in the government's actions as well as in the Egyptians' hearts, and this will make the nation ready . . . for a constitution and then independence." Ultimately Muja'is's condemnation of Wardani's act was not rooted in an ethical condemnation of assassination, but in its futility: "For the dagger and a bullet in one person [does not affect] an entire government, and does not reform an entire government." Just as it had indirectly done through Polikivitch's discussion, *al-Ḥurriyya* was endorsing political violence, and interpreting anarchist violence specifically, as an unavoidable (and necessary) manifestation of oppression, but one that should be accompanied by a larger project of social and political reform.

By the end of the first decade of the twentieth century the network around *al-Nūr* and *al-Ḥurriyya* had begun displaying interest for and sometimes overt identification with international leftist movements and ideologies, especially anarchist tenets and icons. This shift was accompanied by a general radicalization of the network's discourse on workers and the beginning of a social analysis that was more class-based. This radical turn was also visible in a number of interconnected topics central to the group's worldview and linked to notions of social and international justice. But what exactly is the significance of such discoveries? First, they serve to challenge the dominant historiographic narrative of absence, namely, the absence of radical, socialist, and leftist movements in Syria before 1919.[94] Not only do the discoveries exposed in this chapter point to a vibrant forum of debates regarding socialism, anarchism, and the like, as well as the articulation of ideas regarding these ideologies, but they also show that, for a variety of local and international reasons, such ideas were synthesized and incorporated into local political discourses and could be implemented as projects. Second, such discoveries shed light on a very specific moment in the history of Syria, one that has often been described as constituting the antechamber of nationalism. In this grand narrative Beirut and Mount Lebanon existed in anticipation of nationalism before 1914. As a consequence of this overriding narrative, calls for social justice, workers' education, social reform, the eradication of sectarianism, the curbing of clerical power, resistance to European political and economic encroachment, and increased local autonomy vis-à-vis Istanbul have all been taken as steps that would inexorably lead to nationalism.

Rather than confirming this interpretation of the unstoppable march toward nationalism, and through the discoveries concerning this vibrant and active radical network, I hope to have underlined the historical contingencies of nationalism as it developed and ultimately triumphed. All the causes embraced and defended by the radical network—mass education, Khairallah's vision of a classless society, anticlericalism, anti-imperialism, and a strong critique of unionist policies in Mount Lebanon—were accompanied by various signs underlining the radical network's allegiance to the Ottoman state, at least until 1909–10. Such signs include *al-Nūr*'s definition of itself as an *Ottoman* periodical, the establishment of *Ottoman* reading rooms, and the organization of *Ottoman* exhibitions in Shuwayr. The point is not to dismiss the strength of nationalist ideas (when chronologically appropriate). Rather, we must resist the temptation of blowing their importance out of proportion. I also wish to emphasize the inextricable connection between the constructions of both radicalism and the brand of nationalism that ultimately emerged, and argue that their intermingling fundamentally shaped the development of both radicalism and nationalism in Beirut and Mount Lebanon.

In all this the radical network's connection to Egypt remains fundamental. It is highly likely that its ideas were known among certain circles in Cairo and Alexandria, and that, reciprocally, those ideas were partly shaped by ideas and experiments in Egypt at the same time. It might be difficult to ascertain that the Syrian network actively and consciously influenced or was influenced by ideas developed in Egypt, yet it is undeniable that there was at least an *informational* connection between members of this network, their publications, their projects, and the cities of Alexandria and Cairo. That is to say, the Syrian network most likely *knew* of certain radical ideas that were floating around in Egypt, and conversely the ideas and activities of that Syrian network were known in certain Alexandrian and Cairene circles.

Al-Nūr had bases in both Cairo and Alexandria; it had a correspondent and more than one contributor in the former and was published in the latter. Therefore it is likely that various members of that network were informed about the latest developments on the Alexandrian scene and simultaneously that the network's actions among Syrians and non-Syrians of Alexandria and Cairo enjoyed a certain visibility. Furthermore the keen interest in the Syrian provinces maintained by Syro-Egyptian periodicals and newspapers such as *al-Ahrām*, *al-Muqtaṭaf*, and *al-Hilāl* led these periodicals to regularly publish articles on various matters pertaining to Syrian reform in general. In other words, projects such as the ones promoted by *al-Nūr*'s network—the establishment of night schools and the agricultural and industrial exhibition mounted by them—were very likely to be covered by the large Syrian periodicals of Egypt. And indeed they were. Both *al-Ahrām* and *al-Muqtaṭaf* devoted articles to the industrial exhibition of 1905 in Shuwayr and sent reporters to cover the event.[95] Thanks to the coverage such events received in major Syro-Egyptian dailies and periodicals, a substantial segment of Alexandria's and Cairo's populations could have known about *al-Nūr*'s ideas and activities, and the other way round. Farah Antun, when he was still based in Alexandria, devoted much attention and a long article to the need to establish agricultural schools in Egypt, which would teach peasants new methods of producing more efficiently and would help them fend off what Antun described as rapacious capitalists waiting to take over peasant land in Egypt.[96] The dissemination of the Syrian network's ideas beyond the geographic borders of Syria was given a boost by the fact that Jirji Baz, one of the network's main characters, occasionally contributed articles to influential Syro-Egyptian periodicals such as *al-Hilāl* and *al-Muqtaṭaf*. At the same time, *al-Nūr*'s network was aware of the latest developments in Egypt thanks to the contribution of writers residing in Egypt, such as Labiba Hashim and *al-Ḥurriyya*'s correspondent in Cairo, Husayn Rida.

The press was not the only forum for the Syrian radical network's Egyptian connection. Virtually every project undertaken by the network around *al-Nūr* (free reading rooms, industrial and agricultural exhibitions, and the Ferrer play) involved Syrians from Egypt visiting Mount Lebanon or Beirut. For instance, Niqula Tuma, a Syrian lawyer and social reformist residing in Egypt, was one of the speakers at the inauguration of the first reading room established by *al-Nūr*'s network in Shuwayr;[97] reporters from *al-Ahrām* and *al-Muqtaṭaf* covered the industrial exhibition; and the famous actor 'Aziz 'Eid, who was based in Egypt and was involved in more than one radical performance, had the lead role in the Ferrer play, which was written and put on by the network.

Hence it is extremely likely that the relationship with Cairo and Alexandria had an impact on the formulation of this network's ideas, and most probably also on the dissemination of its ideas beyond Syria. In fact these connections, as well as the deep similarities that existed between the two brands of radicalism emerging in Beirut and Alexandria, hint at more than a mere informational connection between the cities' radical networks. Indeed the articulation of the ideas promoted by the two radical networks in Beirut and Alexandria, as well as their application, were extremely similar, formulated and implemented within a few years from one another and seemingly unique throughout the Arab provinces of the Ottoman Empire. It is to the second radical network of Italian anarchists, based in Alexandria, that we now turn.

AN ITALIAN ANARCHIST NETWORK IN ALEXANDRIA

In 1898 Pietro Vasai, a thirty-two-year-old Italian anarchist, disembarked in Alexandria after having roamed the Mediterranean for almost three years. Born and raised in Florence, Vasai had joined the very dynamic Tuscan anarchist scene at sixteen, quickly becoming one its most active figures, participating in anarchist and socialist circles and managing one of the most important anarchist periodicals of the time, *La Questione sociale*, founded by Errico Malatesta, the towering figure of Italian anarchism.[98] These were years of serious repressions and crackdowns on anarchists throughout Europe. From the late 1880s until the late 1890s Vasai's life followed the same pattern: anarchist activism—usually in the form of publishing, labor organization, and propaganda work among workers—followed by prison sentences triggering short periods of self-imposed exile, then a return to Italy, and another arrest and prison term. His exiles took him to Switzerland, Tunisia, Barcelona, and perhaps beyond, places where he maintained a dynamic engagement with local anarchist activities. He soon established a wide web of contacts with fellow (mostly Italian) anarchists throughout the world, gaining tremendous respect and making it into the Who's Who of anarchists, as well as having the dubious honor of being classified as a "dangerous anarchist" *(sovversivo* or *anarchico pericoloso)* in Italian police files. He also acquired valuable experience in labor organization and propaganda. Around 1896, after being condemned to yet another round in prison, Vasai appealed for and won a conditional exoneration, a legal device by which subversives were pardoned by the Italian state on condition that they left the country and relocated elsewhere. Vasai relocated to Egypt and eventually made his way to Alexandria, where he would remain until 1914.

Fin de siècle Alexandria was no virgin territory for anarchists. Wittingly or unwittingly, the Ottoman Empire in general, and Egypt specifically, had been harboring European revolutionaries probably since the 1820s, offering asylum to Italian Carbonari as well as participants in the 1848 revolutions fleeing repression from Europe. In the 1870s Italian anarchists began heading there for a number of reasons. For some the Ottoman Empire had come to epitomize tyranny and oppression; a revolution there would lead to its ineluctable destruction and subsequent replacement with, in the words of one prominent anarchist, "a republican federation of the Balkan provinces with Constantinople as a free city."[99] A number of anarchists participated in the liberation struggles of various Ottoman provinces, most notably in Crete in 1866 and in 1896, in the hopes of bringing forth the destruction of this tyrannical entity.[100] Although most anarchists did not hold such beliefs (or were not willing to risk their lives for them), many were deeply interested in the "Eastern Question" and wrote about it.[101] More important for our story, beginning in the 1870s Egypt, deemed more liberal than the rest of the Ottoman Empire, became a chosen destination for Italian (and other) anarchists.

Anarchism had emerged as a major political ideology in Europe, most vibrantly in Italy and Spain, and quickly gained ground throughout the world, from South America to East Asia, at the same time as its proponents were fleeing repression in Europe, which intensified following the wave of bomb attacks and political assassinations in the 1890s. However, Italian anarchist activities in Egypt had fully taken off as early as the late 1870s. By then the Egyptian cities were well plugged into global information and communications networks, and news from all over the world reached them promptly, thanks to the telegraph, news agencies, a reliable postal system, and a plethora of periodicals. People and commodities flocked there with ease and regularity, as the Suez Canal, a fairly extensive railway system, and steamships connected Alexandria to the rest of the world, most notably Italy. For the internationalist, highly mobile anarchists, who were often on the run, access to this kind of infrastructure was vital.

Anarchism in Alexandria: An Early Presence

By April 1876 anarchists in Alexandria were operating a branch of the International Workers' Association (Federazione Italiana dell'Associazione Internazionale dei Lavoratori).[102] In April 1877 this section of the International proclaimed its allegiance to the Universal Socialist Congress of Ghent in Belgium and sent a representative there.[103] Although the line between socialism and anarchism was becoming more rigidly demarcated in Europe around that time, there was still some degree of collaboration. Significantly the Alexandrian branch asked the Universal Socialist Congress to establish a federal office to propagate Socialism in "Oriental regions" through the publication of works in Italian, Illiric, Greek, Turkish, and Arabic. A similar request was made by the Cairene and Greek federations of the International. Although no further details are available on the activities of the International in Egypt, the fact that a delegate was sent from Egypt to attend the Congress further attests to the formal and informal connections linking the anarchist scene in Egypt to global leftist networks and institutions.[104] The establishment of *Il Lavoratore* in 1877, the first Italian anarchist periodical to appear outside Italy, also contributed to building and maintaining ties with the global leftist and specifically Italian anarchist networks. It further confirms the strength of the Italian network in Egypt and its pioneering role within the Italian diasporic anarchist world. This is further illustrated by the presence in Egypt of some of the most prominent Italian anarchists, among them the towering figures of Errico Malatesta and Amilcare Cipriani,[105] both future leaders of the Italian Anarchist Party established in Italy in 1891. In fact in 1882 Malatesta and fellow anarchists seem to have fought on the side of

'Urabi and against the British; when the British occupied Egypt that year, some of them were arrested and others fled.[106]

Malatesta and Cipriani were the big stars who converged on Alexandria, but the motor behind the city's anarchist community was a more modest figure, Ugo Parrini, who had settled in Alexandria by 1877. In the early 1880s Parrini devoted himself to reorganizing the anarchist movement, unifying various splinter groups there and organizing anarchist meetings (such as the one in 1881 that was attended by a hundred anarchists).[107] He also founded a clandestine printing press in Alexandria that lasted until around 1882, which the anarchists used to print manifestos, periodicals, and booklets, such as the one celebrating the anniversary of the Paris Commune.[108] Parrini also founded the Circolo Europeo di Studi Sociali, a study group open to "all those who wished to study the social question."[109] After briefly fleeing (or being forcibly expelled) with the advent of the British Occupation, he returned to Egypt. Not much is known about Parrini's or other anarchists' activities in the city in the 1890s, but by March 1892 they were again numerically significant enough to organize at least one public demonstration with speeches and chants in Moharram Bey. During this demonstration one of Bakunin's manifestos was plastered all over town.[110]

Clearly the city kept attracting Italian anarchists even after the British Occupation and well into the twentieth century, as the sources testify. One practical and legal reason behind Egypt's attractiveness for Italian anarchists was the following: starting in 1898 virtually every European state, a number of North and South American states, and the Ottoman Empire itself decided to attack the threat of anarchism in a concerted manner and combine their efforts in crushing subversives and "fighting terrorism."[111] The expansion of international law for this aim and the establishment of mechanisms allowing police cooperation across the boundaries of national jurisdictions probably set the basis for our modern-day Interpol.[112] Britain, however, refused to participate in the establishment of an international police system in charge of tracking down anarchists; it was the sole dissenter from among the twenty-one countries that met in Rome in 1898.[113] Another set of agreements, known as the Secret Protocol for the International War on Anarchism, was signed in St. Petersburg in 1904, but again Britain did not join. This is not to say that anarchists had it easy in Egypt, but it probably still meant that they weren't as often arrested there as in Italy or France.[114] Egypt's own multiple and rather convoluted legal system of mixed and indigenous courts further complicated matters, often allowing European anarchists to maneuver around the system and play one law against another, thus gaining time and postponing justice. This relative leniency nonetheless did not eliminate the threat of occasional crackdowns, raids, and trials that involved anarchists or people suspected of anarchist sympathies.[115] If anarchists were, in theory at least, more tolerated in Egypt than elsewhere, they were subjected to relentless surveillance, as the British archives and the bulky file on suspected anarchists compiled by the Italian consulate in Egypt eloquently testify. One report dating from 1900 suggests that suspected active anarchists in Egypt numbered around sixty-six, most of whom were employed as masons, carpenters, shop owners, and workers. A handful of them, mostly based in Cairo and Alexandria, were classified as dangerous.[116]

Nonetheless Italian anarchists went to Alexandria to be relatively safe from police and surrounded by friendly anarchists. They were also attracted to the city by the presence of a significant Italian working class, which would be the natural audience for anarchist propaganda efforts. As I discuss at greater length in the following chapter, in the late nineteenth century and continuing well into the twentieth, Italians as well as Greeks, Maltese, Syrians, Armenians, and Jews from the Ottoman Empire, the Austro-Hungarian Empire, and Italy formed networks of labor that circulated throughout the Mediterranean in search of employment. In this geography of migration, few countries attracted Mediterranean workers as much as Egypt. A modernizing state with a booming construction industry—including railways, port expansion, and the famous Suez Canal—developing factories, and a spectacular growth in trade,[117] Egypt was to play the role of a Mediterranean El Dorado, and its two main cities, Cairo and especially Alexandria, constituted sites of convergence for various Mediterranean labor networks for many decades and well into the twentieth century (in fact, until the 1950s.) By the turn of the century there were around 12,000 Italians in Alexandria out of a population of 320,000. The overwhelming majority were workers, and they were employed primarily in the construction industry as carpenters, masons, stone carvers, and painters, as well as in crafts. Many also worked as cooks, servants, shopkeepers, wine distributors, shoemakers, and tailors, and Italian women found jobs as servants and nannies. A large proportion seems to have been seasonally employed, or were in Egypt for a number of years before moving elsewhere (to other parts of North Africa, the Ottoman Empire, the Americas, or back to Italy). Most of the Italian workers lived in mixed neighborhoods, and it was in one such neighborhood, Moharram Bey, a poor neighborhood of Jewish, Arab and European workers at the city's periphery, where "despite the few villas with beautiful gardens sprinkled here and there . . . one can see the misery," that the anarchists' HQ and main activities were.[118]

THOUGHT AND PRAXIS: THE IDEAS AND ACTIVITIES OF ALEXANDRIA'S ANARCHIST NETWORK

Throughout the 1890s and 1900s Vasai, Parrini, and their companions relentlessly busied themselves doing propaganda work among workers, mostly but not exclusively Italian. One of their main aims and accomplishments was to move beyond existing mutual aid societies, deemed not political enough by anarchist standards, and establish what was known as *leagues of resistance*. These were units that helped workers stand up to their employers, strike, and negotiate. Part of their raison d'être was to establish common funds that would help strikers survive without yielding to the financial pressure of having to break a strike and go back to work. Being a typographer, Vasai began his organizational work among fellow typographers and was crucial to the establishment of the Typographers' League, whose members were at the forefront of anarchist activities.[119] Although he had particularly high ambitions for typographers—he wanted them to be at the vanguard of labor militancy and guide other groups—Vasai did not limit his organization work to them, but was active among metalworkers and others.[120] He seems to have been quite successful: in 1902 three different leagues—cigarette rollers, construction workers, and typographers—joined forces and started holding common meetings.[121] Vasai was also instrumental in founding leagues of resistance in Cairo, and his opinion and expertise were often called upon by his anarchist companions based in the capital.[122] He and his companions participated in organizing strikes, going as far as publishing the names of picket crossers and strikebreakers in the periodicals they founded. They also raised funds for workers' widows and sick workers' families and helped widows negotiate financial compensation from their deceased husbands' employers.[123] Other activities included organizing emergency services at the neighborhood level, such as sanitation and health services (for instance, during a cholera epidemic), in which the famous Italian poet Giuseppe Ungaretti, then part of this anarchist scene in Alexandria, also participated. Parrini and Vasai also helped coordinate anarchist meetings and supervised the establishment of study circles around the social question. According to one source, these circles were attended by "anarchists living in Alexandria, and around thirty youths, almost all trade employees *[commis de négoce]* and Jewish."[124] These study groups usually took place in wine shops that were also libraries (such as Parrini's), from which members of the community could borrow books. Enrico Pea, who would later become a well-known author and who was part of the anarchist scene then, recalled being handed a copy of the French anarchist Sebastien Faure's (1858–1942) *I Delitti di Dio* (The Crimes of God, ca. 1901) at one of these makeshift meeting halls during his initiation phase and advised to read it carefully.[125] In his autobiographical novel Pea describes his initiation into the world of anarchists:

> It is best to now look into the true landscape of Moharram Bey.
>
> I had my first anarchist contact in this neighborhood, when I had just arrived in Egypt.
>
> It was really Edmondo, the son of my then boss, an avaricious and tyrannical Austrian, who first spoke to me of "social justice." The son was betraying the father. But as he was young like me, Edmondo, and had been only recently initiated, he lacked the sufficient authority for me to believe him blindly. And I could also contradict him since often he wouldn't find clear reasons to oppose my objections. For that one evening, he took me to Pilade, a Pisan carpenter, right there, in the paved street. . . . I had my first

> lesson on "the future society" from Pilade. I was called a "sympathizer," which is the first grade (even anarchism has its grades). I would become a "compagno" later.[126]

Besides establishing study groups that attracted "excommunicated and subversive people from all parts of the world, who would meet there with their discourses in rebellion from God and society,"[127] the anarchists focused on publishing periodicals and manifestos. At least seven anarchist periodicals were issued between 1877 and 1914 in Alexandria.[128] Vasai in particular put his typographer's skills to good use and produced at least one extant periodical with Joseph Rosenthal, a Jewish anarchist with some Beirut connection who had moved to Alexandria (from Cairo) in 1899.[129] *La Tribune Libre/La Tribuna Libera,* a bilingual periodical founded in 1901, had a publication figure that hovered around a thousand, of which six hundred were sent to Italy.[130] It published translations of texts by Kropotkin, Bakunin, Reclus, and Tolstoi, as well as articles by Italian anarchists such as Malatesta. It also included a section on local matters, discussing local anarchists' initiatives such as talks, meetings, and strikes.

PLUGGING ALEXANDRIA AND EGYPT INTO THE ANARCHIST WORLDWIDE WEB

The fact that such a large percentage of *La Tribuna Libera*'s issues (and those of other anarchist periodicals published in Alexandria) were sent abroad indicates just how much of a global project anarchism was and how connected Alexandria was to this global network.[131] Like many anarchists from the turn of the century, the Italian anarchists in Alexandria functioned—and functioned intensely—on two levels, the global and the local. In fact it would be more accurate to say that theirs was a world in which the two were inextricably linked, cognitively, politically, and socially. Among their primary concerns was to connect—or connect even more firmly—Alexandria and Egypt to the global (and specifically Italian) network that constituted the world anarchist scene and spanned various parts of the Mediterranean and Europe, Italy, and the Americas: Argentina, Uruguay, and Brazil, as well as the United States. Not only were these periodicals distributed locally; they were also sent abroad to fellow anarchists in Naples, Buenos Aires, Paterson, New Jersey, and probably elsewhere. Members of the Egyptian anarchist scene also contributed articles and entries on the situation of anarchism in Egypt to anarchist periodicals in the above-mentioned places, and engaged in discussions with fellow anarchists on the pages of famous anarchist periodicals, such as Jean Grave's *La Révolte*. They followed each other's news closely and with concern, worried about their companions' fate, sent news about individual anarchists and their itineraries, raised funds internationally to support anarchist families abroad, subsidized anarchist periodicals in Italy and abroad, and passionately debated various anarchist theories.[132] The periodicals were central to the establishment and maintenance of this global community and sense of solidarity, a feeling that was also consolidated by the constant circulation of members of this network, who brought with them letters, news, books, and periodicals by fellow anarchists.

Thanks to the presence and activities of Vasai and his companions, Alexandria remained a beacon of Italian anarchism and a necessary stop on the anarchist Grand Tour. Alexandria's anarchists invited famous companions to give talks in their city, and even convinced some of them to settle in Egypt, promoting it as a safe haven and a vibrant center for anarchism. Among these visitors was Pietro Gori, who would also spend many years in Argentina, where he played a central role in the establishment of the first Labor Federation in 1901.[133] Many anarchists settled there for a few years following their companions' invitation. They would quickly get involved in the anarchist scene, founding and managing periodicals and doing propaganda work among workers. Anarchists from all walks of life passed through Alexandria, coming from or on their way to North Africa, Italy, Switzerland, South America, or North America. Even those who were merely transiting for a couple of days would get in touch with Vasai and his companions. One such character was Giovanni Oldani, a traveling photographer who came to Alexandria from Geneva and then Tunis, and whom the Italian consulate described as an "anarchiste convaincu, élève de Gori et ancien compagnon de Vasai et d'Angio. Cet individu fait le tour du monde faisant le métier de photographe ambulant. Il fait partie du 'circolo anarchico internazionale' de Montevideo (Amérique du Sud)."[134] Another was Giulio Bettini, a trader *(négociant)* moving between Rome, Alexandria, and New York, who immediately contacted the local anarchists upon disembarking in the Egyptian city.[135]

THE UPL: A COLLABORATIVE PROJECT BETWEEN ANARCHISTS AND BOURGEOIS RADICALS?

Global and transnational ties were crucial, but anarchists in Alexandria remained profoundly committed to establishing local institutions and connections and disseminating their ideas to larger segments of the local population. One of this network's most remarkable achievements was undoubtedly its crucial role in the establishment of the Université Populaire Libre in 1901.[136] A unique project throughout the Middle East and the Eastern Mediterranean, the UPL, which lasted at least a decade, was based on the model of the French Université Populaire first launched in Paris in October 1899.[137] Although Deherme, the founder of the Parisian Université Populaire, was a lapsed anarchist who sought to distance himself from both anarchism and socialism, he and the popular university project remained strongly influenced by the two movements. Like many of his peers, Deherme was deeply affected by Darwin's natural selection theory, and he wanted to establish through education a caste of "elite workers," or as the Université Populaire's mission statement put it, "l'émergence des plus aptes: l'élite ouvrière." The Université Populaire therefore adhered to a typically hybrid fin de siècle radical ideology, combining belief in mass education and progressive values with a profound distaste for organized workers' politics. Rather than viewing class struggle as a necessary (and desirable) step in the march toward a utopian classless society, the proponents of the Université Populaire argued that a different path was possible: they sought to destroy class divisions by promoting class harmony, which would be cultivated by the joint education of different classes. The cooperation they sought to build between progressive intellectuals and workers was connected to a different conception of workers, one that defied the more rigid (or leftist) definitions of working class to encompass the petite bourgeoisie and white-collar workers generally.

The fact that Alexandria's Université Populaire Libre was founded a mere two years after the establishment of the first Université Populaire in the world is an eloquent testimony to how experimental and cutting-edge the Alexandrian anarchist scene—and in some ways the city itself—was. It initially offered free evening courses for workers (mostly in Italian or French, although initially it did offer some courses in Arabic) and saw its mission as "extending literary and scientific education among the city's popular classes."[138] The UPL actively sought to educate the popular masses about social issues and social activism, enlightening them about social theory (it offered lectures explaining Bakunin's ideas, for instance). The university seems to have been well attended, with the first few classes enrolling an average of fifty-five students.[139] Two years after it was founded, the UPL claimed it had attracted fifteen thousand individuals (including eight hundred women), who in the prior fifteen months had attended courses, conferences, and artistic or literary evenings organized by the university.[140] Besides offering courses, the UPL prided itself on its public reading room, which contained many books and subscribed to radical leftist and anarchist periodicals from France and Italy.

Although it was most likely Italian anarchists, especially Vasai, who first conceived of the UPL,[141] it probably would be fair to claim that the project saw the light thanks to the enthusiastic support it received from a group of Alexandrian notables and public figures, members of the city's Mediterranean and multiethnic bourgeoisie. On the university's founding committee in 1901 sat twenty-one members of Alexandria's most prestigious (and mostly nonindigenous) families, including the Abbate,[142] Aghion, Menasce, and Ralli families. Most of these scions were Italian and Jewish notables (indigenous, European, and Italian Jews), who, despite their radical sympathies, sent their children to receive a solid education at the Jesuit school in Alexandria.[143] Significantly it was the same families, indeed the very same individuals who sat on the board of the municipality, putting forth relatively progressive policies and making sure that the UPL received a regular subsidy from municipal funds. For this caste, such progressive ventures, including low-income housing, theatrical subsidies, and the establishment of a popular university, were signs of Alexandria's modernity and were also in line with the wave of municipal socialism then coursing through the world. Members of this progressive bourgeoisie donated books to the university library and devised and often taught courses or gave lectures at the UPL on topics ranging from sociology to Ancient Alexandria. Indeed lectures and courses were not offered by professional educators, but by lay faculty, in line with the UPL's motto "Let everyone be responsible for teaching what they know and what they think . . . and every reader make his own opinion of things; for it is good that he have under his eyes the pros and cons of every matter"[144]—an attitude very similar to that of the Arabic periodicals discussed in chapter 2. The majority of teachers and lecturers during the first year were French, Italians, and Jews, but we do occasionally find Syrian and indigenous Egyptian names.[145]

The Mission of the UPL and the Ideas It Promoted: Radicalism and Its Limits

Although this initial collaboration between anarchists and bourgeois radicals bore fruit with the establishment of the UPL, the end result was ambiguous and ambivalently radical. The UPL was ultimately profoundly and genuinely radical, and simultaneously profoundly weary of certain notions, discourses, and practices that leftist radicals, especially anarchists, keenly sought to promote. The UPL offered courses on global radical themes and organized lectures on Tolstoi and Anatole France, evolution, the theater, strikes and their role in workers' movements, feminism, social positivism, and theories of progress, which analyzed the works of Saint-Simon, Owen, Fourier, Lassalle, Marx, and Bakunin.[146] The Bakunin lecture seems to have been much appreciated, if our sources are to be trusted.[147] The university's curriculum thus exposed a large number of Alexandria's population to the works and main concepts in the leftist canon and informed them about the latest achievements of unions in Europe, as well as workers' negotiation strategies and the advantages and disadvantages of strikes. Yet at the same time the UPL's radicalism had clear limits.

If a relatively high number of people attended at least one lecture in the first few years of the university's foundation, who were they? Although the UPL was, in theory and according to its charter, open to all "and admitted no distinction of nationality, religion, or language," the reality of the matter a few months later was very different.[148] In fact despite initially offering courses in Arabic its first year, by the end of that year the university was giving only three lessons in Arabic, as compared to forty-one in Italian and twenty-six in French.[149] And Egyptian Muslims, though never a strong presence in the UPL, were almost completely absent (or invisible) within a few months. The handful of Egyptian Muslim names that appear in 1901 as participants, patrons, and lecturers, figures such as Sheikh Hilmy effendi and 'Abdu Badran effendi, who gave lectures in Arabic, including at least one on "The Worker,"[150] seem to have all but disappeared in the following years. These were not the only changes that took place: it appears the UPL attracted mostly nonworkers.[151]

Within a few months it was mostly employees and members of the upper- and middle-class bourgeoisie who were attending the UPL, an audience not very different from those attending some of the *universités populaires* in France.[152] The absence of workers is particularly noticeable given that the UPL had initially called "on all workers' associations to organize courses responding more specifically to the needs and aspirations of workers" and "received with pleasure the delegates of the [the mutual aid organizations] Fratellanza Artigiana and the Società Nazionale whose assistance we are very much relying on."[153] The university prided itself on the collaborative forum it constituted: "The worker, the employee, the employer have something to learn here and something to teach: it truly is a cooperative university that we have founded." Specifically the university underlined its commitment to providing an education to the underprivileged classes, stating as one of its main premises that "even those who cannot contribute to expenses have a right to instruction."[154]

It is not clear what prompted the disappearance of both indigenous Egyptians and workers (if indeed the issue is one of disappearance),[155] yet this dual reorientation seems to have taken place around the same time as Vasai and the other anarchists were being progressively withdrawn from the project. Various statements suggest that workers were actively kept at a distance by the university's administration, which complained that these workers "appartenaient aux partis les plus avancés et . . . étaient plus enclins à la propagande que disposés à suivre des cours."[156] The administration also refused to grant workers' organizations access to the UPL's classrooms to hold meetings.[157] Eventually the university seems to have completely slipped away from the anarchists' control.[158] By 1904 the anarchists were desperately trying to reclaim the UPL; one spy who infiltrated the anarchist group reported to the Italian consulate, "A été fort discuté à propos de l'Université Populaire Libre qui, de jour en jour, tend à devenir une institution bourgeoise, et des propositions ont été faites pour combattre l'invasion de cet élément étranger à la classe ouvrière."[159] To the best of my knowledge they never managed to seize control of the UPL again. However, many of the ideas promoted by them continued to be taught in the evening classes, even if workers stopped attending the UPL, despite the anarchists' relentless attempts to convince workers, especially typographers, to participate.[160]

Whatever the reasons, by its first year the UPL had shifted its attention from workers to a new conceptualization of "classes populaires" and even of "the proletariat." At the same time as it was offering courses and lectures on unionization, strikes, and Bakunin, the university began promoting business courses that would appeal to the petite bourgeoisie. One such course was described as "dedicat[ed] very especially to trade and bank employees who, while already having a practical notion of business, aspire to higher posts."[161] In the eyes of the UPL, this petite bourgeoisie, with its interest in acquiring business-related skills, formed as legitimate a section of the "classes populaires" as did the proletariat.[162] The aim of these business courses was thus to improve the lot of this petite bourgeoisie and prepare it for a new dawn, "l' aurore de jours moins tristes pour les *prolétaires de la bureaucratie.*"[163] The *prolétaires de la bureaucratie* had therefore replaced the *prolétaires de l'industrie.* Bank and trade house directors were also encouraged to push their employees to register, as this would be of obvious interest to them and ensured higher profits.[164]

The UPL's management put forth two different arguments to justify its loss of interest in workers. First, it argued that Egyptian industry was still underdeveloped and that "Alexandrian workers"—by which it most likely referred to workers of all ethnicities, immigrant as well as indigenous—were not as advanced as workers in Europe and were therefore not ready to reap the benefits offered by the UPL. An indicator of the Alexandrian workers' backwardness was the lack of seriousness and durability of their strikes.[165] Second, the main committee of the UPL suggested that class consciousness might not be possible in a composite city such as Alexandria, in whose rare factories "les éléments les plus divers se rencontrent sans se confondre."[166] Indeed the UPL underlined Egypt's "specificity" (the ethnic and religious diversity of its population) from the very beginning. During his inaugural speech President Abbate "demand[ed] of all of the professors, conference givers, adherents, to take into consideration the *special situation of Egypt.* There are here men belonging to all races and all doctrines."[167] The managers of the university would reiterate their call for prudence: "Ici, au milieu de cette population où tant d'élements différents se coudoient et risquent parfois de se heurter, la plus grande prudence est impérieusement nécessaire, au risque de compromettre l'essentiel de l'oeuvre."[168] Thus the UPL was to some extent willing to sacrifice its vision of class cooperation to avoid threatening what it saw as a precarious balance between various ethnicities and religious communities. Rather than advocate class action and the making of a working class through active cooperation between workers of different ethnicities and intellectuals, a project it viewed as "propaganda" to be avoided at all costs, the UPL sublimated class action by suggesting *science* as an effective means for ethnic and religious communities to transcend their differences. This worldview was clearly expressed at the inauguration ceremony in the words of Abbate: "Our goal is to show them [men belonging to all races and all doctrines] *that only science is capable of uniting all intellects* and that beauty *[le beau],* in all its manifestations, is the only object which should cause a unified heartbeat."[169] Two years later the UPL reiterated its faith in science: "Répandre la culture scientifique et littéraire, ce n'était pas prêcher la révolution, c'était préparer les cerveaux à comprendre les vérités scientifiques qui, seules, peuvent assurer le développement intégral des individus."[170]

This emphasis on science as the real liberator of individuals and societies—to be contrasted with party activism or anarchosyndicalism, deemed propagandistic—was not specific to the UPL. As we have seen, it was also perfectly in line with the ethos of the *nahḍa* and its more radical contingent, as well as with the general spirit of the *universités populaires,* their abhorrence of official ideologies and organized propaganda, and their firm belief that it was through *individual reason* and *scien-*

tific thinking that people's minds would blossom. It was also compatible with one important current within anarchism, which privileged intellectual emancipation and rebellion over any kind of political apprenticeship. Hence the UPL viewed its mission as objectively presenting scientific truths (including such controversial and political truths such as Darwinism and the latest sociological theories), while leaving the public to be the judge of these truths and use reason to determine whether they were valid or not. There would be no go-between, no guiding party between these truths and the public; the public had to rely on its own reason: "Le sectarisme est mort: il faut se résigner à la liberté et à la raison. Le peuple a les pièces en mains, et il ne les lâchera plus. Il veut tout voir par lui-même, et juger. Il congédie les traducteurs qui sont les trahisseurs, les médiums de l'Inconnaissable."[171]

If the rallying cry provided by science already constituted a compromise and set limits in terms of class activism and workers' activism, the rest of the UPL's self-perceived mission and the regulations it imposed on the format for discussions within its walls would erode class politics even more. During the inaugural lecture the Comité expressed its desire to "create an intellectual and moral center where all classes of society could meet, cooperate for a common action. . . . We want freedom for all[,] . . . disdain of social distinctions, of ranks, of casts."[172] At the same time, this seemingly revolutionary forum, which displayed an irreverence for social categories, rather than encouraging difference of thought, was meant to emphasize unity, "seeking all that unites the knowledgeable and the ignorant, rich and poor," and avoid conflict.[173] Indeed only discussions that followed a certain format, a very institutional, bourgeois format, would be tolerated, "on condition that politeness and urbanity dominate all discussions."[174] But perhaps most revealing of the UPL's limited interest in a class-based action and cooperation was its emphatic desire to promote some sort of *morality* rather than an explicit political agenda, as it announced its aim: "in one word . . . to make the brain of some and the heart of others run at the same time, *for the development of everybody's soul:* such are the general lines of our program, conforming to that of the first Universités Populaires of Paris."[175]

If class action was relegated to a secondary category, this was due to both local and global factors. The popular universities in various parts of the world could be equally ambivalent about workers' organized politics and class struggle; from that perspective the UPL of Alexandria was not exceptional. At the same time, certain local conditions also explain this shying away from workers' activism. For one, the UPL was the product of both workers' groups and the bourgeoisie. This meant that the university's ties to workers' groups was not as strong and unilateral as those established by other popular universities in other cities—and the managers of the UPL were acutely aware of this difference.[176] In effect the bourgeois element took over and did not allow workers and workers' associations to develop the UPL into a more worker-oriented institution. The consequence of such a standoffish position toward working-class politics was bound to have repercussions on the project's membership; it clearly affected the UPL's success among the working classes, at least in the long run.[177] At the same time, the UPL's experiment serves as an eloquent illustration of the wider corpus of beliefs and practices that made up the global radical moment, including the multiplicity and wide range of interpretations, ad hoc bricolages and alliances, and the resulting tensions over the meaning of radicalism. If, for Vasai and his companions, anarchism meant first and foremost anarchosyndicalism and organizational work among workers, for the bourgeois radicals who ended up in charge of the UPL anarchism and radicalism meant individual redemption through knowledge and science, without which no social liberation would ever be possible (or desirable). Nonetheless, through the UPL leftist ideas indubitably made their way among a rising middle and professional class, even if the discourse promoted by the university's managers allowed ethnicity to override any social concern and to trump class.[178]

But this was not the end of the story of collaboration between bourgeois radicals and anarchists. When, in 1907, three Russians were accused of planning the destruction of a commercial ship in the port of Alexandria, and were subsequently arrested and extradited, no fewer than eighty Alexandrians signed a protest letter.[179] A look at the list of signers, speaking on behalf of "justice and humanity," reveals that most of them had Italian, Jewish, and Russian names and included the usual suspects of the Alexandrian anarchist scene (Rosenthal, Pea, Molco, and Sajous, among others), as well as many members of the notable families (such as Morpurgo and Ades), who described themselves in the petition as "hommes modérés et considérés dans la Cité."[180] In fact of eighty names on the "antideportation" list, twenty were also registered members of the UPL in 1903.[181] A few years later, in 1909, the UPL organized a large gathering to protest the arrest of Ferrer, a sign that the university still adhered to some of global radicalism's basic principles.[182] The radical bourgeois contribution to the UPL probably added visibility as well as viability to the project, guaranteeing not only municipal funding but also coverage by various well-established Alexandrian periodicals (including the Syrian Egyptian Alexandra de Avierino's *Anīs al-Jalīs* and *Le Lotus*).[183] The UPL experiment allowed Alexandria to link itself to another international radical network, that of the popular universities and radical publishing houses in France and Italy, all of which sent books and publications to the UPL's reading room.

THE VEXED NOTION OF IMPACT

The experiment of the UPL aside, what can we make of all the anarchist activity in Alexandria? How can we assess the vexed notion of impact that this Italian network had on Italian working classes in Alexandria, but also more generally on Alexandria workers as a whole and on Alexandrian and even Egyptian society? One could argue that the constant surveillance to which the Italian community in Egypt was subjected and the ongoing reports on anarchist activities until roughly 1914 suggest that the matter was taken seriously at least by the Italian consulate, which might indicate that the network's propaganda work mattered and was deemed dangerous. Earlier I referred to a consular estimate of sixty-six anarchists in Alexandria around 1900. However, other sources suggest that these numbers increased fairly significantly, at least among those who could be labeled sympathizers or novices. Although the number of workers who attended anarchist meetings and joined the leagues was not massive, it was not negligible; between eighty and two hundred attended meetings and were members of various leagues.[184] Occasionally consular reports mention "a huge crowd" attending a talk given by one anarchist or another, such as Pietro Gori's 1904 lecture series on "'bread and liberty in workers' revolutions, which were very warmly received."[185] Obviously success and impact are relative, and different sources paint a different picture. For instance, Italian consular reports from 1902, perhaps as wishful thinking, suggested that there was no need to worry about the study groups that Vasai and others were establishing, and that, like previous attempts, they were doomed to fail.[186] Yet the memoirs of Pea and certain autobiographical essays by Ungaretti, as well as some of the extant periodicals themselves (not to mention the UPL's two hundred or so members), suggest that anarchists were getting their message across despite various hurdles, rivalries, and tensions. Although it is true that many of the anarchist periodicals were short-lived, there were a lot of them, thus guaranteeing a constant flow of anarchist information and propaganda. At least one periodical, which was distributed for free, was expected to have a publication figure of two thousand, an impressive figure for the period and for Egypt.[187] Many of the events organized by the anarchists were quite visible: public demonstrations, distributions of manifestos, and strikes, some of which were reported in the Arabic and foreign-language press. The coverage these events received was not even necessarily positive, but it meant added visibility and free advertising, especially when the periodicals translated and reproduced some of the foreign-language manifestos.[188] Many non-Italian names pop up in conjunction with Italian anarchists and their activities, both in Cairo and in Alexandria. Besides Russian and probably Austro-Hungarian Jews, we find the occasional Greek and Armenian names and the rare Syrian ones (the last within the UPL).[189] Also we know that many of the propaganda talks were given in more than one language.[190] Furthermore, through the UPL, which lasted at least until 1909, some of the anarchists' ideas must have gotten disseminated to a fairly substantial segment of the population, if indeed fifteen thousand people attended the UPL's lectures during the first year. Obviously, though, because so much of the propaganda work was through informal, oral discussions and among nonelites and took place in wine shops or coffee shops, it is very difficult to assess its impact.

If the question of impact is thorny enough when it comes to Italian workers, it is exponentially more difficult to address in the case of non-Italian, and especially indigenous workers. Nonetheless various signs indicate that Italian anarchists were reaching out to and in contact with local Egyptians, indigenous and immigrant. One of these kinds of activities was the distribution throughout the city of multilingual anarchist and socialist tracts that usually appeared in some combination of Italian, Greek, Arabic, Judeo-Spanish, and French. An example is a tract protesting a department store's mistreatment of its workers, published by La Société Internationale des Employés du Caire, in French, Greek, and Arabic.[191] As previously mentioned, as early as 1877 Alexandria's and Cairo's branches of the International Association of Workers had asked the Universal Socialist Congress to publish tracts and booklets in Arabic and Turkish, among other languages.[192] Records also indicate that the multiethnic and multilingual Cairene Typographers' League, which was heavily infiltrated by anarchists, pledged its support to the League of Indigenous Typographers in their efforts to unionize and considered their indigenous colleagues to be serious about labor militancy.[193] The International Association of Cooperation for the Improvement of the Working Classes (Association Internationale de Coopération pour l'amélioration des classes ouvrières), whose political sympathies can be surmised by its name and which was established in 1909 by anarchists in Alexandria, counted both indigenous and nonindigenous Egyptians among its members.[194] The title of a new anarchist periodical *Malesc . . . Bukra!!* (No Worries. . . . Tomorrow!), which supposedly was issued in March 1904 (although there seem to be no extant copies of it), suggests it was bilingual, most likely Arabic and Italian.[195] As previously mentioned, the Université Populaire Libre did occasionally (even if seldom), offer lectures and classes in Arabic, including lectures on workers and workers' issues. Furthermore the connections between the (mostly) Italian anarchists and non-Italians were not limited to indigenous Egyptians and Arabic speakers, but also included reaching out to other linguistic and ethnic minorities by giving talks in Hebrew (Judeo-Spanish?) and Greek, publishing in these languages, and offering workers political support.[196] Less directly, perhaps, the numerous strikes, lockouts, and increased workers' militancy that included efforts to unionize, which took place in Egypt between 1900 and 1914, should be added as indices of collaboration. Many of these initiatives were the result of workers from various ethnic communities working together, but in which nonindigenous workers often played a key role at the organizational level. This increased militancy, especially the use of certain concepts and strategies by various indigenous groups (such as leagues of resistance and night schools for workers), suggest that the methods advocated by the anarchists were being used by a fairly large segment of the working classes and by ideologies that sought to mobilize or interpellate the working class.

Thus we should reassess the verdict made by a contemporary and local anarchist (Roberto D'Angiò) and a historian (Leonardo Bettini), suggesting that these Italian anarchists had no impact on the indigenous population. Writing in 1905 D'Angiò complained that Italian anarchists did indeed put some efforts into reaching out to "the indigenous population," but that they were faced with a lack of interest and indifference on their part. In his words, "The Egyptian working-class, whether because in Egypt one lives relatively better than elsewhere, or because anarchist ideas really horrify it, or due to reasons of climate or Oriental customs, has stayed constantly and stubbornly away from anarchists."[197] In fact the supposed indifference of the indigenous workforce toward anarchism and socialism (especially as they were formulated by Italian militant migrants) was not unique to Egypt. Various Italian anarchist periodicals in São Paulo deplored the attitudes of Brazilian workers to social issues and labor militancy in terms very similar to their compatriots' back in Alexandria and Cairo.[198] The historian Bettini, writing in the 1970s, had a very different take on the anarchists' failure to penetrate the Egyptian local working milieu, which he linked to their inability to come up with a political intervention that was adequate to the existing cultural and political scene. He argued that, rather than adapt their discourse and their actions to suit local indigenous needs, Italian anarchists promoted a model that really suited European working classes.[199] Tellingly, the Egyptian Italian anarchist community appears to have been split on the issue of including and reaching out to non-Italians (indigenous and otherwise). Perhaps the reasons for excluding non-Italians were a combination of racism and stereotypes à la D'Angiò, to which anarchists were not immune, and the fear that other groups of workers (especially indigenous ones) would be willing to take the jobs of striking workers—in other words, that they had no class solidarity.

Vasai at least seems to have been favorable to collaborating with and doing propaganda work among non-Italian workers. In one instance his appeal to his Cairene companions for financial help to establish *La Tribuna Libera* with Joseph Rosenthal went unanswered. The archives suggest that, at least from the perspective of the Jewish anarchists in Cairo, the real reason for this was Rosenthal's Jewish origins. This did not stop Vasai from establishing the periodical and collaborating with Rosenthal on many other occasions. In another instance Vasai and one of his companions, a Frenchman by the name of Constantin Sajous, who was also a typographer, withdrew their membership in the Typographers' League; immediately after, the league specified that membership was limited to nonindigenous workers, suggesting that things had been otherwise during Vasai's participation and supervision.[200] Given these indications, the examples provided in this chapter on multilingual publications, talks, and collaborations between Italian and non-Italian workers all strongly suggest that the Italian anarchists' ideas and praxis were not confined to Italian workers.

ANARCHISM AMONG INDIGENOUS EGYPTIANS

If anarchist ideas were not confined to Italian workers in Egypt, neither were they confined to workers tout court. According to Egyptian police reports, anarchism was a popular ideology among indigenous Egyptians around 1910. Its principles were becoming increasingly familiar and appealing to a wide range of individuals and groups contesting the status quo, especially those actively engaged in anti-British and nationalist activities. Ibrahim al-Wardani, the ardent supporter of Mustafa Kamil, who assassinated Prime Minister Butrus Pasha Ghali in 1910, was said to have mixed with Russian "revolutionaries and anarchists" while studying in Lausanne.[201] Upon his return to Egypt, Wardani played a prominent role in the labor syndicates and workers' night schools affiliated with the Egyptian Nationalist Party (al-Ḥizb al-Waṭani). According to a British source, it was in these workers' night schools that Egyptian "lower classes . . . were taught revolutionary doctrines and systematised hatred of the occupying Power."[202] Furthermore, the British claimed, Wardani had "on several occasions give[n] utterance to anarchist (not socialist) doctrines of an advanced tinge." The report concluded, "This makes his choice as organiser of labour syndicates and preparer of strikes the more significant of the recklessness of these leaders as to the means they are ready to employ for the furtherance of their projects, and emphasises their moral responsibility for any violence that may result."[203] Although Wardani himself vehemently denied the allegations that he was an anarchist, his political thought and actions were more likely than not tainted with anarchist principles. Not surprisingly, Wardani's act and subsequent trial unleashed a wave of panic and triggered a witch hunt and full-fledged investigation of secret societies in Egypt. A special police bureau was established for that task, and it soon transpired that there were at least twenty-six such societies, many of them plotting to conduct political assassinations and other violent political acts.[204] Significantly, one such society was called the Society for the Encouragement of Free Education (Jamʿiyyat al-Tashjīʿ ʿalaʾl-Taʿlīm al-Ḥurr).[205] It had a dozen members: "Half . . . were students at the government schools and the other half were employees and students at al-Azhar. . . . Words were sometimes uttered showing that the youths had anarchist tendencies *[anna lahum muyūl fawḍawiyya]*."[206]

Similar episodes suggest that anarchism was far from confined to a handful of Italian militants; both elites and nonelites incorporated many aspects of anarchism into ambient discourses and practices. However, the issue here is not one of origins: I am certainly not suggesting that this specific network of Italian anarchists is the source of all or even most leftist, revolutionary, and specifically anarchist thought, action, or information that was present in Egypt at the time. Rather, one way to think about this one network of anarchists is that it contributed to the reservoir of anarchist and more generally radical ideas, propaganda, information, and practices in Egypt prior to World War I. Its members might have played a particularly formative and central role in disseminating anarchism among various social, intellectual, and political categories in Egypt, but we simply cannot map this precisely. What is evident, though, is that anarchism and anarchist ideas, in Egypt and elsewhere in the Ottoman Empire, far from being confined to marginal and minority groups, were gaining ground and being synthesized in other revolutionary radical or social movements, which included proto-nationalist, nationalist, trade unionist, and Muslim reformist movements. Specifically, although anarchist and nationalist liberation movements might have been deemed incompatible in different historical contexts, they seem to have had quite a symbiotic relationship in non-Western European settings around the turn of the century. While such a hypothesis deserves to be more seriously investigated, in the case of Egypt suffice it to say that the relationship between nationalism and the (multiple) Left(s) (anarchism and socialism specifically) in pre-WWI Third World contexts (i.e., in the context of colonial domination), and the interaction and exchanges between the Left(s) and nationalist ideology and praxis as it was being constructed in the period under study, fundamentally shaped both ideologies and movements.

CONCLUSION

The story of Italian anarchism in Alexandria sheds light on important features of the city itself and of the Eastern Mediterranean generally. First, it shows that Alexandria was very much integrated into the global world; rather than having a separate, utterly distinctive history that followed a different cadence or was isolated from world trends, the city was in fact a major player and participant in the story of globalization and radicalism. Alexandria's anarchist story is comparable to (albeit different from) that of Rio de Janeiro, for instance, or Paterson, New Jersey. It also confirms the existence of a geography of contestation connecting certain cities through radical networks. From this perspective, the Italian anarchist network was only one of many—including Muslim reformists, Syrian radical intellectuals, Armenians nationalists and socialists—that converged on Alexandria. Hence Alexandria was a crossroads for radical networks that sought to establish a more just society by defending workers' rights and establishing night schools for workers. Not only did these networks converge on the city; they had ample opportunities to intersect there and learn from one another. The various experiments and radical projects that were taking place there were known and had repercussions beyond the city's limits, spreading first throughout Egypt, at least certainly to Cairo and the cities of the Delta, but also throughout the Eastern and Southern Mediterranean. The activities of this anarchist network in Alexandria are a stark reminder of anarchism's omnipresence and importance during the fin de siècle. Although this Alexandrian history has been largely forgotten by historians, it has been preserved in literary works, such as Giuseppe Ungaretti's essays and Enrico Pea's novels. Pea has paid tribute to the city's vibrant anarchist milieu and its combination wine shops and libraries, "frequented by excommunicated and subversive people from all parts of the world, who would meet there with their discourses in rebellion from God and society."[207] If no one now recalls the name of Pietro Vasai, who went back to Italy in 1914 and died there two years later, there is some poetic justice in the fact that his name appears in Pea's book, where he has been immortalized as a man "sick with altruism and tuberculosis."[208]

EPILOGUE: BEIRUT, CAIRO, ALEXANDRIA, AND THE EMERGENCE OF ANALOGOUS RADICALISMS

In this chapter I have analyzed the construction of radical networks in Beirut and Alexandria and dwelt at length on these networks' elaboration of discourses concerning workers and the working classes. My focus has been on the interplay between local and global trends that were to impact the version of radicalism promoted by these two networks. In this study important similarities emerged between the mechanisms of the network and the brands of radicalisms they promoted. First, there was a strong relationship between the radical network and a larger circle of reformers, whether intellectuals or bourgeois. This relationship guaranteed the nonmarginality of these networks and ensured a certain level of dissemination of their ideas throughout society. Second, ideas were combined with praxis. Both networks, through their own contacts or their alliances with powerful institutions and individuals, had the ability to put their ideas into practice and found institutions, especially institutions pertaining to mass education (night schools, popular universities, and free public reading rooms). Third, both networks founded and relied heavily on publications to disseminate their ideas. These publications guaranteed an international connection, since their readership and contributors formed a transnational and global network. In the case of *al-Nūr* and *al-Ḥurriyya,* this international connection to Syrian communities throughout the world and the periodicals' strong connection to Egypt must have contributed significantly to the shift from a purely local and provincial focus to a more global perspective and an interest in and identification with international radical movements, what I have labeled "the international bent."

The similarities between these two networks were not limited to their functioning, but extended to their ideas. Neither of them, at least not while the Italian anarchists collaborated with the bourgeois radicals, adopted class as a dominant unit of social analysis. At the same time, this did not prevent them from promoting some truly radical and leftist ideas. Equally analogous was their novel conception of the working class, which brought together real workers (in the Marxist sense) and middle-class white-collar workers—again, at least through the anarchists' collaboration with bourgeois radicals in Alexandria. Both networks actively sought to educate workers about their rights and ways of improving working conditions through strikes, negotiations with employers, and the formation of workers' unions.

The radicalism of both networks was characterized by a package of issues and theories that all intersected and were interconnected, and whose weight varied from city to city. These issues included anticlericalism, class cooperation, and class harmony between the working and middle classes. Finally, both networks were attracted to the ideas of Darwin and Tolstoi and believed science to be the ultimate equalizer and enlightening force of humanity.

The similarities between the projects implemented in the Beirut and Mount Lebanon area and in Alexandria are so strong as to hint at a connection between them. As previously suggested, this connection might be limited to general knowledge; that is, each network might have known incidentally about the other network's activities. However, there are enough indices to suggest that the connection was quite deep. I have already established the significant connection between *al-Nūr*'s network and Egypt, and have also suggested that the UPL project was quite visible, as it was patronized by a powerful Mediterranean bourgeoisie with contacts with various key institutions, such as the municipality. As we have seen, various periodicals and writers did support and write about the university, among them Alexandra de Avierino, a Syro-Egyptian whose fame was well established in both Egypt and Syria.[209] It is very likely that other periodicals, including *al-Ahrām, al-Muqtaṭaf,* and *al-Hilāl,* covered events sponsored by the UPL. The fact that all these periodicals circulated widely in Syria suggests that the Syrian radical network was familiar with the ideas promoted by the popular university.

Furthermore a small but significant number of Syrians (the majority of whom were either Jews or Greek Catholics) were active within the UPL, both as *adhérents* and lecturers, and it is not unlikely that some of them had a connection to the radical network in Syria.[210] Indeed potential intersections between these radical networks are numerous; for instance, it is no coincidence that the first work in Arabic overtly sympathetic to anarchism dates from 1898 (to the best of my knowledge) and was written by Shibli Shumayyil, a resident of Cairo who was in contact with Alexandra de Avierino.[211] We could also consider the fact that Errico Malatesta was deported from Alexandria and sent initially to Beirut. Or that Ya'qub Sannu'a, the dramatist and writer who had lectured at Deherme's Coopérative des Idées in Paris (which was the name of the first Parisian *université populaire*), had his work published in Beirut after his forced exile from Cairo, and corresponded with some of the Russian anarchists in Geneva (namely, Isabelle Eberhardt throughout 1896).[212] What I am suggesting is that such radical networks could easily be connected institutionally and individually, through a number of radical characters and thanks to a plethora of institutions—the press, the theater, exhibitions, and educational institutions—that linked the two cities and made the circulation of people and ideas a common occurrence. One of this book's main conclusions is that Alexandria, because of its very privileged place on the globalization map, was a particularly privileged site for the construction and convergence of a multitude of radical networks—

intellectual, political and, as we shall see in the following chapter, labor-based. This allowed it to play the role of radical beacon to other cities. To use terminology I developed in chapter 1, Alexandria served as a regional nodal city, whose impact was felt throughout the Eastern Mediterranean, especially in Beirut, thanks to the number and kinds of linkages connecting the two cities.

5

Workers, Labor Unrest, and the Formulation and Dissemination of Radical Leftist Ideas

In the last quarter of the nineteenth century a new form of social contestation appeared in Ottoman cities, particularly the capital, Istanbul, and port cities such as Salonica, Izmir, Alexandria, Beirut, and Tunis. Often described in the local press as a "foreign," "alien," and "European" form of protest,[1] strikes became an increasingly common feature of Eastern Mediterranean urban experience, especially after the 1890s. Indeed between 1872 and 1908 around fifty strikes were recorded throughout the Ottoman Empire (excluding Egypt);[2] in 1902—a year of no specific significance, either in the economic or the political arena—ten strikes took place in Alexandria alone during February and March.[3] The figures were to rise exponentially in the few months after the Young Turk Revolution of July 1908, a period that witnessed an explosion of strikes, mostly concentrated in Istanbul, Salonica, and Izmir, and involving up to 100,000 strikers, half of the urban wage laborers of the empire.[4]

In this chapter I analyze the place of workers in the construction and dissemination of radical leftist ideas. Whereas previous chapters have focused either on institutions or on intellectual or radical militant networks, this chapter is more of a history from below, as it is concerned primarily with workers' dissemination of radicalism, mostly among themselves but also to other segments of the populations of Beirut, Cairo, and Alexandria. Just as Alexandria, Cairo, and Beirut were poles of attraction for radical intellectual networks, they were also sites of convergence and intersection for a multiplicity of labor traditions and workers' networks of contestation. Especially in Alexandria a Mediterranean and even global tradition of labor militancy overlapped and intersected spatially and temporally with a strong local activist tradition among craftsmen. Hence I argue for the need to approach the history of national labor movements in the late nineteenth century and early twentieth from a global perspective; indeed the movement of capital, labor, and information and the establishment of internationalist workers' associations meant that the history of workers in one locality was much more connected to other localities and global affairs, both formally and informally.[5]

What were the reasons behind the emergence and popularity of strikes as a form of labor contestation in Beirut, Cairo, and Alexandria? What do strikes say about social change and labor shifts in these three cities, and the impact of such developments on the attractiveness and dissemination of radical ideas by and among workers? What specific social, political, and economic conjunctures in and between the three cities allowed for the formulation and especially dissemination of leftist ideas by and among workers? Or, to borrow the expression of one labor historian, what were the "complex mediations between a variety of economic, social and cultural phenomena" that helped workers mobilize in favor of radical ideas?[6] The relationship between strikes and radicalism is not necessarily linear. One way of reading strikes is as a form of contentious politics, as defined by Charles Tilly, and a potential expression of radical leftist ideas by workers.[7] Although strikes do not necessarily imply workers' adherence to radical movements and ideologies, they have very often been accompanied by class discourse in many urban societies since the late nineteenth century. Strikes usually reflect a certain degree of mobilization and cooperation between workers, and hence may be seen as an index of working-class formation, activism, and radical militancy. To quote E. P. Thompson, strikes help illustrate just "how present the working class was at its own making," including its own radical politicization.[8] At the same time that strikes illustrate the resonance of radical ideas among workers, their visibility also grants workers major agency in the wider dissemination of radicalism throughout society.

In this chapter I elaborate on some of the themes first broached in the previous chapter. I problematize and analyze the relationship between class and ethnicity—their intersection, overlap, and opposition—in order to examine how radical ideas moved and were exchanged across the multitude of immigrant, migrant, and indigenous workers' networks. Unfortunately I am unable to address the crucial issue of female labor. With a handful of exceptions, this topic has been seriously understudied in Middle Eastern history, and I tremendously regret partaking in this silence.[9] The general silence surrounding the participation of women in the labor force is particularly deplorable given the large presence in Syria and Egypt of female workers in factories and workshops (particularly in textile and tobacco industries), among other places of employment, and hence the fact that women very likely participated in strikes and formulated, consumed, and disseminated radical ideas.[10]

STRIKES AS AN EXPRESSION OF LABOR CONTESTATION

The working classes in Alexandria, Cairo, and Beirut certainly had good reasons for their discontent. I have already dwelt on these issues earlier in this book; suffice it to mention here that in both Egypt and Syria local and global factors had affected the economy and led to uncertainty and instability. In Egypt the economic boom of the late nineteenth century (1893–1907) and the growth in real wages in the 1880s and the first half of the 1890s was interrupted by a mini-depression in the mid-1890s, a brief sharp decline in the ratio between real wages and GDP until the end of the 1890s, and a stock crisis in 1907, with only partial recovery by 1914.[11] Mount Lebanon and Beirut followed a similar economic pattern. The great agricultural depression and low commodity prices of the 1870s were followed by a period of prosperity until the middle of the 1890s, when silk production and export represented the major forms of economic activity in Mount Lebanon. According to a British consular report, the mountain witnessed "a surprising progress in wealth, population and general prosperity," as high income from silk also encouraged the development and revival of manufacturing industries such as shoemaking and soap works.[12] Clearly it was not only the mountain economy that benefited from this growth; inextricably tied to it was Beirut's economy, and the city was to develop an entire infrastructure linking it to silk production centers in Mount Lebanon. Business boomed, and the city prospered.[13] By the 1890s, however, a number of signs concerning the silk industry, such as the inability to produce sufficient eggs for export or even for their own needs from the 1880s onward, triggered insecurity in an industry that employed a great number of people.[14]

I do not wish to give the impression that change in the periphery occurred mostly because of actions triggered by the core, or that workers' militancy was purely reactive to the West. Yet it is undeniable that the impact of Egypt's and Syria's semi-peripheralization and incorporation into the world capitalist system had dramatic repercussions on workers' lives, as attested by a number of serious investigations on the matter.[15] Although sectors, industries, and regions were differently and unevenly affected by this incorporation into the world market, by the early 1880s, and especially after 1882 in the case of Egypt, various Syrian and Egyptian local industries and businesses had been affected by a combination of intertwined local and global factors.[16] These factors led to restructurings, uncertainty, real wage fluctuations, unemployment, and general economic instability, all of which were exponentially exacerbated by the 1907 cotton crash in Egypt.[17] In Cairo, Alexandria, and Beirut there thus emerged a class of discontented, disgruntled workers.

The Need for a Specific Form of Labor Contestation

Although economic grievances certainly contributed to social unrest among workers, they do not on their own explain the popularity of strikes or the very specific mode of social contestation strikes represented. Nor do these grievances explain the appeal and dissemination of radical leftist ideas of which labor militancy, and strikes in particular, are a form of praxis. Rather the adoption of strikes as a method of contestation reflects a series of significant changes and historical developments in the three cities, which can be summarized as follows: (1) the emergence of *common* grievances and interests among workers in various sectors; (2) the weakening or disappearance of various institutions or groups that had previously defended workers' rights; (3) local social flux that led to unstable labor categories and the appeal of radical ideas, while allowing workers in different sectors or geographic areas to establish new communication channels; and (4) global trends that transformed the cities under investigation into poles of attraction for global labor networks.

In cities deeply integrated into the world capitalist system such as Alexandria, Cairo, and Beirut (and Mount Lebanon), few sectors of the economy were immune from fluctuations resulting from their incorporation into the world economy and subsequent encroachments by foreign companies. This was a new phenomenon that warranted new methods of contestation. Whereas in past centuries economic, political, and social factors had occasionally triggered urban unrest, these factors had either concerned specific groups that rebelled and rioted—most commonly Janissaries, but sometimes workers in certain guilds, such as butchers—or they had affected the entire urban population. In other words, such factors usually did not specifically or exclusively affect the entire labor force. In early modern times until the 1830s, that is, right after the abolition of the Janissary Corps and the introduction of the Tanzimat, it was one of the following factors that triggered urban unrest: (1) an increase in prices, leading to bread riots in which the majority of the urban population participated (such as in Damascus in 1757); (2) heavy taxation, resulting in the complete shutdown of an entire city; or (3) power struggles between various military-administrative groups, mostly between the Yerliler and the Kapıkulları. Although artisans were not the main subjects in such episodes of urban unrest, their participation was quite common.[18]

Starting in the late nineteenth century another significant change made strikes particularly appealing and effective. This was the disappearance or erosion of groups whose members had previously defended protesting artisans or had arbitrated between contesting parties, for instance between the rioting urban population and a representative of the state, or guild members and their sheikhs.[19] Until the mid-nineteenth century most of the causes for rioting were either internal or pertained to the guilds' relationship with the state. Hence artisans' rights could be defended by the Janissaries or their issues tackled by the sheikh of the guild.[20] Up until the early nineteenth century ulama, sheikhs, the heads of sufi brotherhoods, and Janissaries spoke and negotiated on behalf of rioters. But by the end of the century they were no longer in a position to do so; the Janissary Corps had been dissolved in 1826, and the power of guilds and their sheikhs had generally been eroded, sometimes by state design—although not absolutely, and with significant exceptions.[21] As workers' contention focused on foreign companies, or at least industries with links to international capital, the defense of workers' rights became increasingly difficult for guilds as well as the Egyptian and Ottoman states. Hence by the late nineteenth century a new kind of labor militancy was needed, one that could defend workers' rights as a group and forcefully express their demands and grievances in the face of foreign interests and an increasingly weak state. Such a method of contestation was also possible because the social organization of labor was undergoing changes that rendered labor categories fluid and porous and facilitated communication between workers in various sectors, industries, and neighborhoods, allowing them to coordinate strikes and mobilize effectively.

Fluid and Porous Categories

In the late nineteenth century and early twentieth the majority of workers in Egypt and the Ottoman Empire were crafts workers and artisans concentrated in small units of production, mostly in homes and workshops and small factories with ten employees or fewer.[22] Their number seems to have been on the rise, in both relative and absolute terms.[23] In fact only a very small percentage of the workforce was involved in factory work in the Ottoman Empire and Egypt, where industrial production before 1914 represented a tiny proportion of the national economy.[24] By one estimate, of a total Ottoman labor force of 9.5 million in 1914, 280,000 workers were employed in manufacturing, and another 200,000 were equally divided between construction and transportation.[25] In the case of Egypt, the census of 1907 reported almost 380,000 workers engaged in industry out of a population of more than eleven million; this figure included 45,000 hand loom weavers and 11,000 railway workers.[26]

How valid is this dichotomy between these various labor (and social) categories, namely, artisans, factory workers, construction workers, industrial workers, and even agricultural workers? We know that throughout the eighteenth and nineteenth centuries there were overlaps between craftsmen, manufacturers, and factory workers in Cairo, Damascus, and Mount Lebanon. It was not uncommon for artisans "[to supplement] their income through work which was in many ways similar to their own: carpentry, weaving, or spinning. The same may be said for other manufactories in branches such as textiles, glassworks, or sugar refining."[27] Factories throughout the nineteenth century employed artisans and members of construction guilds, and Damascene journeymen weavers were increasingly being transformed into factory workers in the mid- and late nineteenth century.[28] There was no rupture between old ways of production and modern mechanized ways, but rather a progressive adaptation of the old into the new and the coexistence of these two forms for long periods of time.[29] Factory work in textiles, for instance, was often similar to work that had been taking place for decades in small workshops, and weavers or other artisans involved in textile making or clothes manufacturing were the obvious contenders for such factory jobs. Factories often employed "aggregates of artisans organized under one roof. . . . The sheer variety of trades present in the factories is striking."[30] When artisans in a collapsing sector went in search of a new profession they were very likely to end up working in factories and on construction sites, doing jobs that did not require specific skills. Rather than completely severing ties with their guild, previous profession, or artisanal customs and culture, artisans-turned-workers most likely transposed many of those ties to their new sites of employment. The maintaining of ties between guilds and small industry was confirmed by Vallet in 1911: "Qu'en un mot, les corporations puissent être considérées comme abolies de fait, c'est possible, mais . . . il subsiste des 'corporations' de fait entre les artisans de la petite industrie. Toute la partie du Caire qui s'étend au pied des anciens remparts entre la citadelle et la mosquée de Qalaoun groupe par quartier les ouvriers d'une industrie donnée."[31]

The lack of rigid boundaries between artisans and factory and construction workers was not limited to their professional life. Throughout the Ottoman Empire artisans and workers in the late nineteenth century "often lived in the same neighborhoods, partook of a common culture, and engaged in similar activities" and did not seem to view themselves as forming separate categories.[32] The picture that emerges is thus one of constant interaction and overlap between craftsmen and factory workers, as they worked, lived, and engaged in cultural practices together. In the Ottoman Empire and Egypt, as well as in many parts of the Mediterranean, if not the world, labor categories, including agricultural work, were indeed very fluid and porous, and the move from crafts to industry was anything but linear. This occupational fluidity was accompanied by tremendous labor migration flows, with some workers engaging in a combination of agricultural, construction, and artisanal work in a single year. This was not necessarily new, but in the late nineteenth century unemployment in agriculture was very high and was accompanied by seasonal migration from Upper Egypt to Cairo and the Delta. For instance, most coal heavers in Port Sa'id in the late nineteenth century were migrant Egyptians from Upper Egypt, "attracted—often during the summer down season and at a time of deepening market relations—by the promise of cash wages comparable to and perhaps higher than those available in agriculture, construction and security."[33] This pattern of employment was most likely the rule rather than the exception, at least in the Mediterranean context.[34]

The fluidity and porousness of these social and labor categories had a number of significant implications for the formulation and dissemination of radical ideas by and among workers. The reshaping of old labor categories, the beginning of the formation of new ones, and the porous boundaries between them meant that social categories were not fixed; they were, almost in a molecular sense, unstable, and hence more likely to be receptive to ideas of contestation and challenge than during more stable times. This instability was one among a series of factors (not least of which were serious economic grievances) that gave a certain resonance to radical ideas among workers. Furthermore porous categories allowed ideas and information to circulate with relative ease; the knowledge or planning of a strike in a textile factory could be conveyed by one artisan working there to other members of his guild employed in a workshop in a different quarter. In cities undergoing such social and economic transformations and restructurings, ideas must have moved relatively seamlessly between labor sectors and categories, allowing for various traditions and networks of contestation—that of artisans, peasants, modern factory workers, and construction workers—to intersect.

The Contagiousness of Strikes

Perhaps one manifestation of this porosity and its impact on the dissemination of radical ideas and social contestation among workers was the contagiousness of strikes across social, labor, and geographic boundaries. Although the scarcity of sources does not allow us to draw a nuanced picture of the mechanisms involved in the spread of strikes, various episodes strongly suggest that some form of contagion did indeed occur between different labor categories. For example, during the three-month period of strikes and protests that erupted in December 1899 in Cairo's tobacco industry, workers in different tobacco factories "coordinated their activities and went on strike at the same time."[35] During one of Cairo's most visible strikes (1901), the European clothing manufacturers *(ṣunnāʿ khayyāti al-thiyāb al-ifranjiyya)* were joined, at meetings as well as demonstrations, by cigarette rollers and other workers, and workers' mobilization was such that the number of demonstrators reached 1,500.[36] In the spring of 1907 striking cabmen in Cairo were joined by carters, silk weavers, butchers, and others in strikes that lasted six weeks and have recently been described as "surely the most significant wave of popular protest prior to the 1919 rebellion in Egypt."[37] In August 1908 striking workers in the Port of Beirut were joined by railroad workers.[38] Similarly in 1911 workers in Cairo's electric, gas, and water companies joined the Cairo tramway company strikers.[39] Examples abound of strikes spilling from factory to factory within a specific sector, from one sector to another, from one neighborhood to another, and from one city to another.[40] Another important feature of strikes, especially after 1908, is the collaboration of "white collar and blue collar workers [who] prepared their petition and went on strike together."[41]

GLOBALIZATION AND LABOR CONTESTATION

That craftsmen were active participants in popular protest is certainly undeniable (and expectable). Some researchers have argued that "protests by workers in factories did not have some special role in the vanguard of popular protest and the emergence of mass politics in Egypt. . . . The collective actions of those inside and outside of factories were of complementary importance, reinforced each other, and responded to similar political opportunities."[42] Yet at the same time certain new sites and sectors constituted privileged spaces of contestation. These spaces—ports, railroad companies, tramway companies, and textile and tobacco factories—had a number of distinguishing features: they were intimately connected to the regions' integration into the world capitalist system;[43] they were among the earliest sites of contestation; they were frequent and visible sites of contestation; and they occasionally were in some sense exemplary sites of contestation. In other words, it seems that workers in these sectors and sites often advised, assisted, and led contesting workers in other sectors.[44]

As had been the case elsewhere in the Ottoman Empire and the southern Mediterranean (especially North Africa), the first and largest strikes in Syria and Egypt occurred in and over newly created spaces (ports, railways, and tramways) that very quickly became contested spaces.[45] Port cities in particular had a high concentration of such sectors as they emerged as "the privileged locales of contact with the world capitalist economy . . . [and] captured and reflected in concrete form the entire episode of incorporation."[46] In Egypt the coal heavers of Alexandria went on strike in April 1882, and in the late 1890s a series of strikes paralyzed the ports of Port Sa'id and Alexandria.[47] The port of Beirut was the stage of labor unrest almost as soon as the Compagnie du Port was established in 1893.[48] The ongoing efforts of the French-owned and -managed Compagnie du Port (which by 1913 employed two hundred to three hundred workers) to control and regulate port activities at sea, on the docks, and at customs level clashed with the interests of an entire subproletariat of indigenous porters and *mahonniers* (stevedores), who feared that their means of subsistence was under threat.[49] Throughout the empire the *mahonniers* and porters *(ḥammāl)* were the bêtes noires of European merchants and their consuls, who deemed them a riotous, rowdy crowd standing in the way of efficiency and hanging on to obsolete guild norms.[50]

In fact a study based on data covering the period 1870–1996 and pertaining to labor unrest throughout the world has shown that, for the entire period covered by the study, "transportation labor unrest is the largest category, surpassing even manufacturing. . . . Indeed, the percentage of total labor unrest accounted for by transportation workers surpassed all other categories in every decade except three: the 1870s and 1930s . . . and the 1990s. . . . Labor unrest among ship and dockworkers account for 52% of the total transportation labor unrest mentions over the entire 1870 to 1996 period." For the period that interests us, the transportation categories are shipping and docking and railroads.[51]

The labor militancy linked to ports (especially docks) might have been connected to a number of factors. First, transport workers have historically possessed strong bargaining power, as the "relative fortunes of capitalists in different locations . . . are greatly impacted by the development of new transportation networks . . . , as well as by the disruption of existing transportation networks, including disruptions caused by workers' struggles."[52] Second, various forms of employment coexisted in ports; while a large number of workers were employed in the construction of the port itself, many premodern jobs had survived and had to adapt to much larger freights, a new infrastructure, and a completely novel (and European) management system. Third, these various forms of employment followed different tempos; as one historian of Marseilles points out, "Sur les ports et les docks, l'activité évolue plus fortement, selon les arrivées et les départs des navires: il s'agit d'un secteur sensible aux variations, à la concurrence. . . . Les entrepreneurs fonctionnent par conséquent avec deux types d'ouvriers: un groupe fixe, les *abonnés,* et un groupe variable, les *accidentels*. . . . C'est parmi ces manoeuvres et journaliers . . . entièrement soumis aux variations conjoncturelles que la concurrence est la plus forte, et les conflits les plus fréquents et violents."[53] It seems that dockworkers (as well as agricultural workers, construction workers, and gas workers) were often recruited as "casual, seasonal or project laborers, whose working lives were characterized by forms of discontinuity: by episodic work periods, by frequent changes of employer, and often of work site and sometimes of geographical locale as well."[54]

The new sectors that were most prone to labor unrest had important characteristics in common, many of which were linked to globalization. To start with, they employed large numbers of workers.[55] Because they were sites of contention throughout the world, and given their deep connection to international capitalism, they mattered, and disturbances there received much coverage in the international press. By the late nineteenth century workers in cities connected to global information networks had gained unprecedented access to news about the rest of the world. Through newspapers and plays and by word of mouth they learned more about labor unrest, strikes, and workers' gains throughout the world than ever before, and this knowledge must have contributed to workers' militancy. Thus the increase in strikes between 1900 and 1914 in the Eastern Mediterranean is both in line with and connected to the exponential rise of strikes throughout the rest of the world during the same period, and specifically to the movement of information about them.[56] The radicalizing effect of the rapid movement of information between one part of the world and another was not lost on contemporary observers. *Al-Muqtaṭaf* alluded to it in 1889, complaining, "News [of strikes in Europe in October 1889] come to us as quickly as thunderstorms, as if it were among the most difficult political issues to resolve."[57] The French consul of Beirut realized the subversive effect of news circulation between cities, especially pertaining to workers' militancy; reporting in 1908 on labor unrest at the Compagnie du Port, he speculated that "la nouvelle, récemment publiée par l'agence Fournier, que les ouvriers des ports de Constantinople, Smyrne et Salonique se sont mis en grève ne peut qu'encourager le mouvement."[58] The Ottoman Foreign Ministry seems to have reached the same conclusion, as attested by the Ministry's nervous and regular reports on strikes in various corners and industries of the world.[59]

POPULAR ANTI-IMPERIALISM

Another shared characteristic of these sectors and sites of contestation is that they were European-owned and -managed.[60] Many studies have explained conflicts between workers and employers in terms of proto-nationalism or, anachronistically, nationalism. The notion of *popular anti-imperialism* seems more suitable and useful, alongside what I unhappily call *localism,* that is, the emergence of a discourse and subsequent form of social mobilization calling for resistance against direct or indirect imperialism.[61] This popular anti-imperialism and localism brought together various protest groups that contested the shared authority of indigenous elites and foreigners and denounced the illegitimacy of rulers and social elites allying themselves with European interests. These groups had a wide array of grievances and reasons to mobilize, but popular anti-imperialism allowed them to temporarily set aside significant differences and make *foreignness* their common enemy. Foreignness did not refer exclusively to foreigners, but included foreign capital and foreign practice. It could therefore be used to delegitimize natives who contested local tradition or practice, and also those who no longer had the interests of the land and its indigenous inhabitants at heart, just as we saw in some of the monologues that were popular in turn-of-the-century Egypt.[62]

Workers who went on strike in European-owned sectors and sites in Beirut, Cairo, and Alexandria in the late nineteenth century and early twentieth did not necessarily articulate proto-nationalist ideas or programmatically articulate the destruction of empires and an end to colonialism or call for foreigners to abandon these sites and return them to their indigenous owners. Rather they criticized the companies' imposition of *foreign practice,* which was new, or contrary to guild customs, or opposed to decisions collectively made by workers, or actually contrary to Ottoman law. Such a discourse is vividly illustrated in the strike that shook the Compagnie du Port de Beyrouth in 1908. During this incident workers bitterly complained that the company had violated their guild's rules by appointing its own *chefs de service* and inflicting punishment on guild members, a right exclusively reserved to the sheikh of the guild.[63] In the petition they submitted to their employer, the strikers' main accusation against the company was that it was "only Ottoman in name" ("française de fait et ottomane de nom") and that it threatened Ottoman customary practices and welfare.[64] In the late nineteenth century and early twentieth strikes often erupted when workers felt the company was meddling in their affairs and challenging customary practices or collective decisions, rather than out of a programmatically articulated nationalism or anti-imperialism. To suggest that such episodes were more localist and popular anti-imperialist than proto-nationalist does not diminish their significance nor their mobilizational power. On the contrary, it was precisely because of this localist rallying cry that workers were able to effectively challenge the authority of foreign companies and mobilize popular and institutional support. Indeed strikes in European-owned and -managed sectors indubitably enjoyed the support of large segments of the urban population, manifested in a particularly visible, intense, and passionate way. Support came from common people, entire neighborhoods, and various segments of the population, including indigenous merchants.[65]

In more than one instance popular support for strikers also came from urban institutions, such as municipalities and local governorships. The municipality of Beirut actively sought to protect the rights of local workers employed in European-owned companies. It often sided with workers against their employers, provoking the companies' wrath. On more than one occasion the wali of Beirut tried to defend porters' rights by interceding on their behalf with the Compagnie du Port. In 1893 the newly established port company retained only a small number of the porters previously employed by the local customhouse before the company took over. The wali of Beirut, Khalid Bey, intervened and asked the concession holder of the port, M. de Perthuis, to recruit all the porters who had previously been employed by the old customhouse.[66] Thirteen years later the municipality intervened on behalf of Sa'id Kaddourah, "chef d'équipe d'ouvriers du port ayant été sans raison suspendu de ses fonctions," and asked the port company to reemploy him.[67] In 1912 tensions rose so high between the municipality and the Beirut gas company that the company directly accused the municipality of fomenting labor unrest. That year a vitriolic telegram was sent to Istanbul by the director of the Beirut gas company, accusing the municipality of encouraging workers to strike and threatening to stop providing gaslight to the city if the imperial government did not intervene and defend the company's rights: "La municipalité s'alliant avec divers perturbateurs ameute public répandant bruits les plus malveillants *pousse nos ouvriers à la grève*. . . . La municipalité et les perturbateurs continuent activement leur campagne de malveillances espérant nous *intimider jetant le trouble parmi nos ouvriers et dans nos usines*. . . . Gouvernment impérial étant fortement intéressé à protéger capitaux travaillant dans l'Empire nous sollicitons votre haute intervention."[68]

In some instances the support expressed by local populations almost turned labor strikes into full-fledged urban spectacles and riots. During the Cairo Tramway Company strike of July 1911 strikers in Bab al-Hadid, Bulaq, Giza, and 'Abbasiyya held banners with logos enjoining the population to support them and carried boxes for contributions. Their calls were answered: families took to the streets, demonstrating alongside workers, and a whole show was mounted with a parade, an orchestra, and carts to collect donations in popular neighborhoods.[69] When the Tramway Company decided to challenge strikers by running some of its lines, segments of the population decided to show their support in a more hands-on fashion: in various popular neighborhoods such as Husayniyya, Bulaq, and 'Abbasiyya, inhabitants stopped the carriage and beat the riders and set it on fire.[70] In 1894 workers, administrators, and merchants joined forces in an uprising against the

Compagnie du Port de Beyrouth, as "une coalition des employés et portefaix de l'ancienne douane, des autorités locales et du commerce tout entier se forma contre la nouvelle entreprise; les bâtiments de la douane furent envahis, le personnel de la compagnie maltraité et chassé, et les services furent repris tels qu'ils existaient auparavant."[71]

The mobilizing channels strikers used to rally popular support as well as those used by their supporters to express their solidarity with workers combined carnavalesque methods such as parades with alternative ways of using and appropriating institutions such as the press. Sometime, perhaps in the 1870s, newspapers began publishing *shakāwa* (petitions and complaints) written on workers' behalf, exposing their grievances and making their demands public.[72] Not much is known about the writing process itself, or whether the idea of submitting a copy of the petition to periodicals came from strikers or from the newspaper itself. Nevertheless by the first years of the twentieth century such a procedure had become fairly common practice.[73] At the same time the press became a forum for people to demonstrate their support with strikers. Perhaps one of the most remarkable illustrations of the press's appropriation by workers and the plebe generally was the petition sent by the residents of Bulaq in 1911, signed by "ahāli Bulaq" (the people or residents of Bulaq, a neighborhood of Cairo). Having addressed the initial petition in the form of a telegraph to the khedivial Qaimaqam in Alexandria, the inhabitants of Bulaq proceeded to send a copy to *al-Mu'ayyad,* which published it. The telegram expressed the residents' "discontent at the damage to public interest *[ta'ṭīl maṣāliḥ al-jumhūr]* due to the stubbornness of the director of the Tramway company against the just demands of the workers," and their wish for government intervention "for the sake of the workers and the inhabitants of the capital."[74] Evidently the idea of a neighborhood writing a petition was in itself not new; the novelty lay in the publicity acquired by the publication of the petition in a newspaper. This made the petition public knowledge and public property and allowed workers to turn the press into a court for the people.

GLOBALIZATION, LABOR MIGRATIONS, AND THE MEDITERRANEAN: SHIFTING THE PARADIGM FROM FOREIGN TO MIGRANT WORKERS

Localism and general opposition to European encroachment thus partly explain the predominance of strikes and labor militancy in global sites and sectors. Such explanations are not comprehensive, though, given that it was foreigners themselves who conducted a large number of strikes against foreign and European employers. Indeed such sites and industries (ports, railway and tramway companies, and the construction and tobacco industries) had more in common than merely being managed and owned by Europeans; throughout the world, the Mediterranean, and more specifically the Ottoman Empire and Egypt they employed large numbers of migrant and immigrant workers from various Mediterranean regions.[75] In the case of Egypt, the workers came not only from Upper Egypt but also from Italy, Greece, Malta, Syria, and other parts of the Ottoman Empire. Much of the literature on these industries—most prominently the cigarette industry in Egypt and the Ottoman Empire—has acknowledged the significant presence of foreign labor but has classified the subject by explicitly or implicitly concluding that foreign workers (problematically described as "European") were more politically savvy and attuned to working-class politics than the indigenous population.[76] However, little research has been done on the roots of this politicization, its implications for local labor militancy, and the relationship between this nonindigenous proletariat and the Egyptian working class.[77] I seek to fill this gap by analyzing the relationship between global migrations and social contestation, specifically labor militancy.

Between 1870 and 1914 large numbers of people migrated and immigrated throughout the world in search of work. In fact the unparalleled circulation of labor—even compared to today—constituted one of the defining features of the wave of globalization in the period under study.[78] During that period the demand for labor was so great that trains transporting migrant workers to one country or city were sometimes rerouted to more profitable destinations.[79] The Mediterranean world was, as a whole, an important player in these mass migrations, and some of its regions were particularly affected.[80] On the sending end, Italy and Syria (especially Mount Lebanon) were among the regions proportionally most affected by emigration during that period, and certain villages in Italy and Mount Lebanon saw large percentages of their population emigrate to North and South America. By one estimate fourteen million laborers emigrated from Italy alone between 1870 and 1914, becoming what the historian Donna Gabaccia has termed "workers of the world."[81]

Emigration, immigration, and migration were not solely transatlantic. Starting in the late nineteenth century and continuing well into the twentieth many Mediterranean cities became poles of attraction for, among others, a plethora of Mediterranean immigrant workers. Marseilles, with its large Italian working class,[82] and Izmir, Salonica, Tunis, and Alexandria saw their populations swell, partly as a consequence of rural and internal migration, but also because of trans-Mediterranean labor migration. Greeks and Italians, Maltese, Syrians, Armenians, and Jews from the Ottoman Empire, the Austro-Hungarian Empire, and Italy formed networks of labor that circulated throughout the Mediterranean in search of employment. These labor migrations were mostly from the northern to the southern shores of the Mediterranean, in a reverse trend to that which would follow a hundred years later—albeit it with serious differences, not least of which are our present world's stringent immigration laws, a world order allowing for the exclusion of undesirables, and a very different balance of power between exporting and importing nations.

Between 1870 and 1890 workers from the Balkans, Italy, and Spain flocked to Egypt, North Africa, and various parts of the Eastern Mediterranean and Anatolia, where the increase in real wages was the highest around the Mediterranean periphery.[83] Some settled for long periods in their host city; others were seasonal or traveling migrants *(gens de passage)*.[84] Beirut (and Syria generally) constituted one pole of attraction for migrant labor—among others, Italian workers and southern, central, and eastern European Christians and Jews involved in craftwork.[85] The reports of the Alliance Israélite Universelle branch in Beirut, a secular institution that sought to educate, emancipate, and modernize Oriental Jews and initiate them into the principles of the French Enlightenment,[86] indicate that the association was establishing apprenticeship programs in Beirut for Jews from Palestine and Syria as well as central and eastern Europe. Significantly this apprenticeship in Beirut targeted central and eastern European Jews—German, Austrian, Polish, and Romanian Jews are mentioned—who either had already moved to Palestine or were in Syria, perhaps on their way to Palestine.[87] The aim was to provide training in a big city for carpenters, masons, tailors, and even porters.[88]

Beirut occupied a relatively modest place on the map of labor migration compared to Cairo and Alexandria. In this geography of migration few countries attracted Mediterranean workers as much as Egypt. I have already described some of the main reasons behind Egypt's attractiveness and the resulting convergence of various Mediterranean labor networks there: the incorporation into the world economy and consequently a booming construction industry, developing factories, and spectacular growth in trade. The first serious injection of immigrants into Egypt came during the boom of 1860–70. By 1897 between 15 and 20 percent of Alexandria's 320,000 inhabitants were Mediterranean and the city was home to native Egyptian as well as Greek, Italian, Armenian, Maltese, and Syrian workers, among others.[89] These Mediterranean workers were engaged in all kinds of professional activities, in crafts as well as small-scale manufacturing, but the ports, railways, and tobacco factories were unique in one respect: they employed high concentrations of nonindigenous workers. The census of 1897 estimated the presence of this nonindigenous labor force at a mere 5 percent in industry, commerce, and services, most of them working in industries in Alexandria and Cairo.[90] In some sectors the percentage was much higher; a good 50 percent of the workers in Alexandria's Autofage foundry were Italian, around 20 percent of construction workers were nonindigenous (mostly Italian), and a similar percentage of nonindigenous workers were employed in clothing manufacturing.[91] The figures for this trans-Mediterranean proletariat, in both absolute and relative terms, were to increase over time. According to one estimate, approximately 25 percent of Egypt's railroad workers were foreign in 1907; this translated into roughly five thousand foreign workers in the largest urban sector of employment.[92] By 1917 southern European workers represented around 20 percent of workers in Alexandria's industrial sector.[93] Needless to say, many of these trans-Mediterranean immigrant workers in Egypt were not quite foreign—or at least not foreign in the same way—since they were *Ottoman* subjects.[94] Indeed in certain sectors, especially the tobacco industry and tailoring, Ottoman workers—Greeks, Armenians, Syrians, and Jews from the Balkans—made up a large proportion of the labor force. In one of the strikes organized by the tailors of Cairo in 1901, slogans were chanted in Ottoman Turkish as tobacco workers and tailors paraded throughout the streets of the capital. With names such as Khayyat, Labotado, Lefanto, Cattawi, Shouareth, Kodel, 'Arman, Marchakian, Otiri, Khishda, and Diyano, the strikers proudly carried the multilingual banner of their association, with their logo written in Arabic, Italian, Greek, Judeo-Spanish, and Armenian. Nor were they a small group; by the time the demonstrators reached Midan al-Opera in Cairo they numbered around three thousand.[95]

International Labor Migration and Radicalism

Immigrant and migrant workers were thus employed in large numbers by certain sites and industries. They were particularly active and even overrepresented in strikes, both as common participants and as leaders. Indeed foreign names constantly appeared in conjunction with strikes and were particularly visible at the top organizational level as names of spokesmen, instigators, and organizers.[96] Foreigners were at the forefront of mobilizing their fellow workers for collective action, publishing petitions in newspapers, and circulating multilingual tracts and manifestos promoting socialist, anarchist, or anarchosyndicalist ideas.[97] What were the factors behind the militancy of migrant workers? A number of features seem to have made migrant and immigrant workers lean toward radicalism and labor activism: (1) their connection to internationalist movements and networks, such as the Second Socialist International, and anarchist networks; (2) the link between migration and unemployment; (3) their privileged access to information; and (4) the special relationship between immigrant workers and immigrant intellectuals.

Throughout the world immigrant and migrant workers seem to have been more aware of the advantages of establishing connections with internationalist movements, networks, and organizations than were their more stable counterparts (many of whom were themselves internal migrants).[98] From that perspective Egypt was no exception. Not only had its trans-Mediterranean migrant workers previously participated in or been exposed to labor contestation and strikes, but many of them formally belonged to various global and internationalist radical networks and organizations. One such network was established by leaders of the Second International Socialist, who in the early 1890s began looking into the idea of organizing migrant and emigrant workers. In 1893, after long debates on the issue, the International Socialist passed a motion asking various socialist parties in the world (most prominently the Italian Socialist Party) to carry out propaganda and organizational campaigns among emigrant workers and actively promote their affiliation with labor unions in host countries.[99] Various labor organizations that had been the fruit of local initiative sought to join these internationalist and global networks for increased protection and funding. In Cairo the Ligue des Employés du Caire, which had five hundred members and was founded around 1905 to "defend the interests of employees against capitalists," wrote to the Office of the Socialist International in Brussels, asking the Office to "point the League to the attention of international socialists so that they take interest in it."[100] Roman Hanssen, who wrote the letter on behalf of the League's president, Mr. Delbourgo, underlined the association's need for guidance:

> Je me permets d'attirer votre attention sur une ligue qui a été fondée dernièrement au Caire pour défendre les intérêts des employés contre les capitalistes. Elle compte 500 membres, existe depuis dix mois et s'occupe spécialement de régler les conflits entre ouvriers et patrons. Eloignée de tout parti organisé et par conséquent sans aucune direction, la Ligue s'adresse à vous, afin que vous l'assistiez par tous les moyens possibles (conseils et collaborations), pour émanciper les employés, afin que ceux-ci comprennent qu'ils ne sont pas des esclaves mais possèdent les mêmes droits que les autres citoyens. Nous vous serions bien reconnaissants si vous vouliez aussi attirer l'attention des socialistes internationaux sur la ligue des Employés du Caire et les prier de s'intéresser à elle.[101]

Through this connection to internationalist organizations immigrant workers could plug into "communications networks capable of organizing collective action."[102] Potentially they could also affect the brand of radicalism that was brewing in such cities, perhaps seeking to align it with a certain European and institutional or official interpretation of socialism.

Professional insecurity was another factor that most likely contributed to the radicalization of migrant and immigrant workers. Little is known about migrants' recruitment processes and professional networks in Egypt and Syria. It seems that workers went wherever they could find work, and that work contracts were not the norm.[103] In some cases there might also have been more systematic recruitment mechanisms, such as placement offices or recruiters who would go from town to town arranging for workers' transportation and promising, if not delivering, employment; these mechanisms remain to be systematically investigated.[104] More often than not, though, people left their town in Italy, Syria, or the Balkans, following the footsteps of friends or relatives, upon hearing news of employment opportunities in one part of the world or another. The memoirs of Giovanni Veltri describe what must have been a common story among migrants. An uneducated man from Calabria, Veltri decided to immigrate to Africa, as he put it, in 1883 at the age of fifteen and left his hometown accompanied by a couple of friends and cousins. Disembarking in Tunis they contacted a contractor friend who advised them to head to Souk Ahras in Algeria. Finding no work there either, they moved from one Algerian town to another before learning railway construction skills from fellow Grimaldesi in North Africa and briefly working on a railway line there. Finally Veltri decided to leave North Africa and try his luck in the American Northwest.[105] If his autobiographical novel is to be trusted, Panait Istrati (1884–1935), a half-Greek, half-Romanian jack of all trades, left his native Romania and headed to Egypt following in his best friend's footsteps. He was at various times a painter, a cabaret waiter, and a pastry chef in Cairo and Alexandria before deciding to head to Mount Lebanon. Accompanied by a compatriot he met in Egypt, Istrati spent months painting and decorating houses in the village of Ghazir. He most likely engaged in various political activities as well; according to one biographical source, Istrati was active in revolutionary movements throughout the world and was one of the founders of the Romanian Socialist Party in 1909.[106]

These two examples point to a general feature of migrant labor: that employment was often volatile and could come to a sudden end, as large construction projects were abandoned halfway for lack of funding or simply terminated without prior notice.[107] Many migrant workers were in fact prospective workers who had no guarantee of being employed. Many Italians headed south and east, lured by the possibilities of recruitment by railway or port companies and convinced they would easily be recruited; they were often disappointed. In the late 1890s and for the following twenty-five years Italian consuls in various Mediterranean cities deplored their compatriots' rush south and did their best to dissuade workers from heading to Egypt and Syria in search of employment in large infrastructure projects, especially railroad construction. One report sent by the Italian consulate in Beirut in 1896 did not mince words:

> Many Italian workers come here from Smyrne and from other place in Turkey, hoping to find work in the railroad construction, and they find themselves instead condemned to turn back, disillusioned, or to opt for the streets, unemployed and deprived of every means. To how many letters sent to me from Anatolia and Macedonia, have I replied that there were no jobs here in Syria. Yet filled with false information, many workers have ventured to these other shores. It is urgent that it be publicly known, in an explicit manner, what the state of public works in this region is truly like.[108]

Another report sent that same year from the consul in Alexandria warned of the large numbers of Italian workers who converged there only to find themselves unemployed and on the streets, prompting the Ministry of Foreign Affairs to "invite [Italian] workers to abstain, at least for now, from trying to find work in Egypt."[109] Time and again similar grim warnings were sent from Italian consuls around the Eastern Mediterranean, reminding prospective emigrants of the fate of their compatriots who had ventured east only to remain unemployed, "leading a life of laziness," or having to contend with miserable salaries.[110]

The frantic reports written by Italian and other consuls throughout the Southern and Eastern Mediterranean indicate that the potential for labor subversion and radical militancy among a roaming, migrant, and often unemployed labor force was not lost on local observers. It is highly likely that the relationship between transience and unemployment, on one hand, and potential trouble in the form of labor militancy, on the other, was not a mere figment of consular imagination. A number of studies on workers corroborate this association between migration and subversion, not only around the Mediterranean but throughout the world. Michelle Perrot's study on workers in late nineteenth-century France indicated that police reports labeled as most dangerous "ces ouvriers nomades qui paraissent n'avoir d'autre but que de semer la discorde partout où ils passent" and concluded that "le migrant est, par définition, suspect; l'instabilité sent l'immoralité."[111] Besides police anxieties, Perrot has argued, this association between migration and subversion rested on known facts, such as "l'influence excitante des étrangers, belges surtout, dans l'industrie du Nord de la France."[112] This association between movement and radicalism was found in various parts of the world, in the metropoles as well as in colonies.[113]

In the late nineteenth century and early twentieth perhaps no group of migrants was as effectively engaged in migrating globally *and* spreading radical ideas and participating in radical movements as Italian workers, who, in the words of two historians, "probably came clos[er] to being an international revolutionary proletariat than any other group of workers."[114] The rather panicky tracking of Italian railroad workers in the Ottoman Empire and the constant background checks involving the shuttling of lists of names across Europe and beyond, whose purpose was to identify and purge anarchist and socialist workers, seem to corroborate the Italians' reputation as an international revolutionary proletariat on the move. The letter the Ottoman consul in Genoa sent to the Ministry of the Interior in Istanbul provides one eloquent example of the fear Italian migrant workers elicited and the kind of surveillance to which they were subjected: "Vu le nombre considérable d'ouvriers italiens qui se trouvent engagés dans le service de nouvelles voies ferrées de l'empire, et d'autre gens de cette catégorie qui se rendent continuellement en Europe dans le même but, les autorités impériales feraient bien d'exercer à leur égard une surveillance active et rigoureuse."[115] This kind of suspicion was evidently not limited to Italians, but Italian workers do seem to have been singled out as particularly promising troublemakers.[116]

The fact is, even when immigrant workers had not participated in strikes prior to their arrival in their host country and had no ties with internationalist workers' organizations, they seem to have known about instances of labor unrest occurring wherever they had compatriots—which was usually everywhere. Workers belonging to diasporic migrant communities, Italians, Greeks, Syrians, and Armenians, were plugged into formal and informal networks of information through the press, but also by word of mouth. In some cases the combination of roaming foreigners with locals who had come back after traveling and working in other parts of the world was deemed particularly explosive. In the words of one worried French observer based in Mount Lebanon:

> Les nombreuses grèves qui, depuis l'établissement de la constitution, se sont déclarées un peu partout dans l'Empire ottoman sont d'un exemple trop facile pour ne pas tenter un jour la population séricole du Liban et de la Syrie. Les meneurs ne manqueraient point, soit parmi les indigènes rentrés, sans avoir fait fortune, des républiques americaines où les questions ouvrières donnent lieu à de si fréquents conflits, soit parmi ces Européens sans moyen d'existence défini qui rodent un peu partout en Syrie et dont quelques-uns même s'emploient de temps à autre, comme chauffeurs ou mécaniciens, dans certaines filatures de la région. [117]

All this suggests that there was an almost intrinsic relationship between mobility and internationalist ideas. More specifically, workers, because they represented the majority of migrants and immigrants at the turn of the century, and even if they did not adhere to such ideologies, had a very strong chance of being exposed to, and hence of carrying information on the internationalist idea that affected them most: labor militancy and various brands of leftist radical ideology that were being formulated and disseminated at the time.

Migration also seems to have led to the construction of a special relationship between immigrant workers and immigrant intellectuals and professionals. Various immigrant professionals and intellectuals spoke and negotiated on behalf of striking workers. Many historians have associated the rapprochement between a rising professional middle class and workers, and have identified the role of this middle-class intelligentsia in labor negotiations and representation as a trademark of nationalist politics starting in 1908 in Egypt. It seems that such a practice preceded nationalist politics and was widespread among immigrant communities. In Cairo and Alexandria Greek and Syrian professionals and intellectuals—doctors, journalists, and lawyers—became the spokespeople for workers, negotiated on their behalf with their employers, and generally defended their rights, a practice that "may well have been a way of enhancing the respectability of, and thereby winning broader support for, the new unions."[118] For instance, Dr. Kyriazi led and spoke on behalf of the cigarette rollers' union in Cairo in 1899, and Dr. Pastis led the clothing workers of that city a few years later. Similarly Syrian professionals such as the lawyers George Saidawi in Cairo and Antun 'Arqash in Alexandria represented workers in their negotiations with companies and petitioned for their rights.[119] Indeed throughout the world immigration seems to have predisposed workers and radical intellectuals and professionals to a rapprochement as immigration demarcated class lines somewhat differently. As Charles Tilly has suggested, immigration triggers a series of "continuous processes of collective transformation involving the use of old social networks and categories to produce new ones"; whereas categories "stay put," networks "migrate . . . [and] create new categories."[120] This rapprochement between workers and intellectuals in the host country may have been linked to mechanisms regulating the integration of migrants into a new social setting; perhaps the initial unit of integration in Alexandria came primarily through one's ethnic or religious group, and hence allowed for more interaction between intellectuals and workers than would have been the case in the old country. Robert Ilbert has suggested that Alexandria's Freemason lodges offered a privileged space of encounter between non-indigenous workers and their notables.[121] An analysis of the mechanisms regulating the interaction between immigrant workers and professionals or intellectuals is beyond the scope of this book, yet the number of times a Greek or Syrian professional interceded and negotiated on behalf of striking workers (Greek, Syrian, or more often than not "mixed") certainly suggests that immigrant workers at times enjoyed a privileged relationship with intellectuals, and that this helped them articulate their grievances and organize themselves more effectively.

THE TOBACCO INDUSTRY: A MEDITERRANEAN CULTURE OF CONTESTATION

One industry in particular illustrates the relationship between globalization, migrant labor, and labor militancy. The tobacco industry, one of Egypt's leading factory industries and largest employers, was one of the sectors most persistently affected by strikes in Cairo and Alexandria in the first years of the twentieth century, as well as being the sector employing one of the highest percentages of women.[122] Indeed one historian referred to the "particulière combativité des ouvriers de cigarettes" in Egypt, and another took Cairo's cigarette workers' strike of 1899 as the starting point for the emergence of Egyptian working-class militancy (if not history).[123] Both internal and external factors predisposed tobacco factories to become sites of contention. On a global level the increased mechanization of factories, especially after 1907, as well as the integration of Egypt and various parts of the Ottoman Empire into the world market affected cigarette making throughout the empire particularly severely and led to its decline and to many layoffs.[124]

In Egypt most of the workers employed in the tobacco industry came from Macedonia and Syria, and their immigration was linked to the establishment of the Régie de Tabac Ottoman in 1884. Macedonia and Syria—specifically the regions around Ladiqiyya, Beirut, and parts of Mount Lebanon—were central regions for the cultivation and export of tobacco, as well as relatively important producers of cigarettes. Throughout the empire the company supplied tobacco cultivators with substantial interest-free loans, and hence effectively prevented tobacco merchants and local landholders from financing cultivation. As it began manufacturing and selling its own products, it forced out already established manufacturers and sellers who were simply unable to compete. As a consequence, around three hundred tobacco factories were shut down throughout the empire, and many tobacco workers, mostly of Greek origin, emigrated to Egypt beginning in the 1870s.[125] The big blow for Syria and Mount Lebanon came with the Régie's decision in the 1880s to transfer tobacco cultivators from the Sham provinces to Anatolia and the European parts of the empire. As a consequence, Syria also lost a significant part of its tobacco-related labor force.

In Egypt, throughout the Ottoman Empire, around the Mediterranean, and beyond, the cigarette industry seems to have produced a culture of contestation and an inclination toward radical politics.[126] Throughout the Ottoman Mediterranean tobacco workers engaged in strikes and labor unrest and were involved in various political movements of the Left—syndicalist, socialist, and anarchist.[127] In some cities (Salonica perhaps figuring at the top of the list of Ottoman cities) tobacco factory workers were the focus of serious educational projects in the early twentieth century, as well as politicization efforts and propaganda work by socialist and anarchist organizations. Among the seventeen brochures produced by the printing press of the Fédération Ouvrière de Salonique in 1914, found in its "bibliothèque socialiste," the tobacco industry was the only industrial sector that received coverage; it was the subject of essays with titles such as "Le procès des ouvriers du tabac" and "Le lock-out du tabac industriel."[128] It would also not be surprising to discover that, like their fellow tobacco workers in North, Central, and Latin America, Ottoman and Egyptian tobacco workers engaged in the practice of having a reader, who would read novels, newspapers, and pamphlets to fellow workers in factories.[129] This culture of contestation and high degree of class consciousness and politicization that characterized tobacco workers were not unknown to the Ottoman state, which did its best to prevent propaganda material produced by tobacco workers in places such as Manastir, and destined for workers throughout the empire, from entering the empire.[130] Egypt thus was no different from the rest of the Ottoman Empire, the Mediterranean, and the world when it came to having particularly politicized, organized, and class-conscious tobacco workers. There too tobacco workers disrupted production for long stretches of time from the late nineteenth century onward, organized the first recorded strike in Cairo and the second one in Alexandria, coordinated strikes between various factories, and formed the first union. Most significant, at least in Cairo and Alexandria, tobacco workers played a mentoring role when it came to labor unrest, advising workers in other sectors on striking and negotiation tactics.[131]

One of the distinguishing features of the cigarette industry in Egypt was the relatively important presence of Syrian workers, a factor that helps explain their high visibility in labor organization and unrest in that sector.[132] The facts are telling: the cigarette workers' strike of 1903 in Cairo was led by a Syrian; the earliest Egyptian workers' organization was an association of Syrian and Egyptian Workers, al-Jamʿiyya al-Iqtiṣādiyya al-Sharqiyya li ʿUmmāl al-Lafāʾif bi Miṣr (the Eastern Economic Association in Egypt for Cigarette Workers), established in 1896; and when cigarette rollers advised striking tailors and lent them their support in 1901, Syrians (tobacco workers or professionals who were sympathetic to the workers' cause) were there to give speeches and help maintain the momentum of the strike.[133] Whereas Syrians in Egypt have been portrayed as middlemen in the fields of business and administration,[134] the participation of Syrian workers and, in may instances, their leadership in militant activities within the tobacco industry suggest that they might have been important liaisons between nonindigenous and Egyptian workers. In any case, it is highly likely that their shared language facilitated the communication and coordination of militant action with the indigenous working class—not that many of the other nonindigenous workers did not speak Arabic (a point to which I will return). As immigrants and like their Greek, Italian, and Armenian counterparts, Syrian workers in Egypt were most likely plugged into networks of social contestation in Egypt as well as in Syria and throughout the world.

CLASS AND ETHNICITY: THE INTERACTION BETWEEN INDIGENOUS AND NONINDIGENOUS LABOR

Working and Striking Together

A number of Syrian workers may have played the go-between and provided a communication channel to share contestation strategies and radical ideas between indigenous and nonindigenous workers. How often did workers from different ethnic groups communicate, mobilize, and act together? How fluid were the boundaries between workers belonging to various ethnic groups? Did ideas, concepts, militancy, activism, or even workers themselves move between all these different ethnic groups? And how did the relationship between workers from different ethnicities impact the dissemination and brand of leftist radical ideas? In my analysis of the Italian anarchist network based in Alexandria I began tackling these questions, but it is now time to do so more systematically. First, let us consider the hotly debated issue of ethnic labor, or, more accurately, the existence of a split labor market, which made sectors, positions, and wages dependent on workers' place in a certain implicit racial hierarchy.

Until the 1970s a number of historians maintained that an ethnic division of labor existed among Ottoman workers, especially in the industrial arts, and that certain ethnic groups dominated certain professions.[135] However, recent studies have challenged this notion, and so have various accounts by workers on life in Alexandria, Cairo, and Istanbul.[136] The memoirs and biographical writings of Pea and Istrati depicted worksites employing a mix of indigenous and migrant workers of various ethnicities. Istrati's Greco-Romanian narrator works on a construction site with indigenous and immigrant workers, and Pea claimed, "[The indigenous people *(il popolo)*] have worked in fields for centuries. They are the people who work with me . . . at the Port, at the office, inside the boiler. They are like me, oppressed by social injustice."[137] This picture has been corroborated by contemporary studies on workers' conditions and by information concerning the collaboration of workers from different ethnicities during strikes and for the establishment of associations.[138]

All this, however, does not necessarily eliminate the existence of different salaries and hierarchies based on ethnicity; these hierarchies might have been eroded in given sectors at given times, but a fair number of sources point to differences in salaries between indigenous and foreign workers in various professions. Of course neither foreign nor indigenous workers were homogeneous categories. Divisions and hierarchies among cabbies in Cairo between local Egyptian Cairenes, migrants from Upper Egypt, Sudanese, and Berbers are illustrated by the petitions sent to the police and the minister of the interior by the Upper Egyptians asking for a separate head (sheikh) and complaining of discrimination by the Arab sheikh of their guild.[139] Similarly, some foreigners were more foreign than others, and this was reflected in the positions they occupied as well as their salaries.

Indeed the fates of all these categories (local and foreign, foreign and less foreign, etc.) were inextricably linked to one another, and their wages and places within the labor hierarchy were determined in relation to the Other.[140] In some sense, it was employers themselves (and mostly European employers) who created the two categories of foreign and indigenous labor by favoring the former over the latter and consistently discriminating against the latter in terms of wages and job hierarchy.[141] But these categories were in flux as well and could be negotiable, especially if the state or a consul decided to fight for the rights of a given ethnicity or nationality. The correspondence between various ministers and state board members on one hand, and the railway and telegraph companies on the other, illustrates the kind of battles (and occasional successes) that went on in the period under study. In 1883 the president of the Council of Ministers, Cherif Pasha, upon hearing of the retirement of Mr. George, "sous-inspecteur des télégraphes égyptiens," firmly insisted that his successor be "un Egyptien, et non un étranger. Depuis que les télégraphes égyptiens existent, et notamment depuis que l'inspection générale en est confiée à Mr Flayer, des Egyptiens ont dû être formés et il n'est pas à supposer qu'on ne trouve parmi eux quelqu'un qui soit en état de remplir les fonctions de sous-inspecteur."[142] A few years later the president of the Railway Board, Takwor Pasha Agopian, scribbled in the margins of a memo that he did not see why there should be a distinction between Egyptian and foreign workers.[143]

Although more research needs to be done, proceeding case by case as well as sector by sector, the evidence suggests that sectors created by foreign capital (such as ports, railways, tramways, and tobacco factories) had a strong labor hierarchy based on ethnicity and that this fact had repercussions on workers' militancy and their involvement in strikes. The imposed hierarchy and discrimination against indigenous workers often led to strikes and protests. For example, in 1900 indigenous workers at Alexandria's tramway company went on strike protesting against the fact that certain positions, such as *mufattishīn* (ticket controllers), were available only to non-Egyptians, and that it was precisely in these positions that opportunities for professional advancement existed. In 1893 Beirut's indigenous *mahonniers* went on strike protesting against the Compagnie du Port's preferential employment of foreign workers.[144] At the same time, resentment between indigenous and non-indigenous workers went both ways. While indigenous workers in Cairo, Alexandria, and Beirut felt that immigrant workers had taken over their turf, occupied higher echelons of employment, received higher wages, and generally enjoyed better treatment by company owners, immigrant workers also resented their indigenous counterparts who were catching up, quickly acquiring new skills and often willing to work for lower wages.[145] In 1877 a British observer noted, "The best work [in wood, but also in bricklaying and masonry] in Cairo and Alexandria is all done by foreigners, at wages double, or even treble those paid to native hands." But he also pointed out that indigenous workers were catching up in quite a few sectors:

> [The railway engineering work] is chiefly done by Englishmen, at wages ranging from 8p to 25£ a month, or by Frenchmen or Germans at from twenty to thirty per cent less. But in this craft natives have, within the past few years, qualified to an extent which has sensibly reduced the number of Europeans employed, with the result that both on the railways and in fixed factories, a large proportion of the engine-drivers are now Egyptians, receiving from 8p to 19£ a month. In the other trades Maltese take the lead in respect alike of skill and wages, receiving as ordinary workmen, 5s, or as foremen, from 6s to 8s a day; Frenchmen, Italians, and Greeks ranking next, at from 3s to 5s per diem.[146]

In Alexandria the relatively low real wages for foreign skilled workers compared to wages in Cairo might have added to the level of resentment of immigrant workers toward locals.[147] Perhaps a good way for migrant workers to break the competition was to make sure their indigenous counterparts did not settle for wages that threatened their recruitment opportunities or their salaries. In other words, it was often to the economic advantage of migrant and immigrant workers to initiate indigenous workers into a certain terminology of labor rights, share with them international methods of labor contestation and negotiations, and help them unionize and organize strikes.

Italian consular reports from the first years of the twentieth century nervously noted that "strikers' socialist agitation" had appeared in Egypt and was gaining ground among various nationalities, including indigenous workers. According to these reports, the Cairo cigarette workers' strikes of 1901 had not presented a serious threat, given that Greek subjects constituted the overwhelming majority of strikers; their demands had not been met, and they had failed to get the participation of indigenous workers. Things were different in 1902, however; the strikes were no longer limited to Greeks but had spread to other nationalities (specifically to Italian and indigenous workers), and to other sectors as well.[148] The reports also pointed out that foreign workers, Greeks and some Italians, convinced the workers employed at the Soussa tobacco factory, all of whom were indigenous Egyptians, to go on strike, a phenomenon that the writer of the report deemed to be "rather serious."[149] The British also were worried by the spread of strikes to the indigenous working class; in fact one report, again on the cigarette rollers' strike of 1902, is worth quoting at length:

> The strike of the cigarette-rollers, which followed shortly on that of the tailors, has, in some respects, been more serious. The broad facts of this case are as follows: almost all the large manufacturers of cigarettes are Greeks. About a year or so ago, a strike occurred amongst their workmen, who are principally Greeks and Syrian Christians. The result was that a Syndicate was formed amongst all the leading manufacturers, who agreed that they would all accord identical terms to their workmen. A small firm, Messrs Soussa Brothers, did not join this Syndicate at the time; their business was purely local and did not attract much attention. Messrs Soussa employ mainly native workmen, who are less skilled than Europeans, but who work at much lower rates. Being, therefore, able to undersell the members of the Syndicate, they recently secured a very large order for the delivery of cigarettes in South Africa. This alarmed both the members of the syndicate and their workmen. The result was that strong pressure was exerted by the Greek workmen to prevent the natives accepting Messrs Soussa's terms. Some of these men, being, more often than not, terrorized by the Greeks, struck; others, under police guard, continued at work. Riots occurred in the streets. A very rigorous system of picketing was adopted by the Greeks against the native non-strikers. In this case, therefore, there was manifestly a serious risk that the racial aspect of the affair would be brought into strong prominence.[150]

This example illustrates how, in the long run, strikes and workers' militancy could not remain confined to either foreigners or indigenous Egyptians, given how linked their employment opportunities and conditions were. It also suggests that ethnicity and class were inseparable markers, regardless of the overemphasis on ethnicity in many consular reports as the main factor behind tensions and conflicts.

After Work: Multiethnic Living

Workers of various ethnicities had to deal and communicate with one another in the workplace, and they also had many other opportunities for daily contact. In both Cairo and Alexandria different ethnic groups shared the same densely populated neighborhoods, a picture confirmed by censuses, personal memoirs, and historical research. For example, in the Jewish quarter of Alexandria lived Jews from the Greek islands (Chios and others) as well as Orthodox Greeks, whereas the Maghribi quarter was inhabited mostly by working-class Egyptians and Italians.[151] Some have argued that the degree of interaction was in fact quite limited; other contemporary and nearly contemporary narratives of life in Cairo and Alexandria have on the contrary painted a much more vivid picture of domestic and social interaction. The commonality of encounters can also be seen in the emergence of a lingua franca and widespread (if perhaps limited) multilingualism among workers, a phenomenon found in port cities around the Mediterranean.[152] One contemporary source in Alexandria commented, "L'Italien . . . est très répandu. . . . Les porteurs arabes mêmes le baragouinent un peu. C'est en Italien également que notre cafetier, Ibrahim, nous dit son plaisir de nous recevoir dans sa baraque."[153] Another source mentioned that Greek, Italian, and indigenous Egyptian domestic servants employed by the Benakis family spoke a number of shared languages between them and with their employers.[154] Historians have also underlined multilingualism and the emergence of lingua francas; Ilbert argued that both indigenous and non-indigenous workers "spoke a specific idiom composed of Greek, Arabic and Italian, which they all understood and which shows the regularity of contacts," and other researchers have suggested that Maltese came to constitute a lingua franca in Alexandria.[155] As one historian felicitously put it, Alexandrians were "promiscuous language users."[156]

I previously discussed the importance of the neighborhood coffeehouse as a multiethnic working-class *lieu de sociabilité* and a favorite space within a larger multiethnic "working-class public sphere" in Alexandria, Cairo, and Beirut.[157] Workers gathered there to relax and enjoy some entertainment, but also to discuss politics and plan strikes.[158] Popular plays, monologues, and songs from the early twentieth century depicted—and sometimes berated—the coffeehouse as a space where class and ethnic barriers were momentarily erased.[159] It was mostly neighborhood people who patronized coffeehouses; as a consequence, coffeehouses in mixed neighborhoods had a multiethnic, multireligious clientele, whereas those in more homogeneous neighborhoods had a homogeneous clientele.[160] Although the mechanisms of labor mobilization (especially during strikes) remain obscure, it is very likely that the networks mobilizing workers were based on residential and neighborhood ties rather than occupational, class-based, or ethnic ties. At least these were the mechanisms of social mobilization in other cities during social movements, for instance during the Paris Commune.[161] Such a hypothesis is quite plausible. Indeed we have seen the importance of the neighborhood as a unit of social contestation (and general socialization); it was initially through its quintessential spaces—the coffeehouse, the street, the workshop—that workers exchanged information and ideas, militated, mobilized, and rallied popular support. The fact that many working-class neighborhoods were ethnically mixed provided a continuous communication channel and allowed for the dissemination of radical ideas between different categories of workers.

RETHINKING ETHNICITY AND FOREIGNNESS

Is it possible that this entire discussion on ethnicity is based on an anachronistic understanding of what ethnicity meant for people at that time? And how did class affect the conception of ethnicity? What exactly was Ottoman identity, and what was its significance for Ottoman workers?[162] What did the adjective *Greek* or *Italian* mean for workers in Cairo and Alexandria in the late nineteenth century, or, for that matter, in Anatolia, Greece, and Italy? Was it primarily a linguistic identity? A consular and legal one? What was the significance of *foreignness*, when many of Alexandria's foreign Greek, Italian, and other workers had known nothing but Egypt? Pea, describing his Alexandrian half-Italian, half-Spanish friend Pipicco, who frequented the anarchist grounds of the Baracca Rossa, wrote that he "knew nothing about Italy . . . nor Spain. He was born here, educated at the school of the 'ignorant' who do not say mass. . . . Pipicco *lacked nationality;* he was *figlio del paese.*"[163] There must have been many such Alexandrians who "lacked nationality" and functioned in a language of their own, incorporating words, expressions, and hand gestures from various Mediterranean cultures. According to Pea, "[They made Alexandria a] Babel . . . which . . . convinced me of the uselessness and damnation of homelands."[164] A recent study on multiethnic Alexandria between 1880 and 1914 has argued that foreignness, especially in a colonial context post-1882, "was above all a position of privilege. If patterns of use and outcome before the courts are used to measure such privilege, it becomes clear that foreignness was not simply determined by birth." Rather it was determined on "a case-by-case basis. The decision to grant consular registration or an identity document to an individual was often the product of incomplete evidence or inconsistent principles. In many cases, foreign and local appeared to be incommensurate rather than counterpart categories. . . . On an individual scale, then, foreignness was a partial and intermittent quality."[165]

The issue of *cosmopolitanism* (a term that probably obscures more than it explains) in cities such as Alexandria is, of course, at the heart of the matter. And yet most discussions of cosmopolitanism that have raged about Alexandria and many other Levantine port cities of the time have not specifically addressed the question "Whose cosmopolitanism?," but have eliminated class as a category of investigation.[166] This is a particularly heavy silence, since workers represented the majority of immigrants and foreigners residing in these cosmopolitan cities. Although an in-depth analysis of cosmopolitanism is beyond the scope of this book, I would like to at least argue for the necessity of tackling the issue of working-class cosmopolitanism and suggest directions for further study.[167]

Ilbert, for one, argues that workers transcended their ethnic identities in order to improve their work conditions, but that in times of crisis ethnic allegiance and later nationalism superseded class interests.[168] He reaches this conclusion concerning turn-of-the-century Alexandria in hindsight, as he extracts an entire history of workers' activism and interaction in the late nineteenth century and early twentieth from one specific period, 1919–21, during which class solidarity was set aside to the advantage of ethnic allegiance.[169] And yet the relationship between ethnicity, nationalism, and labor militancy surely changed over time and was different in 1907, 1914, and 1919. Specifically, nationalism and its relationship to the masses and workers changed dramatically during this period, as nationalism itself began to emerge and take shape and as it shaped and was shaped by radicalism and socialism, as well as other mass ideologies developing at the same time. Furthermore why should one event (namely, the purported victory of ethnicity and nationality over class in 1919) be deemed more telling than various instances of multiethnic collaboration among workers, to the extent that it overrides them? To phrase it differently, just as class solidarity did not always transcend ethnic barriers, neither was it a situation in which, to quote a historian working on the late nineteenth-century Maghrib, "communal identity [always] won out over common economic interests."[170]

As expected, although workers from various ethnicities interacted and collaborated in many instances, the image that transpires from that period is far from one of perfect harmony and cooperation. The limits of interaction between indigenous and nonindigenous labor are evident, and various facts and narratives suggest that relations between these two groups, and more generally between indigenous Egyptians and Europeans,[171] were marred by an underlying racism of southern European working classes toward their Egyptian equivalent. Examples of tensions and conflicts between Egyptians, Italians, Maltese, Syrians, and Greeks, workers or otherwise, also abound. Pea's memoirs allude to this prevalent racism in (even) anarchist and socialist nonindigenous workers' perception and treatment of indigenous workers, and a number of historians have concluded that "overall, nationalism and labor market competition taken together meant that quite severe violence, even death, was a threat and a reality on Cairo's building sites in the second half of 1907."[172] This kind of confrontation and violence was certainly not specific to Egypt, nor was it specific to colonial or semicolonial situations; ethnic relations between French and Italian dock workers in Marseilles around the same period were even more marred by racism and violence, with French employees attacking Italian workers, demanding their expulsion and replacement by French workers. Starting in 1870 French workers' associations became increasingly mobilized around anti-Italian rhetoric and action, mounted strikes protesting the use of foreign labor, circulated petitions, and organized public meetings to encourage popular and political support and push for measures discriminating against foreign labor.[173] Examples abound for the rest of the world as well, the United States included. What was different in the case of Egypt was the existing balance of power. Partly because they did not have the backing and infrastructure of an independent state behind them, Egyptian indigenous workers certainly never had the same possibility of excluding foreign workers and did not have access to the same means of violence that French workers in France had; at the same time, the overwhelming majority of Italian, Greek, and other nonindigenous workers did not have the backing of the local state either, or of another powerful state. When striking Greek cigarette rollers were summarily expelled from Egypt, they had nobody to appeal to and could do little but ask an Athenian newspaper to publicize their fate.[174] There were certainly other factors at play; the state might not have mattered that much, ultimately, compared to the interests of international companies or the internal regulating mechanisms of a global or at least Mediterranean labor market. Still, the possibilities for violence and the possibilities for one-upmanship were very different, and relatively reduced. Again, this does not mean that racism and a strong sense of racial hierarchy were absent; however, politically and structurally such sentiments could not lead to the same measures or affect ethnic relations the same way as they did in strong, independent states or in a colonial (and settler) context such as Algeria. I am certainly not suggesting that class solidarity, workers' militancy, and working-class cosmopolitanism were necessarily more natural in such a context, nor that they were easier than in other contexts; rather the meanings of *class* and *ethnicity* in cities such as Cairo and Alexandria perhaps need to be explored using lenses different from those used for studying class and ethnicity in colonial contexts or in the contexts of strong states.

CONCLUSION

How can the interplay between the two dynamics of class and ethnicity, a subject that has often been oversimplified at the expense of one force over the other, be analyzed more accurately in cosmopolitan, multiethnic cities?[175] How did the experience of migration (or rather, the multiple experiences of migrations) affect this interplay?[176] What were the implications of such complex phenomena on the formulation and dissemination of radical leftist ideas? Throughout this chapter I have argued that the role of workers in the formulation and dissemination of radical ideas requires tracking and following such ideas, information, and forms of militancy as they moved between and within cities. Such social and intellectual mappings question the validity of various categories and resulting dichotomies regarding labor groups, as these groups were far from rigid and stable: first, the dichotomy between different sectors of employment, and second, that between indigenous and nonindigenous labor. The removal of such barriers is a necessary step for gaining insight into the kind of working-class culture that emerged in cities such as Alexandria in the late nineteenth century. Furthermore the interplay between class and ethnicity resulted in the emergence of very specific brands of socialism, anarchism, and general radicalism in multiethnic and migrant cities such as Cairo, Alexandria, and Beirut. These brands may profoundly differ from many of the official Western interpretations of socialism that systematically sought to ignore the shaping influence of ethnicity and nationality in the making of local socialisms and radicalisms. Finally, migration and immigration should clearly be viewed as another central factor constantly affecting and changing preexisting social networks, categories, and relations within the host society as well as the old country.

Conclusion

Deprovincializing the Eastern Mediterranean

SITUATING AND DEFINING RADICALISM IN THE EASTERN MEDITERRANEAN

This book has traced the formulation and dissemination of radical ideas in and between the cities of Beirut, Cairo, and Alexandria in the late nineteenth century and early twentieth. I devoted particular attention to socialism, anarchism, and their various permutations and interpretations. Succinctly put, I conclude that these ideologies (or some variation of them) had self-conscious proponents in these cities and, perhaps more important, that socialist and anarchist ideas were constantly being discussed, disseminated, and reworked among various segments of these cities' populations. Such a depiction challenges the dominant historiographic narrative of absence concerning radical, socialist, and leftist movements and ideas in Egypt and Syria before World War I. More than that, I suggest that radicalism was alive and well in the three cities in question.

The story of radicalism in each of these Eastern Mediterranean cities is part of a much larger story. A deep connection existed between the brands of radical ideas and activities in these cities and the movements of various social and intellectual networks connecting them and establishing a geography of contestation, or a special radical trajectory linking Beirut, Cairo, and Alexandria. This web of networks helps explain the strong similarities between the brands of leftist thought, projects, and militant practices that emerged. Yet this radical trajectory was not isolated within the world region of the Eastern Mediterranean, but was connected to wider radical webs, particularly those formed by immigrant and diasporic networks connecting the Eastern Mediterranean to North and South America and southern Europe. In fact the link between radicalism and globalization has been a central argument of this study. Radicalism, I have argued, was simultaneously an indicator and a shaper of the foundational wave of globalization that was characterized first and foremost by extensive and unprecedented circulation and movement of people, commodities, capital, information, and ideas. The movement of people and information through the press, the theater, and labor networks was not one among equals: it followed a geography often (if not mostly) dictated by empires and capitalism. It was the cause and consequence of a greatly expanded labor market (in fact a global, or almost global market), and it resulted in entangled webs of people on the move as well as increased communication channels between them. Thus globalization also meant shared concerns, shared resistance, and the emergence of a shared (or very similar) vocabulary, repertoire, and conceptualization of labor, of society, and of radical politics. It also led to the establishment of diasporic webs with unprecedented possibilities to communicate, organize, and share visions of a new social and world order through the printed word as well as by word of mouth. Beirut, Cairo, and Alexandria figured prominently within this global story, attracting, molding, and refracting numerous networks whose members articulated and promoted a plethora of radical ideas and practices.

Besides being very much related to movement, radicalism in the late nineteenth century and early twentieth was also linked to the rise of new genres, new forums, and new spaces, such as the press and the theater. Within and beyond the nexus constituted by the three Eastern Mediterranean cities, these two institutions established and relied on networks of intellectuals and dramatists and allowed for the circulation of people and radical ideas and the making of a radical canon. Radicalism also went hand in hand with movements of contestation and the emergence of new classes that envisioned different social and world orders. At home members of these new classes, individually as well as collectively, sought to challenge the authority of traditional elites. Part of this challenge came in the construction of a discourse promoting an alliance between the middle and working classes and the formation of a united body that would put a halt to political, economic, cultural, and social damage inflicted by traditional elites who were unfit to rule. The search for, experimentation with, and bricolage of ideas that challenged the existing social order at home and the right of traditional elites to rule was often accompanied by a contestation of the existing world order. Hence many of the radical networks and movements discussed in this book combined anticolonial discourses with radical leftist ideas and opposed political and economic imperialism, which they saw as intrinsically linked. The fact that these various radical ideas and networks—anarchist, anticolonial, revolutionist—often intersected and were entangled allowed for the kinds of eclectic bricolages that were so typical of the fin de siècle. Beirut, Cairo, and Alexandria (especially the latter two) served as nodal points, harboring and bringing together local radicals and political exiles and militants from different parts of the Mediterranean and beyond, guaranteeing the circulation of printed material and providing the necessary conditions, spaces, and institutions for the exchange and synthesis of ideas and practices. Such encounters and exchanges took place in coffeehouses, clubs, associations, salons, and study circles, as well as on quays, on construction sites, and in workshops. They led to the forging of links and occasionally lifelong connections between radicals, workers, and intellectuals from various continents.

CULTURE AND POLITICS BEFORE WORLD WAR I

Radicalism emerged in the Eastern Mediterranean at a time of momentous political and economic changes, which ushered in new ways of reconfiguring society and prompted a rethinking of major social and political themes. Such themes included the relationship between state and society and the relationship between various social categories or classes. The three decades before World War I were a period of great optimism, when envisioning a different society was possible and even, in some cases, imperative. The realization that the social order was changeable and malleable was not confined to elites or to new intellectual classes. Certainly in Eastern Mediterranean cities workers actively shaped the language, media, and spaces of contestation and the culture of radicalism that spread in these cities. In the theater and songs, in coffeehouses, in the workplace, and on the streets workers in various sectors promoted a plethora of radical ideas. Although many of them could not read, workers found ways to learn about events and opinions from newspapers and periodicals; they also utilized the printed word fairly successfully to promote their demands and come up with their own definitions and interpretations of what social justice meant and what kind of radical change they were interested in promoting. Through the mediation of literate skilled workers or of sympathetic radical intellectuals or members of the middle class, workers effectively used the printed word to rally support for their strikes, denounce unjust employers, and generally to petition for more rights. Even when they didn't actively try to take over the discursive space of the periodical, they invariably spilled over or barged into the lives of middle-class readers. The periodical provides one example among many of the institutions and media that emerged in the late nineteenth century and provided the physical and discursive spaces for new conceptualizations of the public and the social, where elites and nonelites could in fact interact, whether or not the interaction was planned and desired.

In other words, the history of radicalism in the fin de siècle Eastern Mediterranean suggests that in terms of the production and consumption of radical culture, the boundaries between middle classes and working classes might not have been as rigid as previously thought. This is not to minimize the importance of class and how class informs culture, but rather to underline that the whole meaning, structure, and conception of class were taking shape and constantly mutating during this period, and that this allowed spillovers between categories. It is perhaps in the study of radicalism that such interactions are most visible.

Radicalism was thus the product of intellectuals as well as of popular classes. It was a package of ideas that worked at different registers; some of the discussions among radical intellectuals were highbrow and took place in learned circles and in cutting-edge and newly emerging disciplines (sociology, urban planning, political economy); others took place among radical peasants, artisans, and construction and industrial workers, many of whom were more interested in praxis than in theory. Various radical ideas and ideologies were promoted and published in periodicals designated for experts and members of new liberal professions; others were disseminated through much more accessible periodicals, some of which explicitly sought to reach the masses, or through pamphlets. The printed word was certainly not the only vehicle for the articulation of radicalism; many radical ideas were expressed on stage, in coffeehouses, and in mutual aid societies and at night schools.

Radicalism was in part the appropriation by emerging classes and categories of discursive spheres that had hitherto been reserved for traditional sources of authority, namely, political and cultural elites. At the same time, another kind of appropriation was taking place. The appropriation of socialism and anarchism by networks of intellectuals, dramatists, and workers and their recasting, reinvention, and ultimate subversion of these two European ideologies in ways that made them appealing to local audiences sheds light on the very active participation of peripheral locals in the making of a global world. Appropriation is perhaps not the only way to think of these processes by which socialism and anarchism were indigenized, however; radicals actively and increasingly envisioned their societies as an intrinsic part of a larger entity: the colonized world, the Muslim world, the diaspora (for instance, Syrian or Italian), the working classes of the world, or the world writ large.

The study of Eastern Mediterranean radicalism thus contributes to *deprovincializing* the history of the Arab world and the Eastern Mediterranean by shedding light on the complex processes behind the emergence of global consciousness and solidarity. The study also underlines the presence and vibrancy of a universalist, secularist, and leftist discourse of radicalism and resistance, which has been obscured by the preoccupation of historians with the emergence of nationalist discourses and, in the past two decades, Islamist discourses. Furthermore writing the history of radicalism before World War I brings to the fore the intermingling of leftist radicalism with Islamist, nationalist, and anticolonialist discourses and networks, an intermingling that fundamentally shaped each one of these ideologies. Hence even for historians mostly concerned with the emergence and development of nationalist or Islamist movements, the story of radicalism is an integral and extremely formative part of these movements.

HISTORICIZING AND CONTEXTUALIZING NATIONALISM

The study of radicalism breaks ranks with the past several generations of studies of nationalism in the region because it argues that nationalism coexisted, competed, and grew symbiotically with its relationship to other forms of political and social contestations in the Eastern Mediterranean, specifically radicalism. Rather than depict nationalism as a dominant, or even fully articulated, fully formed ideology in the period under study, this study has shed light on the plethora of ideologies, ideas, and practices that circulated in the fin de siècle in the Eastern Mediterranean, especially in the three cities in question. Specifically the *nahḍa,* which has been viewed predominantly as an era of nationalist awakening, cultural if not political per se, is here enlarged beyond this framework and viewed instead as part of a global radical moment, in which many *nahḍa* intellectuals engaged with and contributed to the making of a global radical culture. The discoveries concerning this active radical scene underline the historical contingencies of nationalism as it developed in the period under study and as it ultimately triumphed. They challenge nationalist teleological historiography on fin de siècle Syria and Egypt and question the validity of the nationalist straitjacket that has been forced upon various causes, such as calls for social justice, workers' education, social reform, the eradication of sectarianism, the curbing of clerical power, and the opposition to European political and economic encroachment. Instead radicalism and nationalism both constituted movements of contestation that sought to transform themselves into mass movements, and both of them evolved concomitantly, their intermingling profoundly shaping their development.

In this book I have contested one dominant historiographic assumption, namely, that social reform began with nationalist thinkers and politicians and had virtually no antecedents. I have shown that various radical groups and networks besides nationalists—most prominently socialists, anarchists, and radical reformists—were organizing and educating workers by founding night schools and other institutions. These radical reformists, who were middle-class professionals and intellectuals (lawyers, journalists, and others), worked on creating a crucial alliance with workers and sought to turn them into a force foreign companies and European colonialism had to reckon with. Not only that, but in Beirut, Cairo, and Alexandria leftist radical reformist networks actually preceded nationalists in conceiving and implementing projects of social reform. Hence one of my main conclusions is that, although nationalists surely played a central role in calling for social reform and casting workers as a sociopolitical entity (later imagined as "the nation"), they were not the first, nor the only, nor initially the most influential group to do so.

RADICALISM AND BEYOND: THE HISTORIES OF THE EASTERN MEDITERRANEAN IN THE LATE NINETEENTH CENTURY

The late nineteenth century witnessed the emergence of a global set of concerns and concepts in which radicalism occupied a central place. Nonetheless radicalism was only one manifestation, albeit an important one, of this global moment. Beyond shedding light on radicalism, I hope this book has demonstrated the necessity of adopting a global perspective on the intellectual, social, and labor histories of the late nineteenth-century Eastern Mediterranean. None of these histories can be fully understood without sketching the movements of intellectuals, workers, periodicals, and books beyond individual cities, and in fact across a sea and an ocean, though not at the expense of local connections, institutions, and networks, nor of other trajectories. I am thinking here particularly of the important story of intellectual linkages throughout the Muslim world, especially between the Eastern Mediterranean and the Indian subcontinent in the late nineteenth century, which still awaits more research. In the case of Middle Eastern labor history, my adoption of a global lens allows me to argue that the Eastern Mediterranean in the late nineteenth century and early twentieth was part of, and intrinsically connected to, larger labor markets in the Mediterranean and even beyond. In the process various assumptions about local mechanisms and factors behind workers' militancy are nuanced or challenged: the Marxist bias against artisans' politicization and militancy; the notion of strikes as imported by foreign workers; and the imposition of a nationalist straitjacket on workers' radical history. Rather, the emergence of strikes and the dissemination of radical ideas by and among workers emerged as a result of interconnected local and global social and economic factors, which caused labor categories to be particularly fluid and unstable, triggered discontent among workers, and expanded communication channels between them. These channels allowed for the circulation of ideas and practices, including radical ideas pertaining to strikes and workers' militancy.

Finally, a word about the end of the story: for both the Eastern Mediterranean and the world writ large, World War I marked a watershed. It brought with it devastation and a new world order, the end of certain empires (most important for our story the Ottoman Empire) and the consolidation of others, either through classical means or through the imposition of the mandate system. It also ushered in new political configurations, such as new states and new nation-states, and during and after the war led to much stricter control over people's mobility. Finally, it triggered a communist revolution and the emergence of an official, state-sponsored ideology of exporting, assisting, and universalizing this revolution on a global scale. Such massive changes could not but impact the global radical moment that has been the subject of this book.

This is not to say that anarchism and other, more hybrid kinds of radical experimentations that blossomed before World War I disappeared; however, the consolidation of the nation-state and of communism as *the* official, triumphant state ideology and the proliferation of national communist parties, together with increased surveillance, control of borders, and occasionally stringent immigration laws in the Mediterranean and parts of North and South America, fundamentally affected the brands of radicalism that proliferated in the 1920s and later. The story of radicalism did not end then, but the foundational moment of its genesis was over.

APPENDIX

AL-MUQTAṬAF

On Socialism and Anarchism

"Ta'līm al-nihilist," *al-Muqtaṭaf* 4 (1879): 289–92.
"Fasād madhhab al-ishtirākiyyīn," *al-Muqtaṭaf* 14 (March, 1890): 361–64.
"Al-Ishtirākiyyūn wa'l-fawḍawiyyūn," *al-Muqtaṭaf* 18 (August 1, 1894): 721–29, 801–7.
"Ārā' al-'ulamā': Ishtirākiyyū Almānya," *al-Muqtaṭaf* 19, (April 1895): 313–14.
"Ḍarar al-ishtirākiyya," *al-Muqtaṭaf* 19 (June 1895): 478.
Khalil Thabit, "Al-Ishtirākiyyūn al-dīmuqrātiyyūn," *al-Muqtaṭaf* 25 (August 1900): 146–51.
"Elisée Reclus," *Al-Muqtaṭaf* 30 (December1905): 960.
"Numuww al-ishtirākiyya," *al-Muqtaṭaf* 31 (June 1906): 530.
"Bāb al-masā'il: Francisco Ferrer," *al-Muqtaṭaf* 36 (March 1910): 297.
"Francisco Ferrer," *al-Muqtaṭaf* 36 (April 1910): 344–46.
"'Adad al-ishtirākiyyīn," *al-Muqtaṭaf* 38 (February 1911): 203.
Shibli Shumayyil, "Al-Ishtirākiyya al-ṣaḥīḥa," *al-Muqtaṭaf* 42 (January 1913): 9–16.
"August Babel," *al-Muqtaṭaf* 43 (October 1913): 362–66.
"Bāb al-masā'il," *al-Muqtaṭaf* 44 (January 1914): 93–94.
Salama Musa, "Al-Fawḍawiyya 'an zu'amā'iha," *al-Muqtaṭaf* 44 (January 1914): 25–28.

On Strikes and Labor Conflicts

"Mashākil dhawī al-a'māl: Ta'aṣṣub aṣḥāb al-ma'āmil wa al-'ummāl," *al-Muqtaṭaf* 11 (May 1887): 454–60.
"Ḥall mashākil al-'ummāl wa aṣḥāb al-a'māl," *al-Muqtaṭaf* 11 (June 1887): 517–20.
"Ḍiyā' al-amwāl bī i'tiṣāb al-'ummāl," *al-Muqtaṭaf* 14 (October 1889): 27–29.
"I'tiaāb al-'ummāl," *al-Muqtaṭaf* 27 (January 1902): 64–66.
As'ad Dāghir, "Istidrāk," *al-Muqtaṭaf* 27 (January 1902): 95.

"I'tiaāb al-aunnā'," *al-Muqtaṭaf* 27 (February 1902): 95.
Najib Shahin, "Al-I'tiṣāb wa ḥayawiyyat al-'umma," *al-Muqtaṭaf* 27 (February 1902): 160–61.

On Workers

"Ujūr al-'ummāl," *al-Muqtaṭaf* 17 (July 1893): 708–9.
"Sharikat al-'ummāl," *al-Muqtaṭaf* 28 (January 1903): 61–63.
"Al-Kutub wa'l-'ummāl," *al-Muqtaṭaf* 31 (August 1906): 649–53.
Shibli Shumayyil, "Al-'Ummāl fi'l-qadīm," *al-Muqtaṭaf* 42 (November 1913): 487–89.

AL-HILĀL

On Socialists and Anarchists

"Al-Fawḍa fi Faransa," *al-Hilāl,* January 15, 1894, 317.
"Al-Fawḍawiyyūn fi Italya," *al-Hilāl,* February 1, 1894, 348.
"Al-Fawḍa fi Faransa," *al-Hilāl,* March 1, 1894, 412–14.
"Manshūr fawḍawī 'aqīm," *al-Hilāl,* April 1, 1894, 475.
"Al-Fawḍawiyya," *al-Hilāl,* September 15, 1897, 71.
Salim Yusef, "Al-Ishtirākiyya wa'l-nīhiliyya," *al-Hilāl,* December 15, 1897, 290–94.
"Mu'tamar al-fawḍawiyyīn," *al-Hilāl,* January 1, 1899, 219.
Amin Qattit, "Al-Ishtirākiyyūn," *al-Hilāl,* October 1, 1900, 20–21.
"Al-Fawḍawiyya fi'l-Islām," *al-Hilāl,* October 1, 1901, 7–8.
Sa'id Abu Jamra, "Al-Fawḍawiyyūn fi'l-Islām: ṭā'ifat al-ḥashghāshīn," *al-Hilāl,* November 1, 1901, 83–86.
"Mustaqbal al-anarshiyya," *al-Hilāl,* February 1, 1902, 285.
"Al-Ishtirākiyya wa numuwwuha," *al-Hilāl,* June 1, 1906, 563.
"Al-Ishtirākiyya: Madhhab shāi' fi Europa," *al-Hilāl,* January 1, 1908, 252.
"Al-Ijtimā'iyya wa'l-Ishtirākiyya," *al-Hilāl,* February 1, 1908, 265–82.
"Al-Ishtirākiyyūn fi'l-'ālam," *al-Hilāl* (February 1908): 315.
"Francisco Ferrer wa'l-ishtirākiyya fi Isbānya," *al-Hilāl,* November 1, 1909, 114–18.
Salama Musa, "Tārikh al-ishtirākiyya fi Ingliterra: Wa ḥāl al-'ummāl fiha wa'l-i'tibār bi masā'ilihim," *al-Hilāl,* March 1, 1910, 335–38.
"Al-Ishtirākiyyūn fi'l-'ālam," *al-Hilāl* (February 1911): 315.
"Al-Ishtirākiyyūn fi'l-'ālam," *al-Hilāl* (April 1912): 442.

On Labor Issues

"Al-Jam'iyya al-iqtiṣādiyya al-sharqiyya li 'ummāl al-lafā'if bi Miṣr," *al-Hilāl,* July 1, 1896, 877.
"I'tiṣāb al-'ummāl fi Faransa," *al-Hilāl,* November 1, 1892, 100–101.
"'Amalat al-sagāyir fi Miṣr," *al-Hilāl,* July 15, 1894, 698.
"Al-'Ummāl wa aṣḥāb al-a'māl: Tārikh al-'ilāqa baynahum," *al-Hilāl,* May 1, 1912, 466–75.

On the Literary Canon

"Zola," *al-Hilāl,* February 15, 1897, 441.
"Zola," *al-Hilāl,* February 15, 1898, 469.
Esther Lazari Moyal, "Zola," *al-Hilāl,* October 15, 1903, 63.
"Riwāyat Maxim Gorki," *al-Hilāl,* May 1, 1907, 504.

NOTES

INTRODUCTION

1. The term has not been exclusively associated with the Left. There is also Conservative Radicalism and Islamic Radicalism, but I am limiting myself here to the Radical Left.

2. Giddens, *Beyond Left and Right,* 1.

3. On the 1870–1920 wave of globalization, see, among others, Bayly, *The Birth of the Modern World 1780–1914;* Hopkins, *Globalization in World History;* Owen and Pamuk, *A History of Middle East Economies in the Twentieth Century,* 4–5; Owen, "Using Present Day Notions of Imperialism, Globalization and Internationalism." On urban changes in Beirut, Cairo, and Alexandria, see, among others, Fawaz, *Merchants and Migrants in 19th Century Beirut;* Hanssen, *Fin-de-siècle Beirut;* Ilbert, *Alexandrie 1830–1930;* Reimer, *Colonial Bridgehead;* Volait, "Making Cairo Modern (1870–1950)"; Arnaud, *Le Caire.*

4. Burke, "Changing Patterns of Peasant Protest," 34. For protest and resistance in the Hawran, see Schilcher, "Violence in Rural Syria in the 1880s and 1890s," in which the author argues that the last twenty years of the nineteenth century witnessed protests and literally warfare between the peasants, landlords, and the Ottoman state, which was linked to the Syrian hinterland's integration into the world capitalist system and thus the impact that trends in world markets would have on it. See especially the section titled "Phase Three (1890): Radical Populism in Jabal Hawran," during which period the peasants, mostly Druze but also some Christians, set up a commune ('Ammiyya) and actually received the backing of Mustafa 'Asim Pasha, the governor of Damascus, who "support[ed] them in their disputes over cultivation rights against their land controllers, contractors, and shaikhs" (62–65). After the Ottoman state literally waged war on them in 1895–96, a general uprising ensued, followed by a detente around 1900.

5. Chaichian, "The Effects of World Capitalist Economy on Urbanization in Egypt, 1800–1970," 28. More recently, see Gran, " 'Passive Revolution' as a Possible Model for Nineteenth-

century Egyptian History"; Schulze, "The Egyptian Peasant Rebellion, 1919," in which the author argues that "regions such as southern Upper Egypt . . . were integrated into the [colonial system, by which he means 'the systematic restructuring of a regional economy, whereby the ultimate goal is to integrate it into a superimposed division of labor, hierarchized and centralized on the basis of capitalist production', and which was taking place from 1820 until World War I] by providing the needed reserves of migratory labor for cotton cultivation areas of the delta" (172–73).

6. Chaichian, "Effects of World Capitalist Economy," 30. One feddan equals 1.038 acres.

7. Chaichian, "Effects of World Capitalist Economy," 30–31.

8. According to Roger Owen, "The Rapid Growth of Egypt's Agricultural Output, 1890–1914," 92–93:

> Just over half the agricultural population of Upper Egypt was calculated as 'landless' in 1917. The other half, which did possess some land, was confined to growing lower-value crops, mostly foodstuffs, during the autumn and winter months. The result was a huge reserve army of seasonal labor which, even as early as 1888–9, involved a migration of between half a million and 800,000 men and boys. Many were involved in the annual cleaning of the Delta canals, but many others were brought down the Nile by labor contractors to work the fields and harvest the cotton.

9. Khater, *Inventing Home*, 8.

10. This is very engagingly described by Khater in *Inventing Home*.

11. Burke, "Changing Patterns of Peasant Protest," 32.

12. Kasaba, "Migrant Labor in Western Anatolia, 1750–1850," 113.

13. See the various reports by the British Benevolent Society (signed "S.[?] J. Davis, almoner of British Benevolent Society"), addressed to the British consul in Alexandria, on poor British subjects needing repatriation from Egypt. Cases included Maltese, the "members of a roving theatrical company that came out from England," "distressed railway men from South Africa (Durban)," and "a half educated nursery governess" from England. PRO (Kew), FO 78/5164 Turkey (Egypt) Consular and Commercial, Consuls at Alexandria, 1901. See, for example, letter from British Benevolent Society, "Expenditure in repatriating from Alexandria distressed British subjects—January 1 to June 30 1901."

14. On Alexandria, see Hanley, "Foreignness and Localness in Alexandria, 1880–1914," 234.

15. See Dār al-Wathā'iq (Cairo), Majlis al-Wuzarā', Naẓarat al-Dākhiliyya, 8/1 al-Bulīs [police] mutafarriqāt, File 2, on Qānūn al-musharradīn (vagrants) [1894]:

> Les dispositions de l'article 2 relatives aux vagabonds mises aux paragraphes . . . sont applicables aux personnes suspectes qui, étant valides, n'exercent habituellement aucun métier et n'ont pas de moyens d'existence, quoiqu' elles aient un domicile fixe. La police en leur donnant l'avertissement leur ordonnera de se mettre au travail dans un délai de 10 jours au moins et de 20 jours au plus. Si l'avertissement reste sans effet l'individu sera déféré au parquet pour l'application de la peine. (Signed, "[Khedive] Abbas Hilmi, Abdīn palace, 7 Cha'bān 1311 [February 13, 1894]")

See Torpey, *The Invention of the Passport;* Harper, "Empire, Diaspora and the Languages of Globalism, 1850–1914," 148.

16. Bayly, "'Archaic' and 'Modern' Globalization in the Eurasian and African Arena, ca. 1750–1850," 54.

17. Dumont, "Freemasonry in Turkey," 481.

18. See Shirine Hamadeh's brilliant analysis of the expansion of public spaces in eighteenth-century Istanbul, *The City's Pleasures.*

19. On the role played by coffeehouses in Eastern Mediterranean cities in the nineteenth century, see Kırlı, "The Struggle over Space"; Desmet-Grégoire and Georgeon, *Cafés d'orient revisités.* On the souk, see, among many, Mermier, "Souk et citadinité dans le monde arabe."

20. See, for instance, the photograph in Georgeon, "Lire et écrire à la fin de l'Empire ottoman," 177.

21. This reading was most famously articulated in Antonius, *The Arab Awakening.*

22. I am much indebted to Julia Clancy-Smith for this expression.

23. Sassen, *Global Networks, Linked Cities.*

1. THE LATE NINETEENTH-CENTURY WORLD

1. This point is compatible with Chris Bayly's argument that

> a kind of international class structure was emerging. . . . The ruling groups, professions, and even working classes of different societies looked more and more similar, were subject to similar types of pressure, and began to harbor similar aspirations. Convergence, uniformity, and similarity did not mean, again, that all these people were likely to think or act in the same way. At the very least, though, they could perceive and articulate common interests which breached the boundaries of the nation-state, even if they were profoundly influenced by it. (*The Birth of the Modern World 1780–1914,* 21)

2. Bayly, *Birth of the Modern World,* 168.

3. Karl, "Creating Asia."

4. See the many publications of the Secrétariat du Bureau Socialiste International, such as *L'Internationale Ouvrière et Socialiste,* 1: 81–83, which has information on socialist periodicals sponsored by the International in Argentina.

5. Not surprisingly the typographers and printers' secretariat is the first (1889), "a trade that represented *par excellence* the aristocracy of the most skilled workers, who were the first to organize themselves." Dreyfus, "The Emergence of an International Trade Union Organization (1902–1919)," 40.

6. There is an extensive literature on the difference between anarchism, anarchosyndicalism, and revolutionary syndicalism, but this is a debate that is beyond the scope of this book. For more information, see Hall and Garcia, "Urban Labor," 166; van der Linden and Thorpe, *Revolutionary Syndicalism.*

7. I am borrowing this expression from Richard Jensen, "The United States, International Policing and the War against Anarchist Terrorism, 1900–1914," in *Terrorism and Political Violence* 13, no. 1 (2001): 16, quoted in Deflem, "'Wild Beasts without Nationality,'" 277.

8. For anarchism in China, see Arif Dirlik's work, notably *Anarchism in the Chinese Revolution* and "Vision and Revolution." For anarchism in Japan, see Plotkin, *Anarchism in Japan.* For the Philippines and Cuba, see Anderson, *Under Three Flags.* For India and the Indian diaspora, see Ramnath, "Two Revolutions, the Ghadar Movement and India's Radical Diaspora, 1913–1918." For anarchism and anarchosyndicalism in South Africa, see van der Walt, "Bakunin's Heirs in South Africa." There is a very extensive literature on anarchism in Italy and Spain, as well as in North and South America.

9. On Spanish anarchism in the diaspora, see Moya, *Cousins and Strangers,* which connects Spain and particularly Barcelona to South America. On anarchism in the Italian diaspora, see the work of Donna Gabaccia, including *Italy's Many Diasporas,* especially chapter 5, "Nationalism and Internationalism in Italy's Proletarian Diasporas, 1870–1914"; Turcato, "Italian Anarchism as a Transnational Movement, 1885–1915." On England, see the following rather telling report: "The anarchist section of the community in England consists almost entirely of foreigners. During the last dozen years, of the total number registered about 3% are natives of this country, so if aliens were deported the anarchist movement would have few adherents here." FO 881/8518, confid. 8518, Correspondence respecting the measures to be taken for the prevention of anarchist crimes, 1902, Inclosure 2 no. 2, memorandum signed E. R. Henry and dated January 7, 1902.

10. See Nataf, *La Vie quotidienne des anarchistes en France, 1880–1910,* 154.

11. Fowler, *Japanese and Chinese Immigrant Activists,* 36–37.

12. Fowler, *Japanese and Chinese Immigrant Activists,* 51.

13. Anderson makes a similar argument: "[Anarchism] was open to 'bourgeois' writers and artists—in the name of individual freedom—in a way that, in those days, institutional Marxism was not. Just as hostile to imperialism, it had no theoretical prejudices against 'small' and 'ahistorical' nationalisms, including those in the colonial world. Anarchists were also quicker to capitalize on the vast transoceanic migrations of the era." Anderson, *Under Three Flags,* 1.

14. Quoted in Hobsbawm, *Revolutionaries,* 78. Francisco Ferrer y Gardia (1859–1909) was a Spanish anarchist and freethinker who came under attack from the Spanish government and Church and was condemned to death in 1909. The following chapters examine the reception of Ferrer's ideas and news of his death in Beirut, Cairo, and Alexandria.

15. An argument made, in the case of Spain, by David Ortiz, but one that seems to fit the attitude of anarchists in other parts of the world as well. See Ortiz, "Redefining Public Education," 82–84.

16. Ortiz, "Redefining Public Education," 84.

17. In 1877 "Carlo Cafiero and Enrico Malatesta provoked a peasant uprising in southern Italy in which tax records were burned and the overthrow of the king proclaimed." Fleming. *The Geography of Freedom,* 131.

18. Fleming. *The Geography of Freedom,* 127–31.

19. See, for example, Cuban anarchists' use of the theater to spread their ideas, especially among women. Shaffer, "The Radical Muse."

20. See Gabriel, "Performing Persecution."

21. Best et al., *L'Affaire Ferrer,* 20.

22. According to Nataf, "En 1889, à l'occasion de l'Exposition universelle, une 'conférence

internationale anarchiste' se tient à la salle du Commerce, 94 faubourg du Temple. Personne n'ayant prévu quoi que ce soit . . . la réunion se déroule dans un désordre indescriptible." Nataf, *Vie quotidienne des anarchistes en France,* 134–35.

23. On discussions pertaining to the notion of civilization, see Aydın, *The Politics of Anti-Westernism in Asia* and "A Global Anti-Western Moment?"

24. I am borrowing this expression from Beth English's review of Tom Goyens, *Beer and Revolution.*

25. See, for instance, Tager, "Politics and Culture in Anarchist Education."

26. Ortiz, "Redefining Public Education."

27. Tager, "Politics and Culture in Anarchist Education."

28. For the Chinese context, see Dirlik, "Vision and Revolution," 129. Many of these are very similar to those that appear in this book.

29. For a fascinating analysis of how Mechnikov, a Russian anarchist, discovered mutual aid in Japan and incorporated it into anarchist thought, and how this "led him to refashion anarchism, transforming it from a Bakuninist ideology of primordial and violent destruction of the existing social and political structures into an evolutionary construct for developing a civilization on the basis of mutual aid," see Konishi, "Reopening the 'Opening of Japan.'"

30. Christian Geulen has described Piotr Kropotkin's concept of mutual aid as a "combin[ation of] Darwin's evolution theory with Proudhon's concept of 'mutualité,' in order to sketch out a possible social development, in the course of which the selective pressure of a brutal nature would lead to a just and peaceful social order among human beings." Geulen, "The Common Grounds of Conflict," 77.

31. See, for instance, Garcia-Bryce, "Politics by Peaceful Means."

32. Rose, *The Intellectual Life of the British Working Classes,* 58.

33. For example, in 1894 the Association for Literary Production (Jam'iyyat al-intāj al-adabi) was established in Alexandria by employees of the Egyptian post office. The association also put on theatrical performances. Zaidan, *Tārīkh ādāb al-lugha al-'arabiyya,* 87.

34. Moya, "Immigrants and Associations," 839.

35. Moya, "Immigrants and Associations," 842.

36. Harland-Jacobs, *Builders of Empire.*

37. Karpiel, "Freemasonry, Colonialism, and Indigenous Elites."

38. One of the splits seems to have occurred between those who viewed Masonry as compatible with deism and religion, and those who didn't. The former seem to have been connected to the British or Scottish lodges, whereas the latter were overtly anticlerical, specifically anti-Catholic (and by extension, in the case of Beirut and Mount Lebanon, anti-Maronite). The anticlerical lodges tended to be French, Spanish, and Italian. Jessica Harland-Jacobs makes this distinction and dates the split to 1878 between the Anglo-Saxon and the Latin lodges, when the Grand Orient de France decided to admit atheists into the brotherhood. See Harland-Jacobs, *Builders of Empire,* 288.

39. Bose, *A Hundred Horizons.*

40. For a recent study on the nexus between anti-imperialisms, pan-nationalisms, and nationalisms, see Conrad and Sachsenmaier, *Competing Visions of World Order.*

41. Aydın, *Politics of Anti-Westernism in Asia.*

42. Anderson, *Under Three Flags,* 1.

43. Errico (or Enrico) Malatesta was a leading anarchist activist and thinker whose importance among anarchist circles throughout the world was tremendous. He headed the Italian Anarchist Party at one point and was elected secretary of the Anarchist International in 1907. For more information on Malatesta, his life and work, see, among others, Richards, *Errico Malatesta;* Nettlau, *A Short History of Anarchism;* Droz, *Dictionnaire biographique du mouvement ouvrier international;* Masini, *Storia degli anarchici italiani nell' epoca degli attentati.*

44. To quote the French sentence, "Que doit penser ce pauvre petit de la civilisation française et de sa supériorité sur la civilisation arabe?" *Les Temps Nouveaux* (Paris), May 18, 1907, 5.

45. *Les Temps Nouveaux,* January 11, 1908, 7.

46. There were serious divisions among anarchists regarding the acceptability of political assassination. Kropotkin, for one, was against it, but Elisée Reclus accepted it. See Fleming, *The Geography of Freedom,* 132.

47. In February 1878 Vera Zasulitch shot the chief of police in St. Petersburg; in May and June two attempts were made on the life of the kaiser; in October an assassination attempt against Alfonso XII of Spain failed; and in November it was the turn of King Umberto of Italy to be attacked. A decade later Paris was rocked by a series of explosions and political assassinations that lasted two years, from March 1892 to 1894, and ended up killing the French president Sadi Carnot (at the hands of an Italian anarchist). Four years later it was the turn of the Austrian empress, and in 1900 that of the Italian king Umberto I. Non-European cities and heads of states were not spared either; U.S. President McKinley was killed by an (Italian) anarchist in 1901, and in the Ottoman Empire Istanbul was the stage of Armenian bomb attacks in 1894–96.

48. On Indian revolutionaries who went to Paris to learn the art of bomb making from Russian nihilists, see Sharma, *Role of Revolutionaries in the Freedom Struggle,* 57.

49. Ghosh, "Terrorism in Bengal," 273–75.

50. Ramnath, "Two Revolutions," 8.

51. Anderson, *Under Three Flags,* 2. It is worth quoting him at length:

> The near-simultaneity of the last nationalist insurrection in the New World (Cuba, 1895) and the first in Asia (the Philippines, 1896) was no serendipity. Natives of the last important remnants of the fabled Spanish global empire, Cubans (as well as Puerto Ricans and Dominicans) and Filipinos did not merely know about each other, but had crucial personal connections and, up to a point, coordinated their actions—the first time in world history that such trans-global coordination became possible. Both were eventually crushed, within a few years of each other, by the same brutish would-be world hegemon.

52. Bayly, "Distorted Development," 142.

53. "Khārijiyya: Shay' 'an al-hind," *Al-Ḥurriyya,* July 24, 1909, 14.

54. Bayly, "Distorted Development," 142. See also Bose, "Representations and Contestations of 'India' in Bengali Literature and Culture."

55. See, for instance, Schneer, "Anti-imperial London."

56. See Bonakdarian, "Iranian Constitutional Exiles and British Foreign-Policy Dissenters, 1908–9."

57. See Egger, *A Fabian in Egypt;* Haroun, *Shibli Shumayyil,* 90.

58. Dirlik, *Anarchism in the Chinese Revolution,* 14.

59. Dirlik, *Anarchism in the Chinese Revolution,* 25.

60. Blair, "Local Modernity, Global Modernism."

61. On Charles Gide, see Marc Penin, *Charles Gide 1847–1932: L'esprit critique* (Paris: l'Harmattan, 1998), as well as Pierre-Yves Saunier's review of Penin's book on the H-Urban website (September 1998).

62. Charles Gide's *Principes d'économie politique* was translated and printed in Istanbul in Ottoman Turkish in 1911 by Hasan Hamit, Hasan Tahsin, and Mustafa Zühtü. The first Arabic edition I found appeared in 1925, but it is quite likely that parts of Gide's articles or part of his book had been translated earlier. The discussion in *al-Ḥurriyya* (discussed in chapter 4) on mutualism and a new rapport between workers and owners sounds very similar to Gide's ideas. Gide's ideas were also summarized and cited in *L'Egypte contemporaine,* an influential social science periodical that was initially published in Cairo in 1909. The American University of Beirut's library has quite a few of Gide's titles in English and French, the oldest of which was published in English in 1903–4 in Boston, and which was most likely acquired then (since later editions are available as well).

63. See Nataf, *La Vie quotidienne des anarchistes en France, 1880–1910,*48; Dreyfus, "Léopold Mabilleau et le mouvement mutualiste français," 104–5.

64. Andreucci, "Italy," 206.

65. See, for instance, Saunier, "Sketches from the Urban Internationale, 1910–50." See also Payre and Saunier, "Municipalités de tous pays, unissez vous!"

66. Horne, "Le libéralisme à l'épreuve de l'industrialisation," 13–14.

67. See, for example, the work of Salama Musa. For secondary sources, see *Review* 12, no. 3 (1989), published as *The French Revolution and the World-System* (Binghamton, NY: Fernand Braudel Center for the Study of Economics, Historical Systems, and Civilization), especially the articles by Maurice Agulhon, "The Heritage of the Revolution and Liberty in France," 405–22, and Patrice Higonnet, "Jacobinism and the World-System," 423–35. See also Heidrich, *The French Revolution of 1789;* Ra'if Khuri's classic *Modern Arab Thought; Les Arabes, les Turcs et la Révolution Française;* Brown, *Har Dayal,* 49; Ramnath, "Two Revolutions."

68. On 1848, see Bayly, *Birth of the Modern World,* 4. On the Paris Commune, see Eichner, "Vive la Commune!"

69. For instance, it was partly "exiles who had fled from the aftermath of the Paris Commune or Bismarck's anti-socialist laws of 1878 [who] began to introduce the [British] popular radicals to the work of Lassalle, Marx, and Proudhon. The popular radicals, prompted by such influences, began to develop an economic analysis of capitalist exploitation." Bevir, "Republicanism, Socialism, and Democracy in Britain," 357.

70. See Eichner, "Vive la Commune!," and chapter 4 of this book.

71. Anderson, *Under Three Flags,* 1.

72. Harper, "Empire, Diaspora and the Languages of Globalism," 154.

73. See, for instance, the reference to Elisée Reclus's work in Tamimi and Bahjat, *Wilāyat Bayrūt,* 2: 43, as well as his obituary in the Arabic press, discussed in chapter 2.

74. Anderson, *Under Three Flags,* 28; Pascale Casanova, *La République mondiale des lettres,* cited in Anderson.

75. Ibrahim Shihadi Farah translated the first of these short stories, which initially appeared in Russian in 1899. This subject is discussed at length in chapter 2.

76. Strauss, "Who Read What in the Ottoman Empire (19th–20th Centuries)?," 54, 62. Strauss points out that this Turkish version of Dumas's *Monte Cristo* "has rightfully been regarded as the first 'real' translation of a novel from a western language." The translator was Teodor Kasap (1835-97). Strauss also mentions an Armenian version, as well as an imitation of Dumas's best-seller into Judaeo-Spanish; the imitation, *A Little Monte Cristo,* "seems to have been one of the first novels published in that language" in Salonica in 1850.

77. See the section in chapter 3 of this book on the performance of *Le Juif errant* in Beirut in 1911. On Sue's work in Ottoman languages such as Armenian and Greek, see Strauss, "Who Read What in the Ottoman Empire," 52–54. The novel *Juif errant* plays an important role in turning people against religion. The famous anarchist Ravachol is said to have "sous l'influence du Juif errant, d'Eugène Sue, . . . récus(a) la religion." Nataf, *Vie quotidienne des anarchistes en France,* 203.

78. Taylor, "Shakespeare and Radicalism," 358.

79. See, for instance, Reid, "Syrian Christians, the Rags-to-Riches Story, and Free Enterprise."

80. Rose, *Intellectual Life of the British Working-Classes,* 55.

81. See chapter 4 in this book.

82. Rose, *Intellectual Life of the British Working-Classes,* 55.

83. Eley, *Forging Democracy,* 43. See Musto, "The Rediscovery of Karl Marx."

84. See Farah Antun, "Al-dīn wa'l-'ilm wa'l-māl," *al-Jāmi'a,* June 1903, 258. For Salama Musa, see his booklet *Al-Ishtirākiyya,* as well as S. Hanna and Gardner, *Arab Socialism,* 53–54.

85. Anderson, *Under Three Flags,* 29.

86. See, for example, Eley's remark that only 4.3 percent of borrowings from workers' libraries in Germany were in the social sciences, compared to over 63 percent in fiction, and that "works by Marx and Engels . . . were mainly absent from the chosen reading." Eley, *Forging Democracy,* 43.

87. Eley, *Forging Democracy,* 43–44. Eley also pointed out that "even if Marx's own writings were hard to get hold of, there were many commentaries about them—some three hundred titles in Italy alone from 1885 to 1895, or over two books a month on Marxism and socialism for a decade."

88. On the Arabo-Muslim word, see Sajdi, "Print and Its Discontents."

89. Anderson, *Under Three Flags,* 2.

90. Sohrabi, "Global Waves, Local Actors."

91. See Eley, *Forging Democracy:* "By the early 1900s, the map of Europe was entirely occupied by socialist parties, providing the main voice of democracy, anchored in popular loyalties and backed by increasingly impressive electoral support" (26).

92. Manning, "1789–1792 and 1989–1992," paragraph 68.

2. THE *NAHḌA* AND THE PRESS

1. The term *ishtirākiyya* first appeared two decades earlier, in the Beiruti *al-Bashīr* and *al-Jinān,* and in Egyptian periodicals in 1878–80. See M. Kerr, "Notes on the Background of

Arab Socialist Thought"; Wahba, "The Meaning of *Ishtirakiyah*"; Glass, *Der Muqtaṭaf und seine Öffentlichkeit,* 557–58. *Al-Muqtaṭaf*'s own first article on socialism and nihilism (lumped together) appeared in 1879 ("Taʿlīm al-Nihilist," *al-Muqtaṭaf* 4 [1879]: 289–92), but the periodical seems to have resumed its coverage of radical movements and ideas only in 1890. For a list of articles that appeared in *al-Muqtaṭaf* and *al-Hilāl* on socialism, anarchism, and related topics, see the appendix. For studies on *al-Muqtaṭaf,* see Farag, "*Al Muqtataf* 1876–1900," as well as Dagmar Glass's monumental *Der Muqtaṭaf und seine offentlichkeit.* Due to my linguistic limitations, I am unfortunately unable to make much use of Glass's study. For a review of it, see Hamzah.

On *al-Hilāl,* see Philipp, *Gurgi Zaidan,* as well as relevant sections in his *Syrians in Egypt 1725–1975;* Dupont, *Girgi Zaydan, 1861–1914.* Albert Hourani's brilliant study on the period and on these periodicals' owners, *Arabic Thought in the Liberal Age,* remains a classic.

2. See appendix.

3. An argument generally made by Donald Reid, whose article on Syrian Christian socialists is an important contribution to an otherwise very understudied topic. See Reid, "The Syrian Christians and Early Socialism in the Arab World."

4. On the existence of "a wide range of literacies," see N. Hanna, "Literacy and the 'Great Divide' in the Islamic World, 1300–1800."

5. Georgeon, "Lire et écrire à la fin de l'Empire ottoman," especially 170–73.

6. Georgeon, "Lire et écrire à la fin de l'Empire ottoman," 173.

7. According to one historian of the press in the Middle East:

> When the Syrian Salim al-Hamawi's weekly *al-Kawkab al-sharqi* came out in Alexandria in 1873, twenty friends of Syrian origin in al-Mahalla al-Kubra joined together to pay one franc each for a 20 franc subscription. [Similarly] a group of young Sunnis in Baghdad in the late 1870s organized the same kind of collective effort to purchase a single subscription of *al-Muqtaṭaf.* Forty years later, in 1918, a similar phenomenon was depicted as still "quite common" in Syria: "every four or five men use one journal, which one of them purchases and reads, walking along the road, while the others listen. Or, the one who paid for it (an exorbitant sum!) reads while the others wait until he is through and then circulate it among themselves." (Ayalon, *The Press in the Arab Middle East,* 158)

8. Georgeon, "Lire et écrire," 178, my translation.

9. "Fasād madhhab al-ishtirākiyyīn" (Rottenness [or Corruptness] of the Doctrine of the Socialists), *al-Muqtaṭaf* 14 (March 1890): 361–64.

10. Various historians, including Farag, Reid, and Philipp, have seen *al-Muqtaṭaf* and specifically Nimr and Sarruf as fully embracing liberal economic thought and being unmitigated pro-capitalists. I would argue that in fact the two authors' views on the subject were more nuanced and less unchanging than that, and that their promotion of Samuel Smiles's self-help philosophy has been misread, a point I made in chapter 1.

11. "Fasād madhhab al-ishtirākiyyīn," *al-Muqtaṭaf* 14 (March 1890): 261–64.

12. "Fasād madhhab al-ishtirākiyyīn."

13. "Fasād madhhab al-ishtirākiyyīn."

14. Such as the letters written by the French anarchist Auguste Valiant, condemned to death for throwing a bomb at the French Parliament. Reproduced in *al-Hilāl,* March 1, 1894, 412–14.

15. Reid makes the same point and dates *al-Hilāl's* conversion to around 1908. Reid, "Syrian Christians," 180.

16. "Socialism as a whole is not compatible with natural occurrences *[min al-umūr al-muṭābiqa li majāriyyāt al-ṭabī'a],* and for that, it will not be able to establish a basis in society *[lan taqūma lahu qā'ima].*" "Socialism and Nihilism," *al-Hilāl,* December 15, 1897, 290–94. *Al-Hilāl* repeated the same argument in "Socialists," *al-Hilāl,* October 1, 1900, 20–21, and in "Count Tolstoi," *al-Hilāl,* May 1, 1901, 425–29.

17. "Count Tolstoi."

18. Recall that in its 1890 article *al-Muqtaṭaf* used terms such as *fasād* and *mufsid* (corruption and corrupting) time and again to describe socialism. On the other hand, *al-Hilāl* suggested that by turning to anarchism socialists had been "corrupted and led astray" *(ufsidū wa uḍlilū)* by it. "Socialism and Nihilism," *al-Hilāl,* December 15, 1897, 290–94. See "Al-Fawḍawiyya," *al-Hilāl,* September 15, 1897, 71. The periodical's opinion on anarchism would also change and become more nuanced with time. See Khuri-Makdisi, "Levantine Trajectories."

19. For *al-Hilāl* the struggle for a more equal distribution of wealth was a wasted battle because natural differences between people's abilities meant that even if wealth inequalities were to be reversed and wealth redistributed equally, the situation would soon revert back to inequality. "Count Tolstoi," *al-Hilāl,* May 1, 1901, 425–29.

20. "Count Tolstoi." Similarly, *al-Muqtaṭaf* argued that the main path to reforming society and decreasing its inequalities was through widespread education, which "[decreases] the differences between classes of people *[ṭabaqāt al-nās].*" "Fasād madhhab al-ishtirākiyyīn," *al-Muqtaṭaf* 14 (March 1890): 261–64.

21. While reiterating the futility of wealth distribution, *al-Muqtaṭaf* sought to explore other aspects of socialism and eventually linked socialism primarily to reform: "Socialism is an ancient principle, for all the reformists in the past until now have aimed to reform government . . . so that everybody would become comfortable *[rāḥa]* and live in ease. "Al-Ishtirākiyyūn wa'l-fawḍawiyyūn," *al-Muqtaṭaf* 18 (August 1894): 721–29. Ironically even Shibli Shumayyil, who considered himself and was considered a socialist, reassured his readership that socialism was not about wealth distribution. See Shumayyil, "Al-Ishtirākiyya al-ṣaḥīḥa," *al-Muqtaṭaf* 42 (January 1913): 9–16.

22. "Al-Ishtirākiyyūn wa'l-fawḍawiyyūn," *al-Muqtaṭaf* 18 (August 1894): 721–29, my emphasis.

23. "Al-Ishtirākiyyūn wa'l-fawḍawiyyūn." *Al-Muqtaṭaf* attributed the weakness of socialism to the inability of its proponents to "limit themselves to curing the weaknesses [or defects] of the social body *['ilal al-hay'a al-ijtimā'iyya]* in matters that concern everybody and harm nobody. . . . They went overboard in their demands and have turned away from some natural rights. . . . They helped in some ways, and were detrimental in others."

24. "Fasād madhhab al-ishtirākiyyīn," *al-Muqtaṭaf* 14 (March 1890): 261–64.

25. Khalil Thabit, "Al-Ishtirākiyyūn al-dīmuqrātiyyūn," *al-Muqtaṭaf* 25 (August 1900): 146–51.

26. Thabit, "Al-Ishtirākiyyūn al-dīmuqrātiyyūn."

27. Thabit, "Al-Ishtirākiyyūn al-dīmuqrātiyyūn."

28. At the same time, the article criticized more anarchist-leaning socialists. "Francisco Ferrer wa'l-ishtirākiyya fi Isbānya," *al-Hilāl*, November 1, 1909, 114–18.

29. "Francisco Ferrer wa'l-ishtirākiyya fi Isbānya," 115–18. The article argued that the wave of protests in Spain served as a warning to the government that it should not neglect its duties toward the people: "[The Spanish government] learned that the people are alive, and will not . . . be patient with oppression for long; perhaps it will launch reforms in such a way that it addresses the socialists' demands and decreases the ambitions of politicians and religious figures."

30. "Francisco Ferrer wa'l-ishtirākiyya fi Isbānya," 116.

31. "Francisco Ferrer wa'l-ishtirākiyya fi Isbānya," 116.

32. Donald Reid states that *al-Hilāl* started adopting a more favorable view of socialism around 1908. Reid does not mention any favorable shift in *al-Muqtaṭaf*'s coverage. In fact he argues that *al-Hilāl* "picked up" where *al-Muqtaṭaf* stopped, and that "*al-Muqtaṭaf* remained one of the main Arabic commentators on socialism until 1908, when it was gradually replaced by Jurji Zaydan's *al-Hilāl*." Reid, "The Syrian Christians and Early Socialism," 180.

33. "Al-'Ummāl wa Aṣḥāb al-Māl: Tārikh al-'ilāqa baynahum," *al-Hilāl*, May 1, 1912, 466–75. For the articles in *al-Muqtaṭaf*, see appendix.

34. "Bāb al-masā'il," *al-Muqtaṭaf* 44 (January 1914): 93–94.

35. According to Philipp, the term *al-nahḍa* first appeared in *al-Muqtaṭaf* in 1888 in an article about the development of Arab medicine, but was most likely already familiar to the periodical's readership. Philipp, *Gurgi Zaidan*, 6.

There is a very extensive bibliography on the *nahḍa*. For the classic Arab nationalist narrative on the *nahḍa* and the period under study, see Antonius, *The Arab Awakening*. For general discussions, see Buheiry, ed., *Intellectual Life in the Arab East, 1890–1919;* Hourani, *Arabic Thought in the Liberal Age;* Hourani, "Forty Years After"; Sharabi, *Arab Intellectuals and the West;* R. Khuri, *Modern Arab Thought*. For more recent works that seek to frame the *nahḍa* in discussions on modernity and problematize it, see 'Azmah et al., *'Aṣr al-nahḍa*. For works making use of recent discussions in the fields of cultural studies and literary theory, see Guth, "*Wa hakadha kana ka-iblis.*"

36. Reformists throughout the Ottoman Empire argued that reform had become urgent due to the unequal and exploitive relationship between East and West. In Roussillon's words, "La nécessité et l'urgence de la réforme [en Egypte] s'y sont d'emblée formulées et y ont été vécues dans le cadre d'une relation inégale avec l'Autre." Roussillon, *Entre réforme sociale et mouvement national*, 13.

37. Roussillon, *Entre réforme sociale et mouvement national*, 11.

38. The conflict between secular and religious institutions is vividly illustrated in the clashes between recently established *majālis milla* (communal councils) and local clergies. See, among others, Hakim-Dowek, "The Origins of the Lebanese National Idea, 1840–1914"; Eddé, "Démographie des Maronites à Beyrouth au XIXème siècle," especially 19–20; Davie, "La Millat grecque-orthodoxe de Beyrouth 1800–1940," 164–65. For some of the *nahḍa*'s main ideas on education, see the selection of lectures and articles on the subject by key *nahḍa* figures such as Butrus al-Bustani, Shahin Makariyos, Shibli Shumayyil, Muhammad Kurd 'Ali, and Labiba Hashim in Y. Q. Khuri, *Maqālāt wa khutab fi'l-tarbiya*.

39. See "Socialism and Nihilism," *al-Hilāl,* December 15, 1897, 290–94, in which the author claims that socialism "accompanied humanity from its first civilization . . . from Elias of Chalcedonia . . . to Plato's Republic . . . and the Asyneans [?], in pre-Christian Syria." As for anarchism, see "Al-Fawḍawiyya fi'l-Islām," *al-Hilāl,* October 1, 1901, 7–8, where the author argues, "Anarchism did not appear in Islam under the same manifestation as in Europe, but it appeared, in a similar way to today's anarchism, under different manifestations." Interestingly the same argument appears in 1917 in a book in which the twelfth-century Assassins' branch of the Ismailis, and their assassination of the Seljukid grand vizier Nizam al-Mulk, is taken to be "proof that they are anarchists [nihilists, Nihiliste]." Tamimi and Bahjat, *Wilāyat Bayrūt,* 2: 69.

40. The relationship between old and new forms of biography deserves a study of its own. Noteworthy contributions to this topic include Fay, *Auto/Biography and the Construction of Identity and Community in the Middle East.* The obsession with biographies was a feature of *al-Muqtaṭaf,* as it reflected the editors' deep belief in individual accomplishment and the contribution of great figures to civilization. For a more comprehensive discussion of biographies and their role in *al-Muqtaṭaf,* see Farag, "*Al-Muqtataf* 1876–1900," 167–68.

41. For a detailed "who's who" in socialism and anarchism, see "Al-Ishtirākiyyūn wa'l-fawḍawiyyūn," *al-Muqtaṭaf* 18 (August 1894): 721–29. The article describes in positive terms the life and work of Robert Owen, Saint-Simon, Fourier, Louis Blanc, Proudhon, Robertus, Lasalle, Marx, Bakunin, Kropotkin, and Reclus.

42. See *al-Hilāl*'s article "Zola," February 15, 1897, 441. Another article that appeared a year later on the Dreyfus Affair evidently mentions Zola and examines his role in it: *al-Hilāl,* February 15, 1898, 469. The periodical also published and advertised a book on Zola's writings by Esther Lazari Moyal (1873–1948), a Beiruti Jew who had settled in Cairo: *al-Hilāl,* October 15, 1903, 63.

"Count Tolstoi," *al-Hilāl,* May 1, 1901, 425–29. *Al-Hilāl* was particularly interested in Tolstoi's theories on the social body's corruption by wealth and consequently the need for wealth distribution. The Russian author was very much en vogue among radicals all over the world due to his social and controversial religious views and his subsequent excommunication by the Russian Church in 1901. Before *al-Hilāl, al-Jāmi'a* devoted long articles on Tolstoi; his picture even graced the cover of one of its issues. See the articles that appeared in *al-Jāmi'a* in October 1900 and January and February 1901, 648–52.

43. *Al-Muqtaṭaf* showed a serious interest in strikes, wavering between condemnation and endorsement. It condemned them in the 1880s and 1890s, but it published more sympathetic articles in the early years of the twentieth century. See Khuri-Makdisi, "Levantine Trajectories," chapters 1, 4.

44. "Al-Ishtirākiyya wa numuwwuha," *al-Hilāl,* June 1, 1906, 563. The exaltation of Japan by Ottoman, and specifically Arab intellectuals and rulers as illustrating the possible progress of an Eastern secular country had a long history that actually predated Japan's victory over Russia in 1905. See Khuri-Makdisi, "Levantine Trajectories," chapters 2, 3.

45. "Ferrer," *al-Hilāl,* November 1, 1909, 115. "For this reason, the voices of socialists are only heard when they come to the defense against injustice or protest against tyranny . . . as they did yesterday at the execution of Francisco Ferrer."

46. "Ferrer," 114.

47. *Al-Hilāl* linked the rise of socialism to industrial inventions "that enriched factory owners," as well as to the American and French revolutions. The two factors "led to the appearance of many thinkers who examined the difference in wealth between workers and capitalists . . . [and] came up with various opposing solutions to this problem." "Ferrer," 114–15.

48. On this connection, see chapter 3.

49. The damage caused by sectarianism was a dominant leitmotiv in the *nahḍa*'s worldview. See, among others, Butrus al-Bustani's implicit references to sectarianism and its damage to the social body in a lecture he gave at the Syrian Scientific Society of Beirut in 1869: "Khitāb fi'l-hay'a al-ijtimā'iyya wa'l-muqābala bayna al-'awā'id al-'arabiyya wa'l-ifranjiyya," in Y. Q. Khuri, *A'māl al-jam'iyya al-'ilmiyya al-sūriyya 1868–1869*, 204–17, especially the section titled "Al-Hay'a al-ijtimā'iyya," 204–7.

50. On Salim Naqqash's writings on *al-hay'a al-ijtimā'iyya*, see chapter 3.

51. "Al-Ishtirākiyyūn wa'l-fawḍawiyyūn," *al-Muqtaṭaf* 18 (August 1894): 721–29.

52. Shibli Shumayyil, "Al-Ishtirākiyya al-ṣaḥīḥa," *al-Muqtaṭaf* 42 (January 1913): 9–16, reprinted in *Ḥawādith wa khawāṭir*, 105–12. In fact Shumayyil had been writing articles on socialism for some time before that and had published them in a number of periodicals, including family-owned ones. The best known among Shumayyil's relatives was his nephew Rashid Khalil Shumayyil (1855–1928), founder of *al-Baṣīr* (Alexandria, 1897). Other close relatives included his brother Amin (1828–97), founder of *al-Ḥuqūq*, one of the first law journals in Egypt; Qaysar, founder of *Majallat al-Samīr;* and Sabi', founder of *Majallat al-Tasliya.* See Tarrazi, *Dhikra qudamā' ṭalabat al-madrasa al-baṭrakiyya bi Bayrūt 1865–1938*, 13–15. Shumayyil encountered various criticisms for his "audacious" articles on socialism, including his article in the Beiruti *al-Akhbār* in 1908 defending socialism and its principles. Al-Sa'id, *Thalāth lubnaniyyīn fi'l-Qāhira*, 61–63.

53. One of the most remarkable figures of the *nahḍa*, Shibli Shumayyil has yet to fully receive the scholarly attention he deserves. A native of Kfar Shima in Mount Lebanon, Shumayyil first attended the Patriarchal School in Beirut before studying medicine at the Syrian Protestant College and graduating from its first medical class (1871). He then pursued his studies in Paris and eventually ended up in Egypt, initially settling in Tanta, where he practiced medicine for ten years, before moving permanently to Cairo and issuing the medical periodical *al-Shifā'*, published by *al-Muqtaṭaf*'s printing press. Shumayyil's claim to fame rests on his efforts to popularize Darwinism and especially evolutionary theory in the Arab world starting in the 1880s. For more information on Shumayyil, see, first and foremost, Georges Haroun's magisterial study *Shibli Shumayyil.* See also relevant sections in Reid, "Syrian Christians"; Elshakry, "Darwin's Legacy in the Arab East"; Hourani, *Arabic Thought in the Liberal Age*, 245–59; al-Sa'id, *Thalāth lubnaniyyīn fi'l-Qāhira.*

54. For a more detailed analysis of Shumayyil's "Al-Ishtirākiyya al-ṣaḥīḥa," see Khuri-Makdisi, "Inscribing Socialism into the *Nahḍa.*"

55. Shumayyil, "Al-Ishtirākiyya al-ṣaḥīḥa," 105–12.

56. See Bozarslan, "Les Courants de pensée dans l'Empire ottoman, 1908–1918"; Mardin, *The Genesis of Young Ottoman Thought.*

57. Fleming, *The Geography of Freedom*, 122. Incidentally, a biographical article on Elisée Reclus's life and thought appeared in *al-Muqtaṭaf* upon his death. See "Elisée Reclus," al-*Muqtaṭaf* 30 (December 1905): 960.

58. Ludwig Büchner (1824–99) was the author of *Darwinismus und Sozialismus; oder, Der Kampf um das Dasein und die moderne Gesellschaft* (Leipzig: E. Gunther, 1894). His work was highly popular among leftist circles in Europe at that time, as part of a trend of thinking on socialism and political economy in general in the context of evolutionary theory; his theory on the unity of all beings was particularly influential. Shumayyil started seriously reading about Büchner and his views on Darwinism when he was in Paris in the 1870s, and he later published a plethora of articles explaining Büchner's theories and commenting on them, as well as a translation of his *Six Lectures on the Theory of Darwin,* which was first published by al-Mahrusa, the Alexandrian printing press owned by the Syrian radical thinker, playwright, and theatrical director Salim Naqqash. For an explanation of Büchner's theories, see Hourani, *Arabic Thought in the Liberal Age,* 248–49. See also Elshakry, "Darwin's Legacy in the Arab East."

59. In Shumayyil's words, "Socialism is a modern teaching, although its roots are ancient." "Al-Ishtirākiyya al-ṣaḥīḥa," (True Socialism), in *Ḥawādith wa khawāṭir,* 105.

60. Shumayyil, "Al-Ishtirākiyya al-ṣaḥīḥa," 111.

61. According to one estimate, the circulation figures for these periodicals hovered around 10,000, at least for *al-Hilāl* in 1897. See Ayalon, *The Press in the Arab Middle East,* 45. Glass also estimates the circulation of these periodicals as being quite low. Glass, *Al-Muqtaṭaf und seine Offentlichkeit,* 10–11.

62. A glance at other periodicals and how often they would reproduce articles that initially appeared in *al-Muqtaṭaf* or *al-Hilāl* gives a sense of how canonical the two periodicals had become among Egyptian audiences. See, for example, the periodical *al-Muḥīṭ,* published in Cairo by 'Awad Wasif, whose section " 'Ālam al-Siḥāfa" (The World of the Press) very often included an article of interest from *al-Muqtaṭaf* or *al-Hilāl.*

63. Accardo and Corcuff, *La Sociologie de Bourdieu,* 42.

64. On universal values, see Bourdieu's comment, "L'exercice du pouvoir symbolique par un groupe, une classe, une nation, a pour objectif d'imposer comme une vérité universelle et allant de soi un arbitraire culturel." Accardo and Corcuff, *La Sociologie de Bourdieu,* 42.

65. Hisham Sharabi has coined the term *vocational intellectuals* to describe members of this class. He defines vocational intellectuals as "those whose roles as intellectuals were lifelong careers." Sharabi, *Arab Intellectuals and the West,* 4.

66. Khalidi, "Society and Ideology in Late Ottoman Syria," 125 (although Khalidi is concerned with Arabists specifically).

67. To use Durkheim's concept. On the concept of collective consciousness, see Curtis and Petras, *The Sociology of Knowledge.*

68. Established in 1857 in Beirut, this influential learned society's self-proclaimed goal was to strengthen knowledge, found schools, and encourage thought. Its members lived all over the Middle East and included various government ministers, such as the ministers of finance and of education (*ma'ārif*); various consuls, Levantine and others, throughout the Empire; and the usual literary suspects, including the Bustanis, Yazijis, Taqlas. On the members of the Syrian Scientific Society, Abu-Manneh writes that it was "first established . . . as a kind of cultural club by a group of *littérateurs* from Beirut. The new society, however, had a wider membership, Muslim and non-Muslim, with many young men in their early twenties, and with members from almost all the other towns in Syria and Palestine, including Damascus.

Cairo and Alexandria were also represented, presumably by members from among the Syrian communities in the two cities." Abu-Manneh, "The Province of Syria, 1865–1888," 19. The Syrian Scientific Society published various articles on progress and civilization, and its publications were circulated and read throughout the empire, especially Syria and Egypt. For a compilation of talks and publications, see Y. Q. Khuri, *Aʿmāl al-jamʿiyya al-ʿilmiyya al-sūriyya.*

69. For biographies of owners and founders of Arabic periodicals in Egypt and the Americas, see Tarrazi, *Tārīkh al-ṣiḥāfa,* vols. 1 and 2. For the press in Egypt specifically, see Zakhura, *Al-Sūriyyūn fi Miṣr,* and relevant sections in Philipp, *Syrians in Egypt. Al-Ahrām* provided an extreme example of this trend. Tarrazi, *Dhikra qudamāʾ ṭalabat al-madrasa al-baṭrakiyya bi Bayrūt,* 11–15.

70. The overlap between the professional and the personal, and especially the familial, is a strong recurrent feature among *nahḍa* intellectual networks. Perhaps no institution embodied this better than *al-Muqtaṭaf,* many of whose contributors were related, either through blood or through marriage alliances. To begin with, Shahin Makariyos, the printer of *al-Muqtaṭaf* and one of the periodical's directors, was married to Faris Nimr's sister. He was also the father-in-law of Khalil Thabit, who contributed articles sympathetic to socialism. Sarruf's wife, Yaqut Barakat, had a sister married to Asʿad Daghir, at one point *al-Muqtaṭaf*'s correspondent in Damascus and a contributor of antisocialist articles to the periodical (see his 1902 articles, discussed in the following pages). Another sister of theirs married Rizqallah al-Barbari, the author of the first article on evolution in *al-Muqtaṭaf* and a regular contributor to the periodical. See Farag, "*Al-Muqtataf* 1876–1900," 92–95, 110–17; Glass, *Al-Muqtaṭaf und seine Öffentlichkeit.* Similarly *al-Jāmiʿa* was run by Farah Antun, his sister Rosa, and her husband, Niqula Haddad, and Amin al-Rihani's sister was married to Naʿum Mukarzil, the owner of the New York–based *al-Huda.*

See Yves Gonzales-Quijano's very perceptive article on the emergence of a new and *modern* kind of author in the Arab world in the late nineteenth century: "Littérature Arabe et Société," 448.

71. See Lasch, *The New Radicalism in America, 1889–1963.* Christophe Charle makes a similar argument about the rise of the intellectual in France by tying it to the Dreyfus Affair, and hence radical politics. Charle, *Naissance des intellectuels 1880–1900,* 7.

72. In certain villages of Mount Lebanon as much as a quarter of the population emigrated. See Hourani and Shehadi, *The Lebanese in the World,* especially the essays by Engin Akarlı ("Ottoman Attitudes towards Lebanese Emigration, 1885–1910"), Albert Hourani, ("Lebanese and Syrians in Egypt"), Charles Issawi ("The Historical Background of Lebanese Emigration, 1800–1914"), and Alixa Naff ("Lebanese Immigration into the United States: 1880 to the Present"). See also Karpat, *Ottoman Population, 1830–1914.*

73. It is equally remarkable that these educational institutions in Beirut not only trained and subsequently lost educated Syrians who left for Egypt, but they also gained students from various part of the Ottoman Empire, specifically Egypt, and provided them with the modern education previously described. Indeed a nonnegligible number of Shawām, Syrians who settled in Egypt, sent their children to study in Beirut, especially at SPC and the Patriarchal School. Based on the lists of students enrolled at the Collège Patriarcal Grec-Catholique de Beyrouth in 1895–96, I have calculated that out of roughly 190 students, 50 were from Beirut, 40 from Egypt (15 from Cairo, 12 from Alexandria, 13 from various Delta towns), 24 from

Mount Lebanon, 14 from present-day Syria (the overwhelming majority from Damascus), and 13 from present-day Turkey (4 from Istanbul, 3 from Alexandretta, 2 from Mersin, and 1 from Izmir). The majority of Egyptian students attending the Patriarchal School were Greek Catholic Shawām (with last names such as Bulad and Zananiri), but a few Egyptian Muslims and Jews also sent their sons to study there. "Liste des étudiants, 1895–1896," Archives du Collège Patriarcal Grec-Catholique de Beyrouth, Beirut.

74. AUB Archives, Syrian Protestant College's 39th Annual Report of 1904, 32–33. Out of almost 600 SPC graduates still alive in 1904, 270 were residing in Syria, 198 were established in Egypt, 48 in other parts of the Ottoman Empire, and 45 were in the United States. "Number and Geographical Distribution of Graduates of the Syrian Protestant College 1870–1904," 31. The same was true of graduates of the Medical School at Beirut's Saint Joseph. There, between 1887 and 1907, of the 350 students who graduated, 220 were originally from Syria, but only 150 of them remained there; the remaining graduates ended up in Egypt, which "ne fournit que 60 diplômés et elle en reçoit 115." Nigarendé, "Beyrouth, Centre Medical," 44–45.

75. In the United States alone, twenty-one Arabic publications appeared between 1892 and 1907, seventeen of them in New York. Among the longest lasting and most influential was *al-Huda,* which was founded in New York in 1898. Syrians made up the overwhelming majority of Arabic speakers in North and South America, and they produced virtually all of the Arabic publications. See Naff, "Lebanese Immigration into the United States," 154; Tarrazi, *Tārīkh al-ṣiḥāfa,* vol. 2, part 4.

76. Daghir, *Qāmūs al-ṣiḥāfa al-lubnāniyya 1868–1974,* 396–495; Tarrazi, *Tārīkh al-ṣiḥāfa,* vol. 2, part 4, pp. 6–40, 108–10.

77. For studies on Syrians in Egypt, see Barbotin, "Les Syriens Catholiques en Egypte 1863–1929"; Dahir, *Hijrat al-shawām ila Miṣr;* Hasanayn, *Dawr al-shāmiyyīn al-muhājirīn ila Miṣr fi al-nahḍa al-adabiyya al-ḥadītha;* Hourani, *Arabic Thought in the Liberal Age;* Hourani, "Lebanese and Syrians in Egypt"; Philipp, *Gurgi Zaidan,* Philipp, *Syrians in Egypt.* For earlier works on Syrians in Egypt, see the various *tarājim* types, very popular in the late nineteenth century and early twentieth, which were compilations of Syrians' success stories in Egypt, for instance, Jirji Zaidan, *Tarājim mashāhīr al-sharq;* Zakhura, *Al-Sūriyyūn fi Miṣr.*

78. In Egypt as well the private press was subjected to some form of regulation through co-optation, censorship, and banning, but it certainly was much milder than in the rest of the empire during Abdülhamid's rule. As has often been pointed out, the press in Egypt was relatively free under the British Occupation, as Lord Cromer saw in it "a mere safety-valve for public opinion." Philipp, *Syrians in Egypt,* 97.

79. A press law, devised in 1909 and amended no fewer than five times between 1912 and 1914, made it possible to ban newspapers and imprison and flog journalists (Ayalon, *The Press in the Arab Middle East,* 68). In the period 1909–14 virtually every Arabic-language newspaper issued in Egypt or in the Americas was forbidden entry into the empire at one point or another for criticizing the Young Turks or "inciting Arabs against Turks." See, for instance, the following documents prohibiting various periodicals from entering the empire: BBA DH.ID.79, 31, 1331.L.9 Tahrirat (1); BBA DH-SYS 55–2, 14, 5.7.1330; BBA DH-SYS 55–1,15, 8.2.1329.

80. See, for example, Daoud Barakat, "Lettre Ouverte au Mutsarref du Liban, Traduction d'un article du journal arabe *al-Ahram* du Caire (no 1216 du 27 décembre 1906, édi-

tion hebdomadaire), Annexe à la dépêche no. 4 du 12 janvier 1907," reproduced in Ismail, "Consulat Général de France à Beyrouth (1897–1907)," in *Documents diplomatiques et consulaires relatifs à l'histoire du Liban et des pays du Proche-Orient du XVIIè siècle à nos jours,* 17: 362. In this open letter the editor of *al-Ahrām,* Daoud Barakat, reminded the *mutasarrif* that *al-Ahrām* was "untouchable": "*Al-Ahram* a mille correspondants qui écrivent à votre barbe et à la barbe de votre fils, ce vendeur de justice."

81. Among the various networks of exiled reformists was the network formed by the social, religious, educational, and charitable institutions al-Maqāṣid and al-'Urwa al-Wuthqa, the Muslim reform movement of Abduh, Afghani, and Rida. The presence and role of Muslim reformists was particularly strong there, and they also contributed to linking very closely Beirut and Cairo. Afghani, 'Abduh, and their school of thought also attracted many non-Muslims, such as the Syrian Christians Adib Ishaq and Salim Naqqash and the Egyptian Jew Ya'qub Sannu'a, who maintained regular contact with them during their common years of exile in Paris. See Sheikh Muhammad Rashid Rida, "The Second Syrian Trip," initially published in Rashid Rida's *al-Manār* (Cairo), 21 (1918–20), reprinted in Rida, *Riḥlat al-Imām Muhammad Rashid Rida.* See also chapter 3 of this book. On 'Abduh, see Hamzah, "La pensée de 'Abduh à l'âge utilitaire." On Rida, see Hamzah, "L'intérêt général (maslaha 'âmma) ou le triomphe de l'opinion."

82. This point is discussed further in chapter 4.

83. See AUB Archives (Beirut), "A Statement 1883 by the President to the Board of Manager" (signed and dated "D. Bliss, July 10, 1883"), in "Annual Reports, Board of Managers, Syrian Protestant College, 1882–3," 69–75. For studies on the Lewis Affair, see Elshakry, "Darwin's Legacy in the Arab East"; Farag, "*Al-Muqtataf* 1876–1900"; Meier, *Al Muqtataf et le débât sur le Darwinisme;* S. Jiha, *Darwin wa azmat sanat 1882 fi'l-kulliya al-ṭibbiyya;* Kedourie, "The American University of Beirut," especially 85–87. There are few contemporary sources on the Lewis Affair. Meier mentions *al- Muqtaṭaf's* "brief and laconic report" on the topic in an 1883 issue, as well as a few letters sent by readers pertaining to the origins of the Lewis Affair.

84. A statement by the president of SPC to the board of managers in 1883 sternly summarized the consequences of the Lewis Affair from the perspective of the missionaries: "The year 1882–3 will long be remembered as one of discord and rebellion." "Annual Reports, Board of Managers, Syrian Protestant College, 1882–3."

85. In his memoirs Zaidan stated that many of the students who first went on strike against the Lewis Affair (many of whom eventually left the college altogether) were Freemasons. In fact the four men associated with *al-Muqtaṭaf* and *al-Hilāl,* namely, Sarruf, Nimr, Makariyos, and Zaidan, all had a more or less serious connection to freemasonry in Beirut and Cairo. See Philipp, *Gurgi Zaidan,* 22–23. Nadia Farag also claims that Nimr was master of the Beiruti Masonic Lodge, was elected master in two lodges in Egypt as well, and received a gold medal, and that Makariyos was even more prominent in Freemason circles, holding meetings and hosting Masons in his house in Cairo and authoring seven books on freemasonry (four of which were published by *al-Muqtaṭaf*'s press). Farag, "*Al-Muqtataf* 1876–1900," 44, 55.

86. For a global perspective on Darwinism and its universality in the late nineteenth century, see Christian Geulen's fascinating chapter, "The Common Grounds of Conflict: Racial Visions of World Order 1880–1914," especially 80–81, where the author argues that in the late nineteenth century evolutionism had become

> a universal theory—concerning everybody and therefore adaptable by everyone [which was] understood in most parts of the world as a new philosophy of and for the modern world rather than as scientific study on the origins of biological life. . . . Darwin's evolution theory and evolutionary racial thinking provided both a direct access to the most advanced knowledge of modernity and a way to articulate alternative visions of what was called and generally admired as evolutionary progress.

87. Shibli Shumayyil, the greatest promoter of Darwinism (and socialism) in the Arab world, was initiated into Darwin's various theories around 1870 at SPC. See Shumayyil's introduction to *Majmūʿa,* reprinted in *Ḥawādith wa khawāṭir,* 261.

88. Musa, *Tarbiyat Salama Musa,* 52.

89. Zaidan seems to have been quite sympathetic to Darwinism as well, applying evolutionary theory to language in his first book in 1886. According to Philipp, Darwinism would, "with time, attain an increasingly important position in his thinking." Philipp, *Gurgi Zaidan,* 22.

90. Dodge to Bliss, February 13, 1885, in *Record of the Board of Managers of the Syrian Protestant College,* quoted in Farag, "*Al-Muqtataf* 1876–1900," 262.

91. This goes against what Nadia Farag writes concerning *al-Muqtaṭaf's* authorship. Farag maintains that articles appearing in *al-Muqtaṭaf* and authored by contributors "were always signed, and [that] the journal was very much against a policy of anonymity. . . . Even readers' letters were generally not published unless signed." She also claims that between 1884 and 1889 most of the writing was done either by Sarruf or by Nimr—and almost never by the two of them writing together—and that after the foundation of *al-Muqaṭṭam* in 1889 Sarruf wrote most of the articles that appeared in *al-Muqtaṭaf.* Farag, "*Al-Muqtataf* 1876–1900," 92–93. Even if this were the case with *al-Muqtaṭaf,* many, if not most, other periodicals remained very much a communal project into which friends and relatives pooled their efforts in the production of articles and translations, whether or not they signed their contribution. We should also remember that *al-Muqtaṭaf* occupied a privileged space and enjoyed specific favors after it moved to Egypt, given that Sarruf and Nimr were close to the British administration in Egypt and supported the British presence there.

92. "Bāb al-Zirāʿa Seção Agricola," *al-Farāʾid* (São Paulo), January 1, 1911, 18.

93. See, for instance, the Brazilian *al-Farāʾid*'s reproduction of an article on Mahmud Şevket Paşa, the Ottoman war minister, which had appeared in *al-Hilāl: Al-Farāʾid,* August 1911, 203–5. Or see its reproduction of a poem by the American Ella Wheeler Wilcox, "The Richman's Son and the Pauper's Son," initially published in New York in *The Journal* and translated into Arabic by Asʿad Rustum. See also the memoirs of Jirji Zaidan, who recalled receiving articles sent by friends from various parts of the globe. Philipp, *Gurgi Zaidan,* 209.

94. *Al-Muqtaṭaf* claimed to have covered one specific topic, political economy, after hearing of its readers' interest in it: "We have spoken . . . to two famous men in Egypt, and have learned through them the readers' interest in this science." "Al-Raʾs māl," *al-Muqtaṭaf* 11 (January 1887): 214.

95. See *al-Muqtaṭaf's* April 1911 issue. As for Farah Antun's *al-Jāmiʿa,* which was published in Alexandria, it claimed to have received in its first four issues in 1899 thirty-one let-

ters from readers in Alexandria, fourteen from Cairo, ten from Beirut, and five from Brazil. Reid, *The Odyssey of Farah Antun,* 56–57.

The trajectory of these periodicals is fascinating in and of itself. Sometimes friends and relatives living on different continents would offer one another yearly subscriptions to a specific periodical. To give one example, in 1909 an annual subscription to *al-Ḥurriyya* (published in Beirut) was offered by a Syrian in Haiti to his relatives back in Mount Lebanon. *Al-Ḥurriyya,* October 9, 1909, 191.

96. *Al-Hilāl*'s readers in Brazil were instructed to either send subscription payments directly to Cairo or make a transfer from one of the big banks in Brazil to a bank in a European capital or Beirut, if a transfer to an Egyptian account was not possible. Another option was to send banknotes in the currency of "any country of the great powers" *(al-duwal al-ʿuẓma),* make a transfer to one of the merchants in Egypt or Syria, or send a postal order. *Al-Hilāl,* August 1, 1899, 648. As for *al-Muqtaṭaf,* it had agents in Cairo, Alexandria, Damanhur, Tanta, al-Fayyum, Minia, Asiyut, Tahta, Beirut, Tripoli, Damascus, Jerusalem, Jaffa, Homs, Aleppo, Sidon, and Hama, as well as in Brazil, Argentina, the United States, Mexico, Canada, and Cuba. Farag, "*Al-Muqtaṭaf* 1876–1900," 86. The same held for minor periodicals, such as Jirjis al-Khuri al-Maqdisi's *al-Mawrid al-Ṣāfi,* published in Beirut and distributed in Brazil through its agent. *Al-Farā'id,* December 1911, 227.

97. "Socialism and Nihilism," *Al-Hilāl,* December 15, 1897, 290–94, question from Salih effendi Yusuf (Rawda) and Najib effendi Bannut (Beirut).

98. "Socialists," *al-Hilāl,* October 1, 1900, 20–21, question from Amin effendi Qattit, São Paulo.

99. "The Future of Anarchism," *al-Hilāl,* February 1, 1902, 285, question from Ibrahim effendi Shihadi Farah, São Paulo.

100. "Count Tolstoi," *al-Hilāl,* May 1, 1901, 425–29.

101. Interestingly Khawaja Niqula Ibrahim Nasr wrote from Pennsylvania, inquiring whether there existed a compilation of socialists' and communists' works and whether there existed a book, *in Arabic,* clarifying their ideas. *Al-Muqtaṭaf* answered that, to the best of its knowledge, such a book in Arabic did not exist. "Bāb al-masā'il: al-ishtirākiyyūn wa'l-ijtimāʿiyyūn," *al- Muqtaṭaf* 44 (January 1914): 93–94.

102. Knowlton, "The Social and Spatial Mobility of the Syrian and Lebanese Community in São Paulo, Brazil," 292.

103. Tarrazi broke them down into eighty-two newspapers and thirteen magazines. For comparative purposes, the United States came second, with a total of seventy-nine publications. Tarrazi, *Tārīkh al-ṣiḥāfa,* 2: 493.

104. Rafful Sa'adah's translation of some of Tolstoi's work, under the title *Mā huwa al-dīn,* was printed in *al-Maṭbaʿa al-Sharqiyya* in São Paulo in 1903, after having been serialized in the periodical *al-Munāẓir* in São Paulo. As for Gorki's work, the translator was Ibrahim Shihadi Farah, the owner of the periodical *al-Farā'id* (São Paulo). The first of these short stories, initially published in Russian in 1899, was titled "Twenty-Six Men and a Girl" ("Dvadsat' shest' i odna") and was about lost ideals, and other essays by Gorki were serialized in *al-Farā'id* in 1911. The translation appeared as a book in 1906.

105. "Al-Fawḍawiyyūn fi'l-Islām: ṭā'ifat al-ḥashshāshīn," *al-Hilāl,* November 1, 1901, 83–86, written by Dr. Saʿid Abu Jamra, São Paulo.

106. According to one study on anarchism in Brazil, "Anarcho-syndicalism was the most influential ideological force in the Brazilian labor movement. From 1906 to 1920, its adherents formed the backbone of the militant leadership, edited most of the labor press, and dominated the activity and organization of the unions." Maram, "Anarchists, Immigrants, and the Brazilian Labor Movement, 1890–1920," 80.

The role of Italian diasporic anarchism in the formulation and dissemination of radical ideas in Beirut, Cairo, and especially Alexandria is covered in depth in chapter 4.

107. Rotellini, *The Press of the State of São Paulo, 1827–1904,* 20.

108. Hannun, *Marāthi al-Labaki,* 93. The eulogy underlined the fact that *al-Munāẓir*'s readers were not "slaves of inherited principles or prisoners of religious beliefs . . . or [were fed] articles praising the ruler or the patriarch . . . the wealthy or. . . religious men."

109. He was also the author of a book on sexually transmitted diseases published in Arabic twice by *al-Hilāl*'s press, in 1902 and again in 1910.

110. 'Abdou, *Dr Abdou's Travels in America,* 364.

111. "Bāb Mashāhīr al-Rijāl: Tolstoi, al-Faylasūf al-Rūsi al-Shahīr," *Al-Farā'id* (São Paulo), January 1911, 1–4, 29–35; "Tolstoi, Mā Aftakiruhu fi'l-Ḥarb," *Al-Farā'id,* January 1911, 36–39; "Qaṣīdat Hafiz li Tolstoi," *Al-Farā'id,* January 1911, 43–44.

112. *Al-Farā'id,* August 1911, 180–88. Ferri had studied with Cesare Lombroso, the famous Italian criminologist, but unlike his teacher, he examined the social causes behind crime, such as destitution and alienation, rather than adhering to Lombroso's racialist explanations.

113. *Al-Farā'id,* December 1911, 269.

114. M. Jiha, *Farah Antun,* 28.

115. For example, when Amin al-Rihani lived in Cairo in 1905, he would send copies of his articles that had appeared in Egyptian periodicals to his friends who owned periodicals in New York or São Paulo. See his letter to Jamil Ma'luf, Cairo, May 15, 1905, in *Rasā'il 1896–1940,* 57. In another example, Rihani's friend in Cairo, George Hubayqa, distributed Rihani's work on the French Revolution to newspaper and periodical publishers in Cairo, including *al-Muqaṭṭam, al-Ahrām, Miṣr,* and *al-Mu'ayyad.* See letter from George Hubayqa, September 1, 1903, in A. al-Rihani, *al-Rihani wa mu'āṣirūhu,* 48.

116. Antun mentioned socialism's contribution to both "democratic principles" and "weaker nations" in an article in *al-Jāmi'a,* in which he connected social injustice with an unjust world order that featured imperialism. See his article "Al-qarn al-'ishrūn wa mā fa'alahu al-qarn al-tāsi' 'ashar," *al-Jāmi'a,* January 1, 1900, 460.

117. This was the case for his novel *Al-dīn wa'l-'ilm wa'l-māl,* which he serialized in 1903, in which workers (*al-'ummāl*) protest against their exploitation by capitalists (*rijāl al-māl*). In this novel socialism is presented as the most natural option for workers. "Al-dīn wa'l-'ilm wa'l-māl," *al-Jāmi'a,* June 1903, 258.

118. "Italy and Its Birth," *Al-Jāmi'a,* August 1900, 261. In contrast, the assassination of U.S. President McKinley by anarchists prompted Shumayyil to argue that anarchists committing high-profile assassinations, especially against heads of state, were useful because they were consciously committing murder in order to attract the public's attention to the system's injustices. See Shumayyil, "Al-Qatl al-ijtimā'ī" (Social Murder), *al-Baṣīr* (1901), reprinted in *Al-Duktūr Shibli Shumayyil,* 147–49.

119. A. al-Rihani, *Al-Rīḥāniyyāt,* 1: 17, lecture delivered at the Jam'iyyat al-Shubbān al-Mārūniyyīn, New York, February 9, 1900, my emphasis.

120. Rihani, letter to Na'um [Mukarzil], al-Frayke, November 18, 1906, in *Rasā'il Amin al-Rihani, 1896–1940* (2nd ed.), 104.

121. The periodicals included Shibli Mallat's *al-Naṣīr,* based in Mount Lebanon and Beirut, Muhammad Kurd 'Ali's *al-Muqtabas,* and Na'um Labaki's *Munāẓir* in São Paulo.

122. Rihani, letter to Na'um [Mukarzil], in *Rasā'il Amin al-Rihani* (2nd ed.), 104.

123. "Tolstoi," *al-Jāmi'a,* August 1901, 143–44. Antun would also read Rafful Sa'adah's translation of another Tolstoi short story, "The Kreutzer Sonata," in *al-Munāẓir. Al-Jāmi'a,* June 1903, 256.

124. Hannun, *Marāthi al-Labaki,* 161.

125. "Tidhkār intiqāl al-Jāmi'a," *al-Jāmi'a* (New York), July 1, 1906, 23–27.

126. See Rihani's (extremely long) letter to Na'um Labaki, 1901, in *Rasā'il 1896–1940* (2nd ed.), 407–14.

127. Rihani, letter to Na'um Labaki, 1901, in *Rasā'il 1896–1940* (2nd ed.), 22, my emphasis.

128. See, for instance, Musa, "Ta'līm al-umma," *al-Muqtaṭaf,* October 1, 1910, and Glass's discussion of the exchange in *Der Muqtaṭaf und seine Öffentlichkeit,* 564–70.

129. For the number of periodicals founded by Syrians in Egypt, see Philipp, *Syrians in Egypt,* 98; Hourani, "Lebanese and Syrians in Egypt." According to most estimates (mostly based on the Egyptian censuses), Syrians in Egypt made up around 0.3 percent of the total Egyptian population in 1907, and roughly 3 percent of the population of Cairo and Alexandria.

130. Shumayyil, *Ḥawādith wa khawāṭir,* 255.

131. Shumayyil published his articles on socialism in a number of periodicals, including family-owned ones such as his nephew Rashid's *al-Baṣīr* (Alexandria, 1897).

132. Rihani, letter to Jamil Ma'luf, Cairo, May 15, 1905, in *Rasā'il 1896–1940,* 57.

133. *Al-Shifā', al-Maḥrūsa,* and *al-Muntakhab* were all used in the School of Medicine of Qasr al-'Ayni in Cairo and in SPC, and *al-Muqtaṭaf* also played a similar role. Haroun, *Shibli Shumayyil,* 103.

134. As illustrated by the central role Syrians and Lebanese in Egypt and Brazil played in calling for the establishment of an independent Syria and Lebanon, and also during the King Crane Commission of 1919. See Buheiry, *Intellectual Life in the Arab East, 1890–1939,* specifically the essay by Stefan Wild, "Negib Azoury and His Book *Le Réveil de la Nation Arabe,*" 92–104.

135. Tim Harper's conclusion is worth quoting at length:

> Paradoxically, notwithstanding the power of European world systems and their "empires of information," there were perhaps more people participating in globalization, more people consciously thinking and acting on a global basis, and from more centres, than at any time since. The *fin-de-siècle* was the highwater mark of long-distance migrations. It was also perhaps an era when it was very much easier to take part in these debates than later. The globalization of European imperialism was an extension of the nation state. The globalism I have

> tried to describe was not. (Harper, "Empire, Diaspora and the Languages of Globalism, 1850–1914," 158)

136. Harper has written about the emergence of a new diasporic public sphere (1890–1920), most evident in port cities (his essay focuses on port cities of the Indian Ocean), describing it as

> a world where events far afield . . . were a common currency for all. Ideas of political community were not imagined solely around the territorial or administrative boundaries of imperial rule, powerful though these colonial categories were. They were based on harder connections and were international in outlook. Here, old and new "diasporic public spheres" came together through the expanded role of lingua francas and the fetish for translation. Their concerns were a long way away from those of the "imagined communities" of modern nation statehood . . . yet this globalist ethos was not solely the preserve of the strategically positioned elite. What is striking is how deeply the networks described here reached. (Harper, "Empire, Diaspora and the Languages of Globalism, 1850–1914," 156–57)

3. THEATER AND RADICAL POLITICS

A longer version of this chapter appeared as Ilham Khuri-Makdisi, "Theater and Radical Politics," CCAS Occasional Papers, Georgetown University, 2006.

1. "Li Ferrer," *al-Ḥurriyya,* October 30, 1909, 230. This is the first study and, with the exception of contemporary sources, the first mention of this performance and of Middle Eastern reactions to Ferrer's death. The primary sources themselves are scarce; in *La Syrie* Khairallah very hastily mentions the play, although the author's own participation in it and his support for Ferrer are almost certain. A much richer, if clearly biased source for this episode is *al-Ḥurriyya,* a periodical issued in Beirut in 1909 by Daud Muja'is, one of the writers of the Ferrer script and among the main instigators of the Ferrer episode. *Al-Ḥurriyya* devoted four articles over the span of four weeks to the play and its repercussions, as well as reports on demonstrations against the Spanish state and Church throughout Europe and quotations by leftist figures such as Jean Jaurès about Ferrer himself. *Al-Ḥurriyya* and the radical network around it are the subjects of the following chapter.

2. The first school established by Francisco Ferrer opened in Barcelona in 1901, the same year a comparable educational institution was established in Alexandria, the Université Populaire Libre. The UPL is discussed later in this chapter and in chapter 4.

3. Including parts of the Ottoman Empire. In Salonica a big demonstration took place in solidarity with Ferrer in October 1909. Paul Dumont, "Naissance d'un socialisme ottoman," in *Du socialisme ottoman à l'internationalisme anatolien,* 73–84.

4. For an analysis of this episode, see Best et al., *L'Affaire Ferrer.*

5. 'Aziz 'Eid was not just any actor. A Syrian by birth, 'Eid was the first among three chief creators of the modern popular theater in Egypt. His career took off when he joined Iskandar Farah's troupe in the early twentieth century. Although his reputation was as a Vaudeville-type performer, 'Eid seems to have had a predilection for controversial roles. In 1908 his troupe

performed Ibrahim Najjar's *Masraḥiyya fi sabīl al-istiqlāl* in Cairo, which was banned because it was highly critical of Muhammad Ali and was accused by the authorities of "wanting to plant the seeds of divisions between Egyptians and Turks." 'Awad, *Al-Tārīkh al-sirri li'l-masraḥ qabla thawrat 1919,* 15–18. See also Landau, *Studies in the Arab Theater and Cinema,* 86.

6. Petro Pauli was the director of the two periodicals *al-Waṭan* and *al-Murāqib.* Tarrazi, *Tārīkh al-ṣiḥāfa,* vol. 1, part 2, 184. The other performance in question was Amin al-Rihani's *Abdulhamid fi Atina,* which was described as having "a sound social purpose in which [Rihani's] aim was to criticize habits and traditions and religious and 'national' intolerance *[al-ta'aṣṣub al-dīni wa'l- qawmi].*" 'Aziz 'Eid played the role of Abdülhamid. "Al-Tamthīl al-'arabi," *al-Ḥurriyya,* October 9, 1909, 180–81.

7. "Masraḥiyyat Francisco Ferrer," *al-Ḥurriyya,* November 13, 1909, 253–58. It was highly unlikely that this was indeed the first world performance of a Ferrer play; in fact one such play was performed at Gaité Montparnasse in Paris in October 1909. See Best et al., *L'Affaire Ferrer,* 20.

8. "Masraḥiyyat Francisco Ferrer," 253–58.

9. "Masraḥiyyat Francisco Ferrer," 254. The Marrakech campaign refers to the Spanish-Moroccan war launched by Spain in 1908, against which there were many demonstrations in Spain in July 1908.

10. All seem to have been in *fuṣḥa* rather than colloquial Arabic.

11. "Masraḥiyyat Francisco Ferrer," *al-Ḥurriyya,* November 13, 1909, 258.

12. "Masraḥiyyat Francisco Ferrer," 258.

13. See Felix Faris, "Min ajlihi," *al-Ḥurriyya,* November 27, 1909, 283–85:

> The play was a criticism of the Spanish clergy, so why did the local clergy get up in arms? . . . The clergy here is not one united group; each group among them has positive and negative traits; Jesuits are different from local monks, monks are different from priests, and the Ottoman state is different from the Spanish one. Therefore, the clergy in this country does not deserve the fate that history has thrust upon the Spanish clergy, except if the [Syrian] clergy behaves in a similar fashion [to the Spanish clergy] (God forbid). If this were to happen, we would strike the one tyrant in all countries. [The clergy] complained . . . accusing us of diverging from religion. They are mistaken, for we are stronger in faith and follow more closely the laws of Christ than those who reside in palaces and drape themselves in crimson garbs [i.e., high ecclesiastical dignitaries].

14. Khairallah, *La Syrie,* 110.

15. For a description of a theater in Beirut, see the memoirs of Pietro Perolari-Malmignati, who traveled to Syria in the 1870s:

> Entering the house that serves as a theater, we cross a room . . . and through a wooden staircase, we arrive at our bench, a sort of naked table, without varnish or color. . . . It is quite small. . . . The theater, a nondescript room, is full of people. I did not expect to find so many, and it seems to me to indicate a certain civilization, that there should be in Beirut so many people willing to spend two francs to attend a comedy. There are no women among the spectators . . .

> and most of the audience is Muslim, because the author of the comedy is Muslim. . . . The governor and other people are sitting right in front of the stage, smoking a water-pipe. The top of the small stage is decorated with a sun with yellow rays, the crescent with a star in the middle and, on the side, Ionian columns. (Perolari-Malmignati, *Su e giu' per la Siria,* 154)

16. Even government employees in Alexandria established their own theatrical company (Sharikat al-tamthīl) in 1903. Najm, *Al-Masraḥiyya fi'l-adab al- 'arabi al-ḥadīth 1847–1914,* 173. Najm provides information on fourteen theatrical associations *(jam'iyyāt al-tamthīl)* in existence between 1885 and 1914 in Egypt, of which seven were in Alexandria and three in Cairo. According to the author, these associations did not limit themselves to performing plays, but also discussed and studied them. To these fourteen associations must be added performance troupes that were associated with clubs, associations, and schools (182–86).

17. On the etymologies of these terms and their various use, see *al-Muqtaṭaf* 69 (July 1926), reproduced in al-Khatib, *Naẓariyyat al-masraḥ,* 1: 353–54.

18. Al-Tahtawi, "Fi muntazahāt madīnat Bārīz," 17–25.

19. Al-Tahtawi, "Fi muntazahāt madīnat Bārīz," 17–25.

20. More precisely, although this play is generally considered the first play performed in Arabic in the Arab East, Moreh and Sadgrove have uncovered an earlier one produced by Abraham Daninos, an Algerian Jew, performed in Algiers in 1847. Moreh and Sadgrove, *Jewish Contributions to Nineteenth Century Arabic Theatre,* 1.

21. M. Naqqash, introduction to *Muqaddima li "Arzat Lubnān,"* 2: 415–20.

22. M. Naqqash, *Muqaddima li "Arzat Lubnān,"* 2: 415–20.

23. M. Naqqash, *Muqaddima li "Arzat Lubnān,"* 2: 416.

24. M. Naqqash, *Muqaddima li "Arzat Lubnān,"* 2: 415–20.

25. M. Naqqash, *Muqaddima li "Arzat Lubnān,"* 2: 415–20.

26. M. Naqqash, *Muqaddima li "Arzat Lubnān,"* 2: 418.

27. S. Naqqash, *Al-Jinān,* 1: 39–47.

28. S. Naqqash, *Al-Jinān,* 1: 41.

29. S. Naqqash, *Al-Jinān,* 1: 41.

30. S. Naqqash, *Al-Jinān,* 1: 41, my emphasis.

31. S. Naqqash, *Al-Jinān,* 1: 41.

32. "It is said . . . that the people of Egypt . . . [are so welcoming that they] make the stranger forget about his own country." S. Naqqash, *Al-Jinān,* 1: 44.

33. S. Naqqash, *Al-Jinān,* 1: 44–46.

34. See, for example, Mohammad Kurd 'Ali, "Al-Tamthīl fi'l-Islām," *al-Muqtabas,* Muḥarram 1324 (1906), in Khatib, *Naẓariyyat al-masraḥ,* 1: 143–44.

35. S. Naqqash, *Al-Jinān,* 1: 41: "'Ala annana nazīduha taḥdīdan [kalimat al-tamaddun] fa naqūlu annaha . . . wāsiṭat taqsīm arzāqihim wa mā baynahum bi qisṭ wa 'adl."

36. Al-Afghani's radicalizing influence on the development of the theater was continued by two of his most active disciples, Salim Naqqash and Adib Ishaq, both of whom were central figures in the world of the theater. Even when they turned to journalism and established newspapers (*Miṣr, al-Tijāra,* and *al-Maḥrūsa,* all issued in Alexandria), their interest in theater never faded and they continued to report and comment on theatrical activities. On al-

Afghani, see Hourani, *Arabic Thought in the Liberal Age*, 103–20; Keddie, *An Islamic Response to Imperialism;* Keddie, *Sayyid Jamal ad-Din al Afghani.*

37. On Ya'qub Sannu'a, see Gendzier, *The Practical Visions of Ya'qub Sannu'.*

38. *Al-Jinān* 6 (March 1875), cited in Sadgrove, *The Egyptian Theatre in the Nineteenth Century,* 56.

39. See *al-Ahrām,* December 20, 1876, cited in Sadgrove, *The Egyptian Theatre in the Nineteenth Century,* 126.

40. See, for instance, Salim Hamawi's letter to the editor in *al-Ahrām,* December 30, 1876, quoted in Sadgrove, *The Egyptian Theatre in the Nineteenth Century,* 135.

41. For example, tickets for *Fi sabīl al-dustūr* (1908) could be purchased from *Maktabat al-Hilāl* in Faggala. 'Awad, *Al-Tārīkh al-sirri li'l-masraḥ,* 88.

42. See, for instance, *al-Ahrām*'s attempts to gather support for Qordahi's troupe, in Sadgrove, *The Egyptian Theatre in the Nineteenth Century,* 155–56.

43. See *al-Ahrām*'s article dated November 23, 1880, in which the author "inquired as to when an Arabic troupe would be seen and when Arabs would make an effort to support an Arab troupe. He hoped that the (European) theatrical activities in Cairo and Alexandria would 'stimulate self-respect amongst the inhabitants of the port [Alexandria] so that they would contribute [financially] to the troupe [to enable it] to present plays in their language.'" Quoted in Sadgrove, *The Egyptian Theatre in the Nineteenth Century,* 150.

44. The reasons for focusing on Alexandria's municipality partly have to do with the availability and accessibility of municipal archives. The archives of Beirut's municipality were probably destroyed during the Civil War (1975–90). The archives used for this section are those of the Municipality of Alexandria (Archives de la Municipalité d'Alexandrie, AMA), which are typed memos and reports from the meetings held by the municipality between 1892 (the year of its foundation) and 1914. These reports were from the Délégation Municipale (referred to as DM) or the Commission Municipale (CM); both are in French. On Alexandria's municipality, see Reimer, *Colonial Bridgehead.*

45. See Sammarco, *Il Contributo italiano nella formazione dell'Egitto moderno.*

46. A report in the municipality archives on theater attendance singled out the Italian working class: "La population ouvrière, *italienne, entre autres,* fréquente le théâtre: il ne faut donc point que le théâtre soit éloigné . . . pour que la population qui ne peut pas prendre de voitures et qui ne peut pas faire cinq km à pied, puisse s'y rendre après son travail." Stross, AMA/DM, May 4, 1910, 8, my emphasis.

47. See, for instance, AMA/DM, June 15, 1892; AMA/DM, November 23, 1893; AMA/DM, November 30, 1909. Between 1892 and 1912 lengthy and fairly passionate debates on the theater took place at least twice a year.

48. AMA/DM, November 21, 1894, 215–16.

49. See, for instance, AMA/DM, July 6, 1909: "Subvention pour la troupe arabe de Al Tamthil al 'asri' dont le directeur est Salim Atalla," or AMA/DM, December 18, 1912: "Allocation d'une subvention au théâtre arabe de Georges Abyad . . . sa troupe étant entre toutes la plus importante et la mieux comprise."

50. Including a certain Abani bey, who most probably was Sulayman Qabbani, the author and compiler of *Bughiyat al-mumaththilīn* and at one point an actor himself. It seems rather unlikely that there would be two Sulayman Qabbanis at that time in Alexandria. Un-

fortunately we have virtually no information on him. *Bughiyat al-mumaththilīn* is discussed at length in a later section of this chapter.

51. See, for instance, AMA/DM, October 28, 1896; AMA/DM, November 29, 1899.

52. The idea of a municipal theater was first suggested in 1906, but it took many years to decide on its location and to resolve various logistical matters. Debates on these issues were still raging in 1910. AMA/DM, January 2, 1906.

53. AMA/DM, November 30, 1909.

54. AMA/DM, May 4, 1910, 8.

55. See AMA/DM, June 15, 1892, in which one of the municipal members argued that the theater was a source of wealth for the city and would create employment for a large number of people. A similar argument was made as early as 1875 by *al-Jinān*. See Sadgrove, *Egyptian Theater,* 56.

56. See, for instance, AMA/DM, August 1, 1894, 168: "Alexandrie est bien plus propre que beaucoup de villes d'Europe, beaucoup plus par exemple que Trieste, Marseille, Naples, Toulon." See the debate in 1902 on a medical congress to be held in Alexandria and the role of the municipality in facilitating this event: "La ville d'Alexandrie ne peut faire moins que certaines petites localités d'Europe." AMA/DM, November 26, 1902.

57. On this topic, see AMA/CM, November 7, 1906: "Si le gouvernement consentait à céder [un terrain], à un prix tout à fait de faveur [pour bâtir des maisons bon marché] . . . on aurait ainsi résolu, comme l'ont déjà fait beaucoup de grandes villes d'Europe, qui ont traversé des crises pour les mêmes causes, la question de permettre à la classe la plus laborieuse de la population, de vivre non écrasée par les loyers, en respirant un air pur et en respectant les lois de l'hygiène."

58. Najm cites thirty-three small troupes (many of which were short-lived) that were formed in Egypt between 1887 and 1908; in the 1890s alone, thirteen such troupes were established. These troupes were usually religiously mixed, including Syrian Christians, Muslims, and Copts. Najm, *Al-Masraḥiyya fi'l-adab al-'arabi al-ḥadīth,* 168.

59. By "every school," I am referring to non-Quranic schools, because I assume that they were not bitten by this theatrical frenzy. To give a few examples, students at the Beiruti Ottoman School of al-Rashidiyya put on theatrical performances, and so did al-Maqāsid students. See Muhammad Yusuf Najm, ed., *Masraḥiyyat al-Shaykh Ibrahim al-Ahdab* (Beirut: Dar Sader, 1985), 20. As for the Jewish School in Beirut, it seems to have been famous for its plays. See Sadgrove, *Jewish Contributions to Nineteenth Century Arabic Theatre,* 78. Schools in Alexandria and Cairo also regularly put on performances. See, for example, the plays performed at Alexandria's Saint-François-Xavier in *Saint-François-Xavier,* 26.

60. In fact when the vilayet of Beirut ordered that political newspapers be monitored by the government and theatrical plays sent to Istanbul to be checked before they could be performed, *al-Ahrām* commented that this would mean a severe financial loss for benevolent associations: "After this, there will be no more theaters remaining in our country . . . and it is no secret that plays in Beirut are some of the most important resources that benevolent associations rely on to help the poor and needy. . . . This law . . . has closed the doors of this source." Yaghi, *Fi juhūd al-masraḥiyya al-'arabiyya,* 52.

61. Niqula al-Naqqash, introduction to M. Naqqash, *Muqaddima li "Arzat Lubnān,"* 2:421.

62. Sadgrove, *The Egyptian Theatre in the Nineteenth Century,* 151.

63. For instance, in 1876 al-Ahdab was summoned to perform a play in the house of two Beiruti notables, Hajj Muhieddin and Hasan al-Bayhum, in celebration of the wedding of one of their sons. Najm, *Masraḥiyyat al-Shaykh Ibrahim al-Ahdab,* 20.

64. Ibrahim al-Muwaylihi was one such patron. Sadgrove, *The Egyptian Theatre in the Nineteenth Century,* 58.

65. Such as the Politeamas in Alexandria, which was being built in April 1881 on al- 'Attarin Street. Sadgrove, *The Egyptian Theatre in the Nineteenth Century,* 70.

66. Sadgrove, *The Egyptian Theatre in the Nineteenth Century,* 129.

67. Qasimi and al-'Azm, *Qāmūs al-ṣināʿāt al-shāmiyya,* 1: 131–32.

68. Bulbul, *Al-Masraḥ al-sūri fi mi'at sana 1847–1946,* 118–19.

69. Sadgrove, *The Egyptian Theatre in the Nineteenth Century,* 151.

70. In Shiyyah, a working-class village close to Beirut that fell under the jurisdiction of Mount Lebanon, members of the local charitable association wrote to Maronite Archbishop Yusuf al-Dibs in 1899 informing him of their intention to found their own theater and asking his permission to build it on the vacant land next to the local Maronite church. They also asked for the theater building to be turned into church *waqf* (charitable and religious endowment) if the association were to be dissolved in the future. Interestingly the term *Maronite* does not appear in the name of the association; we do not know whether or not it was a religiously mixed group, although all the names of its active members were Christian. Al-'Umda wa'-l a'ḍa' al-'āmila li'l-Jam'iyya al-Khayriyya bi'l-Shiyyah, letter addressed to Bishop Yusuf al-Dibs, January 25, 1899, Archives of the Maronite Bishopric of Beirut (nonclassified).

In 1894 Jam'iyyat al-intāj al-adabi (Association for Literary Production) was established in Alexandria by employees of the Egyptian post office under the presidency of Salim 'Atallah. It was to last for many years, and even held occasional performances at the Qordahi Theater. Zaidan, *Tārīkh ādāb al-lugha al-'arabiyya,* 4: 87. See also Najm, *Al-Masraḥiyya fi'l-adab al-'arabi al-ḥadīth,* 178. Intriguingly there was also an amateur troupe called the Troupe of the National (or Patriotic) Peasant (Jawq al-Fallāh al-Waṭani) that was founded in Alexandria in 1895 and performed *Cleopatra* in Samnod in April of the same year. Unfortunately we lack any information about it. Najm, *Al-Masraḥiyya fi'l-adab al-'arabi al-ḥadīth,* 179.

71. To give an idea of its intensity, Salama Hijazi's troupe, probably the most important troupe in Egypt in the early twentieth century, went to Syria four times between 1906 and 1911, that is, pretty much annually. Bulbul, *Al-Masraḥ al-sūri fi mi'at sana,* 115.

72. Najm, *Al-Masraḥiyya fi'l-adab al-'arabi al-ḥadīth,* 117.

73. In the words of Bulbul, "This is how he [Qabbani] spent the years 1884–1900, moving between Damascus and Egypt, and bringing back actors, stage designers, and so on." *Al-Masraḥ al-sūri fi mi'at sana,* 35.

74. Najm, *Al-Masraḥiyya fi'l-adab al-'arabi al-ḥadīth,* 111. Most women recruited in the 1870s and 1880s were not initially professional actresses, but once in a while the head of a troupe would be lucky enough to stumble on women with real talent. Such seems to have been the case with the Beiruti-born Badi'a Masabni, who was to become one of the leading stars of her time. In her memoirs Masabni recalled how she discovered the theater and how the opportunity to join a theatrical performance presented itself. She was then introduced to George Abyad, on tour in Syria and looking to enlarge his cast. Pleased with what he saw, Abyad recruited her. However, Masabni soon moved back to Beirut, where she was intro-

duced to Madame Jeannette, a Frenchwoman who ran "a kind of a cabaret, and had foreign women working for her: French and Romanian and Austrian and German." Masabni would be the only Arab among fifteen female artists. See Masabni, *Mudhakkirāt,* 81, 87, 112.

75. For a list of these troupes, see Bulbul, *Al-Masraḥ al-sūri fi mi'at sana,* 110–14.

76. Salama Hijazi was one among many who spent summers in Syria. Najm, *Al-Masraḥiyya fi'l-adab al-'arabi al-ḥadīth,* 138.

77. A great number (if not the majority) of plays performed by Syrian troupes in Egypt had previously been performed in Syria, specifically Beirut, before that. For examples, see Sadgrove, *The Egyptian Theatre in the Nineteenth Century,* 138.

78. See Masabni, *Mudhakkirāt;* N. Rihani, *Mudhakkirāt Najib al-Rihani.*

79. See this chapter's introduction.

80. *The Masons,* though not overtly sympathetic to freemasonry, was certainly not critical of it. See Shalash, *Al-Māṣūniyya fi Miṣr,* 30–35.

81. This happened at least twice: in December 1909 during a performance by Iskandar Farah and his troupe of *Shuhadā' al-waṭaniyya,* a play written by Victorien Sardou and originally entitled *Patrie,* and again during the performance of the play *Nicola Carter* in Cairo in July 1910. 'Awad, *Al-Tārīkh al-sirri li'l-masraḥ,* 25, 33.

82. Hijazi and Farah had founded a troupe together. Later, after they had gone their separate ways, Farah recruited 'Eid. For details on their professional collaboration, see Najm, *Al-Masraḥiyya fi'l-adab al-'arabi al-ḥadīth.*

83. See Perrot, *Jeunesse de la Grève,* 203; Vertone, "Socialistes et mouvement ouvrier italiens dans la région marseillaise pendant la seconde moitié du XIXe siècle," 97. See also Quesada, *Argentine Anarchism and La Protesta,* 28.

84. *Al-Muqaṭṭam,* July 8, 1910, quoted in 'Awad, *Al-Tārīkh al-sirri li'l-masraḥ,* 42.

85. Reimer, *Colonial Bridgehead,* 155.

86. Farid, *The Memoirs and Diaries of Muhammad Farid,* 25.

87. I am borrowing Geoff Eley's expression. Eley, "Edward Thompson, Social History and Political Culture," 28. See also chapter 5 in this book on the working-class public sphere.

88. Al-Nukhayli, *Al-Ḥaraka al-'ummāliyya fi Miṣr wa mawqif al-ṣiḥāfa wa'l- sultāt al-miṣriyya minha min sanat 1882 ila 1952,* 73. The spokesman was Jirji Tannus. On Tannus and his theatrical activities, see Najm, *Al-Masraḥiyya fi'l-adab al-'arabi al-ḥadīth,* 171.

89. Nukhayli, *Al-Ḥaraka al-'ummāliyya fi Miṣr,* 42.

90. Unfortunately we lack precise information on this topic; in the case of Egypt, theatrical performances were banned in 1888, but it is not known when the ban was lifted. In Syria the ban was imposed in the late 1880s and lifted in 1906.

91. Sadgrove, *The Egyptian Theatre in the Nineteenth Century,* 80.

92. Qasimi and al-'Azm, *Qāmūs al-ṣinā'āt al-shāmiyya,* 1: 131–32.

93. See Hattox, *Coffee and Coffeehouses.*

94. It is not clear when laws concerning the theater in Egypt and in the Ottoman Empire were first formulated; Najm refers to a body of laws specific to the theater and dating back to 1874, but it is likely that there was an earlier set of rules and regulations dating back from the Tanzimat period. *Niẓām al-Masraḥ* (1874), reproduced in Najm, *Al-Masraḥiyya fi'l-adab al-'arabi al-ḥadīth,* 21–22.

95. *Niẓām al-Masraḥ.*

96. *Niẓām al-Masraḥ.*
97. *Niẓām al-Masraḥ.*
98. *Niẓām al-Masraḥ.*
99. *Niẓām al-Masraḥ.*
100. "Deuxième annexe au procès verbal de la Commission Municipale du 29 juin 1904: Règlement sur les théâtres arrêté par la Commission Municipale dans sa séance du 29 juin 1904," AMA/DM, June 29, 1904, 201.
101. "Deuxième annexe au procès verbal de la Commission Municipale du 29 juin 1904," Article 1.
102. "Deuxième annexe au procès verbal de la Commission Municipale du 29 juin 1904," Article 23.
103. Yaghi, *Fi juhūd al-masraḥiyya al-ʿarabiyya,* 52.
104. Exceptions to the rule could be found, however; for instance, whereas *al-Liwāʾ, al-Jarīda,* and *La Réforme* opposed the government crackdown on the theater in 1910, *al-Waṭan* was in favor of such practices. State-owned newspapers obviously reflected the official version, whereas other papers had clear political affiliations.
105. *Al-Ahrām,* August 20, 1908, in ʿAwad, *Al-Tārīkh al-sirri li'l-masraḥ,* 12.
106. Interestingly works of Shakespeare, Molière, Racine, Voltaire, and Dumas, to name just a few, were translated more than once, sometimes within a year or two. There are many possible explanations for this phenomenon. The translations took place in different cities and were not well advertised and marketed, which meant that every locus of theatrical life (at an urban or even at a literary group level) needed to have its own translation and adaptation for the stage. Also some translations were deemed mediocre, and the challenge was picked up by another translator to produce a better version. Some translations were in *fuṣḥa,* whereas others were in colloquial Arabic; Sadgrove suggests that Jalal's translations of Molière's and Racine's plays were in the Egyptian dialect, whereas the Syrian translations were in *fuṣḥa* and were set to music and song, a feature absent from Jalal's translations. Sadgrove, *The Egyptian Theatre in the Nineteenth Century,* 102. Whatever the reasons, the multiple translations indicate the popularity of such works and their canonical status.
107. The first Arabic play performed in Alexandria was *Abu'l-Hasan al-mughaffal aw Hārūn al-Rashīd,* based on a story in *A Thousand and One Nights.* The play, which was first staged in Beirut in 1850 by Marun al-Naqqash, was performed by his nephew Salim's troupe in Beirut before being staged by the same company at the Zizinia Theater of Alexandria in December 1876. Sadgrove, *The Egyptian Theatre in the Nineteenth Century,* 128.
108. See, for instance, al-Ahdab's plays. For an introduction to these plays, see Najm, *Masraḥiyyat al-Shaykh Ibrahim al-Ahdab.*
109. The production of scripts exclusively for the theater seems to have been the exception rather than the rule. Many, if not most of the plays performed around 1900 were adaptations to the stage of a *riwāya,* a confusing term, as it designated both novel and script. Besides translations and adaptations from the classical European theatrical repertoire, most plays performed were either adaptations of novels written in Arabic or novels translated and adapted from French and occasionally English. Hence even when the script itself is not available, we have an idea of the topics addressed by the play if it was adapted from a European or an Arabic novel. The overlap between novel and script is conveyed quite vividly in Farah

Antun's article "Fann al-riwāya," in which he constantly jumps between the read and the acted *riwāya.* See Farah Antun, "Fann al-riwāya" (The Art of the Novel/Play), *al-Jarīda,* part 8 (1906): 305–11, reproduced in M. Jiha, *Farah Antun,* 173–82.

110. For instance, in 1881 Khayyat' s company presented in Alexandria a play titled *The Unjust Suffer Adversities,* which seems to have been based on Voltaire's *Mérope.* Sadgrove, *The Egyptian Theatre in the Nineteenth Century,* 154. Another of Voltaire's plays, *Proteus,* was translated and performed by Jirji Tannus in Cairo between 1904 and 1908 and in Jerusalem in 1908, sponsored by the Grand Lodge of Jerusalem. See ʿAwad, *Al-Tārīkh al-sirri li'l-masraḥ,* 88; Najm, *Al-Masraḥiyya fi'l-adab al-ʿarabi al-ḥadīth,* 171.

111. Victorien Sardou (1831–1908), whose *Patrie,* written in 1869 and set in the late sixteenth century, glorified the Flemish rising against the Spanish king and combined constitutional, patriotic, and anticlerical themes, was immensely popular in Beirut, Cairo, and Alexandria in the early twentieth century, both as text and as play. One of the lines in the play is "Nous ne voulons pas de roi-despote, soldat brutal, moine avide." On this play's performance in the three cities, see ʿAwad, *Al-Tārīkh al-sirri li'l-masraḥ,* 25.

112. *Ibn al-shaʿb,* one of Alexandre Dumas's plays. It was a "political and literary play" about an actor in nineteenth-century England and an attack on social inequalities. It was translated by Farah Antun as *Nubūgh wa ikhtilāl, aw riwāyat fannān.* ʿAwad, *Ittijāhāt siyāsiyya fi'l- masraḥ qabla thawrat 1919,* 75, 101.

113. Taylor, "Shakespeare and Radicalism."

114. The play *Hanā' al-muḥibbīn,* which enjoyed great popularity in the 1890s, provides a good example. Its plot revolves around the classical premise of a seemingly impossible love story between two people from different backgrounds, with the father of the would-be bride invariably opposed to the wedding. Written by Ismaʿil ʿAsim in *fuṣḥa,* this play, which offered a biting social critique of class rigidity and patriarchy, seems to have enjoyed great popularity. It was performed twice in Cairo in 1893 by the popular troupe of Iskandar Farah, and later in Cairo and in towns of the Delta by other troupes, including Salama Hijazi's and George Abyad's. ʿAsim, *Al-Aʿmāl al- kāmila,* 3.

115. Qabbani, *Bughiyat al-mumaththilīn,* 39–52.

116. ʿAsim, *Al-Aʿmāl al- kāmila,* 3.

117. For an example of his anti-imperialist work, see his play *Sultan Salaheddin and the Kingdom of Jerusalem,* written in 1914. On this play, see Najm, *Al-Masraḥiyya fi'l-adab al-ʿarabi al-ḥadīth,* 329. For an example of his socialist work, see his play *Miṣr al-jadīda wa Miṣr al-qadīma* of 1913.

118. On the impact of the French Revolution on Ottoman thinkers generally, see the special issue of *Revue des mondes musulmans et de la Méditerranée* devoted to that subject: Panzac, *Les Arabes, les Turcs et la Révolution française.* Also see R. Khuri, *Modern Arab Thought.*

119. For example, "The Marseillaise" was sung during the performance of Antun Shuhaybar's *Muddaʿī al-sharaf,* which was performed in Beirut's Jewish School in the 1890s. Moreh and Sadgrove, *Jewish Contributions to Nineteenth Century Arabic Theatre,* 90.

120. For instance, Dumas's *Ange Pitou* and Sardou's *Robespierre* (1895), as well as an adaptation of Rihani's work on the French Revolution. The popularity of these plays can be gauged by the number of times they were performed and their scripts read. See Najm, *Al-Masraḥiyya fi'l-adab al-ʿarabi al-ḥadīth.*

121. See George Hubayqa's letter to Rihani: "I distributed your book on the French Revolution among various dailies: *al-Muqaṭṭam, al-Ahrām, Miṣr, al-Waṭan, al-Khazzān, al-Ra'ī al-'ām, al-Rā'id al-miṣri, al-Mu'ayyad.* Yussuf [Rihani, Amin's brother, who lived in Cairo for three years] took a copy and I sent another one to the khedivial press. That is, ten copies, except the ones you sent me personally, which still remain with me. I could not follow the dailies to see what they have written about [your book]. . . . I am sending you the article in *al-Muqaṭṭam* which reviewed it." George Hubayqa, letter to Rihani, Cairo, January 9, 1903, in A. Rihani, *Al-Rihani wa mu'āṣirūhu,* 48.

122. Musa, *Tarbiyat Salama Musa,* 52, my emphasis. It is interesting to compare this view of French literature and French drama as revolutionary to the view of a French priest based in Alexandria around the late nineteenth century and early twentieth. Reporting on the "corrupt morals" of Alexandrians and their lack of interest in religious matters, the priest complained, "Tout ce qu'il y a de mauvais dans la littérature française, arrive à Alexandrie. On lit tout, et on ne trouve d'attrait au théâtre que s'il est équivoque, grossier, scabreux, etc." Unsigned letter, n.d., Archives Saint-François-Xavier (ASFX), 519 C (1).

123. Musa, *Tarbiyat Salama Musa,* 55–57.

124. On this topic, see the writings of Adib Ishaq and many others in R. Khuri, *Modern Arab Thought.* For a broader, non-Arab Ottoman context, see Mardin, *The Genesis of Young Ottoman Thought;* Hanioğlu, *Preparation for a Revolution;* Bozarslan, "Les Courants de pensée dans l'Empire ottoman, 1908–1918."

125. Shibl Damos, letter to Rihani, May 28, 1901, in A. Rihani, *Al-Rihani wa mu'āṣirūhu,* 25. Damos was most likely writing from Fort Wayne, Indiana, where he and his brother were based.

126. According to Bozarslan, when the news of the Unionist coup reached Istanbul, Dr. Ahmed Bey entered the School of Medicine singing "The Marseillaise" at the top of his lungs. Bozarslan, "Les Courants de pensée dans l'Empire ottoman," 148. Engin Akarlı also mentions that Yusuf Pasha, the mutasarrif of Mount Lebanon (1907–15), did not hesitate before the Young Turk Revolution of 1908 "to order the arrest and punishment of even a few youths for chanting the *Marseillaise* and liberal slogans in their remote villages." Akarlı, *The Long Peace,* 73.

127. Or, as Hannah Arendt suggested, it was the *continuation* of the French Revolution:

> If it is true, as Marx said, that the French Revolution had been played in Roman clothes, it is equally true that each of the following revolutions, up to and including the October Revolution, was enacted according to the rules and events that led from the fourteenth of July to the ninth of Thermidor and the eighteenth of Brumaire. . . . It was not in our time but in the middle of the nineteenth century that the term "permanent revolution," or even more tellingly *révolution en permanence,* was coined (by Proudhon) and, with it, the notion that "there never has been such a thing as several revolutions, that there is only one revolution, selfsame and perpetual." (Arendt, *Essay on Revolution,* 44)

128. George Hubayqa, letter to Rihani, Cairo, January 9, 1903, in A. Rihani, *Al-Rihani wa mu'āṣirūhu,* 47–50. Unfortunately nothing is known about Hubayqa. He might have been the same Hubayqa as the one whose name appears on the membership list of Alexandria's Université Populaire Libre in 1901–3.

129. Hubayqa, letter to Rihani.

130. Antun Gemayyil was *al-Ahrām's* editor. The play, written in 1908, was a one-act celebration of the 1908 coup, glorifying the roles of Niyazi Bey and Enver Bey in bringing about the constitutional revolution. It was staged during a literary Ottoman party in Cairo in August 1908 by a troupe of young Syrian literati. 'Awad, *Ittijāhāt siyāsiyya fi'l- masraḥ*, 76. In December 1908 the play *Fatāt al-dustūr* was performed in Cairo or Alexandria in the Teatro 'Abbas: "When Alfonse effendi Zakkur [clearly a Syrian] acted the role of Midhat Pasha, the audience clapped very hard . . . and cried" (83).

131. Most notably the Spanish "revolution" celebrated in the Ferrer play.

132. Jamil Ma'luf, letter to Rihani, Zahle, July 5, 1909, in A. Rihani, *Al-Rihani wa mu'āṣirūhu*, 99.

133. Rihani, letter to Munir Bek, president of the Commercial Court in Beirut, Frayke, 1908, in A. Rihani, *Rasā'il 1896–1940*, 125. It is not clear whether Rihani's play ever got performed; Landau asserts that it was produced in Beirut in 1909, which means that it took some months of negotiations before Rihani got his way. Landau, *Studies in the Arab Theater and Cinema*, 249 n. 456.

134. On this important theme, see, among others, Hanioğlu, *Preparation for a Revolution;* Bozarslan, "Courants de pensée dans l'Empire ottoman."

135. This was not the first time, but during that period it was becoming more of a trend. In 1873 Namik Kemal and his friends ended up in exile because they had performed a play based on the Turco-Russian War and the public had gotten overly excited by it. Mardin, *The Genesis of Young Ottoman Thought*, 66–67.

136. Performed by Hasan Kamil, who generally seems to have recited many monologues with a social agenda. See *Al-Bank al-Zirā'i*, in Qabbani, *Bughiyat al-mumaththilīn*, 78–80.

137. See FO 407, E 143, Confidential (8223), part 60, Further Correspondence respecting the Affairs of Egypt (1902), 8–9, No 13:

138. The authors of the play were Hafiz Ibrahim and Isma'il Sabri. Salama Hijazi turned it into a musical and distributed the roles. It was first performed in Damascus by his troupe, and then performed in Cairo by George Abyad's troupe in 1912 in the Khedival Opera Theater, and very likely in Alexandria and Beirut as well. See Bulbul, *Al-Masraḥ al-sūri fi mi'at sana*, 118–19; Qabbani, *Bughiyat al-mumaththilīn*, 118.

139. Quoted in Bulbul, *Al-Masraḥ al-sūri fi mi'at sana*, 118–19.

140. As previously mentioned, such was the fate of the troupe performing *Ḥādithat jarīḥ Bayrūt* in 1911 in Damascus. The actors in the Ferrer play were luckier: they were put on trial but were acquitted.

141. This chapter focuses on the tensions between Church and stage because they seem to have been particularly strong in Beirut and Mount Lebanon. However, we should keep in mind that there were occasional clashes between *'ulama* and the stage as well. There does not seem to have been a unified position by the Muslim clergy on the topic. *'Ulama* could be as supportive of the theater as they could vociferously oppose it, and some *'ulama* and sheikhs wrote their own plays. The plays seem to have been dealt with case by case. For a lengthy discussion on the theater by *'ulama*, see *al-Ḥaqā'iq* 2 (1911), parts 1–7, reproduced in Khatib, *Naẓariyyat al-masraḥ*, 1: 173–223.

142. There was an impetus among all communities for the establishment of a secular

body representing them, *majlis al-milla,* which often challenged the Church's management of communal affairs.

143. See chapter 2. Also see Rihani's letters from 1899, 1900, and 1901 on journalistic feuds among the Syrian press of the Americas on that issue. A. Rihani, *Rasā'il 1896–1940,* 21–23.

144. See, for instance, the epic disputes that raged between *al-Bashīr,* the mouthpiece of the Jesuits and, by extension, of the Maronite clergy, and *al-Muqtaṭaf.*

145. As commented on by *al-Bashīr,* the mouthpiece of the Jesuits in Beirut, "The students donned the garb of girls and women, and displayed in front of the audience the passion of ardent love and expressions of longing directed at their beloved boyfriends. . . . While we approve of moral plays . . . and acknowledge their benefit for students, we do not agree on them appearing in theatres *[malā'ib]* dressed as girls and women, uttering words of love from their mouths, because of the lethal venom [of such action] for the morality of the young." *Al-Bashīr*, September 4, 1888, 934, quoted in Moreh and Sadgrove, *Jewish Contributions to Nineteenth Century Arabic Theatre,* 76–77.

146. To give only one example, a clash erupted between the students and the clerical teaching body at the Hikma Maronite School of Beirut during a prize distribution that was accompanied by a play on Joseph. BBA BEO BEYRUT 269, Beyrut Gelen, telegraph 188, 1311 [1894]. See also the letter from the Syriac-Catholic patriarch to the wali of Beirut in which the patriarch "expresses his displeasure at the performance of a play in French which offends Christian sentiments." This letter was most likely a copy of the petition signed by various bishops and sent to the wali on February 25, 1322 (1904–5). Greek Orthodox Archives of Beirut, Beyr 1594.

147. See Makdisi, *The Culture of Sectarianism;* Fawaz, *An Occasion for War.* In Makdisi's words, "For the Maronite Church, the Kisrawan revolt [of 1858] could not have come at a more awkward moment. In 1858, Patriarch Bulus Mas'ad had convened a Maronite council at Bkirke in an effort to lay the moral, spiritual, and educational basis for a modern Maronite clergy and community. Therefore, as the Church was positioning itself as the sole representative of the Maronite 'nation'—as it was deliberately cultivating a self-consciously modern image—it was paralyzed by a popular movement that, according to an advisor to the Patriarch, threatened the *ta'ifa* with 'destruction'" (103).

148. Hakim-Dowek, "The Origins of the Lebanese National Idea, 1840–1914," 273.

149. "Al-yahūdi al-tā'eh," *Al-Bashīr,* March 24, 1911, 2. Jirjis Dimitris Sursock (1852–1913) was a dragoman in the German consulate in Beirut. See "Note adressée par M. Cambon à M. Cruppi, ministre des Affaires Etrangères, sur l'incident anti-jésuite à Beyrouth," Paris, May 22, 1911, in Ismail, *Documents Diplomatiques,* 18: 362–65. Sursock was a friend of Amin al-Rihani, whom he saw on a regular basis and with whom he exchanged various letters. One letter suggests that Rihani was also a Freemason: "My dear respected Brother, I received some of the kararis (decoration-like) from Egypt, and they are masonic; I will send you a few." Letter from Jirji Dimitri Sursock, Beirut, April 10, 1906, in A. Rihani, *Al-Rihani wa mu'āṣirūhu,* 73.

150. See *Lisān al-Hāl,* March 29, 1911; *al-Bashīr,* March 24, 1911.

151. BBA DH-SYS 64–24, #9, 6.5.1329 [April 18, 1911]. For a reproduction of the petition, see Khuri-Makdisi, "Theater and Radical Politics."

152. At least fifty-seven copies of it, typed and in Arabic, were sent to the Ministry of the Interior in Istanbul, each one of them containing between forty and ninety seals or signatures. In other words, if, on average, sixty-five people signed each petition, thirty-seven hundred individuals signed the same letter of protest.

153. Among others, see Beinin, *Workers and Peasants in the Modern Middle East;* Lockman, "Imagining the Working Class."

154. Briefly, the UPL was founded as a collaborative effort between Italian militant anarchists based in Alexandria and members of a progressive and cosmopolitan elite, many of whom were on the municipal board of the city. See relevant sections on the UPL of Alexandria in chapter 4.

155. The Parisian Université Populaire was connected to the establishment of the Théâtre civique in June 1897. Mercier, *Les Universités populaires, 1899–1914,* 31. The link between the university and the Egyptian theater was further strengthened by Ya'qub Sannu'a's connection to the Parisian Coopération des Idées, a progressive organization presided over by Deherme, the founder of the *universités populaires.* After his exile to Paris in 1878, Sannu'a continued writing plays and stayed in contact with Egyptian dramatic figures and reformists. (He himself had been a member of al-Afghani's circle in the 1870s and remained a convinced reformist.) Sannu'a's lecture in October 1902 at the Coopération des Idées indicates that the Egyptian dramatist had ties with progressive and anarchist circles in Europe; it is highly likely that he even played a central role in pushing for the establishment of a UPL branch in Alexandria.

156. The subject of a detailed study in chapter 4.

157. Between 1904 and 1909 (if not later) almost every member of that circle was involved in the theater at some point. Theatrical reviews were also a regular feature in *al-Nūr* and its continuation, *al-Ḥurriyya.* The reviews pertained to plays performed in Beirut and Mount Lebanon, as well as in Cairo, where Husayn Wasfi Rida, the two periodicals' correspondent, was based.

158. A sentiment expressed by Husayn Rida, who wrote, "I read a lot about the drama of socialism with [the murder of] its leader Ferrer; I saw authors write [about it] very powerfully; however they could not move me the way I was moved [when I saw the play]." H. Rida, "Fi'l-ṭariq," *al-Ḥurriyya,* November 20, 1909, 270–73.

159. See, for example, Marun Naqqash's view on the theater as discussed earlier in this chapter.

160. *Al-Ahrām,* March 10, 1882, quoted in Sadgrove, *The Egyptian Theatre in the Nineteenth Century,* 155–56.

161. "Al-Tamthīl al-'arabi: Nahḍatuhu al-akhīra 'ala yadd al-janāb al-'ālī," *al-Hilāl,* May 1, 1910, 464.

162. Qabbani, *Bughiyat al-mumaththilīn.* Many of the monologues were in colloquial Arabic, often combining Syrian and Egyptian dialects.

163. Of seventeen monologues, five are authorless, three are by Dr. Ibrahim al-Shududi, one by Amin Taqiyyeddin, one by George Alfa, one by Khalil Mutran, one by Tanios 'Abduh (all most likely Syrians); another is by Fu'ad Salim (origin unknown), one by Ahmad Muharram, one by Mahmud Khayrat, and one by Isma'il Sabri and Hafiz Ibrahim.

164. *Al-Iqdām,* March 30, 1908, quoted in 'Ezzeddin, *Sīrat muthaqqaf thawri,* 32. We do

not know whether such a party existed, but the fact that Shududi could have been a member of such a party is suggestive of his radical sympathies.

165. N. Rihani, *Mudhakkirāt Najib al-Rihani,* 16.

166. One gathering at Shumayyil's house brought together a handful of people, including Tanios Effendi ʿAbduh, "the poet." Shumayyil quoted in Razzuq, *Ḥawādith wa khawāṭir,* 255. ʿAbduh also translated *Hamlet.* See Qabbani, *Bughiyat al-mumaththilīn,* 16.

167. Ibrahim Shududi, *Shubbān al-Azbakiyya,* in Qabbani, *Bughiyat al-mumaththilīn,* 39–52.

168. "T'lā'i al-gadaʿ māshi mḥalfaẓ, khāyif ʿala rūhu min al-ʿayn fī hudūmho mashdūd wa mqammat, raḥ yanfaliq min ʿujbihi ithnayn wa'l-bantalūn rah yinsharmat, min kitr dayqho ʿala'l-fakhdhayn." Shududi, *Shubbān al-Azbakiyya.* A similar description of the dandy—perfumed, wearing skin-tight pants, and swinging his hips—appears in one of Amin Taqiyyeddin's monologues: *Fatā al-ʿaṣr,* in Qabbani, *Bughiyat al-mumaththilīn,* 63–66.

169. Shududi, *Shubbān al-Azbakiyya,* 43.

170. See Ibrahim Shududi, *Waṣf al-mar'a al-sharqiyya,* in Qabbani, *Bughiyat al-mumaththilīn,* 53–63. The work uses Arabicized French and Italian expressions.

171. Shududi, *Waṣf al-mar'a al-sharqiyya,* 56.

172. Shududi, *Shubbān al-Azbakiyya,* 52.

173. Upper-class women offered the only hope for an otherwise unreformable upper class. Whereas upper-class wives also depleted their husband's capital (hence damaging the Egyptian economy), female education could put an end to this trend. One of Ibrahim al-Shududi's monologues begins on a very misogynistic tone, accusing upper-class Westernized women of ruining their husbands by playing poker and generally leading a life of laziness and leisure, and even neglecting their children. However, the tone suddenly changes to reveal the author's sympathy toward women who not only take care of men in their capacity as mothers and wives, but are full of potential and could equal, if not actually surpass men. The truth was that upper-class men were useless and spent all their time and money in tavernas: "What does it mean: it is permissible for a man to spend his nights in khans, drinking, gambling continuously, playing the roulette for hours?" If women were superficial and uneducated, it was the men's fault: "From where would [women] get an education, while the people in our country are asleep; go and educate them in school so that they don't remain similar to animals and that they surpass us in knowledge." Shududi, *Waṣf al-mar'a al-sharqiyya,* 53–63.

174. Shududi, *Shubbān al-Azbakiyya,* 53; *Al-Bank al-Zirāʿi,* 80.

175. *Ibn al-dār,* in Qabbani, *Bughiyat al-mumaththilīn,* 85.

176. Ismaʿil Sabri and Hafiz Ibrahim, *Jarīḥ Bayrūt,* in Qabbani, *Bughiyat al-mumaththilīn,* 122. The same advice appears in another monologue: "Roll up your sleeves . . . follow the Japanese model." *Ibn al-dār,* 85. Japan's victory over Russia in 1905, the first victory of an Eastern over a Western power, had an immense impact on Ottoman society, as it triggered hope for the East's revival and triumph over Western imperialism. Hafiz Ibrahim composed a famous poem, "The Japanese Maiden," celebrating the victory of Japan over Russia, and Mustafa Kamil wrote a book, *The Rising Sun,* on the same topic. See Farag, "*Al-Muqtataf* 1876–1900," 308. In some cases, the infatuation with Japan and the belief that it was the ultimate proof of an Eastern country's ability to progress and be secular even predates the Russo-

Japanese War. Farag's work on *al-Muqtaṭaf* shows how, starting in 1880, the periodical held the belief that "the case of Japan was unique and, without it . . . one would have given up the idea of Progress in the East as hopeless." The periodical devoted many articles to Japan, which "had only yesterday emerged from the dark ages," and compared Japan's remarkable accomplishments to Egypt's lagging behind in secularism, intellectual independence from Europe, and industrialization. Farag, "*Al-Muqtataf* 1876–1900," 307–17. See also Aydin, *The Politics of Anti-Westernism in Asia.*

177. Sabri and Ibrahim, *Jarīh Bayrūt,* 122, my emphasis. This play was performed on March 19, 1912, at the Opera, Cairo.

178. This was the self-proclaimed aim of the amateur troupe established in Alexandria in 1894 by employees of the Egyptian post under the presidency of Salim 'Atallah. Zaidan, *Tārīkh ādāb al-lugha al-'arabiyya,* quoted in Najm, *Al-Masraḥiyya fi'l-adab al-'arabi al-ḥadīth,* 178.

179. Such were the rules and regulations of the amateur troupe established in Alexandria by Egyptian post office employees.

180. "Ū'ā min'l-bunūk; dol wa āḥyāt abūk nāwyīn yilḥasūk wa yisfū'l-madīna." *Al-Bank al-Zirā'i,* 78. Interestingly it is the city rather than the nation that was the chosen unit in this monologue.

181. *Al-Bank al-Zirā'i,* 78.

182. George Alfa, *Al-Azma al-iqtiṣādiyya,* in Qabbani, *Bughiyat al-mumaththilīn,* 89–90.

183. "It is my blood and yours which they [the Agricultural Bank and the pashas] have sucked." *Al-Bank al-Zirā'i,* 78.

184. Shududi, "*Shubbān al-Azbakiyya,*" 41, 51–52.

185. Qabbani, *Bughiyat al-mumaththilīn,* 131. As previously mentioned, there were many articles in the press on how to behave in the theater. The middle class wished to monitor and regulate the behavior not only of audiences, but of the cast as well. Qabbani, for instance, emphasized the need for actors to have "proper manners" (*muhadhdhab al-akhlāq,* 36).

186. See *Min kitāb iyyāk,* translated into Arabic by Ibrahim Ramzi, in Qabbani, *Bughiyat al-mumaththilīn,* 133.

187. "Al-Tamthīl al-'arabi," *al-Hilāl* (1905), reprinted in Khatib, *Naẓariyyat al-masraḥ,* 1: 145–54.

4. TWO RADICAL NETWORKS

1. We do not know whether *al-Ḥurriyya* was issued past 1910. In referring to a specific issue of the periodical, I will cite only the second date appearing on the cover (the two dates follow different calendars). For instance, *al-Ḥurriyya,* October 15 and October 30, 1909, will be cited as *al-Ḥurriyya,* October 30, 1909.

2. One such source is Khairallah Khairallah's *La Syrie* (1912); the author himself was a member of this network. Khairallah devoted a mere five pages to "socialist ideas [which] had their echo and their partisans [and] had, for a moment, their popularity and their triumph" in Syria between 1904 and 1912 (110).

3. See Hakim-Dowek, "Origins of the Lebanese National Idea," and Rihani's letter to Faris Mushriq, August 3, 1906, in *Rasā'il Amin al-Rihani* (2nd ed.), 98.

4. Iskandar 'Azar was a member of the Beiruti Lijnat al-Iṣlāḥ (Reform Committee), which

was founded by Midhat Pasha in the 1870s and included such illustrious intellectuals as Ibrahim al Yaziji, Salim Naqqash, Adib Ishaq, and Abdelqadir al-Qabbani. Diyet, *Ṣiḥāfat al-Kawakibi,* 77.

5. My deep gratitude to Dyala Hamzah for her help in tracing the Rida family connection. Labiba Hashim was the cofounder and coeditor with Alexandra Avierino of *Anīs al-jalīs,* which was published in Alexandria between 1898 and 1908, as well as *'Ayn Shams* and *Majallat fatāt al-sharq.* Felix Faris was the founder of *Lisān al-ittiḥād* (Beirut) and a participant in the Ferrer Affair. The contributors to *al-Nūr* and *al-Ḥurriyya* constantly engaged with him, but did not always agree with his views. Most of the network's members seem to have become suspicious of the Unionists soon after the 1908 revolution, whereas Felix Faris remained a convinced Unionist until at least 1914. See Rihani, *Rasā'il Amin al-Rihani,* 396. See also Tawq, *Majmū'at Felix Faris.* Shibl Damos was the founder in 1898 of the periodical *al-Iṣlāḥ,* which came out in New York (date unknown). He resided in Fort Wayne, Indiana, in the early 1900s. Albert al-Rihani, ed., *Rihani wa mu'āṣirūhu.*

6. See Rihani's correspondence with these various figures, especially during the years 1904–9, when a great deal of his extant correspondence (at least the published correspondence) was with people from this network. Rihani, *Rasā'il Amin al-Rihani* (2nd ed.), 47–137; Rihani, *Rasā'il 1896–1940.* See also "Al-Tamthīl al-'arabi," *al-Ḥurriyya,* October 9, 1909, 180–81, one of various articles on Rihani.

7. Members of this network dedicated articles and speeches to Farah Antun. See, for example, Jirji Baz's lecture "Al-Ādāb," *al-Nūr,* October 15, 1904, 284.

8. Muja'is eulogized Labaki for the soundness of his opinions and his constant commitment to telling the truth on controversial matters. "Ḥadīth al-Ṣuḥuf," *al-Ḥurriyya,* January 15, 1910, 388–89.

9. For instance, they all gathered in Beirut in 1910 at a ceremony attended by 250 people commemorating the life and death of Salma Nasif Trad, a highly educated woman and a passionate defender of women's rights. During this event virtually every person associated with the Ferrer play of 1909 gave a speech. See Tarrazi, *Tārīkh al-Ṣīḥāfa,* vol. 1, section 2, p. 184.

10. According to Philipp, Shams al-Birr was the Beiruti branch of the YMCA. Founded in 1869 by Nimr and Makariyos, it counted many SPC students among its members, as well as Jurji Zaydan, Cornelius Van Dyck, Edwin Lewis, and Ya'qub Sarruf. Philipp, *Gurgi Zaidan,* 22. Whether or not it was connected to freemasonry, Shams al-Birr does not seem to have been a conventional YMCA, since at one Sunday school meeting various speakers (including Shibli Damos) gave talks on the Ottoman Constitution and people's support for it. See *al-Ḥurriyya,* February 5, 1910, 440.

11. See, for instance, the following advertisement that appeared time and again throughout 1909, and in many languages, in *al-Ḥurriyya:* "This office is prepared to translate and draft various letters and articles, legal, commercial or political, to and from Arabic, Turkish, French, English and Italian. The administration of this periodical will be the go-between with that office." *al-Ḥurriyya,* January 1909, 360.

12. *Lisān al-ḥāl,* November 10, 1909, 1. The coverage of the network by the two Egyptian-based periodicals is addressed later this chapter.

13. *Al-Nūr* was a passionate promoter of the theater and conceived of it as the artistic form with the highest social relevance. See "Taqrīd wa intiqād," *al-Nūr,* July 15, 1905, 30–32.

14. The Christian Iskandar 'Azar, for instance, made donations to the Beiruti Muslim benevolent association al-Maqāṣid. See *Al-Fajr al-Ṣiddīq li jam'iyyat al- maqāṣid al-khairiyya fi Bayrūt,* 10–26.

15. In its very first issue, in 1904, *al-Nūr* assured the mutasarrif of Mount Lebanon, Muzaffer Pasha, of its intent to serve Lebanon, at the same time asserting that "*al-Nūr* was founded to be fully Ottoman and patriotic." *al-Nūr,* June 15, 1904, 2.

16. A reformist, Muzaffer Pasha found himself at odds and in conflict with the Maronite patriarchate, with which "a total rupture in relations occurred after 1904. To counter the opposition of these circles, Muzaffer encouraged and supported the movement of disaffection against Church and notables in the Maronite northern sectors, supporting the formation of Masonic lodges and so-called Maronite charitable organizations, which served as the backbone of what often came to be referred to as the 'liberal anti-clerical party.'" Hakim-Dowek, "The Origins of the Lebanese National Idea, 1840–1914," 260–61.

17. In October 1907 *al-Nūr* was still being issued in Alexandria, at the Syrian Jirji Gharzuzi's printing press, but it had at least three administrative offices: one in Alexandria, one in Cairo, and one in Batrun (North Lebanon). Additionally the periodical had a *wakīl* (agent) in Beirut, Na'um Frayha.

18. Muja'is himself insinuated that, although the mutasarrif Muzaffer Pasha was sympathetic to their work, he asked the periodical's owners to limit themselves to apolitical topics such as agriculture and industry. This prompted Muja'is and Mushriq to publish *al-Nūr* in Alexandria. "Bayn-al manāẓir wa'l-manāra," *al-Nūr,* April 15, 1906, 450.

19. As previously mentioned, Syrian emigrants, especially from Egypt, Brazil, Haiti, and the United States, represented a significant proportion of *al-Nūr*'s readership (and later *al-Ḥurriyya*'s), and upon their return to the old country, permanently or temporarily, many of them participated in events organized by the periodicals. Daud Muja'is specifically targeted their support financially and politically. "Ayyuha'l-ikhwān al-muhājirīn al-kirām," *al-Nūr,* September 15–30, 1905, 265.

20. Rihani spent a month in Alexandria in 1907, staying with his brother Yusef. This was one among many long visits to Egypt. See his letter to his sister Sa'da, al-Ramleh [Alexandria], March 1907, in Rihani, *Rasā'il Amin al-Rihani, 1896–1940,* 571–73. Felix Faris worked for a time as a translator in the Alexandria municipality. Shibli Shumayyil contributed articles to and engaged in discussions with Shibli Mallat's periodical, *al-Waṭan.* In one article Shumayyil forcefully argued that society could be reformed only by abolishing religion and patriotism *(al-waṭan)* and advocated universalism and the making of "citizens of the world": "Yaj'al al-'ālam dīnan wāhidan wa waṭanan waḥīdan." Shibli Shumayyil, "Ila Jarīdat al-Waṭan fi Bayrūt" (1910), in *Al-Duktūr Shibli Shumayyil,* 221.

21. A word about the nomenclature pertaining to workers *(al-'ummāl)* on the pages of *al-Nūr* and *al-Ḥurriyya:* the singular *'āmil* and *fā'il* were used interchangeably to refer to a worker; the term *ṭabaqa 'āmila* (working class) was in use by 1910. See K. Khairallah, "Risāla fi uṣūl al-'umrān," *al-Ḥurriyya,* March 5, 1910, 501. I do not recall seeing this term used earlier. Another term in use was *abnā' al-sha'b* (the people's sons), but it had a different, more populist connotation.

22. As reported in the night school's manifesto: *al-Nūr,* December 1, 1904, 444.

23. See *Beyrut Vilayeti Salnamesi,* 237–38, the section titled "Leyli Mekteb-i idadiye talabanin şarait-i intihab ve kubulu."

24. "Al-Awqāf," *al-Nūr,* July 15, 1905, 6–7.

25. See "Swīsra fi Lubnān," *al-Nūr,* January 1, 1907, 8.

26. Archives de l'alliance Israélite Universelle (AIU) / Liban: "Communauté: (1868 et 1904–8)," Box 1: "Divers: comités scolaires, adjoints, clubs, oeuvres, communautés, 1868–1930," letter from Angel, January 12, 1900, 4.

27. See, for example, "Ma'raḍ al-iflās" (The Exhibition of Bankruptcy), *al-Nūr,* July 15, 1905, 6–7, or the rubric "Miskīn al-Ḍa'īf" (Pity the Weak), which appeared regularly, as well as the rubric "Al-Masākīn," on poor migrants from the countryside. The language used to describe poverty could be quite graphic. In one case the author wrote that he "saw the monster attacking the weak and eating the poor." "Miskīn al-Ḍa'īf," *al-Nūr,* September 15 and 30, 1905, 138.

28. Arnstein, *Britain Yesterday and Today,* 192–93.

29. I am using *al-Nūr*'s terminology. It is important to underline the Ottomanist component of this call for reviving the economy; in 1904 it certainly was not linked to a call for any form of independence, but was part of a call to rally the population of the region and mobilize it in defending its economic, cultural, and political spheres from European encroachment. Hence by *al-Ṣinā'a al-dākhiliyya* the network around *al-Nūr* was referring to the local Syrian economy, with the understanding that Syria constituted a region and an integral part of the Ottoman Empire.

30. A hypothesis further supported by the fact that *al-Nūr*'s mailing address was in Shuwayr. The opening of a night school in Shuwayr was decided by the Committee of the Public Good of Shuwayr (Jam'iyyat al-Khayr al-'Āmm fi'l-Shuwayr) in late 1904 and was reported by *al-Nūr,* December 1, 1904, 444. The night school received enthusiastic support on the pages of *al-Nūr,* which printed its program, rules, and regulations twice within the span of four months (December 1904 and March 1905).

31. As reported in the night school's manifesto. *Al-Nūr,* December 1, 1904, 444.

32. *Al-Nūr,* December 1, 1904, 444. The March report on the school mentions thirty students who registered in the first month of the school's existence, their ages between 15 and 40: "Taqwīm Jam'iyyat al-Khayr al-'Āmm," *al-Nūr,* March 15, 1905, 639.

33. "Al-Faqīr wa'l-madrasa," *al-Nūr,* September 15–30, 1905, 182.

34. Starting around 1880 reading rooms mushroomed in many regions of Egypt and Syria, including Mount Lebanon. However, although reading rooms had existed before 1904, *al-Nūr*'s network seems to have been among the first, if not *the* first, to promote their establishment en masse and systematically.

35. One long article, appearing over many weeks, traced great libraries in history, from ancient to modern times, emphasizing the link between libraries and civilizational achievements. See Jirji Nicola Baz, "Al-Muntadayāt al-'arabiyya wa'l-makātib al-'umūmiyya," *al-Nūr,* July 31, 1905, 52–54.

36. "Ghuraf al-qirā'a al-'uthmāniyya," *al-Nūr,* October 31, 1904, 296–301.

37. "Ghuraf al-qirā'a al-majjāniyya," *al-Nūr,* April 30, 1905, 709.

38. "Ghuraf al-qirā'a al-'uthmāniyya," *al-Nūr,* October 31, 1904, 296–301, my emphasis.

39. An article written in 1904 perhaps most clearly illustrates this trend. Deploring in

passing the injustice behind foreign workers' wages being three times higher than those of local workers, the author swiftly generalized his argument on the unequal power relationship between Europeans and locals, and ended up writing predominantly on foreign missionaries' attempts to educate indigenous Christians about "true" Christianity. See *al-Nūr,* November 15, 1904, 321–28.

40. "Sikkat al-ḥadīd wa-mustakhdimūha," *al-Nūr,* February 15, 1906, 340–41, my emphasis. The disclaimer made by *al-Nūr,* in which the periodical clarified that its intention was not to trigger strikes, sounds more like a veiled threat.

41. In one article the author compared the way the superintendents treated workers in silk factories to "the way a pig herder treats pigs. . . . The worker has to accept all sorts of abuses and insults." "Ma'āmil al-ḥarīr wa-'amalatuha," *al-Nūr,* February 1907, 125. Two years later *al-Ḥurriyya* wrote about "those who snatch away the last morsel soaked in blood from the mouth of the orphan, or . . . take the harvester's harvest or the worker's salary by force, those are the sons of Nero and Abdülhamid." "'Ala'l-ru'ūs al-mutamarrida," *al-Ḥurriyya,* July 28–August 15, 1909, 81.

42. "Ḥālatuna al-'ilmiyya wa'l-ṣinā'iyya," *al-Nūr,* April 1, 1906, 420.

43. See, for instance, Khairallah's sequence of articles titled "On the Origins of Civilization." One of his articles explained what "capital" *(ra's al-māl)* meant, and its relation to labor: "Risāla fi uṣūl al-'umrān: Fi ra's al-māl," *al-Ḥurriyya,* January 15, 1910, 385–87. In another article he explored the pros and cons of gain distribution among workers, capitalists, and the intermediate person: "Dhayl fi taqsīm al-arbāḥ," *al-Ḥurriyya,* January 22, 1910, 398–99. In a third article he explained the mechanisms of supply and demand, import and export: "Risāla fi uṣūl al-'umrān," *al-Ḥurriyya,* January 29, 1910, 415.

44. Khairallah, "Dhayl fi taqsīm al-arbāḥ," 398–99.

45. Khairallah, "Dhayl fi taqsīm al-arbāḥ," 398–99; K. Khairallah, "Risāla fi uṣūl al-'umrān," *al-Ḥurriyya,* March 12, 1910, 511. In another article Khairallah discussed the advantages of establishing savings funds for workers; he emphasized the fact that this practice was widespread in "civilized countries." See Khairallah, "Risāla fi uṣūl al-'umrān," *al-Ḥurriyya,* March 5, 1910, 500.

46. Khairallah, "Risāla fi uṣūl al-'umrān," 511, my emphasis.

47. Khairallah, "Dhayl fi taqsīm al-arbāḥ," 398–99.

48. Khairallah, "Risāla fi uṣūl al-'umrān."

49. "Al-Ma'raḍ al-ṣinā'i fi Zahle," *al-Muqtaṭaf,* September 1909), 886–87. The exhibition was organized by Faris Mushriq and his friends.

50. "Risāla fi uṣūl al-'umrān," *al-Ḥurriyya,* February 5, 1910, 435. He made a similar argument in "Risāla fi uṣūl al-'umrān," *al-Ḥurriyya,* January 29, 1910, 416.

51. Nonetheless antagonism toward the Committee of Union and Progress did not emerge immediately after the 1908 revolution. Indeed the group around *al-Nūr* was quite favorable to the Unionists in 1908, and Muja'is and Mushriq were both members of the Radical Party, which was vocally anticlerical and received the Unionists' support. However, by late 1909 members of the *al-Nūr* and *al-Ḥurriyya* network, like many Syrian reformists and radicals, had become disenchanted with the Unionists. See Khuri-Makdisi, "Levantine Trajectories," 213, note 91.

52. "Al-Ta'ṣṣub al-dīnī," *al-Nūr,* July 15, 1905, 9–13.

53. "Ḍayf ka'l-mushīb," *al-Nūr,* June 15 ,1904, 19–23. See also *al-Nūr,* November 15, 1904, 321–28.

54. "Al-Madāris al-ḥaqiqiyya wa shiddat ḥājatina ilayha," *al-Nūr,* July 15, 1904, 68.

55. Beginning in the fall of 1905 and continuing throughout 1906, many articles were published in *al-Nūr* under the rubric "Al-iṣlāḥ al-ikliriki" (The Reform of the Clergy), emphasizing the need to reform both Maronite and Orthodox clergies. Specifically the periodical argued for the need to reform the management of Church *awqāf* (pious foundations) and suggested that the church sell its *waqf* properties and build income-generating establishments that would provide stable income and could not be meddled with. "Al-Baṭrakiyya al-antāqiyya al-urthūduksiyya," *al-Nūr,* November 30, 1905, 299.

See Labiba Hashim's article in which she denounces "men of the clergy [who] want to keep the people's eyes shut . . . and generally wish to treat us as if we were children": Labiba Hashim, "Majlis al-sinūdus al-milli," *al-Ḥurriyya,* September 11, 1909, 150. See also Emile Khuri's article on the clergy, in which he denounces the corruption among members of the clergy and accuses them of stealing from the poor as well as from the rich: Emile Khuri, "Min ajl al-dīn," *al-Ḥurriyya,* November 27, 1909, 281–83.

56. Felix Faris, "Min ajlihi," *al-Ḥurriyya,* November 2, 1909, 283–85.

57. Faris, "Min ajlihi."

58. See also Hakim-Dowek, "Origins of the Lebanese National Idea," 273.

59. Hakim-Dowek, "Origins of the Lebanese National Idea," 265.

60. Owen, *New Perspectives on Property and Land in the Middle East,* xi; Quataert, "Rural Unrest in the Ottoman Empire, 1830–1914," 39.

61. For an analysis of these claims and rebellions based on Musha' in the Hawran, see A. Hanna, *Al-'Āmmiyya wa'l-intifāḍa al-fallāhiyya 1850–1918 fi Jabal Hawrān;* Schaebler, "Practicing Musha'."

62. Khater, "'House' to 'Goddess of the House,'" 335.

63. Schaebler, "Practicing Musha',"

64. See Makdisi, *The Culture of Sectarianism.*

65. See BBA A.MTZ.CL 5/206 1325.7.28 (23) and BBA A.MTZ.CL 2/60 1310.8.8 (90). Many of the documents revolve around land that is contested between villagers on one hand, and the Maronite clergy or a city merchant on the other.

66. "Fi'l-ṭarīq," *al-Ḥurriyya,* September 4, 1909, 111.

67. "Fi'l-ṭarīq," 112.

68. See BBA A.MTZ.CL 5/206 1325.7.28 (23), on various claims over the *waqf* of Mar Ruhana monastery in 'Aramūn.

69. *Al-Ḥurriyya,* February 26, 1910

70. See, for example, Stefaneski effendi Polikivitch, "Falsafat al-qanābil," *al-Ḥurriyya,* August 15, 1909, 86–87, in which the author attacks the "sanctity of the clergy, which sacrifices most of its people, leaders, God and his religion, in order to please a leader [the mutasarrif of Mount Lebanon]" (87).

71. "'Ala'l-ru'ūs al-mutamarrida," *al-Ḥurriyya,* August 15, 1909, 82.

72. Hakim-Dowek, "Origins of the Lebanese National Idea," 324.

73. See Hanioğlu, *Preparation for a Revolution,* 121; Kansu, *The Revolution of 1908 in Turkey,* 3, 52; Sohrabi, "Global Waves, Local Actors."

74. According to Paul Dumont, Salonica's first celebration of May 1 took place in 1909, which is surprisingly late, given that the city's socialists and workers' unions were quite militant. However, unlike the Dbayeh celebration that was conducted by a handful of *gens d'élite,* a large number of people, including workers, participated in Salonica's May 1. See Dumont, "Naissance d'un socialisme ottoman," 76.

75. Khairallah, *La Syrie,* 110. Khairallah wrote that all three organizers were forced to leave Syria: "L'un s'en alla en Amérique, l'autre vint s'abriter à Paris, et le troisième est perdu on ne sait où, sur les grandes routes du monde." It is possible that he himself was one of these organizers.

76. Significantly this event seems to have been very visible since the gathering site was a popular relaxation place. Khairallah, *La Syrie,* 110.

77. See Khuri-Makdisi, "Levantine Trajectories," chapter 2.

78. "Falsafat al-qanābil," *al-Ḥurriyya,* August 1, 1909, 85.

79. Bozarslan and Hanioğlu have both discussed the influence of anarchism on late Ottoman political thought, and specifically on the Young Turks, but have framed it rather narrowly, mostly focusing on its use of terrorism and political violence rather than analyzing its ideology. However, their work indicates how resonant anarchism was during the Hamidian era, at least in Istanbul. The authors point out that the Turkish Anarchist Society was established in 1901 in Istanbul, and that a number of prominent Ottoman political figures and thinkers, including Abdullah Cevdet, Yahya Kemal, and Prince Sabahaddin, were influenced by anarchist thinkers such as Elisée Reclus. See Bozarslan, "Les Courants de pensée dans l'Empire ottoman," and Hanioğlu, *Preparation for A Revolution.*

80. The story behind the 'Aley bomb is draped in mystery and rumor. The official investigation yielded that the idea of planting a bomb in the summer residency of the mutasarrif was conceived by some Lebanese working together with the servants of the mutasarrif, at least one of whom was Greek. These "conspirators" formed an organization called the Organization of Lebanese Nihilists in Spite of Themselves (Jam'iyyat al-Nihilist al-Lubnaniyyīn Raghman 'Anhum). *Al-Ḥurriyya*'s mocking tone suggests that the official version on the 'Aley bomb was not entirely credible: "Falsafat al-qanābil," *al-Ḥurriyya,* August 15, 1909, 85–87; "Li-naḍḥak," *al-Ḥurriyya,* October 16, 1909, 198–99.

81. To quote Polikivitch, "[I] hate any criminal anarchist act *[kull 'amal jinā'i fawḍawi]* regardless of what it is, as long as there are legal ways *[ṭuruq mashrū'a]* to change the condition of peoples *[ḥāl al-shu'ūb]* without resorting to terror. Terror should only be used in the most desperate situations as a defense tool against aggression—and this is an occasion for me to remind revolutionary authors *[al-kuttāb al-thawriyyīn]* of the need to distinguish between revolution and anarchy." *Al-Ḥurriyya,* August 15, 1909, 85.

82. *Al-Ḥurriyya,* August 15, 1909, 85.

83. During the "tragic week" of July 26–August 1 1909, which began as a protest in Barcelona against the military draft before turning into radicals rioting against the Catholic Church, eighty churches and religious institutions were destroyed. See Casas, *Anarchist Organization,* 48.

84. See, for instance, the very graphic descriptions of torture and oppression by the Church, which led to the attacks against the clergy hundreds of years later. "Many centuries later, the clerical oppression lit the fire of resentment . . . in the chest of the Spanish poor

[fuqarā' al-Isbān]." As a consequence of this oppression, and the Spanish clergy's "monopoliz[ing] God and hid[ing] him from the Spanish people . . . the rebellion by the Socialists of Barcelona erupted, and they burned fifteen monasteries." "Kayfa thāra al-Isbaniyūl," *al-Ḥurriyya,* September 15, 1909, 132–33.

85. Abdullah Cevdet, "Almanya Imperatoru ve Sultan Hamid" (1896), quoted in Bozarslan, "Les Courants de pensée dans l'Empire ottoman," 290, my translation and my emphasis.

86. Bozarslan, "Les Courants de pensée dans l'Empire ottoman," 289.

87. *Al-Ḥurriyya,* August 15, 1909, 85.

88. "Kharijiyya: Shay' 'an al-hind: Jihād fi sabīl al-Ḥurriyya," *al-Ḥurriyya,* July 24, 1909, 14.

89. "Kharijiyya: Shay' 'an al-hind: Jihād fi sabīl al-Ḥurriyya," 15.

90. "Kharijiyya: Al-Hind 'Ala ṭarīq al-Istiqlāl wa'l-Ḥurriyya," *al-Ḥurriyya,* August 7, 1909, 47.

91. "Li'l Ḥaqq ḥatta 'Ala'l-Salāṭīn," *al-Ḥurriyya,* October 9, 1909, 187–89.

92. "Kharijiyya: Shay' 'an al-hind," *al-Ḥurriyya,* July 11, 1909, 14.

93. "Al-Wardani," *al-Ḥurriyya,* March 13, 1910, 505–8. I will return to the Wardani case later in this book.

94. See the introductions to this book and to this chapter, and the discussion of various historiographic characteristics pertaining to the left in Syria and in the Arab world. On Syria specifically, see A. Hanna, *Al-Ḥaraka al-'ummāliyya fi Suriyya wa Lubnān, 1900–1945;* A. Hanna, *Min al-ittijāhāt al-fikriyya fi Suriyya;* Buwari, *Tārīkh al-ḥaraka al- 'ummāliyya wa'l-naqābiya fi Lubnān 1908–1946;* Couland, *Le Mouvement syndical au Liban 1919–1946.*

95. Various leading periodicals of Egypt, at their head *al-Ahrām* and *al-Muqtaṭaf,* praised the project and encouraged the public to visit it. "Shukr wa i'tidhār," *Taqwīm, al-Nūr,* September 15–30, 1905, 286. In fact *al-Muqtaṭaf* had been promoting the establishment of craft schools and later of technical schools ever since the 1880s, both in Syria and Egypt. Jirji Zaidan was also interested in this topic, as the notes on the subject in his notebooks attest. See AUB archives (Beirut): J. Zeidan 1861–1914, AA7 box 1.

96. Farah Antun, "Madāris zirā'iyya bi ṭuruq jadīda: Wa idkhāl hādhihi al-ṭarīqa ila'l-quṭr al-miṣri -iqtirāḥ," *al-Jāmi'a,* February 1903, 36–41.

97. "Ghuraf al-qirā'a al-'uthmāniyya," *al-Nūr,* October 31, 1904, 301. Niqula Tuma (1857–1905) was a Syrian reformist, journalist, and lawyer. A graduate of the Patriarchal School in Beirut, he moved to Egypt in the 1870s and was a member of Miṣr al-Fatāt, the reformist political organization founded in 1879 in Alexandria by Salim al-Naqqash, Adib Ishaq, and 'Abdallah an-Nadim. He worked in government departments in Beirut and Alexandria and was involved in journalistic ventured in these cities as well as in Cairo, where in 1887 he founded *al-Aḥkām,* the first Arabic legal magazine. Philipp, *Syrians in Egypt;* Reid, *Lawyers and Politics in the Arab World, 1880–1960,* 55.

98. Unless otherwise specified, most of the information on Pietro Vasai before he reaches Egypt in 1898 comes from Antonioli et al., *Dizionario Biografico degli Anarchici Italiani,* 2: 658–59.

99. These were the words of Amilcare Cipriani, who participated in the 1866 and 1896 Candian insurrections and wrote an article in 1897 ("Crete and the Eastern Question"), ar-

guing that these events were revolutionary and would lead to the collapse of the Ottoman Empire. Masini, *Storia degli anarchici,* 93–94.

100. The participation of anarchists in nationalist struggles was a serious point of contention among anarchist groups. Malatesta, for one, was strongly opposed to anarchist involvement in the Balkan imbroglio or in Panhellenic projects. Masini, *Storia degli anarchici,* 94.

101. Besides Cipriani's article, Elisée Reclus delivered a paper on the Eastern question and on the Ottoman Empire in 1876. Fleming, *The Geography of Freedom,* 116.

102. The International Workers' Association (IWA) was established in the 1860s. Between 1873 and 1876 the various groups within the IWA split along Marxist and anarchist lines. It is quite clear that the Alexandrian branch followed the anarchist model and network rather than the socialist. The IWA's membership in Egypt included Ugo Parrini, on whom more will be said later. According to Bettini, there was also a branch of the International in Port Sa'id, and anarchists were in the process of establishing a women's branch *(una sezione femminile)* in Cairo, as well as a (mixed) branch in Ismailia. Bettini, *Bibliografia dell'anarchismo,* 281, 282, n. 7.

103. The representative was a certain Andrea Costa, who a few decades later would shed his anarchism and become a respectable socialist. See chapter 1, on Costa's visit to Tunis; Bettini, *Bibliografia dell'anarchismo,* 281.

104. Ugo Parrini, "Nostre corrispondenze," *Il Risveglio,* April 22, 1877, reprinted in Bettini, *Bibliografia dell'anarchismo,* 28.

105. On Amilcare Cipriani's anarchist activities, see Nettlau, *A Short History of Anarchism;* Droz, *Dictionnaire biographique du mouvement ouvrier international;* Masini, *Storia degli anarchici.* Milza describes him as "un vétéran des combats menés par les garibaldiens en Crète et en Grèce . . . et aide de camp . . . lors des évènements du printemps 1871 [la Commune] . . . A partir de [1880], on le retrouve continument mêlé aux combats des mouvements ouvriers italiens et français, jusqu'à sa mort survenue à Paris en 1918." Milza, *Voyage en Ritalie,* 187–89.

106. It is not altogether clear whether Italian anarchists effectively ended up fighting alongside 'Urabi. According to Parrini's firsthand account, they certainly tried. In *Dizionario biografico degli anarchici Italiani* Antonioli et al. are adamant about Malatesta's participation in it, his arrest by the British, and his liberation early 1883 (2: 59). According to the memoirs of a lapsed anarchist from Alexandria, Enrico Pea, the president of the Italian Workers' Association in Alexandria sent a letter to the new government under Prime Minister Sami Pasha al-Barudi supporting the 'Urabi insurrection and denouncing foreign intervention. Pea, *Vita in Egitto* (1995).

107. Bettini, *Bibliografia dell'anarchism,* 282.

108. *Decimo anniversario della Comune di Parigi: Parole di un socialista italiano,* reprinted in Bettini, *Bibliografia dell'anarchism,* 282–83.

109. *Decimo anniversario della Comune di Parigi,* 282–83.

110. Reported by Parrini, who participated in (if not organized) this demonstration. See "Un Vecchio" [I. U. Parrini], *L'Anarchismo in Egitto,* in *La Protesta umana,* a.II, n.36 (November 21, 1903), reprinted in Bettini, *Bibliografia dell'anarchismo,* 307.

111. Masini, *Storia degli anarchici,* 121–22.

112. Deflem, "'Wild Beasts without Nationality.'"

113. Deflem, "'Wild Beasts without Nationality,'" 278. See "Mu'tamar al-fawḍawiyyīn," *al-Hilāl,* January 1, 1899, 219, which describes the attempts by European states to organize an international police force to combat anarchism, but pointed out that Britain, Switzerland, and Belgium refused to participate in it. It is very likely that Egypt, being under British rule, was also exempt from such international cooperation and its fight against international anarchism.

114.Ottoman officials jealously noted that the Egyptian police were much more effective at arresting anarchists than the Ottoman police were, accusing the latter of pretending to ignore that anarchists even existed. See BBA/HR.SYS 1760/10, Washington, April 26, 1898, from Ali Ferrouh Bey to Tevfik Pacha, Ministre des Affaires Etrangères.

115. Vasai was often one of the first suspects to be rounded up on such occasions. For example, he was among the individuals arrested and tried in a very visible trial in 1904 for printing manifestos "inciting revolt" *("eccitanti alla rivolta")* and for planning on issuing anarchist periodicals. MAEI, Roma, Ambasciata dal Cairo (1904), Busta 87, 10.

116. MAEI, Roma, Ambasciata dal Cairo (1904), Busta 86, Metodo di sorveglianza sugli anarchici italiani in Egitto, Fondi asseguenti ai Regio Console, Agenti nella Polizia italiana al servizio dell'Egitto, Lista di anarchici redatta dall R Agenza e proveniente dai R R Consolati in Egitto.

117. Owen and Pamuk, *A History of Middle East Economies in the Twentieth Century,* 4–5.

118. Pea, *Vita in Egitto,* 169.

119. "Dalla lega dei tipografi, nella quale gli anarchici abbondano e che sono quelli che piu puntualmente si recano alle riunioni." MAEI, Roma, Busta 87, May 28, 1902, "Informazioni segrete pervenute al R. Consolato in Alessandria e da questo trasmesse alla R. Agenzia Diplomatica in Cairo." See also 4.8.1902, confidentielle 183.

120. MAEI, Roma, Ambasciata al Cairo, Busta 88 (1904), Anno 1902, Affare: Scioperi e questioni relative leghe operaie, "Riservata anarchici (1031)."

121. "Riservata anarchici (1031)."

122. "Riservata anarchici (1031)."

123. MAEI, Roma, Busta 87, May 10, 1902, confid 121.

124. MAEI, Roma, Ambasciata dal Cairo, Busta 86, Pos. 68, 1903, Circolo di studi sociali al Cairo, Circoli ed associazioni anarchiche.

125. Pea, *Vita in Egitto,* 54.

126. Pea, *Vita in Egitto,* 53–54.

127. Pea, *Vita in Egitto,* 170.

128. See Bettini, *Bibliografia dell'anarchismo:* on various periodicals (81–88); on "Points for the history of Italian anarchism in Egypt" (281–88); "Un Vecchio" (An Oldie [Parrini]), "Anarchism in Egypt," in *La Protesta umana* (San Francisco) November 21, 1903 (303–7). Bettini relied extensively on material published in anarchist periodicals worldwide.

129. Rosenthal's identity remains shrouded in mystery. One author claims that Egyptian security files listed him as Russian, whereas other reports assert he was Swiss, Italian, or German. Rosenthal himself insisted he was Egyptian. However, both Bettini and Ilbert maintain that Rosenthal was Syrian: "Lebanese," according to Bettini, *Bibliografia dell'anarchismo,* 82; "bijoutier juif né à Beyrouth d'origine russe," according to Ilbert, *Alexandrie 1830–1930,* 629. The archives of the Italian consulate in Egypt designated him at times as "Israelite and

Austrian subject," and other times as "Russian." Rosenthal became one of the founders of the Egyptian Socialist Party in 1921, which became the Egyptian Communist Party in 1923.

130. MAEI, Roma, Ambasciata al Cairo 1904, Busta 84, [periodicals] Caire le September 16, 1901, confid. 156.

131. On this topic, see Turcato, "Italian Anarchism as a Transnational Movement, 1885–1915."

132. "Mention a été faite à l'égard des évènements de Paterson et on attend avec une vive anxiété de connaitre le sort touché au compagnon Galleani Luigi," n.s, MAEI, Roma, Ambasciata dal Cairo (1904), Busta 87, Universita popolare libere in Egitto / Universita popolare libera in Alessandria. See *La Protesta Umana* (San Francisco), October 22 1903, which appealed to anarchists in San Francisco to send money to M. Angelilio's parents because Angelilio was incapacitated (or arrested) in Alexandria, and his parents, who were in Italy, were in dire straits.

133. On Pietro Gori, see Ruth Thompson, "Argentine Syndicalism: Reformism before Revolution," in van den Linden and Thorpe, eds., *Revolutionary Syndicalism*, 169.

134. MAEI, Roma, Ambasciata dal Cairo, Busta 86, "Miscellanea," "Caire 17.12.1904, confid. 387.

135. MAEI, Roma, Ambasciata dal Cairo, Busta 84, Anni 1900–1904 (Anarchici), letters A-G. Betti Giulio, Ministère de l'intérieur, süreté, Caire 8.8.1903, confid. 328.

136. On the UPL and anarchists in Alexandria, see Gorman, "Anarchists in Education."

137. It is not clear how long the UPL lasted. Poffandi's *1909 Indicateur Egyptien* states that it was still running that year (25). Other sources mention that the UPL's auditorium hosted a pro-Ferrer meeting in October 1909. See Bettini, *Bibliografia dell'anarchismo*, 87. On the Université Populaire in France, see Lucien Mercier, *Les Universités populaires, 1899–1914*.

138. Université Populaire Libre d'Alexandrie (UPL), *Revue des Cours et Conférences, Année 1902–1903*, 295.

139. *Le Lotus*, 3 (June 1901): 130–38, quoted in Ilbert, *Alexandrie 1830–1930*, 683.

140. UPL, *Revue des Cours et Conférences*, 302. By another estimate, female participation was around 10 percent of the total participation figure. See Balboni, *Gli Italiani nella civiltà egiziana del secolo XIX*, 89–90.

141. According to Bettini, the UPL of Alexandria, which he says had a long and flourishing life, saw the light mostly thanks to the initiative of the anarchists Vasai and Galleani, who wrote its status laws. Bettini, *Bibliografia dell'anarchismo*, 285, n. 18.

142. On Onofrio Abbate Pasha (1825-?), a doctor originally from Palermo who came to Alexandria in 1846, see Danovaro, *L'Egypte à l'aurore du XXème siècle*, 76.

143. The same surnames appear among students at Alexandria's Saint-François-Xavier in 1908 and UPL members in 1902–3. Many Italian Jews in Egypt, North Africa, and the Middle East seem to have come from Livorno. On the migration of Italian Jewry from Livorno in the nineteenth century, see Milano, *Storia degli ebrei italiani nel Levante;* Iacovella, "La Presenza italiana in Egitto."

144. UPL, *Revue des Cours et Conférences*, 61–62.

145. Such as George Doumani, Alexandre de Zogheb, Sheikh Hilmi effendi, and 'Abdu Badran effendi.

146. The lecture on Bakunin was given by a certain Rampin in Italian. UPL, *Revue des Cours et Conférences,* 50.

The university's wide selection of courses and lectures provided a basic classical education, which included the works of Molière and Racine, as well as a discussion of more modern issues and language courses. Interestingly French lessons were specifically designed for Russian immigrants. Balboni, *Gli Italiani nella civiltà Egiziana del Secolo XIX,* 3: 90–92. English was taught by Prof. Ernest Hobsbaum, who might have been a relative of Eric Hobsbawm (who was born in 1917 in Alexandria and whose full name is Eric Ernest Hobsbawm).

Anatole France was a strong supporter of the *université populaire* project. His work was quite influential in the Levant and was often mentioned in anarchist writings. Among the very few books that Pea mentioned in his autobiography was France's *Ile aux Penguins,* which was also serialized in the anarchist periodical *Les Temps nouveaux* (Paris).

147. UPL, *Revue des Cours et Conférences,* 106.

148. *La Réforme,* May 27, 1901, quoted in Ilbert, *Alexandrie 1830–1930,* 683–84.

149. Danovaro, *L'Egypte à l'Aurore du XXème siècle,* 68–69. His name does not actually appear in that of the adherents, but Balboni's does (he wrote the preface to Danovaro's work).

150. The lecture was mentioned in *La Tribuna Libera* , October 20, 1901. MAEI Roma, Ambasciata d'Italia in Egitto, Busta 87 (1900–1904), Stampa Anarchica.

151. By the administration's own admission, "les ouvriers manuels fréquentent très peu les cours et les conférences. A vrai dire ils ne les ont jamais fréquentés." UPL, *Revue des Cours et Conférences,* 295.

152. For comparative purposes, workers' participation made up between 25 and 60 percent of the French Université Populaire membership, depending on the case. Mercier, *Les Universités populaires,* 75.

153. UPL, *Revue des Cours et Conférences,* 295.

154. UPL, *Revue des Cours et Conférences,* 3. Nonetheless the UPL accepted and encouraged contributions.

155. The organizers of the UPL suggested that perhaps the lower classes *(classes populaires)* were not interested in joining that project: "L'université a été fondée 'pour aider à la diffusion de la culture scientifique et littéraire parmi les classes populaires de notre ville'; . . . il s'agit de savoir si les classes populaires ont répondu à notre appel." UPL, *Revue des Cours et Conférences,* 295.

156. UPL, *Revue des Cours et Conférences,* 295.

157. UPL, *Revue des Cours et Conférences,* 298.

158. Vasai's name still appeared among the adherents of the UPL in 1903, which meant that he hadn't severed ties with the institution by then. Assemblée générale annuelle, May 10, 1903, rapport du comité, 308.

159. MAEI, Roma, Ambasciata dal Cairo (1904), Busta 87, Università popolare libere in Egitto / Università popolare libera in Alessandria.

160. Università popolare libere in Egitto / Università popolare libera in Alessandria.

161. "L'Enseignement professionnel au point de vue du commerce et de la banque: Leçon d'ouverture du cours supérieur de comptabilité de M. G. de Beaupuis, 25–10–1902," in UPL, *Revue des Cours et Conférences,* 10.

162. "La signification du terme 'classes populaires' est plus large. L' université s'adresse à

tous ceux qui travaillent, aux employés de commerce, de banque, à tous les fonctionnaires. Il y a là un prolétariat aussi intéressant que celui des ouvriers manuels. C'est dans cette classe de travailleurs que nos adhérents se recrutent surtout; c'est dans cette classe de travailleurs que se trouve la majeure partie des élèves inscrits à nos cours et de nos auditeurs libres." UPL, *Revue des Cours et Conférences,* 295.

163. UPL, *Revue des Cours et Conférences,* 48, my emphasis.

164. UPL, *Revue des Cours et Conférences,* 61.

165. UPL, *Revue des Cours et Conférences,* 295.

166. UPL, *Revue des Cours et Conférences,* 295.

167. UPL, *Revue des Cours et Conférences,* 3.

168. UPL, *Revue des Cours et Conférences,* 298.

169. UPL, *Revue des Cours et Conférences,* 3; my emphasis.

170. UPL, *Revue des Cours et Conférences,* 295.

171. UPL, *Revue des Cours et Conférences,* 58.

172. UPL, *Revue des Cours et Conférences,* 2.

173. UPL, *Revue des Cours et Conférences,* 2.

174. UPL, *Revue des Cours et Conférences,* 2.

175. UPL, *Revue des Cours et Conférences,* 2.

176. In the words of the UPL's managers, "L'université est une institution qui a l'instruction pour but. Elle est sortie non pas seulement du sein des groupes ouvriers, mais aussi des milieux bourgeois. . . . Elle ne peut pas paraître favoriser un des partis en présence lorqu'un conflit éclate. Dans les villes où l'université populaire est née du syndicat ouvrier, il en va tout autrement, elle est une branche de l'activité intellectuelle dans la maison du peuple." UPL, *Revue des Cours et Conférences,* 298.

177. The bourgeois radicals who ran the UPL justified this policy of keeping workers' organizations at bay by arguing that it made no sense for the UPL to back workers in a country where political parties did not exist, but that the university still wanted to attract workers and had approached the "rare existing workers societies, most of which are mutual help societies." UPL, *Revue des Cours et Conférences,* 295.

178. Recall the founders' goals of "spreading literary and scientific education among the city's popular classes" and offering free access to education to all those who could not afford it otherwise.

179. The incident involved an "agent provocateur" and his (successful) attempts at convincing Alexandria's Russian immigrant revolutionaries (many of whom fled to Egypt after the failed revolution of 1905) to engage in acts of sabotage against the Russian state. The details of this plot are provided in *L'Arrestation des trois Russes en Egypte,* 4–7.

180. *L'Arrestation des trois Russes en Egypte,* 15. Molco and Sajous were the owners of the publishing house Sajous et Molco, which published this document and other radical documents, such as *Risorgete!,* the atheist propaganda paper distributed for free. If the writers of the petition are to be believed, "le sentiment [de protestation] ne tarda pas à être géneral, partout spontané et dans toutes les classes" (8).

181. See "Liste des adhérents," in UPL, *Revue des Cours et Conférences,* 304–8.

182. Bettini, *Bibliografia dell'anarchismo,* 87.

183. UPL, *Revue des Cours et Conférences,* 304.

184. See MAEI, Roma, Ambasciata dal Cairo, Busta 88 (1904), Anno 1902, Affare: Scioperi e questioni relative leghe operaie.

185. MAEI, Roma, Ambasciata dal Cairo (1904), Busta 86, Roma, March 11, 1904, ministero dell'interno direzione gen. della PS Gabinetto 4680.

186. "Devono servire come centri di propaganda; ma e probabile che anche questo tentativo abbia la sorte che hanno avuto gli altri consimili degli anni precedenti." MAEI, Roma, Ambasciata dal Cairo, Busta 86, Pos. 68. 1903, Circolo di studi sociali al Cairo, Circoli ed associazioni anarchiche, various documents.

187. A document at the MAEI, Roma suggests a figure of two thousand printed copies of *L'Idea,* an anarchist periodical to be based in Alexandria and whose production was being debated in 1909, to be distributed for free. See MAEI, Roma, Ambasc. dal Cairo, Busta 120, Anni 1909–10, unsigned, Cairo, August 15, 1909, "Questionario."

188. In Egypt a Greek man published an anarchist pamphlet in March 1894 in Cairo celebrating the anniversary of the Paris Commune of 1871: "Unite, o oppressed workers . . . and long live the social revolution and anarchism." He was arrested and taken to court. "Manshūr fawḍawi 'aqīm," *al-Hilāl,* April 1, 1894, 475. This was one example among many of anarchist activities among indigenous and nonindigenous, non-Italian groups in Egypt.

189. See, for example, Ambasciata d'Italia Egitto, 87, 1900–1904, Universita Popolare Libera Cairo, "Questo R. Consolato informa la R. Agenzia diplomatica d'Italia che il nominato Mahera Panos [in the following document, he appears as Machera, Panos], anarchico, e di nazionalità greca, fa il fornitore in legno, e lavora al Bazar Mouror [?]. L'anarchico KaraRache Paolo e armeno, fa l'incisore nello stabilimento Parvis."

190. Ambasciata dal Cairo, Busta 120, Anni 1909–1910, le Caire le 12.7.1909, no 359, réunion des adhérents de l'Association internationale de coopération pour l'amélioration des classes ouvrières: "Y assistaient 100 ouvriers environ—des discours ont été prononcés dans différentes langues, par le socialiste Grando Facio, et les anarchistes Nicolas Dumas et Salamon Goldenberg."

191. The tract, which attacks the department store Tiring for exploiting its workers, was printed by the Societé Internationale des Employés du Caire and was published between 1900 and 1914. For the text itself, see Khuri-Makdisi, *Levantine Trajectories.*

192. Parrini, "Nostre corrispondenze," *Il Risveglio,* April 22, 1877, reprinted in Bettini, *Bibliografia dell'anarchismo,* 28.

193. MAEI, Roma, Ambasciata dal Cairo, Busta 120, Anni 1909–10, Stampa sovversiva P 17, Caire 23.1.1911, confid. No 861.

194. MAEI, Roma, Ambasciata dal Cairo, Busta 120, Anni 1909–10.

195. MAEI, Roma, Ambasciata dal Cairo (1904), Busta 86, 1899 processo in Alessandria d'Egitto contro diversi anarchici, Roma, March 11, 1904, ministero dell'interno direzione gen della PS Gabinetto 4680.

196. For instance, "Les anarchistes du Caire ont decidé de donner désormais, dans la salle d'études, trois conférences par semaine, l'une en langue italienne et deux autres en langues hébraique et grecque." MAEI, Roma, Ambasciata dal Cairo, Busta 86, Confidentielle no 103, Cairo, 2.4.1904. See also MAEI, Roma, Ambasciada dal Cairo, Busta 88, Anno 1902, affare: Scioperi e questioni relative, leghe operaie e scioperi, Cairo, January 6, 1902, Ministère de l'intérieur, division de la sûreté, no 4 confid., "Parrini parlera en italien et peut-être en grec."

197. Roberto D'Angiò, *Il Libertario* (La Spezia), October 19, 1905, reprinted in Bettini, *Bibliografia dell'anarchismo*, 285.

198. See de Seixas, *Mémoire et oubli*, 24.

199. Bettini, *Bibliografia dell'anarchismo*, 284–85.

200. "Quelques renseignements sur le mouvement ouvrier d'Alexandrie: Les anarchistes Vasai et Sajous ont cessé de faire partie de la Ligue de résistance entre les ouvriers typographes. Sajous ouvrira, sous peu, en son nom, un petit établissement typographique. La Ligue de résistance a été réformée sous la direction des anarchistes Albano et Bertuzzi. *Les ouvriers indigènes ne peuvent pas en faire partie*." MAEI, Roma, Ambasciata dal Cairo, Busta 88 (1904), Anno 1902, affare: Scioperi e questioni relative leghe operaie, Cairo, March 25, 1903, confid. 137, my italics.

201. Police report C. 140, Abidin 1910, quoted in Badrawi, *Political Violence in Egypt 1910–1924*, 149. See also PRO 30/57/36, Kitchener papers, Mr. Cheetham to Sir Edward Grey, June 30, 1911, reprinted in Burdett, *Arab Dissident Movements 1905–1955*, 135–44, especially 139.

202. FO 407/175, part 72, Further correspondence respecting the affairs of Egypt and the Sudan, 1910, no 66, p. 138, Gorst to Grey, confidential, Cairo, May 6 1910, Enclosure 2 no 82, p. 154, Memorandum by Dr. Nolan on the Wardani case.

203. FO 407/175, part 72, Gorst to Grey, 138.

204. FO 407/175, part 72, Gorst to Grey, 169. Although many of these "plots" turned out to be hoaxes, Badrawi argues that the degree to which they were taken seriously reflects the state's profound insecurity about subversive movements and anarchism specifically, as well as the popularity of such ideas.

205. According to a British Foreign Ministry report on Egyptian secret societies written in 1911, the president of this organization was a tailor, Ahmad Ibrahim al-Sarrawy; among the society's thirteen members, six were students of government schools. The report states, "On a perquisition made at the house of the secretary [Ismail Farag, a lawyer's clerk], papers were seized which showed that he had been, since 1909, [a] member of a secret society of anarchists, which had in view the assassination of the editor of *al-Mu'ayyad*, who was at the time on open war with the Nationalists." The report also classified the organization's goal as "ostensibly [being] the collection of money for Sheikh Shawish's scheme of national education." PRO 30/57/36, Kitchener papers, Mr. Cheetham to Sir Edward Grey, June 30, 1911, in Burdett, *Arab Dissident Movements 1905–1955*, 139.

206. Badrawi, *Political Violence in Egypt 1910–1924*, 84. Badrawi adds that the expression *lahum muyūl fawḍawiyya* became very popular in police reports after the Wardani case (106, n. 30).

207. Pea, *Vita in Egitto*, 170.

208. Pea, *Vita in Egitto*, 107.

209. Alexandra de Avierino, owner and chief editor of the literary magazines *Le Lotus* (1900–1) and *Anīs al-Jalīs* (1898–1924), played a dynamic role in Egypt's feminist movement. Avierino was very active in the Alexandrian literary and feminist scenes, writing essays and plays and translating novels from French into Arabic. She was the vice president of the Alliance of Women for Peace and the Egyptian delegate to the Exposition Universelle of 1900, and she participated in various feminist congresses. She had close connections to many of

the radical figures who have appeared in this book so far; she collaborated with Labiba Hashim on the production of a couple of periodicals and was also close to Shibli Shumayyil. In fact according to Haroun, Avierino almost became Shumayyil's fiancée. Haroun, *Shibli Shumayyil,* 65. Avierino's communal affiliation is not very clear. Ilbert suggests she came from "une famille juive locale, anciennement protégée par l'Autriche" (*Alexandrie 1830–1930,* 683), but in fact she seems to have been born in Beirut to a Syrian orthodox family, as suggested by her membership in the Alexandrian Greek Orthodox association Jam'iyyat Yadd al-Iḥsān in 1906. See *Jam'iyyat Yadd al-Iḥsān.*

210. Besides Alexandra de Avierino, the list included a few clearly Syrian names, including Hobeika, Houry, Malhame, Naggiar, Phares, Sarkis, Tabet, Zananiri, and de Zogheb. It is possible Hobeika might have been the same person enamored of revolutions and corresponding with Rihani. See George Hubayqa, letter to Rihani, Cairo, January 9, 1903, in A. al-Rihani, *al Rihani wa mu'āṣirūhu,* 47–50.

211. On Shumayyil, see chapter 2. On his writings sympathetic to anarchism and anarchists, see his article "Kitāb Fawḍawi," first published in Rashid Shumayyil's Alexandrian *al-Baṣīr.*

212. Eberhardt, *Lettres et Journaliers,* 25.

5. WORKERS AND LABOR UNREST

1. This description was not limited to the early years of strikes, but appeared time and again until 1914. For example, in 1902 *al-Ahrām* accused local cigarette rollers of "aping" European workers, warning them, "This is a corrupting *[fāsid]* imitation, and damaging to them," and *al-Liwā',* the official organ of the Watani Party, commented that the 1900 strike in Cairo "seem[ed] strange in the East." Quoted in 'Ezzeddin, *Tārīkh al-ṭabaqa al-'āmila al-miṣriyya,* 66. Similar comments appeared in the Istanbuli press. For an analysis of the press's reaction to the 1908 strike waves in the capital, see Quataert, "Ottoman Workers and the State, 1826–1914," 29.

2. Beinin, *Workers and Peasants in the Modern Middle East,* 78. See also Quataert, "Ottoman Workers and the State," 2; Karakışla, "The 1908 Strike Wave in the Ottoman Empire."

3. Ilbert, *Alexandrie 1830–1930,* 647.

4. By one count, around 110 strikes erupted between July and December 1908. Quataert, "Ottoman Workers and the State," 2. Beinin itemized these strikes as following: 39 in Istanbul, 31 in Salonica, and 13 in Izmir. Beinin, *Workers and Peasants,* 78.

5. To illustrate how connected local labor histories are to global trends, research conducted on strikes throughout the world (although it is not quite clear how comprehensive it really is) has shown that certain years witnessed explosions of labor unrest. For the period 1860–1914 these peak years were 1889–90 and 1911–12. For a review of theories and research in global labor history, see van der Linden, "Global Labor History and the Modern World-System," especially 438.

6. Savage, "Class and Labour History," 61.

7. McAdam, Tarrow, and Tilly, *Dynamics of Contention,* 4–5. As William Sewell has cautioned, we should resist the urge to think of class discourse as being "naturally attractive" to workers:

> Class discourse is only one of several discourses available to workers to conceptualize and act out their place in society and the State. Even workers involved in class institutions are interpellated (to use the Althusserian term) by various other discourses: unreconstructed Radical democracy, reformist meliorism, self-help, Toryism, nationalism, various religious ideologies, consumerism, and so on. These rival discourses may coexist not only in the same class, but in the same mind. (W. H. Sewell, "How Classes are Made," 72)

8. Thompson, *The Making of the English Working Class,* 8.

9. For the few works that address female labor, see Khater, *Inventing Home;* Zainebaf-Shahr, "The Role of Women in the Urban Economy of Istanbul, 1700–1850." For a more complete bibliography on that topic, see Zainebaf-Shahr, n. 1.

10. See Quataert, "Social History of Labor in the Ottoman Empire," 27. Quataert also points out that "the presence of female labor in manufacturing was common place in the 19th century and before, but the size of females' role in export production is striking." Not surprisingly these female workers were among the worst paid in the Ottoman industrial workforce. Quataert, "Ottoman Manufacturing in the Nineteenth Century," in *Manufacturing in the Ottoman Empire and Turkey, 1500–1950,* 90. In the case of Mount Lebanon, the silk industry in 1911 employed twelve thousand women out of a total labor force of fourteen thousand. See Ducousso, *L'Industrie de la soie en Syrie et au Liban,* 134, 155; Owen, "The Silk-Reeling Industry of Mount Lebanon, 1840–1914"; and especially Khater, "From 'House' to 'Goddess of the House' " and *Inventing Home.* For a fascinating study of migrant female workers to Tunis, see Clancy-Smith, "Gender in the City." On migrant female workers to Alexandria, an interesting phenomenon was that of wet nurses: "The movement of wet nurses that [Sarasua] describes compares with that from Slovenia to Egypt in the second half of the nineteenth century, where the women concerned earned the special name of 'alexandrinke' because most of them undertook migrations to Alexandria that, unlike those to Madrid, would last a lifetime." A. Barbic and I. Miklavcic-Brezigar, "Domestic Work Abroad: A Necessity and an Opportunity for Rural Women from the Goriska Borderline Region in Slovenia," in J. H. Momsen, ed., *Gender, Migration and Domestic Service,* quoted in Sharpe, introduction to *Women, Gender and Labour Migration,* 5–6.

11. Between 1870 and 1890 Egypt had the highest increase in real wages out of all Mediterranean countries, with an annual growth of 3.11 percent during these two decades. See Williamson, "Real Wages and Relative Factor Prices around the Mediterranean, 1500–1940," table 3.4, "Real wage performance in the Mediterranean Basin by decades, 1870s-1930," figure 3.11, "Real wages/GDP per capital, Egypt, Serbia and Turkey, 1880–1939," 63, 72; Owen, *Cotton and the Egyptian Economy, 1820–1914,* 269.

12. See Owen, *The Middle East in the World Economy, 1800–1914,* 154–65. For more information on the place of silk in Mount Lebanon's economy during the nineteenth century, see Labaki, *Introduction à l'histoire économique du Liban;* Ducousso, *L'Industrie de la soie en Syrie et au Liban.*

13. See Fawaz, *Merchants and Migrants in 19th Century Beirut.*

14. Owen, *The Middle East in the World Economy,* 156–7. Around the turn of the century the silk industry employed 180,000 people in Mount Lebanon—14,000 working in fac-

tories and the remaining 165,000 tending to mulberry trees and raising cocoons. By one estimate, fifty thousand mountain families, almost half of the total figure, were completely dependent on silk for their livelihood. Owen, *The Middle East in the World Economy,* 249.

15. See Islamoğlu-Inan, *The Ottoman Empire and the World-Economy;* Kasaba, *The Ottoman Empire and the World Economy;* Kasaba, *Cities in the World System;* Kasaba and Wallerstein, *Incorporation into the World-Economy.*

16. See Beinin, "Egyptian Textile Workers," who argues that "due to the uneven effects of competition from imports, some textile crafts endured with little change"(6). Owen has pointed out that some local handicrafts, far from being decimated by the incorporation into the capitalist world system, actually survived quite well. Owen, *The Middle East in the World Economy,* 289.

17. See Williamson, "Real Wages and Relative Factor Prices around the Mediterranean, 1500–1940"; Owen, *Cotton and the Egyptian Economy, 1820–1914;* Owen, *The Middle East in the World Economy, 1800–1914.*

18. See, for example, Beinin, *Workers and Peasants,* 38, which argues that craftsmen played a very active role in urban revolts during the eighteenth and nineteenth centuries.

19. Edmund Burke III has argued that a new kind of social protest arose around 1900 that asked for the abolition of certain taxes in given cases, as well as requesting the government to abide by sharia and Islamic practices, but where traditional classes that had served as the spokesmen of protesters and had organized them had been eroded. Burke, "Towards a History of Urban Collective Action in the Middle East."

20. Especially after the mid-eighteenth century the Janissary Corps most likely had connections to guilds. On the relationship between Janissaries, artisans, and guilds, see Kafadar, "Yeniçeri-Esnaf Relations"; Kırlı, "A Profile of the Labor Force in Early Nineteenth-Century Istanbul"; Quataert, "Janissaries, Artisans and the Question of Ottoman Decline 1730–1826," 197–203. On guild sheikhs and their role in disputes and during demonstrations in eighteenth-century Cairo, see Raymond, *Artisans et commerçants au Caire au XVIIIème siècle.*

21. This general picture ought to be nuanced, as the dynamics between state and guilds and the development of guilds differed substantively from region to region. In some parts of the empire guilds not only survived; they managed to effectively change and adapt to new economic and social conditions, and even retained some important privileges. Generally, though, by the early twentieth century throughout the empire the power of guilds and of sheikhs of guilds had been seriously weakened. See Quataert, "Labor History and the Ottoman Empire, c. 1700–1922," 103–4; Chalcraft, *Striking Cabbies of Cairo and Other Stories.*

22. Quataert, "Social History of Labor in the Ottoman Empire," 27.

23. Owen, "The Study of Middle Eastern Industrial History," 476; Chalcraft, "The Striking Cabbies of Cairo and Other Stories," 26, 28, 95.

24. Ilbert suggests that there was a difference, in that respect, between Cairo and Alexandria. According to him, the number of industrial establishments in Alexandria rose significantly between 1868 and 1890 (from seven to twenty). While Alexandria was becoming an increasingly industrial city with a concentration of mechanized workshops, Cairo maintained a highly developed artisanal sector. Ilbert, *Alexandrie 1830–1930,* 206.

25. E. J. Goldberg, "The Social History of Egyptian Labor," 172.

26. Egypt, Ministry of Finance, *The Census of Egypt Taken in 1907* (Cairo, 1909), 279–83, quoted in Owen, *Cotton and the Egyptian Economy,* 294–95.

27. Ghazaleh, "Masters of the Trade," 116–17.

28. 'Abbas, *Al-Ḥaraka al-'ummāliyya fi Miṣr,* 29; Vatter, "Militant Textile Weavers in Damascus," 3–6. Roger Owen's research on the Lebanese silk industry in the late nineteenth century and early twentieth has underlined "the extent and complexity of the interrelationships" between the production of silk in factories and small spinners, and the linked fates of their workers. Owen, "The Study of Middle Eastern Industrial History," 477–78.

29. Beinin, *Workers and Peasants in the Modern Middle East,* 19.

30. Chalcraft, *Striking Cabbies of Cairo,* 29.

31. Vallet, *Contribution à l'étude de la condition des ouvriers de la grande industrie au Caire,* 139.

32. Lockman, *Workers and Working Classes,* xxii.

33. See Hansen, *The Political Economy of Poverty, Equity, and Growth,* 55; Chalcraft, "The Coal Heavers of Port Sa'id," 111–12.

34. See, for example, Ramella's study on the Italian wool-producing town of Biella in the late nineteenth century, where he describes the shift from home to factory production as "a long process, governed by numerous microvariables of group life, and strongly conditioned by continuing links with agriculture." Gribaudi's research on early twentieth-century Turin portrayed urban working-class conditions as "a part-way stage in certain existences, and not an eternal destiny, a socially defined and unchangeable condition," in which, among the many immigrants in Turin, some former peasants "returned to their original occupation, some stayed in the city as factory workers, and others again moved up into skilled jobs." Franco Ramella, *Terra e telai, sistemi di parentela e manifattura nel biellese dell'ottocento* (Turin: Einaudi, 1984); Maurizio Gribaudi, *Mondo operaio e mito operaio: spazi e percorsi sociali a Torino nel primo novecento* (Turin: Einaudi, 1987). The discussion comes from Andreucci, "Italy."

35. Shechter, *Smoking, Culture, and the Economy in the Middle East,* 43.

36. *Al-Muqaṭṭam,* November 5, 1901, quoted in 'Ezzeddin, *Tārīkh al-ṭabaqa al-'āmila al-miṣriyya,* 85, and in 'Abbas, *Al-Ḥaraka al-'ummāliyya fi Miṣr,* 54.

37. Chalcraft, *The Striking Cabbies of Cairo and Other Stories,* 164.

38. Couland, *Le Mouvement syndical au Liban,* 46.

39. Couland, "Histoire syndicale et ouvrière égyptienne," 182.

40. Cairo's tramway strike of 1911 seems to have encouraged Alexandria's tramway workers to go on strike the following month. Couland, "Histoire syndicale et ouvrière égyptienne," 182.

41. Karakışla, "The 1908 Strike Wave," 160.

42. Chalcraft, *Striking Cabbies of Cairo and Other Stories,* 197.

43. On the Egyptian case, see Beinin and Lockman, *Workers on the Nile,* 23.

44. On Salonica, see Dumont, *Du socialisme ottoman à l'internationalisme anatolien,* 30.

45. In the Maghrib, in Oran and Algiers, the first strikes took place when a handful of indigenous Algerian dockworkers participated in strikes alongside Spanish and French dockworkers. Gallissot, "Mouvement ouvrier et mouvement national: Communisme, question nationale et nationalisme dans le monde arabe," in *Mouvement ouvrier, communisme et nationalismes dans le monde arabe,* 17. Two of the biggest prewar strikes in Egypt were

launched by tramway workers in Cairo in 1908 and 1911. Tramway workers seem to have been the leading sector of working-class militancy in Egypt until the 1940s. E. J. Goldberg, "The Social History of Egyptian Labor," 173.

46. Keyder, Özveren, and Quataert, "Port-Cities in the Ottoman Empire," 519, 520.

47. See Beinin, *Workers and Peasants,* 66; Chalcraft, "The Coal Heavers of Port Sa'id."

48. Strikes and labor unrest on the quays of Beirut seem to have occurred quite regularly, at least from the 1890s onward. The Beirut Port Company's annual report for 1904 mentioned that fewer strikes among port workers had taken place than in the previous year, an indication that there were strikes in 1903 and 1904. Compagnie du Port de Beyrouth, P8-H-5, "Rapports annuels 1895–1913."

49. See Compagnie du Port de Beyrouth, P8-H-5, "Rapports annuels 1895–1913." The new port, inaugurated in 1894, was the subject of various disturbances, which were noted regularly and very critically by French consular reports. Significantly the same tensions and fears were to be found around the same time in Istanbul, where a primarily French company had been granted the concession to build and operate a modern port.

50. Quataert, *Social Disintegration and Popular Resistance in the Ottoman Empire, 1881–1908,* 95, 102.

51. Silver, *Forces of Labor,* 98–99. For comparative and global perspectives on docks and labor unrest, see Davies et al., *Dock Workers,* vol. 1.

52. Silver, *Forces of Labor,* 100, quoting David Harvey, "Globalization in Question," *Rethinking Marxism* 8, no. 4 (1999): 1–17.

53. Dornel, "Cosmopolitisme et xénophobie," 8.

54. Van der Linden and Thorpe, *Revolutionary Syndicalism,* 7.

55. By one estimate, such trades in Egypt employed between 100,000 and 200,000 workers circa 1914 and were among the country's most valuable sectors between 1897 and 1907. Chalcraft, "The Striking Cabbies of Cairo and Other Stories," 380. For employment figures on the Egyptian State Railway, Egypt's largest employer at the turn of the twentieth century, see Beinin, *Workers and Peasants,* 65. As for the construction industry, beginning in 1897 it was the largest employer of labor outside agriculture, with nearly ninety-five thousand workers in 1907. See Owen, "The Cairo Building Industry and the Building Boom of 1897 to 1907."

56. Silver, *Forces of Labor,* 126. Based on the data compiled by the World Labor Group affiliated with the Fernand Braudel Center at SUNY Binghamton, Silver asserts that "the total number of mentions of labor unrest [in the world] increases from 325 in 1905 to 604 in 1909 and 875 in 1913."

57. "Ḍiyāʿ al-amwāl bi iʿtiṣāb al-ʿummāl" (The Loss of Money [Capital] through Workers' Strikes), *al-Muqtaṭaf* 14 (October 1889): 27–29.

58. M. Fouques-Duparc, consul général de France à Beyrouth, to M. Constans, ambassadeur de France à Constantinople, August 17, 1908, in Ismail, *Documents diplomatiques et consulaires,* 18: 111–12.

59. See BBA HR.SYS. 59/30 (1886; maybe earliest date?), BBA HR.SYS 168/9 (1906), and, on Spanish socialists' declaration of a general strike in 1891, BBA Y.PRK.PT 7/66 (C.29.1308).

60. Around half of the 110 strikes recorded throughout the empire right after the Young Turk Revolution of 1908 were in sectors just created by foreign capital (especially railroads,

tramways, and modernized ports) and employing both Ottoman and non-Ottoman workers. Quataert, "Labor History and the Ottoman Empire," 105. The connection between foreign-owned industry and militancy is further confirmed by the fact that, in September 1908, workers of almost all of the Ottoman railway network went on strike and that "the most important strikes were held in the railways that were in the hands of Western companies." Karakışla, "The 1908 Strike Wave in the Ottoman Empire," 173–74.

61. Burke, "Towards a History of Urban Collective Action." Burke identifies popular anti-imperialism among urban populations of the Ottoman Empire and the Maghrib as "of enormous consequence for the evolution of forms of protest and resistance in the 20th century." I am substituting *localism* for *nativism,* which Cole uses and which is rather problematic, given its association with a certain racist worldview in the case of American history. Cole, *Colonialism and Revolution in the Middle East.*

62. See chapter 3.

63. M. Fouques-Duparc, consul général de France à Beyrouth, to M. Constans, ambassadeur de France à Constantinople, August 17, 1908, in Ismail, *Documents diplomatiques et consulaires,* 18: 111–12.

64. Fouques-Duparc to Constans.

65. Common people—"a Tantawi," "a peasant," "Mustafa from Alexandria"—sent letters to the editors of various newspapers, expressing their support for strikers. See the letters in *al-Mu'ayyad,* August 3, 1911, reprinted in al-Nukhayli, *Al-Ḥaraka al-'ummāliyya fi Miṣr wa mawqif al-ṣiḥāfa wa'l-sulṭāt al-miṣriyya minha min sanat 1882 ila 1952,* 43. In at least one instance, merchants also rallied behind workers. During the porters' strike of 1908 in Beirut, when the Port Company refused to grant strikers their demands and decided to replace them with its own staff, the merchants whose merchandise had to be unloaded refused to grant the company handling rights *(droits de manutention).* Fouques-Duparc to Constans, "Annexe no. 1 à la dépêche no. 91 du 8 octobre 1908," in Ismail, *Documents diplomatiques et consulaires,* 18: 110–13.

66. See Taillandier, consul général de Beyrouth, to M. Develle, ministre des affaires étrangères, July 6, 1893, in Ismail, *Documents diplomatiques et consulaires,* 16: 184.

67. Compagnie du Port de Beyrouth, P9-C, letter signed by Abdulkader Dena [Dana], president of the municipality, April 30, 1906.

68. BBA DH.ID 111–2, no. 1 (1332), Beyrut Osmanlı Havagazı şirketi, doc 2, telegram sent by the director of the gas company Bourdon, 19.4.1332 (1912), my emphasis.

69. Couland, "Histoire syndicale et ouvrière égyptienne," 182.

70. Al-Sa'id, *Tārīkh al-ḥaraka al-ishtirākiyya fi Miṣr 1900–1925,* 52–53.

71. Jullemier, gérant du Consulat Général de France à Beyrouth, to M. Hanotaux, ministre des affaires étrangères, June 9, 1894, in Ismail, *Documents Diplomatiques et Consulaires,* 16: 223. Unsurprisingly Jullemier depicted these port workers as "forming a turbulent population, where many trouble-makers [petty criminals, *malfaiteurs*] are recruited, and which is at the same time dreaded by the public and handled with care *[ménagé]* by the authorities." In this specific case, the fact that the great majority of the four hundred *mahonniers* were Muslims added another dimension to a class-based conflict.

72. In 1877 Alexandria's goldsmiths sent a copy of their petition to Ya'qub Sannu'a's *Abu naddara zarqa* in Paris, which published it in February 1879. Cole suggests that the publi-

cation of the goldsmiths' petition in Paris "was meant to embarrass the government by giving wide circulation among the public to a complaint about injustice." Cole, *Colonialism and Revolution in the Middle East,* 94.

73. For more examples of petitions published by periodicals, see al-Nukhayli, *Al-Ḥaraka al-ʿummāliyya fi Miṣr.* Workers usually petitioned for an eight-hour workday, an increase in their salary, a month's paid holiday, salary payment during illness, and legal protection against physical and verbal abuse. See ʿEzzeddin, *Tārīkh al-ṭabaqa al-ʿāmila al-miṣriyya,* 85. For an example of a petition sent in 1908 to a daily newspaper by striking Beiruti quay employees, see Hanssen, *Fin-de-Siècle Beirut,* 108.

74. *Al-Muʾayyad,* August 3, 1911, reprinted in al-Nukhayli, *Al-Ḥaraka al-ʿummāliyya fi Miṣr,* 42.

75. On immigrant labor flowing into Macedonia in the 1890s, during the construction of the railways of Thessaloniki-Bitola and Thessaloniki-Dedeagac-Istanbul, see Adanır, "The National Question and the Genesis and Development of Socialism in the Ottoman Empire"; Gounaris, "Railway Construction and Labor Availability in Macedonia in the Late Nineteenth Century."

76. I prefer to use the term *trans-Mediterranean* or *Mediterranean.* Many of the workers were not from Europe (such as Syrian and Armenian workers in Egypt), and neither they nor their host country thought of them as European, a term that mostly designated western Europeans and did not include southern Europeans and Ottoman subjects.

77. In fact some historians have written about strikes and foreign labor in terms very similar to those used by contemporary witnesses who opposed strikes a century ago. See, for example, Asʿad Daghir's article "Iʿtiṣāb al-ʿummāl," *al-Muqtaṭaf* 27 (January 1902): 65:

> One reason [for the Cairene tailors' strike of December 1901] is the rowdiness *[ṣiyāʿ]* of the people of the ready-to-wear industry *[makhāzin al-malābis al-jāhiza],* and the natural readiness of the majority of workers to strike, because they are foreigners who are used to this. . . . The majority of strikers are foreigners: Greeks and Italians and others; there is only a small number of national workers *[al-ʿummāl al-waṭaniyyūn],* Egyptians and Syrians, among them. Therefore, it is a foreign Western strike with no connection to us except for its location.

The same idea was expressed by the nationalist leader Muhammad Farid, who, upon hearing of a strike, bemoaned the fact that "this European disease has spread to Egypt." Chalcraft, *Striking Cabbies of Cairo,* 171.

78. Strikwerda, "Capitalists, Immigrants, and Populists," 206.

79. In one such incident Italian workers headed to France were lured to change their destination by German recruiters. Strikwerda, "Capitalists, Immigrants, and Populists," 218.

80. However, the Mediterranean's place as an exporter of labor pales in comparison to South and East Asia, a point made by Adam McKeown in "Global Migration 1846–1940."

81. Gabaccia and Ottanelli, *Italian Workers of the World,* 6. See also Gabaccia, *Italy's Many Diasporas.*

82. On Italian immigration to Marseilles, see W. Sewell, *Structure and Mobility;* Milza, *Voyage en Ritalie.*

83. Williamson, "Real Wages and Relative Factor Prices around the Mediterranean, 1500–1940," 61–63. Not only was the increase in real wages the highest around the Mediterranean, but the figures Williamson gives for real wages themselves indicate that the wages of both urban unskilled and skilled workers between 1850 and 1880 were higher in Istanbul than in most cities of Italy and Spain (56–57).

84. On international seasonal migration, Vallet notes that since 1907 there had been "un mouvement d'émigration temporaire de la population rurale de l'Italie du Sud en Egypte. Des paysans de la Pouille et de la Calabre profitent du moment oǔ les travaux des champs sont suspendus (novembre à mars) pour venir louer leurs services à des entrepreneurs égyptiens." Vallet, *Contribution à l'étude de la condition des ouvriers*, 117.

85. The presence of an Italian working class in Beirut is attested by the existence in 1897 of an Italian aid association, the Società italiana di beneficenza. "Società Italiana di Beneficenza," in *Bollettino del Ministero degli Affari Esteri*, 47–55.

86. On the mission of the Alliance Israélite Universelle throughout the Orient, see Chouraqui, *L'Alliance Israélite Universelle et la renaissance juive contemporaine, 1860–1960;* Rodrigue, *French Jews, Turkish Jews.*

87. Archives de l'Alliance Israélite Universelle–Liban, "Communauté (1868 et 1904–8)," Box 1, "Divers: comités scolaires, adjoints, clubs, oeuvres, communautés, 1868–1930," letter written by Franck, June 23, 1885, 3.

88. The Alliance even suggested that these European Jews, rather than return or head to Palestine, should settle wherever they found jobs in the Ottoman Empire: "Faut-il que tous ces ouvriers formés à Beyrouth retournent à Saffed ou Tibériade? Est-ce indispensable? . . . D'autres ouvriers pourraient peut-être s'établir dans les colonies à Acre, Caiffa, Beyrouth, Tripoli, Lattaquié, Damas, Alexandrie, Mersine, Tarsous, Adana. Mon Dieu, le pays est grand." Archives de l'Alliance Israélite Universelle–Liban, letter written by Franck, June 23, 1885, 3.

89. See Ilbert, *Alexandrie 1830–1930*, 110, 363, 397.

90. Chalcraft, "The Striking Cabbies of Cairo and Other Stories," 106.

91. Ilbert, *Alexandrie 1830–1930*, 206, and figures from the census of 1897, 401.

92. Couland, "Histoire syndicale et ouvrière égyptienne," 180.

93. Ilbert, *Alexandrie 1830–1930*, 402.

94. A law was passed in the 1890s granting citizenship to anybody born in Egypt or any Ottoman subject who had spent fifteen years in Egypt. Although the census of 1897 makes no distinction between Ottoman and Egyptian, the 1917 census does.

95. *Al-Muqaṭṭam*, November 5, 1901, quoted in ʿEzzeddin, *Tārīkh al-ṭabaqa al-ʿāmila al-miṣriyya*, 69–70.

96. The 1909 tramway strike in Cairo was organized by a Syrian wattman (tram driver). Vallet, *Contribution à l'étude de la condition des ouvriers*, n. 1, xi–xii. During the Alexandrian tramway strike of 1911 an Italian worker "stood up and gave a speech inciting the workers to strike. His discourse had a great impact on workers." *Miṣr al-Fatāt*, August 8, 1911, quoted in al-Nukhayli, *Al-Ḥaraka al-ʿummāliyya fī Miṣr*, 69. In Beirut striking workers at the Compagnie du Gaz in 1908 asked for Joseph Rossi to be designated "comme chef de service en ville et Amory comme chef de service à l'Usine." It is not unlikely that Rossi, probably a Levantine or Italian Jew, played a prominent role in organizing strikers or speaking on their behalf. "Revendications du personnel de la Co. du Gaz de Beyrouth (October 2, 1908),

"Annexe no. III à la dépêche no. 91 du 8 octobre 1908," in Ismail, *Documents diplomatiques et consulaires,* 18: 113–14.

97. For instance, a tract protesting a department store's mistreatment of its workers (most likely written between 1900 and 1914) was published by the Société Internationale des Employés du Caire in French, Greek, and Arabic: "Dans un établissement du Caire qui s'appelle de triste mémoire TIRING, On exploite effroyablement les employés! On les tyrannise tous les jours! On menace de renvoi ceux qui osent se plaindre! Pour SAUVER les employés, le public doit intervenir en leur faveur. Il faut qu'il proteste de toute *[sic]* ses forces contre les bas procédés de cette maison. Ne lui permettez plus d'ouvrir ses portes!! N'y faites plus aucun achat!! Boycottez sans relâche TIRING! Ecoutez-nous! Aidez-Nous!" (The Arabic text also contains a few grammatical errors.) My thanks to Dimitris Kastritsis for giving me a copy of this petition.

98. This was certainly the case in Brazil, Argentina, and, to some extent, the United States. On Italian immigrant workers in Brazil and their affiliation with transnational and internationalist workers' organizations, see Gabaccia and Iacovetta, *Women, Gender, and Transnational Lives;* Maram, "Anarchists, Immigrants, and the Brazilian Labor Movement, 1890–1920." On Italian workers in the United States and their affiliation with the International Workers of the World, see D. Goldberg, *A Tale of Three Cities;* Gabaccia's various works, including *Workers of the World.*

99. Milza, *Voyage en Ritalie,* 197. However, in many, if not most, host countries (at least in Brazil and Argentina and apparently in Egypt) it was not socialism but anarchism and anarchosyndicalism that appealed most to immigrant workers.

100. International (Second) Congress Documents, BMS Fr 224 (15a-23a), letter addressed to M. Auguste Bebel at the Bureau Socialiste International, Maison du Peuple, Bruxelles, Rapport du Secretariat pour le mois d'octobre 1905, 6, Roman Hanssen, Le Caire, October 3, 1905.

101. International (Second) Congress Documents, Roman Hanssen (par ordre de la ligue) to D. Delbourgo, président de la Ligue des Employés du Caire, B.P. No 843.

102. F. Cooper, "Port Labour in a Colonial City," 168.

103. Vallet suggests that entrepreneurs in the construction business wishing to recruit foreigners had to contact the offices of the Bourses du Travail, which had a branch in Marseilles, or a similar institution. Vallet, *Contribution à l'étude de la condition des ouvriers,* 116. Italian workers were recruited and brought to the United States mostly through the *padroni* system, which was akin to indentured labor and had connections to organized crime. See Donna Gabaccia, "Class, Exile, and Nationalism at Home and Abroad: The Italian Risorgimento," in Gabaccia and Ottanelli, *Workers of the World,* 28. We do not know whether Italian workers in Egypt were recruited in a similar fashion. Gounaris suggests that Italian workers employed to build railway tracks in Macedonia between the 1870s and 1890s were classified into two groups: "(a) those who were brought by contractors to work on a specific project—the rest of the Europeans should be included in this category as well—and (b) the seasonal migrants who were willing to migrate to any part of the world which seemed to offer prospects for good wages, no matter what risks were involved." Gounaris, "Railway Construction and Labor Availability in Macedonia in the Late Nineteenth Century," 156.

104. It is probably not a coincidence that the five companies in Alexandria that produced soap in 1902 were owned by Syrians and employed "skilled workmen [who were] Syrians."

This might indicate that the workmen were recruited while in Syria and their passage to Alexandria arranged by middlemen working for the five companies in question. See PRO, FO 78/5237 Turkey (Egypt) (Consular and Commercial), Consuls at Alexandria, Gould, Alban, 1902, letter from Arthur R. Brown Alexandria, May 1, 1902, British Chamber of Commerce of Egypt, to A. D. Alban esq., British consul in Alexandria.

105. Potestio, *The Memoirs of Giovanni Veltri.*

106. See Istrati, *Vie d'Adrien Zograffi,* especially the sections "Méditerranée: (Lever du soleil)" and "Méditerranée: (Coucher du soleil)." See also Maricourt, *Dictionnaire des auteurs prolétariens de la langue française de la révolution à nos jours,* 113.

107. In the words of the Italian consul in Beirut:

> There are railroad projects—that is undeniable—but from project to facts, there is a long way to go. The Beirut-Tripoli railroad, besides the fact that it still has not been [fully] approved . . . is only employing local workers, and refuses ours. The bid for the railway Damascus-Beirut and Aleppo, till Birecik, is still at the state of study, but the Ottoman government does not want to give its approval to the trail proposed by the Company, and does not want the Company to accept the trail wanted by the Sublime Porte. As for the Haifa-Hauran-Damascus [line], the work seems to be definitely suspended. (Report by E. de Gubernatis, R. Console generale in Beirut, "Lavori ferroviari in Siria," in *Bollettino del Ministero degli Affari Esteri, Anno 1896,* 672/53)

108. Report by E. de Gubernatis. Similar warnings were issued for Cairo, Alexandria, Port Sa'id, Salonica, and Smyrne. See "Salonicco e Smirne," in Ministero degli Affari Esteri, R. Commissariato dell'Emigrazione, *Bollettino dell'Emigrazione,* 78.

109. "Workers in Egypt," in *Bollettino del Ministero degli Affari Esteri, Anno 1896,* 516/15.

110. For example, the Italian consul in Beirut warned that many workers ended up employed in small enterprises in Mount Lebanon or in the Bekaa and had to contend with miserable wages. *Bollettino del Ministero degli Affari Esteri, Anno 1896,* 53/672. Various reports from around the rest of the Eastern Mediterranean suggest that one reason for this unemployment was that Italian workers were simply unable to compete with local workers and their willingness to accept low salaries. See, for instance, "Egitto," in Ministero degli Affari Esteri, R. Commissariato dell'Emigrazione, *Bollettino dell'Emigrazione,* 79.

111. Perrot, *Jeunesse de la Grève,* 77.

112. Perrot, *Jeunesse de la Grève,* 77.

113. See Torpey, *The Invention of the Passport.* In colonial India "itinerant groups came to be seen as threats, actual or potential, to social stability and regime security" and traditional patterns of circulation came to be seen as a "radical contestation of colonial rule." I. J. Kerr, "On the Move," 100

114. Guerin-Gonzales and Strikwerda, "Labor, Migration, and Politics," in *The Politics of Immigrant Workers,* 25. Although the authors mention that this was the case for Europe and Latin America, it is quite clear that the statement applied to Egypt and the Eastern Mediterranean as well.

115. BBA HR.SYS 1759/2 Ouvriers et employés anarchistes au service des compagnies étrangères dans l'empire, document dated August 10, 1897.

116. See, for example, BBA HR.SYS 1759/2, 2, Brouillon, de Tevfik aux représentants ottomans [sent to St Petersburg, Vienna, Paris, London, Rome, Berlin, Washington, Madrid, Brussels, La Haye, Bucharest, Belgrade, Stettin, Athens, Stockholm, Copenhagen], September 23, 1897:

> Depuis quelque temps, un grand nombre d'ouvriers étrangers viennent dans l'empire pour y être employés aux travaux de construction de chemins de fer. Comme il se peut que parmi ces ouvriers se trouvent aussi des anarchistes ou socialistes, je vous prie de vouloir bien inviter les agents placés sous la juridiction de l'autorité impériale à user de vigilance pour nous aviser le cas échéant de leur départ afin que nous puissions les empêcher de pénétrer dans notre pays.

117. Ducousso, *L' Industrie de la soie en Syrie et au Liban,* 162. See also Khater, "From 'House' to 'Goddess of the House,'" 332; Khater, *Inventing Home.*

118. Beinin and Lockman, *Workers on the Nile,* 53.

119. The Syrian George Saidawi is said to have been the president of the Committee for the Defense of Workers' Rights during the Cairo tramway strike of 1908. Judging him overly sympathetic to workers, the tramway company refused to negotiate with him. Lockman and Beinin, *Workers on the Nile,* 60. Antun 'Arqash was appointed by tramway strikers in Alexandria to present their demands and defend their rights in negotiations with the company's management in 1911. 'Ezzeddin, *Tārīkh al-ṭabaqa al-'āmila al-miṣriyya,* 110. 'Arqash was actually a prominent Alexandrian activist. Born and educated in Beirut, he had moved to Alexandria in 1891, where he was elected to the municipal council in 1912. He is said to have "brought to court many companies, and significantly decreased the load of oppression from the city's inhabitants." Zakhura, *Al-Sūriyyūn fi Miṣr,* 414–15.

120. Tilly, "Transplanted Networks," 81, 84.

121. According to Ilbert, various (nonindigenous) workers joined the Alexandrian Masonic Lodge, which was headed by Tamvacopoulo, a Greek notable, and the Italian lodge La Severa, which was a gathering place for various notables who sat on the Commission for Popular Housing and helped instigate agitation against owners. Ilbert, *Alexandrie 1830–1930,* 649.

122. Perhaps unsurprisingly these Egyptian women, because they mingled with men and especially *foreign* men, had a very bad reputation. In a popular turn-of-the-century Egyptian novella the narrator depicts young women working in the cigarette factories as having particularly loose morals, with "a large number of them [supposedly] illegally married to Greek boys." Lockman, *Imagining the Working Class,* 167; Beinin, *Workers and Peasants,* 68.

123. Couland, "Histoire syndicale et ouvrière égyptienne," 181; 'Abbas, *Al-Ḥaraka al-'ummāliyya fi Miṣr,* 49–53. In December 1899 cigarette workers in Cairo went on strike for three months. By one estimate, nine hundred workers from many factories were involved in this strike. The strike was led by nonindigenous (mostly Greek) cigarette rollers but with the participation and support of Egyptian workers as well.

124. E. J. Goldberg, "The Social History of Egyptian Labor," 169.

125. Shechter, *Smoking, Culture, and Economy in the Middle East,* 32.

126. See Shechter, *Smoking, Culture, and Economy in the Middle East;* Dumont, *Du socialisme ottoman à l'internationalisme anatolien;* Velikov, "Le mouvement ouvrier et social-

iste en Turquie après la révolution Jeune-Turque de 1908." On the militancy of tobacco workers in the United States, see P. A. Cooper, *Once a Cigarmaker;* Mormino and Pozzetta, *The Immigrant World of Ybor City.*

127. Tobacco workers throughout the world were busy educating their fellow workers and politicizing them. Just as they were doing in Salonica, tobacco workers in Florida and Cuba established night schools and opened reading rooms. See Mormino, "The Reader and the Worker"; Mormino and Pozzetta, *The Immigrant World of Ybor City.*

128. Dumont, *Du socialisme ottoman à l'internationalisme anatolien,* 95, n. 15. Other titles on more general topics include *Les Syndicats ouvriers, Le Socialisme en Turquie, La guerre sociale, Socialisme et Judaisme,* and *Chants socialistes,* as well as translations of Maxim Gorki's *The Mother.*

129. On the practice, common especially among cigar makers, of having a reader *(lector)* read aloud in their factories, see Mormino, "The Reader and the Worker"; Manguel, *A History of Reading.*

130. The Ottoman state was apparently aware of the special revolutionary edge of tobacco workers, since in 1911 it issued an order forbidding propaganda material produced by tobacco workers, most likely in Manastir. See BBA DH-SYS 57–1, 23. 6.29. 1329: "Sigara kablarında Hristo Bonef ile Sibka Manastiri resmi ile propaganda yazıları olan sigara kağıtlarının memalik-i osmaniye'ye idhalinin yasaklanması ve bu yasaklara uymayanlar hakkında kanuni takibat yalımasına dair."

131. For example, during the tailors' strike in Cairo in 1901 tailors met with cigarette rollers. It is probable that cigarette activists did not limit their advice to tailors, but also advised workers in other sectors and helped organize them as well. "I'tiṣāb ṣunnā' al- khayyāṭīn," *al-Muqaṭṭam,* November 5, 1901, quoted in 'Ezzeddin, *Tārīkh al-ṭabaqa al-'āmila al-miṣriyya,* 69–70.

132. Syrians seem to have been particularly overrepresented in the tobacco industry in Egypt. In one tobacco factory in Cairo, 43 out of 212 workers were Syrian (i.e., 20 percent). In his study of labor conditions in Egypt, Vallet devoted one case study out of five to a Syrian in a tobacco factory. Vallet, *Contribution à l'étude de la condition des ouvriers,* 7. The archives of the Orthodox Church in Alexandria also confirm the relatively strong association between Syrians and tobacco workers: out of the 637 men who got married in the (Syrian) Orthodox Church in Alexandria between 1869 and 1911, roughly 12 percent were *dakhkhākhīn* (tobacconists), a very high number of whom came from Ladikiyya. Archives of the Greek Orthodox Church of the Dormition, Alexandria, "Al-Akālīl fi kanīsat ṭā'ifat al-Rūm al-Urthūduks li'l-waṭaniyyīn fi sanat 1869–1917," Document II (Marriage Register 1869–1917).

133. On the 1903 strike, see Vallet, *Contribution à l'étude de la condition des ouvriers,* n. 1, xi–xii. The cigarette workers' association, which was said to have a large membership, was established "in order to aid workers materially and culturally [or morally, *al-musā'ada al-māddiyya wa'l-adabiyya*] and defend their interests with factory owners." *Al-Hilāl,* July 1, 1896, 877. Two of the speakers during the 1901 strike, Salim Fifani and Jirji Tannus, were clearly Syrian. See 'Ezzeddin, *Tārīkh al-ṭabaqa al-'āmila al-miṣriyya,* 70.

134. See, for instance, Philipp, *Syrians in Egypt;* Hasanayn, *Dawr al-shāmiyyīn al-muhājirīn ila Miṣr fi al-nahḍa al-adabiyya al-ḥadītha.*

135. See Quataert, "Labor History and the Ottoman Empire."

136. See, for instance, Kırlı, "A Profile of the Labor Force in Early Nineteenth-Century Istanbul." The author argues that occupational specialization was connected to migrants' place of origin rather than ethnic identity.

137. Istrati, *Méditerranée (Lever du soleil)*, 388; Pea, *Vita in Egitto*, 88.

138. During the tailors' strike of 1901, the banner of the tailors' association had the name of the association written in Arabic, Italian, Greek, Hebrew, and Armenian. 'Ezzeddin, *Tārīkh al-ṭabaqa al-'āmila al-miṣriyya*, 85. As for workers' associations, we know of at least two examples of multiethnic associations: the association founded by Syrian Egyptian cigarette rollers in Cairo and the Cairene tailors' association. Many workers' associations were organized along ethnic lines, but it is not clear whether their membership was exclusively so.

139. Chalcraft, *Striking Cabbies of Cairo and Other Stories*, 87.

140. In some sectors non-Egyptians were paid up to 50 percent more than Egyptian workers. See Owen, "The Cairo Building Industry and the Building Boom of 1897 to 1907," 343. In that work, see also table 7, "Daily Average Wages of Egyptian and Foreign Building Workers in Cairo," which shows the wage differences between Egyptian and foreign workers in various construction professions between 1903 and 1913 (342). See also Hansen, *The Political Economy of Poverty, Equity, and Growth*, table 2.2, "Nominal and Real Wages for Construction Workers, by Skill, Sex, Nationality, and Region, 1913," 54. According to this table, in 1913 the foreign skilled males in the construction industry in Cairo made around 55 percent more than their indigenous cohort; the gap was less in Alexandria, where the wages of foreign skilled males were 28 percent more than those of indigenous workers.

141. According to Quataert, Europeans and non-Muslims occupied higher echelons of employment in the European-capitalized enterprises and sectors throughout the Ottoman Empire. Quataert, "Labor History and the Ottoman Empire," 104. This stratification pattern is perhaps most clearly seen in Egypt's tobacco industry, with Greeks constituting the elite hand rollers, alongside some Armenians and Syrians, while indigenous Egyptians (specifically Egyptian *women*) were at the bottom of the ladder. Ironically it seems that it was precisely these Levantine workers who were at the vanguard of labor unrest in the tobacco industry. See Beinin, *Workers and Peasants*, 68.

142. Dār al-Wathā'iq -Majlis al-Wuzarā'- Maṣlaḥat Sikkat al-Ḥadīd 2/1/P. muwaẓẓafīn 1887–1897, Cairo, September 27, 1883, telegram to the president du conseil des ministres, signed Cherif, addressed to Timmermann.

143. Dār al-Wathā'iq -Majlis al-Wuzarā'- Maṣlaḥat Sikkat al-Ḥadīd 2/1/P. muwaẓẓafīn 1887–1897, copy, conseil, copie chemin de fer 18.2.1887.

144. Hanssen, "The Effect of Ottoman Rule on Fin de Siècle Beirut," 125–26.

145. According to the Italian vice consul based in Alexandria in 1890, the economic conditions of Italian workers there had worsened, especially for bricklayers, stone dressers, and carpenters, whose monopoly over these professions was now being challenged. To their great dismay, Italians were being replaced by indigenous labor, who "work for half the salary because they have fewer needs to satisfy; they work more because they are less conscious of their rights and are intelligent enough to acquire the skills of Italian workers." Report from the vice consul T. Carletti, January 4, 1890, in Archivio Storico del Ministero degli Affari Esteri, serie A, b, 29, f. 5, quoted in Rainero, "La Colonia italiana d'Egitto," 137.

146. McCoan, *Egypt as It Is*, 292–98.

147. According to Hansen, the fact that foreign skilled workers in Alexandria and other ports had relatively low real wages was linked to these cities serving as ports of entry for such labor. Hansen, *The Political Economy of Poverty, Equity, and Growth*, 53–55.

148. MAEI, Rome, Ambasciata al Cairo, Busta 88 (1904), Scioperi (p 83)—questioni di massima (?), Cairo, January 16, 1902 (57/16).

149. MAEI, Rome, Ambasciata al Cairo, Busta 88 (1904), Scioperi (p 83)—questioni di massima (?), Cairo, January 16, 1902 (57/16).

150. FO 407, E 143, Confidential (8223), part 60, Further Correspondence respecting the Affairs of Egypt, 1902.

151. Ilbert, *Alexandrie 1830–1930*, 168.

152. On the various lingua francas in Algerian ports during French rule, see Prochaska, "History as Literature, Literature as History," 686, n. 47. Prochaska writes that the lingua franca of the Mediterranean, known as *sabir*, allowed communication between Muslim indigenous populations and foreign Christians. *Sabir* mixed French, Spanish, Italian, and Arabic and was progressively replaced by another lingua franca, *pataouète*, which had little Arabic, thus reflecting the power dynamics in colonial Algeria.

153. Istrati, "*Méditerranée (Lever du soleil)*," 371.

154. Based on Pinelopi Delta's *Premiers Souvenirs*, 217, 162, quoted in Trimi, "La famille Benakis," 88. Delta is the daughter of Immanuel Benakis.

155. Ilbert, *Alexandrie 1830–1930*, 169; Hanley, "Foreignness and Localness in Alexandria, 1880–1914," 298, summarizing and paraphrasing the research of Alexander Borg, "Language," in *Malta : Culture and Identity*, ed. Henry Frendo and Oliver Friggieri (1994), 41.

156. Hanley, "Foreignness and Localness in Alexandria," 60.

157. I am borrowing Geoff Eley's expression. Eley, "Edward Thompson, Social History and Political Culture," 28.

158. For example, the striking tailors of Cairo met in the coffeehouse Alf Layla wa Layla in 1901. "I'tiṣāb ṣunnā' al-khayyāṭīn," *al-Muqaṭṭam*, November 5, 1901, quoted in 'Ezzeddin, *Tārīkh al-ṭabaqa al-'āmila al-miṣriyya*, 69–70. In 1907 the cabbies of Cairo held a number of meetings in coffeehouses throughout the city, where they decided on a general strike. Chalcraft, "The Striking Cabbies of Cairo and Other Stories," 424–25. These are only two examples of what seems to have been a very common occurrence, and one that continued well into the 1940s and even later, as depicted in E. J. Goldberg, *Tinker, Tailor, and Textile Worker*, 23.

159. See Qabbani, *Bughiyat al-Mumaththilīn;* chapter 3 of this work.

160. Georgeon, "Les cafés à Istanbul à la fin de l'Empire ottoman."

161. On the role of neighborhoods in mobilizing Parisians during the Commune, see Gould, *Insurgent Identities*. He argues that, whereas class-based ties formed the essential mobilization factor in Paris during the Revolution of 1848, the networks involved in the mobilization of the Commune were primarily residential and revolved around neighborhood relations. A similar argument is made in Savage, "Class and Labour History."

162. According to one study, "Before 1900, the nature of Egyptian nationality was not articulated in legal terms. It was plain that Egypt was no longer Ottoman, but Ottoman presence lingered in the law courts and the census. If pressed to define their status, local subjects had no alternative but to refer to the Ottoman nationality law of 1869." Hanley, "Foreignness and Localness in Alexandria," 346.

163. Pea, *Vita in Egitto,* 65, my emphasis.

164. Pea, *Vita in Egitto,* 8.

165. Hanley, "Foreignness and Localness in Alexandria," 16, 272. Of course part of the problem is classification. The censuses of 1881 and 1917 created categories of classification that said a lot more about the Egyptian state and British colonialism than they did about people's self-perceptions and identities. On this topic, see 279. See also Sibel Zandi-Sayek's forthcoming work on Izmir, *A World in Flux.*

166. See, for example, Göçek, *Rise of the Bourgeoisie;* Ilbert, *Alexandrie 1830–1930.* Both works focus almost exclusively on notables and the bourgeoisie. Sami Zubaida also dismisses the idea of workers' cosmopolitanism, stating that cosmopolitanism is typically found in "artistic, intellectual and bohemian milieus, but also the world of international business and high finance, and some mafias and underworlds." Zubaida, "Cosmopolitanism and the Middle East," 16.

167. It would be most useful to look at notions and dynamics of cosmopolitanism *beyond* Europe. In this respect, readings on fin de siècle São Paulo, for instance, can be very helpful. This is not to say that working-class cosmopolitanism, if it existed in both São Paulo and Alexandria or if it was constructed as such by elites and working classes, was similar; rather, looking at São Paulo's cosmopolitanism (and its relationship to and distinction from Rio's) helps define some themes worthy of investigation in the case of Alexandria. Interestingly both São Paulo and Rio around the turn of the century took pride in their cosmopolitanism. However, although both the bourgeoisie and the working classes of São Paulo expressed pride at being cosmopolitan and foreign, such sentiments were reserved for Rio's social elites. See de Seixas, *Mémoire et oubli,* 15–16.

168. Ilbert, *Alexandrie 1830–1930,* 649.

169. Ilbert, *Alexandrie 1830–1930,* 649.

170. Liauzu, "The Workers' Movement in North Africa," 198.

171. As Zubaida points out, cosmopolitan Alexandria in the early twentieth century "included a rigorous system of exclusion on buses and trams, and certainly from clubs, some bars and cafés and many social milieus." Zubaida, "Cosmopolitanism and the Middle East," 26.

172. Chalcraft, "The Striking Cabbies of Cairo and Other Stories," 454–56. Pea nonchalantly describes the savage attack and subsequent killing of an Egyptian worker by a dog, an incident that, with one exception, does not seem to have particularly moved the Italian workers who witnessed it. Pea, *Vita in Egitto,* 63. On the other hand, there certainly are instances of Europeans intervening to defend an Egyptian who was being attacked or abused by another European, triggering a split within the European community. See al-Jami'i, *Mudhakkirāt al-Za'īm Ahmad 'Urabi,* 2: 742.

173. Dornel, "Cosmopolitisme et xénophobie," 4–7.

174. The letter, which was published, said the following:

> To the editor, the undersigned having been expelled from Egypt [because they went on strike], on account of the strike of the cigarette makers, and only for that . . . we beg you to have the kindness to support us by your paper, because we are here away from our families and from our children. . . . We are here without food, shelter, and support, not being able to return to Egypt because

> our photographs are exhibited at all the seaports and central provinces of Egypt. We repose, therefore, in the hands of the press, which is competent for the purpose. (FO 407, E 143, Confidential (8223), part 60, Further Correspondence respecting the Affairs of Egypt, 1902, pp 8–9, no 13, enclosure in no 22, extract from the *Acropolis* [Greek newspaper in Athens], February 3, 1902 [translated])

175. On this topic, see Elbaz, "Les Sciences sociales et la question des étrangers," 16.

176. As William Sewell has argued, "Different categories of immigrants had very different experiences. . . . Male immigrants differed from females, long-distance immigrants from short-distance immigrants, Italian-born immigrants from both French-born and other foreign-born immigrants, immigrants early in the nineteenth century from those who migrated later. . . . Immigrants in general differed systematically and significantly from natives, although not always in the ways predicted by the traditional theory." W. Sewell, *Structure and Mobility,* 161.

BIBLIOGRAPHY

ARCHIVAL SOURCES

Alexandria, Egypt

Archives of the Greek Orthodox Church of the Dormition
"Al-Akālīl fi kanīsat ṭā'ifat al-Rūm al-Urthūduks li al-waṭaniyyīn fi sanat 1869–1917," Document II (marriage register 1869–1917)
Municipal Library, Archives de la Municipalité d'Alexandrie (AMA)
Commission Municipale (AMA/CM), 1892–1914
Délégation Municipale (AMA/DM), 1900–1914

Beirut, Lebanon

American University of Beirut, Jafet Library
Syrian Protestant College, "Annual Reports, Board of Managers, Syrian Protestant College," 1879–1899
J. Zeidan 1861–1914, AA7 box 1
Beirut Greek Orthodox Archives
Beirut Maronite Archives, noncatalogued
Collège Patriarcal Grec-Catholique (noncatalogued)
"Liste des étudiants, 1895–1896"
Compagnie du Port de Beyrouth
P8- H-5, "Rapports annuels 1895–1913"
P9-C, "Correspondence"

Cairo, Egypt

Collège de la Sainte Famille
Archives Saint François-Xavier (ASFX), 519 C (1)

Dār al-Wathā'iq al-Qawmiyya-Majlis al-Wuzarā'
Naẓārat al-Dākhiliyya, 8/1 al-Bulīs [police] mutafarriqāt; 8/3/3 al-Bulīs, Shu'ūn Afrād; Maṣlaḥat Sikkat al-Ḥadīd 2/1/P

Cambridge, MA

Harvard University, Houghton Library, International (Second) Congress Documents, BMS Fr 224 (15a-23a)
Harvard University, Widener Library, Archives de l'Alliance Israélite Universelle (AIU)/Liban "Communauté: (1868 et 1904–8)," Box 1, "Divers: comités scolaires, adjoints, clubs, oeuvres, communautés, 1868–1930

Istanbul, Turkey

Başbakanlık Devlet Arşivi (BBA)
BBA Bab-ı Āli Evrak Odası (BEO) Vilayet Gelen-Giden Defterleri
BEO Vilayat Gelen-Giden Defterleri, 260
BEYRUT 269, Beyrut Gelen
BEO A.MTZ.CL Bab-ı Āli Evrak Odası (BEO) Mumtaze Kalemi Cebel-i Lubnan
A.MTZ.CL 5/206; A.MTZ.CL 2/60; A.MTZ.CL 5/206
Dahiliye Nezareti Belgeleri, Idari Kısım Belgeleri (DH.ID)
DH.ID 79,31; DH.ID 111–2, 1
Dahiliye Nezareti Belgeleri, Siyasi Kısım Belgeleri (DH.SYS)
DH.SYS 55–1,15; DH.SYS 55–2, 14; DH.SYS 57–2, 46; DH.SYS 57–1, 23; DH.SYS 64–24, 9
Hariciye Nezareti Siyasi Kısım Evraki Dosya Envanteri (HR.SYS)
HR.SYS 1760/10; HR.SYS. 59/30; HR.SYS 168/9; HR.SYS 1759/1; HR.SYS 1759/2; HR.SYS 1759/3; HR.SYS 1759/4; HR.SYS 1760; HR.SYS 1761/1–36
Yıldız Esas Evrakı (Y.EE)
Y.EE 38/21, 13, 76

London, England

Public Record Office (PRO), Foreign Office Archives, Series FO 407, E 141; FO 407, E. 143; FO 407/164; FO 78/5164; FO 78/5166; FO 407/175; FO 78/5237; FO 78/5239; FO 78/5240; FO 881/8518; FO 83/1970

Rome, Italy

Ministero degli Affari Esteri (MAEI)
Ambasciata dal Cairo, Busta 84, 86, 87, 88

PRIMARY SOURCES, SECONDARY SOURCES, AND REFERENCE WORKS

'Abbas, Ra'uf. *Al-Ḥaraka'l 'ummāliyya fi Miṣr, 1899–1952.* Cairo: Dar al-Katib al-'Arabi li'l-Tiba'a wa'l-Nashr, 1967.
'Abdou, Nagib. *Dr Abdou's Travels in America.* N.p.: n.p., 1908.
Abu-Manneh, Butrus. "The Province of Syria, 1865–1888." In *Problems of the Modern Middle East in Historical Perspective,* ed. Spagnolo.

Accardo, Alain, and Philippe Corcuff. *La Sociologie de Bourdieu: Textes choisis et commentés*. Bordeaux: Le Mascaret, 1986.

Adanır, Fikret. "The National Question and the Genesis and Development of Socialism in the Ottoman Empire: The Case of Macedonia." In *Socialism and Nationalism in the Ottoman Empire 1876–1923*, ed. Tunçay and Zürcher.

Agulhon, Maurice. "The Heritage of the Revolution and Liberty in France." *Review* 12, no. 3 (1989): 405–22.

Akarli, *The Long Peace: Ottoman Lebanon, 1861–1920*. Berkeley: University of California Press, 1993.

Akarlı, Engin. *The Long Peace: Ottoman Lebanon, 1861–1920*. Berkeley: University of California Press, 1993.

———. "Ottoman Attitudes towards Lebanese Emigration, 1885–1910." In *The Lebanese in the World: A Century of Emigration*, ed. Hourani and Shehadi.

Anderson, Benedict. *Under Three Flags: Anarchism and the Anti-colonial Imagination*. London: Verso, 2005.

Andreucci, Franco. "Italy." In *The Formation of Labor Movements 1870–1914: An International Perspective*, ed. van der Linden and Rojahn.

Antonioli, Maurizio, et al., eds. *Dizionario biografico degli anarchici italiani*. Vol. 2. Pisa: BFS, 2003–4.

Antonius, George. *The Arab Awakening: The Story of the Arab Nationalist Movement*. London: H. Hamilton, 1938.

Arendt, Hannah. *On Revolution*. New York: Viking Press, 1963.

Arnaud, Jean-Luc. *Le Caire: Mise en place d'une ville moderne 1867–1907*. Paris: Sindbad, Actes Sud, 1998.

Arnstein, Walter. *Britain Yesterday and Today: 1830 to the Present*. 6th ed. Lexington, MA: D. C. Heath, 1992.

L'Arrestation des trois Russes en Egypte. Alexandrie: Imprimerie Sajous, Molco, 1907.

'Āsim, Isma'il. *Al-A'māl al-kāmila*. Ed. 'Ali Isma'il. Cairo: Dar Zahrat al-Sharq, 1996.

'Awad, Ramsis. *Al-Tārīkh al-sirri li'l-masraḥ qabla thawrat 1919*. Cairo: Matba'at al-Kilani, 1972.

———. *Ittijāhāt siyāsiyya fi'l-masraḥ qabla thawrat 1919*. Cairo: al-Hay'a al-Miṣriyya al-'Āmma li'l- Kitāb, 1979.

Ayalon, Ami. *The Press in the Arab Middle East: A History*. Oxford: Oxford University Press, 1995.

Aydın, Cemil. "A Global Anti-Western Moment? The Russo-Japanese War, Decolonization and Asian Modernity." In *Competing Visions of World Order*, ed. Conrad and Sachsenmaier.

———. *The Politics of Anti-Westernism in Asia: Visions of World Order in Pan-Islamic and Pan-Asian Thought*. New York: Columbia University Press, 2007.

'Azmah, 'Aziz, Sharbil Daghir, Nadim Nu'ayma, and Musa Wahba. *'Aṣr al-nahḍa: Muqaddimāt libirāliyya li'l-hadātha*. Beirut: al-Markaz al-Thaqafi al-'Arabi, 2000.

Badrawi, Malak. *Political Violence in Egypt 1910–1924: Secret Societies, Plots and Assassinations*. Surrey, UK: Curzon, 2000.

Baer, Gabriel. *Fellah and Townsman in the Middle East: Studies in Social History.* London: Frank Cass, 1982.

Balboni, L. A. *Gli Italiani nella civiltà egiziana del secolo XIX.* 3 vols. Alexandria: V. Penasson, 1906.

Barbotin, Anne-Sibylle. "Les Syriens Catholiques en Egypte 1863–1929: Identité et dépersonnalisation." Master's thesis, Université Paris-IV (Sorbonne), 1996–97.

Barbour, Nevill. "The Arab Theatre in Egypt." *Bulletin of the School of Oriental Studies, University of London* 8, no. 1 (1935): 173–87.

Bayly, C. A. " 'Archaic' and 'Modern' Globalization in the Eurasian and African Arena, ca. 1750–1850." In *Globalization in World History,* ed. Hopkins.

———. *The Birth of the Modern World 1780–1914: Global Connections and Comparisons.* Oxford: Blackwell, 2004.

———. "Distorted Development: The Ottoman Empire and British India, circa 1780–1916." *Comparative Studies of South Asia, Africa and the Middle East* 27, no. 2 (2007): 332–44.

Beinin, Joel. "Egyptian Textile Workers: From Craft Artisans Facing European Competition to Proletarians Contending with the State." Paper presented at the Textile Conference IISH, November 11–13, 2004.

———. *Workers and Peasants in the Modern Middle East.* Cambridge, UK: Cambridge University Press, 2001.

Beinin, Joel, and Zachary Lockman. *Workers on the Nile: Nationalism, Communism, Islam, and the Egyptian Working Class, 1882–1954.* Princeton, NJ: Princeton University Press, 1987.

Berkes, Niyazi. *The Development of Secularism in Turkey.* Introduction by Feroz Ahmad. London: Hurst, 1998.

Berque, Jacques. *Egypte: Impérialisme et révolution.* Paris: Gallimard, 1967.

Best, Francine, et al. *L'Affaire Ferrer.* Paris: Centre National et Musée Jean Jaurès, 1989.

Bettini, Leonardo. *Bibliografia dell'anarchismo: periodici e numeri unici anarchici in lingua italiana pubblicati all'estero, 1872–1971.* Vol. 1. Florence: Crescita politica editrice, 1976.

Bevir, Mark. "Republicanism, Socialism, and Democracy in Britain: The Origins of the Radical Left." *Journal of Social History* 34, no. 2 (2000): 351–68.

Beyrut Vilayeti Salnamesi. Beirut: Vilayet Matbaası, 1893.

Blair, Sara. "Local Modernity, Global Modernism: Bloomsbury and the Places of the Literary." *English Literary History* 71 (2004): 813–48.

Bollettino del Ministero degli Affari Esteri, Anno 1896. Rome: Tipografia del Ministero degli Affari Esteri, 1897.

Bonakdarian, Mansour. "Iranian Constitutional Exiles and British Foreign-Policy Dissenters, 1908–9." *International Journal of Middle East Studies* 27 (February 1995): 175–91.

Bose, Sugata. *A Hundred Horizons: The Indian Ocean in the Age of Global Empire.* Delhi: Permanent Black, 2006.

———. "Representations and Contestations of 'India' in Bengali Literature and Culture." In *Nationalism, Democracy, Development: State and Politics in India,* ed. Sugata Bose and Ayesha Jalal. New Delhi: Oxford University Press, 1998.

Bourdieu, Pierre. *Sociology in Question.* Trans. Richard Nice. London: Sage, 1993.

Bozarslan, Hamit. "Les Courants de pensée dans l'empire ottoman 1908–1918." PhD diss., EHESS, 1992.

Braudel, Fernand. *Autour de la Méditerranée.* Paris: Editions de Fallois, 1996.

Brown, Emily C. *Har Dayal: Hindu Revolutionary and Rationalist.* Tucson: University of Arizona Press, 1975.

Buheiry, Marwan, ed. *Intellectual Life in the Arab East, 1890–1939.* Beirut: American University of Beirut Press, 1981.

Bulbul, Farhan. *Al-Masraḥ al-sūri fi mi'at sana 1847–1946.* Damascus: Wizarat al-Thaqafa, 1997.

Burdett, Anita L. P., ed. *Arab Dissident Movements 1905–1955.* Vol. 1, *1905–1920.* N.p.: Archive Editions, 1996.

Burgat, Marie-Claude, ed. *D'un Orient l'autre: Les métamorphoses successives des perceptions et connaissances.* Vol. 1. Paris: Editions du Centre National de la Recherche Scientifique, 1991.

Burke, Edmund, III. "Changing Patterns of Peasant Protest." In *Peasants and Politics in the Modern Middle East,* ed. Kazemi and Waterbury.

———. "Towards a History of Urban Collective Action in the Middle East: Continuities and Change 1750–1980." In *Etat, ville et mouvements sociaux au Maghreb et au Moyen-Orient (Urban crises and social movements in the Middle East and North Africa),* ed. Kenneth Brown et al. Paris: l'Harmattan, 1989.

Buwari, Ilias. *Tārīkh al-ḥaraka al-'ummāliyya wa'l-naqābiyya fi Lubnān 1908–1946.* Vol. 1. Beirut: Dar al-Farabi, 1980.

Cameron, Ardis. *Radicals of the Worst Sort: Laboring Women in Lawrence, Massachusetts, 1860–1912.* Urbana: University of Illinois Press, 1993.

Casas, Juan Gómez. *Anarchist Organization: The History of the F.A.I.* Trans. Abe Bluedstein. Montreal: Black Rose Books, 1986.

Chabelland, Colette, ed. *Le Musée social en son temps.* Paris: Presses de l'Ecole Normale Supérieure, 1998.

Chaichian, Mohammad A. "The Effects of World Capitalist Economy on Urbanization in Egypt, 1800–1970." *International Journal of Middle East Studies* 20, no. 1 (1988): 23–43.

Chalcraft, John. "The Coal Heavers of Port Sa'id: State-Making and Worker Protest, 1869–1914." *International Labor and Working-Class History* 60 (Fall 2001): 110–24.

———. "The Striking Cabbies of Cairo and Other Stories: Crafts and Guilds in Egypt, 1863–1914." PhD diss., New York University, 2001.

———. *Striking Cabbies of Cairo and Other Stories: Crafts and Guilds in Egypt, 1863–1914.* Albany: State University of New York Press, 2004.

Charle, Christophe. *Les intellectuels en Europe au XIXe siècle: Essai d'histoire comparée.* Paris: Seuil, 1996.

———. *Naissance des intellectuels 1880–1900.* Paris: Fayard, 1990.

Chartier, Roger. "Texts, Printing, Readings." In *The New Cultural History,* ed. Hunt.

Chouraqui, Andrée. *L'Alliance Israélite Universelle et la renaissance juive contemporaine, 1860–1960: Cent ans d'histoire.* Paris: Presses universitaires de France, 1965.

Clancy-Smith, Julia. "Gender in the City: Women, Migration and Contested Spaces in Tunis, c. 1830–1881." In *Africa's Urban Past,* ed. David M. Anderson and Richard Rathbone. Oxford: Currey, 2000.

———. "Women, Gender and Migration along a Mediterranean Frontier: Pre-colonial Tunisia, c. 1815–1870." *Gender and History* 17, no. 1 (2005): 62–92.

Clay, Christopher. "Labor Migration and Economic Conditions in Nineteenth-Century Anatolia." *Middle Eastern Studies* 34, no. 4 (1998): 1–32.

Cole, Juan R. I. *Colonialism and Revolution in the Middle East: Social and Cultural Origins of Egypt's 'Urabi Movement.* Princeton, NJ: Princeton University Press, 1993.

Collins, Randall. *The Sociology of Philosophies: A Global Theory of Intellectual Change.* Cambridge, MA: Belknap Press of Harvard University Press, 1998.

Conrad, Sebastian, and Dominic Sachsenmaier, eds. *Competing Visions of World Order: Global Moments and Movements, 1880s—1930s.* New York: Palgrave, 2007.

Cooper, Frederick. "Port Labour in a Colonial City: Mombasa, 1850–1965." In *Dock Workers: International Explorations in Comparative Labour History,* ed. Davies et al.

Cooper, Patricia A. *Once a Cigarmaker: Men, Women, and Work Culture in American Cigar Factories.* Urbana: University of Illinois Press, 1987.

Couland, Jacques. "Histoire syndicale et ouvrière égyptienne." In *Mouvement ouvrier, communisme et nationalismes dans le monde arabe,* ed. Gallissot.

———. *Le Mouvement syndical au Liban 1919–1946.* Paris: Editions sociales, 1970.

Cuno, Kenneth. *The Pasha's Peasants: Land, Society, and Economy in Lower Egypt, 1740–1858.* Cairo: American University of Cairo Press, 1994.

Curtis, James, and John Petras, eds. *The Sociology of Knowledge: A Reader.* New York: Praeger, 1970.

Daghir, Yusuf As'ad. *Qāmūs al-ṣiḥāfa al-lubnāniyya 1868–1974.* Beirut: al-Maktaba al-Sharqiyya, 1978.

Dahir, Mas'ud. *Hijrat al-shawām ila Miṣr.* Beirut: Lebanese University Publications, 1986.

Danovaro, G. D. *L'Egypte à l'aurore du XXème siècle.* Alexandria: Imprimerie Lagoudakis, 1901.

Davie, May. "La Millat grecque-orthodoxe de Beyrouth 1800–1940: Structuration interne et rapport à la cité." PhD diss., Université Paris-IV (Sorbonne), 1993.

Davies, Sam, et al., eds. *Dock Workers: International Explorations in Comparative Labour History, 1790–1970.* Vol. 1. Aldershot, UK: Ashgate, 2000.

Deflem, Mathieu. "'Wild Beasts without Nationality': The Uncertain Origins of Interpol, 1898–1910." In *The Handbook of Transnational Crime and Justice,* ed. Philip Reichel. Thousand Oaks, CA: Sage, 2005.

de Seixas, Jacy Alves. *Mémoire et oubli: Anarchisme et syndicalisme révolutionnaire au Brésil: Mythe et histoire.* Paris: Editions de la maison des sciences de l'homme, 1992.

Desmet-Grégoire, Hélène, and François Georgeon, eds. *Cafés d'orient revisités.* Paris: CNRS, 1997.

Dirlik Arif, ed. *Anarchism in the Chinese Revolution.* Berkeley: University of California Press, 1991.

———. "Vision and Revolution: Anarchism in Chinese Revolutionary Thought on the Eve of the 1911 Revolution." *Modern China* 12, no. 2 (1986): 123–65.

Diyet, Jean. *Ṣiḥāfat al-Kawakibi.* Beirut: Mu'assasat Fikr li'l-Abhath wa'l-Nashr, 1984.

Dornel, Laurent. "Cosmopolitisme et xénophobie: Les luttes entre français et italiens dans les ports et docks marseillais, 1870–1914." *Cahiers de la Méditerranée* (online) 67 (July 2005).

Dreyfus, Michel. "The Emergence of an International Trade Union Organization (1902–1919)." In *The International Confederation of Free Trade Unions,* ed. van der Linden.

———. "Léopold Mabilleau et le mouvement mutualiste français." In *Le Musée social en son temps,* ed. Chabelland.

Droz, Jacques, ed. *Dictionnaire biographique du mouvement ouvrier international.* Paris: Editions ouvrières, 1990.

Ducousso, Gaston. *L'Industrie de la soie en Syrie et au Liban.* Beirut: Imprimerie catholique, 1913.

Dumont, Paul. *Du socialisme ottoman à l'internationalisme anatolien.* Istanbul: Isis, 1997.

———. "Freemasonry in Turkey: A By-product of Western Penetration." *European Review* 13, no. 3 (2005): 481–93.

———. "Jewish, Socialist and Ottoman Organization." In *Workers and the Working Class in the Ottoman Empire,* ed. Tunçay and Zürcher.

Dupont, Anne-Laure. *Girgi Zaydan, 1861–1914: Ecrivain réformiste et témoin de la renaissance arabe.* Damascus: Institut français du Proche-Orient, 2006.

Eberhardt, Isabelle. *Lettres et Journaliers.* Ed. Eglal Errera. Paris: Actes Sud, 1987.

Eddé, Carla. "Démographie des Maronites à Beyrouth au XIXème siècle." PhD diss., Université Saint-Joseph, 1995.

Egger, Vernon. *A Fabian in Egypt: Salamah Musa and the Rise of the Professional Classes in Egypt, 1909–1939.* Lanham, MD: University Press of America, 1986.

Eichner, Carolyn J. "Vive la Commune! Feminism, Socialism, and Revolutionary Revival in the Aftermath of the 1871 Paris Commune." *Journal of Women's History* 15, no. 2 (2003): 68–98.

Elbaz, Mikhael. "Les Sciences sociales et la question des étrangers." In *Les Etrangers dans la ville,* ed. Ida Simon-Barouh and Pierre Simon. Paris: l'Harmattan, 1990.

Eley, Geoff. "Edward Thompson, Social History and Political Culture." In *E. P. Thompson: Critical Perspectives,* ed. Kaye and McClelland.

———. *Forging Democracy: The History of the Left in Europe, 1850–2000s.* Oxford: Oxford University Press, 2002.

Elshakry, Marwa S. "Darwin's Legacy in the Arab East: Science, Religion and Politics, 1870–1914." PhD diss., Princeton University, 2003.

English, Beth. Review of Tom Goyens, *Beer and Revolution: The German Anarchist Movement in New York City, 1880–1914* (Urbana: University of Illinois Press, 2007), posted on H-SHGAPE (May 2008), www.hnet.org/reviews/showrev.php?id=14517.

'Ezzeddin, Amin. *Sīrat muthaqqaf thawri: Al-Mansuri.* Cairo: Dar al-Ghadd al-'Arabi, 1984.

———. *Tārīkh al-ṭabaqa al-'āmila al-miṣriyya: Mundhu nash'atiha ḥatta thawrat 1919.* Beirut: Dar al-Kitab al-'Arabi li'l-Tiba'a wa'l-Nashr, n.d.

Al-Fajr al-Ṣiddīq li jam'iyyat al-maqāṣid al-khairiyya fi Bayrūt: A'māl al-sana al-'ūla. Beirut: Matba'at Thamarat al-Funun, [1297] 1880.

Farag, Nadia. "*Al Muqtataf* 1876–1900: A Study of the Influence of Victorian Thought on Modern Arabic Thought." PhD diss., Oxford University, 1969.

Farge, Arlette. *Subversive Words: Public Opinion in Eighteenth-Century France.* Philadelphia: University of Pennsylvania Press, 1995.

Farid, Muhammad. *The Memoirs and Diaries of Muhammad Farid, an Egyptian Nationalist Leader.* Ed. and trans. Arthur Goldschmidt. San Francisco: Mellen University Research Press, 1992.

Fawaz, Leila. *Merchants and Migrants in 19th Century Beirut.* Cambridge, MA: Harvard University Press, 1983.

———. *An Occasion for War: Civil Conflict in Lebanon and Damascus in 1860.* Berkeley: University of California Press, 1994.

Fawaz, Leila, and C. A. Bayly, eds. *Modernity and Culture: From the Mediterranean to the Indian Ocean.* New York: Columbia University Press, 2002.

Fay, Mary Ann, ed. *Auto/Biography and the Construction of Identity and Community in the Middle East.* New York: Palgrave, 2001.

Fleming, Marie. *The Geography of Freedom: The Odyssey of Elisée Reclus.* Montreal: Black Rose Books, 1988.

Fowler, Josephine. *Japanese and Chinese Immigrant Activists: Organizing in American and International Communist Movements, 1919–1933.* New Brunswick, NJ: Rutgers University Press, 2007.

"The French Revolution and the World-System." *Review* 12, no. 3 (1989).

Gabaccia, Donna. "Class, Exile, and Nationalism at Home and Abroad: The Italian Risorgimento." In *Workers of the World,* ed. Gabaccia and Ottanelli.

———. *Italy's Many Diasporas.* Seattle: University of Washington Press, 2000.

Gabaccia, Donna, and Franca Iacovetta, eds. *Women, Gender, and Transnational Lives: Italian Workers of the World.* Toronto: University of Toronto Press, 2002.

Gabaccia, Donna, and Fraser Ottanelli. *Italian Workers of the World: Labor Migration and the Formation of Multiethnic States.* Urbana: University of Illinois Press, 2001.

Gabriel, Elun. "Performing Persecution: Witnessing and Martyrdom in the Anarchist Tradition." *Radical History Review,* no. 98 (Spring 2007): 34–62.

Gallissot, René, ed. *Mouvement ouvrier, communisme et nationalismes dans le monde arabe.* Paris: Les éditions ouvrières, Cahier du "Mouvement Social" no. 3, 1978.

Ganzoni, T., ed. *Les Echos du Collège Saint-François-Xavier, 1912–3.* Alexandria: n.p., 1914.

Garcia-Bryce, Inigo. "Politics by Peaceful Means: Artisan Mutual Aid Societies in Mid-19th Century Lima, 1860–1879." *The Americas* 59, no. 3 (2003): 325–45.

Gendzier, Irene. *The Practical Visions of Ya'qub Sanu'.* Cambridge, MA: Harvard Middle Eastern Monographs, 1966.

Georgeon, François. "Les cafés à Istanbul à la fin de l'Empire ottoman." In *Cafés d'Orient revisités,* ed. Desmet-Grégoire and Georgeon.

———. "Lire et écrire à la fin de l'Empire ottoman: Quelques remarques introductives." *Oral et écrit dans le monde turco-ottoman. Revue des mondes musulmans et de la Méditerranée,* nos. 75–76 (1995/1–2): 169–79.

Geulen, Christian. "The Common Grounds of Conflict: Racial Visions of World Order 1880–1914." In *Competing Visions of World Order,* ed. Conrad and Sachsenmaier.

Ghazaleh, Pascale. "Masters of the Trade: Crafts and Craftspeople in Cairo, 1750-1850." *Cairo Papers in Social Science* 22, no. 3 (1999).

Ghosh, Durba. "Terrorism in Bengal: Political Violence in the Interwar Years." In *Decentring Empire: Britain, India, and the Transcolonial World,* ed. Durba Ghosh and Dane Kennedy. Hyderabad: Orient Longman, 2006.

Giddens, Anthony. *Beyond Left and Right: The Future of Radical Politics.* Stanford: Stanford University Press, 1994.

Glass, Dagmar. *Der Muqtaṭaf und seine Öffentlichkeit: Aufklärung, Räsonnement und Meinungsstreit in der frühen arabischen Zeitschriftenkommunikation.* Würzburg: Ergon Verlag, 2004.

Göçek, Fatma. *Rise of the Bourgeoisie, Demise of Empire: Ottoman Westernization and Social Change.* Oxford: Oxford University Press, 1996.

Goldberg, David. *A Tale of Three Cities: Labor Organization and Protest in Paterson, Passaic, and Lawrence, 1916–1921.* New Brunswick, NJ: Rutgers University Press, 1989.

Goldberg, Ellis Jay. "The Social History of Egyptian Labor." In *The Social History of Labor in the Middle East,* ed. E. J. Goldberg.

———, ed. *The Social History of Labor in the Middle East.* Boulder, CO: Westview Press, 1996.

———. *Tinker, Tailor, and Textile Worker: Class and Politics in Egypt, 1930–1952.* Berkeley: University of California Press, 1986.

Gonzales-Quijano, Yves. "Littérature Arabe et Société: Une problématique à renouveler. Le cas de la nahda." *Arabica: Journal of Arabic and Islamic Studies* 46, nos. 3–4 (1999): 435–53.

Gorman, Anthony. "Anarchists in Education: The Free Popular University in Egypt (1901)." *Middle Eastern Studies* 41, no. 3 (2005): 303–20.

Gould, Roger. *Insurgent Identities: Class, Community, and Protest in Paris from 1848 to the Commune.* Chicago: University of Chicago Press, 1995.

Gounaris, Basil. "Railway Construction and Labor Availability in Macedonia in the Late Nineteenth Century." *Journal of Modern Greek Studies* 7 (1989): 139–58.

Gramsci, Antonio. "The Intellectuals." In *Selections from the Prison Notebooks.* Ed. and trans. Quintin Hoare and Geoffrey Nowell Smith. New York: International Publishers, 1971.

Gran, Peter. "'Passive Revolution' as a Possible Model for Nineteenth-century Egyptian History." In *Money, Land and Trade: An Economic History of the Muslim Mediterranean,* ed. Nelly Hanna. London: I. B. Tauris, 2002.

Grange, Daniel. *L'Italie et la Méditerranée, 1896–1911.* Rome: Collection de l'Ecole Française de Rome, 1994.

Guerin-Gonzales, Camille, and Carl Strikwerda, eds. *The Politics of Immigrant Workers: Labor Activism and Migration in the World Economy since 1830.* New York: Holmes and Meier, 1998.

Gully, Adrian. "Arabic Linguistic Issues and Controversies of the Late Nineteenth and Early Twentieth Centuries." *Journal of Semitic Studies* 42, no. 1 (1997): 75–120.

Guth, Stephan, "*Wa hakadha kana ka-iblis:* Satan and Social Reform in a Novel by Salim al-Bustani (*Bint al-Laṣr,* 1875)." In *Myths, Historical Archetypes and Symbolic Figures in Arabic Literature: Towards a New Hermeneutic Approach,* ed. Angela Neuwirth et al. Beirut: Orient Institute, 1999.

Hajj, Badr. *Khalil Sa'adah.* London: Riyad al-Rayyis Books, 1987.

Hakim-Dowek, Carol. "The Origins of the Lebanese National Idea, 1840–1914." PhD diss., Oxford University, 1997.

Hall, Michael, and Marco Aurélio Garcia. "Urban Labor." In *Modern Brazil: Elites and Masses in Historical Perspective,* ed. Michael Conniff and Frank McCann. Lincoln: University of Nebraska Press, 1991.

Hamadeh, Shirine. *The City's Pleasures: Istanbul in the 18th Century.* Seattle: University of Washington Press, 2008.

Hamzah, Dyala. "L'intérêt général (maslaha 'âmma) ou le triomphe de l'opinion: Fondation délibératoire (et esquisses délibératives) dans les écrits du publiciste syro-égyptien Muhammad Rashîd Ridâ (1865–1935)." PhD diss., Paris and Berlin: EHESS and Frei Universite, 2008.

———. "La pensée de 'Abduh à l'âge utilitaire: L'intérêt général entre maslaha et manfa'a." In *Modernités islamiques,* ed. M. Charif and S. Mervin. Damascus: IFPO, 2006.

———. Review of Dagmar Glass, *Der Muqtaṭaf und seine Öffentlichkeit. Revue des mondes musulmans et de la Méditerranée* (Yémen Territoires et Identités), nos. 121–22 (April 2008): 296–301.

Hanagan, M. P., et al., eds. *Challenging Authority: The Historical Study of Contentious Politics.* Minneapolis: University of Minnesota Press, 1998.

Hanioğlu, M. Şükrü. *Preparation for a Revolution: The Young Turks, 1902–1908.* Oxford: Oxford University Press, 2001.

Hanley, Will, "Foreignness and Localness in Alexandria, 1880—1914." PhD diss., Princeton University, 2007.

Hanna, Abdallah. *Al-'Āmmiyya wa'l-intifāḍāt al-fallāḥiyya fi Jabal Ḥawrān 1850–1918.* 2nd ed. Damascus: Dar al-Ahali, 1990.

———. *Al-Ḥaraka al-'ummāliyya fi Sūriyya wa Lubnān, 1900–1945.* Damascus: Dar Dimashq, 1973.

———. *Min al-ittijāhāt al-fikriyya fi Sūriyya: Al-nuṣf al-awwal min al-qarn al-'ishrīn.* Damascus: Dar al-Ahali, n.d.

Hanna, Nelly. "Literacy and the 'Great Divide' in the Islamic World, 1300–1800." *Journal of Global History* 2 (2007): 175–93.

Hanna, Sami, and George Gardner. *Arab Socialism.* Leiden: Brill, 1969.

Hannun, Habib, ed. *Marāthi al-Labaki.* Rio de Janeiro: n.p., 1925.

Hansen, Bent. *The Political Economy of Poverty, Equity, and Growth: Egypt and Turkey.* Oxford: Oxford University Press, 1991.

Hanssen, Jens. "The Effect of Ottoman Rule on Fin de Siècle Beirut: The Province of Beirut, 1888–1914." PhD diss., Oxford University, 2001.

———. *Fin-de-siècle Beirut: The Making of a Provincial Ottoman Capital.* Oxford: Oxford University Press, 2005.

Harland-Jacobs, Jessica. *Builders of Empire: Freemasons and British Imperialism 1717–1927.* Chapel Hill: University of North Carolina Press, 2007.

Haroun, Georges. *Shibli Shumayyil: Une pensée évolutionniste arabe à l'époque d'An-nahḍa.* Beirut: Université Libanaise, 1985.

Harper, Timothy. N. "Empire, Diaspora and the Languages of Globalism, 1850–1914." In *Globalization in World History,* ed. Hopkins.

Hasanayn, Ahmad Tahir. *Dawr al-shāmiyyīn al-muhājirīn ila Miṣr fi al-nahḍa al-adabiyya al-ḥadītha.* Damascus: Dar al-Wathba, 1983.

Hattox, Ralph. *Coffee and Coffeehouses: The Origins of a Social Beverage in the Medieval Near East.* Seattle: University of Washington Press, 1988.

Haupt, Georges. *L'Historien et le mouvement social.* Paris: F. Maspero, 1980.

Heidrich, Joachim, ed. *The French Revolution of 1789: Its Impact on Latin America, Asia and Africa.* Berlin: Akademie-Verlag Berlin, 1989.

Higonnet, Patrice, "Jacobinism and the World-System." *Review* 12, no. 3 (1989): 423–35.
Hobsbawm, Eric. *Revolutionaries: Contemporary Essays.* New York: Pantheon, 1973.
Hopkins, Anthony G., ed. *Globalization in World History.* London: Pimlico, 2002.
Hopwood, Derek. *The Russian Presence in Syria and Palestine, 1843–1914: Church and Politics in the Near East.* Oxford: Clarendon Press, 1969.
Horne, Janet. "Le libéralisme à l'épreuve de l'industrialisation: La réponse du Musée social." In *Le Musée social en son temps,* ed. Chabelland.
Hourani, Albert. *Arabic Thought in the Liberal Age.* Cambridge, UK: Cambridge University Press, 1962.
———. "Forty Years After: The Arab Reawakening Reconsidered." In *Emergence of the Modern Middle East,* ed. Albert Hourani. Berkeley: University of California Press, 1981.
———. "Lebanese and Syrians in Egypt." In *The Lebanese in the World,* ed. Hourani and Shehadi.
Hourani, Albert, and Nadim Shehadi, eds. *The Lebanese in the World: A Century of Emigration.* London: I. B. Tauris, 1992.
Hunt, Lynn, ed. *The New Cultural History.* Berkeley: University of California Press, 1989.
Iacovella, Angelo. "La Presenza italiana in Egitto: Problemi storici e demografici." *Altreitalie* 2 (June–December 1994): 60–69.
Ilbert, Robert. *Alexandrie 1830–1930: Histoire d'une communauté citadine.* Cairo: Institut Français d'Archéologie Orientale, Bibliothèque d'étude 112/1, 1996.
———. "*Modèles et vecteurs de la réforme: Le libéralisme des notables.*" In *Entre réforme sociale et mouvement national,* ed. Roussillon.
Iriye, Akira. *Cultural Internationalism and World Order.* Baltimore: Johns Hopkins University Press, 1997.
Islamoğlu-Inan, Huri, ed. *The Ottoman Empire and the World-Economy.* Cambridge, UK: Cambridge University Press, 1988.
Ismail, Adel. *Documents diplomatiques et consulaires relatifs à l'histoire du Liban et des pays du Proche-Orient du XVIIè siècle à nos jours.* Vols. 16–18. Beirut: Editions des Oeuvres Politiques et Historiques, 1979–84.
Issawi, Charles. "The Historical Background of Lebanese Emigration, 1800–1914." In *The Lebanese in the World,* ed. Hourani and Shehadi.
Istrati, *Méditerranée (Lever du soleil).* Paris: Rieder, 1934.
Istrati, Panait. *Vie d'Adrien Zograffi.* Paris: Gallimard, [1934] 1968.
al-Jami'i, Abd al-Mun'im, ed. *Mudhakkirāt al-Za'īm Ahmad 'Urabi.* Vol. 2. Cairo: Dār al-Kutub wa'l-Wathā'iq al-Qawmiyya, 2005.
Jam'iyyat Yadd al-Ihsān. Alexandria: Matba'at Jirji Gharzuzi, 1907.
Jiha, Michel. *Farah Antun.* Beirut: Riyad al-Rayyis, 1998.
Jiha, Shafiq. *Darwin wa azmat sanat 1882 fi'l-kulliya al-ṭibbiyya: Wa awwal thawra ṭullābiyya fi'l-'ālam al-'arabi.* Beirut: Shafiq Jiha, 1991.
Kafadar, Cemal. "Yeniçeri-Esnaf Relations: Solidarity and Conflict." MA thesis, McGill University, 1981.
Kansu, Aykut. *The Revolution of 1908 in Turkey.* Leiden: Brill, 1997.
Karakışla, Yavuz Selim. "The 1908 Strike Wave in the Ottoman Empire." *Turkish Studies Association Bulletin,* September 1992, 153–77.

Karl, Rebecca E. "Creating Asia: China in the World at the Beginning of the Twentieth Century." *American Historical Review*, October 1998, 1096–118.

Karpat, Kemal. *Ottoman Population, 1830–1914: Demographic and Social Characteristics.* Madison: University of Wisconsin Press, 1985.

Karpiel, Frank. "Freemasonry, Colonialism, and Indigenous Elites." Conference proceedings, *American Historical Review*, 2001, www.historycooperative.org/proceedings/interactions/karpiel.html.

Kasaba, Reşat, ed. *Cities in the World System.* New York: Greenwood Press, 1991.

———. "Migrant Labor in Western Anatolia, 1750–1850." In *Landholding and Commercial Agriculture in the Middle East*, ed. Keyder and Tabak.

———. *The Ottoman Empire and the World Economy: The Nineteenth Century.* Albany: State University of New York Press, 1988.

Kasaba, Reşat, and Immanuel Wallerstein. *Incorporation into the World-Economy: Change in the Structure of the Ottoman Empire 1750–1838.* Binghamton: State University of New York Press, 1980.

Kaye, Harvey, and Keith McClelland, eds. *E. P. Thompson: Critical Perspectives.* Philadelphia: Temple University Press, 1990.

Kazemi, Farhad, and John Waterbury, eds. *Peasants and Politics in the Modern Middle East.* Miami: Florida International University Press, 1991

Keddie, Nikki R. *An Islamic Response to Imperialism: Political and Religious Writings of Sayyid Jamal ad-Din al Afghani.* Berkeley: University of California Press, [1968] 1983.

———. *Sayyid Jamal ad-Din al Afghani: A Political Biography.* Berkeley: University of California Press, 1972.

Kedourie, Elie. "The American University of Beirut." *Middle Eastern Studies*, 3 (October 1966): 74–90.

Kerr, Ian J. "On the Move: Circulating Labor in Pre-colonial, Colonial, and Post-colonial India." *International Review of Social History* 51, supplement (2006): 85–109.

Kerr, Malcolm. "Notes on the Background of Arab Socialist Thought." *The Middle East*, special issue of *Contemporary History* 3, no. 3 (1968): 145–59.

Keyder, Çağlar, Eyüp Özveren, and Donald Quataert. "Port-Cities in the Ottoman Empire: Some Theoretical and Historical Perspectives." *Review* 16, no. 4 (1993): 519–58.

Keyder, Çağlar, and Faruk Tabak, eds. *Landholding and Commercial Agriculture in the Middle East.* Albany: State University of New York Press, 1991.

Khairallah, Khairallah. *La Syrie.* Paris: E. Leroux, 1912.

Khalidi, Rashid. "Society and Ideology in Late Ottoman Syria: Class, Education, Profession and Confession." In *Problems of the Modern Middle East in Historical Perspective*, ed. Spagnolo.

Khater, Akram. "From 'House' to 'Goddess of the House': Gender, Class, and Silk in 19th-Century Mount Lebanon." *International Journal of Middle East Studies* 28, no. 3 (1996): 325–48.

———. *Inventing Home: Emigration, Gender, and the Middle Class in Lebanon, 1870–1920.* Berkeley: University of California Press, 2001.

al-Khatib, Muhammad Kamil, ed. *Naẓariyyat al-masraḥ.* Vol. 1. Damascus: Manshurat Wizarat al-Thaqafa, 1994.

Khuri, Ra'if. *Modern Arab Thought: Channels of the French Revolution to the Arab East.* Trans. Ihsan 'Abbas. Ed. Charles Issawi. Princeton, NJ: Kingston Press, 1983.

Khuri, Yusuf Quzma, ed. *A'māl al-jam'iyya al-'ilmiyya al-sūriyya 1868–1869.* Beirut: Dar al-Hamra', 1990.

———, ed. *Maqālāt wa khutab fi'l-tarbiya: 'Aṣr al-nahḍa al-hadītha.* Beirut: Dar al-Hamra', 1990.

Khuri-Makdisi, Ilham. "Inscribing Socialism into the *Nahḍa.*" In *The Making of the Arab Intellectual (1880–1960): Empire, Public Sphere and the Colonial Coordinates of Selfhood,* ed. Dyala Hamzah. New York: Routledge, forthcoming.

———. "Levantine Trajectories: The Formulation and Dissemination of Radical Ideas in and between Beirut, Cairo and Alexandria, 1860–1914." PhD diss., Harvard University, 2003.

———. "The *Nahḍa* Revisited: Socialism and Radicalism in Beirut and Mount Lebanon, 1900–1914." In *Liberal Thought in the Eastern Mediterranean: Late 19th Century until the 1960s,* ed. Christoph Schumann. Leiden: Brill, 2008.

———. "Theater and Radical Politics in Beirut, Cairo and Alexandria 1860–1914." *CCAS Occasional Papers,* Center for Contemporary Arab Studies, Georgetown University, fall 2006.

Kırlı, Cengiz. "A Profile of the Labor Force in Early Nineteenth-Century Istanbul." *International Labor and Working-Class History* 60 (Fall 2001): 125–40.

———. "The Struggle over Space: Coffeehouses of Ottoman Istanbul, 1780–1845." PhD diss., Binghamton University, State University of New York, 2000.

Knowlton, Clark. "The Social and Spatial Mobility of the Syrian and Lebanese Community in São Paulo, Brazil." In *The Lebanese in the World,* ed. Hourani and Shehadi.

Konishi, Sho. "Reopening the 'Opening of Japan': A Russian Japanese Revolutionary Encounter and the Vision of Anarchist Progress." *American Historical Review* 112, no. 1 (2007), online.

Labaki, Boutros. *Introduction à l'histoire économique du Liban: Soie et commerce extérieur en fin de période ottomane (1840–1914).* Beirut: Université Libanaise, 1984.

Landau, Jacob. *Studies in the Arab Theater and Cinema.* Philadelphia: University of Pennsylvania Press, 1958.

Lasch, Christopher. *The New Radicalism in America, 1889–1963: The Intellectual as a Social Type.* New York: Norton, 1965.

Leboutte, René, ed. *Migrations et migrants dans une perspective historique: Permanences et innovations.* Brussels: PIE, 2000.

Liauzu, Claude. "The Workers' Movement in North Africa." In *Social History of Labor,* ed. E. J. Goldberg.

Lockman, Zachary. "Imagining the Working Class: Culture, Nationalism, and Class Formation in Egypt, 1899–1914." *Poetics Today: International Journal for Theory and Analysis of Literature and Communication* 15, no. 2 (1994): 156–90.

———, ed. *Workers and Working Classes in the Middle East: Struggles, Histories, Historiographies.* Albany: State University of New York Press, 1994.

Al-Madrasa al-Kulliyya al-Sūriyya al-Injīliyya [SPC]: Al-Kitāb al-Sanawi, 1884–1890. N.p.: n.p., n.d.

Al-Madrasa al-Kulliyya al-Sūriyya al-Injīliyya [SPC]: Al-Kitāb al-Sanawi, 1891–1901. N.p.: n.p., n.d.

Al-Madrasa al-Kulliyya al-Sūriyya al-Injīliyya [SPC]: Al-Kitāb al-Sanawi, 1902–1911. N.p.: n.p., n.d.

Makariyos, Shahin. *Tārikh al-māṣūniyya al-ʿamaliyya.* N.p.: n.p., 1984.

Makdisi, Ussama. *The Culture of Sectarianism: Community, History and Violence in Nineteenth-Century Ottoman Lebanon.* Berkeley: University of California Press, 2000.

Manguel, Alberto. *A History of Reading.* New York: Penguin, 1997.

Manning, Patrick. *Migration in World History.* New York: Routledge, 2005.

———. "1789–1792 and 1989–1992: Global Interaction of Social Movements." *World History Connected* 3, no. 1 (2005), online.

Maram, Sheldon Leslie. "Anarchists, Immigrants, and the Brazilian Labor Movement, 1890–1920." PhD diss., University of California at Santa Barbara, 1972.

Mardin, Şerif. *The Genesis of Young Ottoman Thought: A Study in the Modernization of Turkish Political Ideas.* Princeton, NJ: Princeton University Press, 1962.

Maricourt, Thierry. *Dictionnaire des auteurs prolétariens de la langue française de la révolution à nos jours.* Amiens: Editions Encrage, 1994.

Masabni, Badiʿa. *Mudhakkirāt.* Ed. Nazik Basila. Beirut: Dar Maktabat al-Hayat, n.d.

Masini, Pier Carlo. *Storia degli anarchici italiani nell' epoca degli attentati.* Milan: Rizzoli editore, 1981.

McAdam, Doug, Sidney Tarrow, and Charles Tilly. *Dynamics of Contention.* New York: Cambridge University Press, 2001.

McCoan, James. *Egypt as It Is.* New York: Henry Holt, 1877.

McKeown, Adam. "Global Migration 1846–1940." *Journal of World History* 15 (2004): 155–89.

McLaughlin, Virginia Yans, ed. *Immigration Reconsidered: History, Sociology, and Politics.* Oxford: Oxford University Press, 1990.

Meier, Oliver. *Al Muqtataf et le débât sur le Darwinisme, Beyrouth 1876–1885.* Cairo: Les dossiers du CEDEJ, 1996.

Mercier, Lucien. *Les Universités populaires, 1899–1914: Education populaire et mouvement ouvrier au début du siècle.* Paris: Les Editions ouvrières, 1986.

Mermier, Franck. "Souk et citadinité dans le monde arabe." In *L'urbain dans le monde musulman de Méditerranée,* ed. Jean-Luc Arnaud. Paris: Maisonneuve et Larose, 2005.

Milano, Attilio. *Storia degli ebrei italiani nel Levante.* Florence: Casa editrice Israel, 1949.

Milza, Pierre. *Voyage en Ritalie.* Paris: Plon, 1993.

Ministero degli Affari Esteri. *Bollettino del Ministero degli Affari Esteri, 1895–1914.* Rome: Tipografia del Ministero degli Affari Esteri, 1896–1915.

Ministero degli Affari Esteri, R. Commissariato dell'Emigrazione. *Bollettino dell'Emigrazione,* vol. 12. Rome: Tipografia Nazionale G. Bertero, 1902.

Mitchell, Timothy. *Rule of Experts: Egypt, Techno-Politics, Modernity.* Berkeley: University of California Press, 2002.

Mola, Aldo. "Le logge 'italiane' in Egitto dall'Unità al fascismo." In *L'Italia e l'Egitto dalla rivolta di Arabi Pascia all'avvento del fascismo,* ed. Rainero and Serra.

Moreh, Shmuel, and Philip Sadgrove. *Jewish Contributions to Nineteenth Century Arabic The-*

atre: Plays from Algeria and Syria. A Study and Texts. Oxford: Oxford University Press, 1996.

Mormino, Gary R. "The Reader and the Worker: *Los Lectores* and the Culture of Cigarmaking in Cuba and Florida." *International Labor and Working-Class History* 54 (fall 1998): 1–18.

Mormino, Gary R., and George E. Pozzetta. *The Immigrant World of Ybor City.* Urbana: University of Illinois Press, 1987.

Morsy, Magali, ed. *Les Saint-Simoniens et l' Orient: Vers la modernité* . Paris: Edisud, 1989.

Moya, José. *Cousins and Strangers: Spanish Immigrants in Buenos Aires, 1850–1930.* Berkeley: University of California Press, 1998.

———. "Immigrants and Associations: A Global and Historical Perspective." *Journal of Ethnic and Migration Studies* 31, no. 5 (2005): 833–64.

Musa, Salama. *Al-Ishtirākiyya.* 2nd ed. Cairo: Mu'assasat Musa li'l-Nashr wa'l-Tawzi', [1913] 1962.

———. *Tarbiyat Salama Musa.* Cairo: Dar al-Katib al-Misri, 1947.

Musto, Marcello. "The Rediscovery of Karl Marx." *International Review of Social History* 52 (2007): 477–98.

Naff, Alixa. "Lebanese Immigration into the United States: 1880 to the Present." In *The Lebanese in the World,* ed. Hourani and Shehadi.

Najm, Muhammad Yusuf. *Al-Masraḥiyya fi'l-adab al-'arabi al-ḥadīth 1847–1914.* Beirut: Dar Bayrut li'l-Tiba'a wa'l-Nashr, 1956.

Naqqash, Marun. *Muqaddima li "Arzat Lubnān"* (1869). In *Naẓariyyat al-masraḥ,* ed. Khatib.

Naqqash, Salim. Article in *Al-Jinān,* August 11, 1875. In *Naẓariyyat al-masraḥ,* ed. Khatib.

Nataf, André. *La Vie quotidienne des anarchistes en France, 1880–1910.* Paris: Hachette, 1986.

Nettlau, Max. *A Short History of Anarchism.* London: Freedom Press, 1996.

Nicolet, Claude, Robert Ilbert, and Jean-Charles Depaule, eds. *Mégapoles méditerranéennes: Géographie urbaine rétrospective. Actes du colloque organisé par l'Ecole Française de Rome et la maison méditerranéenne des sciences de l'homme, Rome, 8–11 mai 1996.* Paris: Maisonneuve et Larose, 2000.

Nigarendé. "Beyrouth, Centre Medical." *Revue du Monde Musulman* (Paris), 8 (1909): 39–52.

al-Nukhayli, Muhammad. *Al-Ḥaraka al-'ummāliyya fi Miṣr wa mawqif al-ṣiḥāfa wa'l-sultāt al-miṣriyya minha min sanat 1882 ila 1952.* Cairo: Matba'at al-Ittihad al-'Am li'l-'Ummal, 1967.

Ortiz, David. "Redefining Public Education: Contestation, the Press, and Education in Regency Spain, 1885–1902." *Journal of Social History* 35, no. 1 (2001): 73–94.

Owen, E. R. J. "The Attitudes of British Officials to the Development of the Egyptian Economy, 1882–1922." In *Studies in the Economic History of the Middle East: From the Rise of Islam to the Present Day,* ed. M. A. Cook. Oxford: Oxford University Press, 1970.

———. "The Cairo Building Industry and the Building Boom of 1897 to 1907." In *Colloque international sur l'histoire du Caire.* Grafenhainichen: VEB Druckerei Gottfried Wilhelm Leibniz, 1969.

———. *Cotton and the Egyptian Economy, 1820–1914: A Study in Trade and Development.* Oxford: Clarendon Press, 1969.

——. *The Middle East in the World Economy, 1800–1914.* 2nd ed. London: I. B. Tauris, 1993.
——, ed. *New Perspectives on Property and Land in the Middle East.* Cambridge, MA: Harvard Middle Eastern Monographs 34, 2000.
——. "The Rapid Growth of Egypt's Agricultural Output, 1890–1914, as an Early Example of the Green Revolutions of Modern South Asia: Some Implications for the Writing of Global History." *Journal of Global History* 1 (2006): 81–99.
——. "The Silk-Reeling Industry of Mount Lebanon, 1840–1914: A Study of the Possibilities and Limitations of Factory Production in the Periphery." In *The Ottoman Empire and the World-Economy,* ed. Islamoğlu-Inan.
——. "The Study of Middle Eastern Industrial History: Notes on the Interrelationship between Manufacturing with Special References to Lebanese Silk and Egyptian Sugar, 1900–1930." *International Journal of Middle East Studies* 16, no. 4 (1984): 475–87.
——. "Using Present Day Notions of Imperialism, Globalization and Internationalism: to Understand the Middle East's Late 19th Century / Early Twentieth Century Past." *MIT Electronic Journal of Middle East Studies* 4 (fall 2003): 4–16.
Owen, Roger, and Şevket Pamuk. *A History of Middle East Economies in the Twentieth Century.* Cambridge, MA: Harvard University Press, 1999.
Pamuk, Şevket, and Jeffrey G. Williamson, eds. *The Mediterranean Response to Globalization before 1950.* London: Routledge, 2000.
Panzac, Daniel, ed. *Les Arabes, les Turcs et la Révolution française. Revue du monde musulman et de la Méditerranée* (Aix-en-Provence), nos. 52–53 (1989).
——, ed. *Les Villes dans l'Empire Ottoman: Activités et societés.* 2 vols. Paris: Editions du CNRS, 1991.
Pascual, Jean-Paul. "Approches de la ville au Levant: Continuités et renouvellements." *Villes au Levant: Hommage à André Raymond. Revue des mondes musulmans et de la méditerranée* (Aix-en-Provence), nos. 55–56 (1990): 9–17.
Payre, Renaud, and Pierre-Yves Saunier. "Municipalités de tous pays, unissez vous! L'Union Internationale des Villes ou l'Internationale municipale (1913–1940)." *Amministrare* 30, nos. 1–2 (2000): 217–39.
Pea, Enrico. *Moscardino, Il Servitore del diavolo, Il Volto Santo.* Ed. Marcello Ciccuto. Turin: Einaudi, 1979.
——. *Vita in Egitto.* Ed. Enrico Lorenzetti. Florence: Ponte alle Grazie, 1995.
Perolari-Malmignati, Pietro. *Su e giù per la Siria: Note e schizzi.* Milan: Fratelli Treves editori, 1878.
Perrot, Michelle. *Jeunesse de la Grève: France 1871–1890.* Paris: Seuil, 1984.
Philipp, Thomas. *Gurgi Zaidan: His Life and Thought.* Beirut: Orient Institut, 1979.
——. *The Syrians in Egypt 1725–1975.* Stuttgart: Steiner Verlag, 1985.
Pignol, Armand. "Les Saint-Simoniens et l'Orient." In *D'un Orient l'autre,* ed. Burgat.
Plotkin, Ira L. *Anarchism in Japan: A Study of the Great Treason Affair 1910–1911.* Dyfed, Wales: Edwin Mellen Press, 1990.
Poffandi, Stefano. *1909 Indicateur Egyptien.* Alexandria: Etablissements Mourès, 1909.
Potestio, John, ed. *The Memoirs of Giovanni Veltri.* Ontario: Multicultural History Society, 1987.
"Procès-Verbal de la séance du 20 Mai 1910." *L'Egypte contemporaine* 1 (1910): 130–31.

Prochaska, David. "History as Literature, Literature as History: Cagayous of Algiers." *American Historical Review* 101, no. 3 (1996): 670–711.
Qabbani, Sulayman, ed. *Bughiyat al-mumaththilīn*. Alexandria: Gharzuzi Press, ca. 1914.
Qasimi, Sa'id, and Khalil al-'Azm. *Qāmūs al-Ṣinā'āt al-Shāmiyya* (selections). In *Naẓariyyat al-masraḥ*, ed. Khatib.
Quataert, Donald. "Janissaries, Artisans and the Question of Ottoman Decline 1730–1826." In *Workers, Peasants and Economic Change in the Ottoman Empire 1730–1914*, 197–203.
———. "Labor History and the Ottoman Empire, c. 1700–1922." *International Labor and Working-Class History* 60 (Fall 2001): 93–109.
———. "Machine Breaking and the Changing Carpet Industry of Western Anatolia, 1860–1908." *Journal of Social History* 3 (1986): 473–89.
———, ed. *Manufacturing in the Ottoman Empire and Turkey, 1500–1950*. Albany: State University of New York Press, 1994.
———. "Ottoman Workers and the State, 1826–1914." In *Workers and Working Classes in the Middle East*, ed. Lockman.
———. "Rural Unrest in the Ottoman Empire, 1830–1914." In *Peasants and Politics in the Modern Middle East*, ed. Kazemi and Waterbury.
———. *Social Disintegration and Popular Resistance in the Ottoman Empire, 1881–1908: Reactions to European Economic Penetration*. New York: New York University Press, 1983.
———. "Social History of Labor in the Ottoman Empire." In *The Social History of Labor*, ed. E. J. Goldberg.
———. *Workers, Peasants and Economic Change in the Ottoman Empire 1730–1914*. Istanbul: Isis Press, 1993.
Quataert, Donald, and Erik J. Zürcher, eds. *Workers and the Working Class in the Ottoman Empire and the Turkish Republic 1839–1950*. London: I. B. Tauris, 1995.
Quesada, Fernando. *Argentine Anarchism and La Protesta*. New York: Gordon Press, 1979.
Rainero, "La Colonia italiana d'Egitto: Presenza e vitalità." In *L'Italia e l'Egitto dalla rivolta di Arabi Pascia*, ed. Rainero and Serra.
Rainero, R. H., and L. Serra, eds. *L'Italia e l'Egitto dalla rivolta di Arabi Pascia all'avvento del fascismo*. Milan: Marzorati, 1991.
Ramnath, Maia. "Two Revolutions, the Ghadar Movement and India's Radical Diaspora, 1913–1918." *Another World Was Possible: A Century of Radical Movements. Radical History Review*, no. 92 (Spring 2005): 7–30.
Raymond, André. *Artisans et commerçants au Caire au XVIIIème siècle*. Damascus: Institut Français de Damas, 1973.
Reid, Donald. *Lawyers and Politics in the Arab World, 1880–1960*. Chicago: Bibliotheca Islamica, 1981.
———. *The Odyssey of Farah Antun: A Syrian Christian's Quest for Secularism*. Chicago: Bibliotheca Islamica, 1975.
———. "The Syrian Christians and Early Socialism in the Arab World." *International Journal of Middle East Studies* 5, no. 2 (1974): 177–93.
———. "Syrian Christians, the Rags-to-Riches Story, and Free Enterprise." *International Journal of Middle East Studies* 1, no. 4 (1970): 358–67.

Reimer, Michael. *Colonial Bridgehead: Government and Society in Alexandria, 1807–1882.* Cairo: AUC Press, 1997.

Richards, Vernon, ed. *Errico Malatesta: His Life and Ideas.* London: Freedom Press, 1965.

Rida, Muhammad Rashid. *Riḥlat al-Imām Muhammad Rashid Rida.* Ed. Yusuf Ibish. Beirut: al-Mu'assasa al-'Arabiyya li'l-Dirasa wa'l-Nashr, n.d.

Rihani, Albert, ed. *Al Rihani wa mu'āṣirūhu: Rasā'il al-udabā' ilayhi.* Beirut: Dar al-Rihani fi'l-Tiba'a wa'l-Nashr, 1966.

Rihani, Amin. *Rasā'il 1896–1940.* Ed. Albert Rihani. Beirut: Dar Rihani li'l-Tiba'a wa'l-Nashr, 1959.

———. *Rasā'il Amin al-Rihani, 1896–1940.* 2nd ed. Ed. Albert al-Rihani. Beirut: Dar al-Jil, 1991.

———. *Al-Rīḥāniyyāt.* Vol. 1. Beirut: Dar al-Rihani li'l-Tiba'a wa'l-Nashr, 1956.

Rihani, Najib. *Mudhakkirāt Najib al-Rihani.* 2nd ed. Cairo: Dar al-Jaib, n.d.

Rodrigue, Aron. *French Jews, Turkish Jews: The Alliance Israélite Universelle and the Politics of Jewish Schooling in Turkey, 1860–1925.* Bloomington: Indiana University Press, 1990.

Roncayolo, Marcel. "Mythes et réalités urbaines à travers le Grand Larousse." In *Mégapoles méditerranéennes* , ed. Nicolet et al.

Rose, Jonathan. *The Intellectual Life of the British Working Classes.* New Haven, CT: Yale University Press, 2001.

Rotellini, Vitaliano. *The Press of the State of São Paulo, 1827–1904.* São Paulo: Venorden, 1904.

Roussillon, Alain. *Entre réforme sociale et mouvement national: Identité et modernisation en Egypte (1882–1962).* Cairo: CEDEJ, 1995.

Sadgrove, Philip C. *The Egyptian Theatre in the Nineteenth Century.* Oxford: Ithaca Press, 1996.

al-Sa'id, Rif'at. *Tārīkh al-ḥaraka al-ishtirākiyya fi Miṣr 1900–1925.* 2nd ed. Cairo: Dar al-Thaqafa al-Jadida, n.d.

———. *Tārīkh al-munaẓẓamāt al-yasāriyya al-miṣriyya 1940–1950.* Cairo: Dar al-Thaqafa al-Jadida, 1976.

———. *Thalāth lubnāniyyīn fi'l-Qāhira: Shibli Shumayyil, Farah Antun, Rafiq Jabbur.* Beirut: Dar al-Tali'a li al-Tiba'a wa al-Nashr, 1973.

Saint-François-Xavier: Le Collège et ses lendemains. N.p.: n.p., ca. 1955.

Sajdi, Dana. "Print and Its Discontents: A Case for Pre-print Journalism and Other Sundry Print Matters." In *Nation and Translation in the Middle East,* ed. Samah Selim. Special issue of *The Translator* 15, no. 1 (2009): 105–38.

Sammarco, Angelo. *Il Contributo italiano nella formazione dell'Egitto moderno.* Alexandria: Angelo Procaccia, 1937.

Sarkis, Yusuf Ilian. *Mu'jam al-maṭbū'āt al-'arabiyya wa'l-mu'arraba.* Cairo: Matba'at Sarkis, [1346–49] 1928–30.

Sassen, Saskia, ed. *Global Networks, Linked Cities.* London: Routledge, 2002.

Saunier, Pierre-Yves. Review of *Charles Gide 1847–1932: L'esprit critique* (Paris: l'Harmattan, 1998). *H-Urban,* September 1998.

———. "Sketches from the Urban Internationale, 1910–50: Voluntary Associations, International Institutions and U.S. Philanthropic Foundations." *International Journal of Urban and Regional Research* 25, no. 2 (2001): 380–403.

Savage, Mike. "Class and Labour History." In *Class and Other Identities,* ed. van Voss and van der Linden.

Schaebler, Birgit. "Practicing Musha': Common Lands and the Common Good in Southern Syria under the Ottomans and the French." In *New Perspectives on Property and Land,* ed. R. Owen.

Schilcher, Linda S. "Violence in Rural Syria in the 1880s and 1890s: State Centralization, Rural Integration, and the World Market." In *Peasants and Politics in the Modern Middle East,* ed. Kazemi and Waterbury.

Schneer, Jonathan. "Anti-imperial London: The Pan-African Conference of 1900." In *Imperial Cities: Landscape, Display and Identity,* ed. Felix Driver and David Gilbert. Manchester, UK: Manchester University Press, 1999.

Schulze, Reinhard C. "The Egyptian Peasant Rebellion, 1919." In *Peasants and Politics in the Modern Middle East,* ed. Kazemi and Waterbury.

Secrétariat du Bureau Socialiste International. *L'Internationale Ouvrière et Socialiste: Rapports soumis au Congrès Socialiste International de Stuttgart 918–24 aoüt 1907.* Vol. 1. Brussels: Bureau Socialiste International, Maison du Peuple, 1907.

Sewell, William. *Structure and Mobility: The Men and Women of Marseille, 1820–1870.* Cambridge, UK: Cambridge University Press, 1985.

Sewell, William H., Jr. "How Classes Are Made: Critical Reflections on E. P. Thompson's Theory of Working-class Formation." In *E. P. Thompson: Critical Perspectives,* ed. Kaye and McClelland.

Shaffer, Kirwin. "The Radical Muse: Women and Anarchism in Early-Twentieth-Century Cuba." *Cuban Studies* 34 (2003):130–53.

Shalash, 'Ali. *Al-Māṣūniyya fi Miṣr.* Cairo: al-Hay'a al-Misriyya li'l-Kutub, 1993.

Sharabi, Hisham. *Arab Intellectuals and the West: The Formative Years 1875–1914.* Baltimore: Johns Hopkins University Press, 1970.

Sharma, I. Mallikarjuna. *Role of Revolutionaries in the Freedom Struggle: A Critical History of the Indian Revolutionary Movements, 1918–1934.* Hyderabad: Marxist Study Forum, 1987.

Sharpe, Pamela. Introduction to *Women, Gender and Labour Migration: Historical and Global Perspectives,* ed. Pamela Sharpe. New York: Routledge, 2001.

Shechter, Relli. "The Egyptian Cigarette: A Study of the Interaction between Consumption, Production, and Marketing in Egypt, 1850–1956." PhD diss., Harvard University, 1999.

———. *Smoking, Culture, and the Economy in the Middle East: The Egyptian Tobacco Market, 1850–2000.* London: I. B. Tauris, 2006.

Sheehi, Stephen. "Inscribing the Arab Self: Butrus al Bustani and the Paradigm of Subjective Reform." *British Journal of Middle Eastern Studies* 27, no. 1 (2000): 7–24.

Shumayyil, Shibli. *Al-Duktūr Shibli Shumayyil: Mabāḥith 'ilmiyya wa ijtimā'iyya.* Ed. As'ad Razzuq. Beirut: Dar Nazir Abbud, 1991.

———. *Ḥawādith wa khawāṭir: Mudhakkirāt al-duktūr Shibli Shumayyil.* Compiled by As'ad Razzuq. Beirut: Dar al-Hamra', 1991.

———. *Kitābāt siyāsiyya wa iṣlāḥiyya.* Compiled by As'ad Razzuq. Beirut: Dar al Hamra', 1991.

Silver, Beverly J. *Forces of Labor: Workers' Movements and Globalization since 1870.* Cambridge, UK: Cambridge University Press, 2003.

Società Geografica Italiana. *Indagini sulla Emigrazione Italiana all'Estero fatte per cura della Società Geografica Italiana (1888–89)*. Rome: Presso la Società Geografica Italiana, 1890.

Sohrabi, Nader. "Global Waves, Local Actors: What the Young Turks Knew about Other Revolutions and Why It Mattered." *Comparative Studies in Society and History* 44 (2002): 45–79.

Spagnolo, John, ed. *Problems of the Modern Middle East in Historical Perspective: Essays in Honour of Albert Hourani*. Reading, UK: Ithaca Press, 1992.

Strauss, Johann. "Who Read What in the Ottoman Empire (19th–20th Centuries)?" *Middle Eastern Literatures* 6 (2003): 39–76.

Strikwerda, Carl. "Capitalists, Immigrants, and Populists: The Impact of Social Conflict and the State on the Origins of World War I." In *Challenging Authority*, ed. Hanagan et al.

Syrian Protestant College. *Annual Reports*. N.p.: 1904–13.

Tager, Florence. "Politics and Culture in Anarchist Education: The Modern School of New York and Stelton, 1911–1915." *Curriculum Inquiry* 16, no. 4 (1986): 391–416.

Al-Tahtawi, Rifaʿat. "Fi muntazahāt madīnat Bārīz." In *Naẓariyyat al-masraḥ*, ed. Khatib.

Tamimi, Rafiq, and Ali Bahjat. *Wilāyat Bayrūt*. Vol. 2. Beirut: Dar Lahd Khatir, 1979.

Tarrazi, Filib di. *Dhikra qudamāʾ ṭalabat al-madrasa al-baṭrakiyya bi Bayrūt 1865–1938*. Saida: al-Matbaʿa al-Mukhallisiyya, 1938.

———. *Tārīkh al-ṣiḥāfa*. Vols. 1 and 2. Beirut: Dar Sadir, n.d.

Tawq, Joseph Khuri, ed. *Majmūʿat Felix Faris: Min udabāʾ al-nahḍa al-ʿarabiyya*. Vol. 2. Beirut: Matbaʿat Ghazir, 2000.

Taylor, Antony. "Shakespeare and Radicalism: The Uses and Abuses of Shakespeare in Nineteenth-century Popular Politics." *Historical Journal* 45, no. 2 (2002):361–64.

Ter Minassian, Anahide. *Nationalism and Socialism in the Armenian Revolutionary Movement*. Cambridge, MA: Zoryan Institute, 1984.

Thompson, Edward P. *The Making of the English Working Class*. London: Victor Gollancz, 1963.

Tilly, Charles. "Transplanted Networks." In *Immigration Reconsidered*, ed. McLaughlin.

Torpey, John. *The Invention of the Passport: Surveillance, Citizenship, and the State*. Cambridge, UK: Cambridge University Press, 2000.

Trimi, Katerina. "La famille Benakis: Un paradigme de la bourgeoisie grecque alexandrine." In *Figures anonymes, figures d'élites: Pour une anatomie de l'Homo ottomanicus*, ed. Meropi Anastassiadou and Bernard Heyberger. Istanbul: Editions Isis, 1999.

Tunçay, Mete, and Erik J. Zürcher, eds. *Socialism and Nationalism in the Ottoman Empire 1876–1923*. London: British Academic Press, 1994.

Turcato, Davide. "Italian Anarchism as a Transnational Movement, 1885–1915." *International Review of Social History* 52 (2007): 407–44.

Université Populaire Libre d'Alexandrie: *Revue des Cours et Conférences, Année 1902–1903*. Alexandria: Librairie L. Schuler, 1903.

Vallet, Jean. *Contribution à l'étude de la condition des ouvriers de la grande industrie au Caire*. Valence: Imprimerie Valentinoise, 1911.

van der Linden, Marcel. "Global Labor History and the Modern World-System: Thoughts at the Twenty-fifth Anniversary of the Fernand Braudel Center." *International Review of Social History 46* (2001): 423–59.

———, ed. *The International Confederation of Free Trade Unions.* Berne: Peter Lang, 2000.
van der Linden, Marcel, and Jürgen Rojahn eds. *The Formation of Labor Movements 1870–1914: An International Perspective.* Vol. 1. Leiden: E. J. Brill, 1990.
van der Linden, Marcel, and Wayne Thorpe, eds. *Revolutionary Syndicalism: An International Perspective.* Aldershot, UK: Scolar Press, 1990.
van der Walt, Lucien. "Bakunin's Heirs in South Africa: Race and Revolutionary Syndicalism from the IWW to the International Socialist League, 1910–21." *Politikon* 31, no. 1 (2004): 67–89.
van Voss, Lex Heerma, and Marcel van der Linden, eds. *Class and Other Identities: Gender, Religion and Ethnicity in the Writing of European Labour History.* New York: Berghahn Books, 2002.
Vatter, Sherry. "Militant Journeymen in Nineteenth-Century Damascus: Implications for the Middle Eastern Labor History Agenda." In *Workers and Working Classes,* ed. Lockman.
———. "Militant Textile Weavers in Damascus: Waged Artisans and the Ottoman Labor Movement 1850–1914." In *Workers and the Working Class,* ed. Quataert and Zürcher.
Velikov, Stefan. "Le mouvement ouvrier et socialiste en Turquie après la révolution Jeune-Turque de 1908." *Etudes Balkaniques* (Sofia), 1 (1964): 29–48.
Vertone, Téodosio. "Socialistes et mouvement ouvrier italiens dans la région marseillaise pendant la seconde moitié du XIXe siècle." In *Gli Italiani nella Francia del Sud e in Corsica (1860–1980),* ed. Emile Témime and Téodosio Vertone. Milan: Franco Angeli, 1988.
Volait, Mercedes. *Architectes et architectures de l'Egypte Moderne (1830–1950): Genèse et essor d'une expertise locale.* Paris: Maisonneuve et Larose, 2005.
———. "Making Cairo Modern (1870–1950): Multiple Models for a 'European-style' Urbanism." In *Urbanism: Imported or Exported? Native Aspirations and Foreign Plans,* ed. Joseph Nasr and Mercedes Volait. London: Willey-Academy, 2003.
Wahba, Mourad Magdi. "The Meaning of *Ishtirakiyah:* Arab Perceptions of Socialism in the Nineteenth Century." *Alif: Journal of Comparative Poetics,* no. 10 (1990): 42–55.
Wild, Stefan. "Negib Azoury and His Book *Le Réveil de la Nation Arabe.*" In *Intellectual Life in the Arab East,* ed. Buheiry.
Williamson, Jeffrey G. "Real Wages and Relative Factor Prices around the Mediterranean, 1500–1940." In *The Mediterranean Response to Globalization before 1950,* ed. Pamuk and Williamson.
Yaghi, Abdulrahman. *Fi juhūd al-masraḥiyya al-'arabiyya: Min Marun Naqqash ila Tawfiq al-Hakim.* Beirut: Dar al-Farabi, 1999.
Yazbak, Yusuf Ibrahim. *Ḥikāyat awwal nuwwār fi'l-'ālam wa fi Lubnān.* Beirut: Dar al-Farabi, 1974.
Zaidan, Jirji. *Tarājim mashāhīr al-sharq.* 2 vols. Cairo: Matba'at al-Hilal, 1922.
———. *Tārīkh ādāb al-lugha al-'arabiyya.* Vol. 4. Cairo: Dar al-Hilal, 1957.
Zainebaf-Shahr, Fariba. "The Role of Women in the Urban Economy of Istanbul, 1700–1850." *International Labor and Working-Class History* 60 (Fall 2001): 141–52.
Zakhura, Ilyas. *Al-Sūriyyūn fi Miṣr.* Cairo: Arabic Press, 1927.
Zakka, Najib Mansur. *Amin ar-Rihani: Penseur et homme de lettres libanais.* Lille: Presses Universitaires de Lille, 1979.

Zandi-Sayek, Sibel. *A World in Flux: Urban Space and Identity Politics in Nineteenth-Century Izmir.* Minneapolis: University of Minnesota Press, forthcoming.

Ziegler, Antje. "Arab Literary Salons at the Turn of the Twentieth Century." In *Understanding Near Eastern Literatures: A Spectrum of Interdisciplinary Approaches,* ed. Verena Klemm and Beatrice Gruendler. Wiesbaden: Reichert Verlag, 2000.

Zubaida, Sami. "Cosmopolitanism and the Middle East." In *Cosmopolitanism, Identity and Authenticity in the Middle East,* ed. Roel Meijer. Surrey, UK: Curzon, 1999.

INDEX

Eastern European Christians, 148
Eberhardt, Isabelle, 133
economic imperialism, 6
economic localism, 23
education. *See* mass education; women's education
educational institutions: development of, 7; global potential of, 46; modernization of, 60. *See also* mass education; schools
Egypt: agricultural work in, 176n8; anti-anarchist measures of, 219nn114–15; anti-imperialist movements in, 26, 109; British Occupation of (1882), 3, 46–47, 49, 110–11, 116, 176n5, 190n78; cigarette industry in, 147; citizenship laws in, 232n94; economic recession in, 136–37; employment figures, 229n55; feminist movement in, 224n209; globalization effects in, 176n5, 176n8; indigenous anarchism in, 129–31; indigenous/nonindigenous tensions in, 162–63; intellectuals in, 87; Italian anarchists in, 24, 47, 115–17 (*see also* Italian anarchist network (Alexandria)); Italian Jewry in, 220n143; IWA in, 218n102; labor categories in, 140–41; land reforms in, 4; leftist movements in, 7; legal system of, 116; migrant labor in, 147, 148–49, 233n103; monoculture in, 4; national identity in, 238n162; nationalism in, 87; political assassinations in, 25; press regulations in, 190n78; reading rooms in, 36, 213n34; secret societies in, 224n205; social problems in, 79; strikes in, 142, 155–56, 158–59, 228–29n45; subversive freedom offered by, 49; Syrian diasporic periodicals in, 46, 48–49, 50, 97; Syrian dramatists in, 72–74; Syrian emigration to, 46–48, 49, 155–56, 212n19; Syrian radical network connected to, 112–13, 132, 133; theater associations in, 198n16; theater political speeches in, 74; theater troupes in, 200n58, 202n77; theatrical regulation in, 202n94; tobacco industry in, 237n141; upper classes in, 89–90, 91, 106, 209n173; 'Urabi insurrection, 218n106; wage levels in, 226n11; women as workers in, 136; worker categories in, 139. *See also* Alexandria; Cairo
Egypte contemporaine, L' (periodical), 181n62
Egyptian Ministry of Education, 75
Egyptian Nationalist Party, 130
Egyptian State Railway, 229n55
'Eid, 'Aziz, 60, 74, 113, 196–97n5, 202n82
eight-hour workday, 231n73
emergency funds, 102
emergency services, 118
emigration, 4–5
employment insecurity, 150–52
England, 2, 22
Enver, Bey, 206n130
ethnicity: class and, 136, 156–60, 161, 163–64; foreignness and, 161–63; labor hierarchies based on, 156–59, 237nn140–41, 145, 238n147; multiethnic associations, 237n138; multiethnic neighborhoods, 159–60, 163–64
Europe: anarchism in, 115; political assassinations in, 25; socialist parties in, 182n91; theater in, 64–67
evolutionary theory: Büchner and, 188n58; Lewis Affair (1882) and, 48; mutual aid and, 179n30; press coverage of, 48; radical networks' belief in, 133; Shumayyil and popularization of, 42, 187n53, 192n87; Université Populaire mission and, 120–21; Zaidan and, 192n89
Exposition Universelle (Paris; 1900), 28, 224n209

Fabianism, 27
factories: artisans employed in, 139–40; labor contestation at, 141–42; mechanization of, 154; women as workers in, 136
al-Farā'id (periodical), 52, 192n93, 193n104
Farag, Nadia, 183n10, 191n85, 192n91, 210n176
Farah, Ibrahim Shehadi, 52, 182n75, 193n104
Farah, Iskandar: Cairo theater of, 73, 75; radical connections of, 74; theatrical troupe of, 196n5, 202nn81–82, 204n114
Farid, Muhammad, 75
Faris, Felix, 61, 95, 197n13, 211n5, 212n20
Fatāt al-Dustūr (Kan'an), 82
Faure, Sebastian, 118–19
Fédération Ouvrière de Salonique, 155
feminism, 211n9, 224n209
Ferrer Affair, 29, 80, 94, 107–8
Ferrer play (1909): actors tried for, 206n140; authorship of, 60, 95, 196n1; clergy's reaction to, 197n13; first performance of, 60–61, 197n7; Middle Eastern reactions to, 196n1; radical networks and, 61–62, 94, 113; reviews of, 208n158; revolutionary fervor during performances of, 83, 84; speeches related to, 211n9

TEXT
10/12.5 Minion Pro

DISPLAY
Minion Pro

COMPOSITOR
Integrated Composition Stytems

INDEXER
Kevin Millham

CARTOGRAPHER
Bill Nelson

PRINTER AND BINDER
Maple-Vail Book Manufacturing Group

Milton Keynes UK
Ingram Content Group UK Ltd.
UKHW040758101124
450942UK00002B/85